THURBERVILLE

The Fisher family gathered for a photo in front of Mike Fisher's old homestead in what is now the south end of Columbus in 1898. Some of the names that Thurber's cousin, Earl Fisher, wrote on the photo in pencil are still faintly visible, although he didn't identify Thurber. Thurber's tiny head is barely visible in the center of the photo above that of Margery Albright, a white-haired woman with a white blouse and black tie around her neck in the second row. Thurber's grandfather, William M. Fisher (black beard, holding a cigar), is in the front row, two people to Albright's left. The two men to his right are his brothers, Milton and Joseph Fisher. Thurber's mother, Mame, is four women to Albright's right in the second row with a white blouse and black tie. Jake Matheny, whom Thurber wrote about in his memories of family gatherings, is in the top row next to the post. (Fisher family photo)

THURBERVILLE

BOB HUNTER

With a Preface by Joe Blundo

Trillium, an imprint of
The Ohio State University Press
Columbus

Library of Congress Cataloging-in-Publication Data
Names: Hunter, Bob, 1951– author. | Blundo, Joe, 1954– writer of preface.
Title: Thurberville / Bob Hunter ; with a preface by Joe Blundo.
Description: Columbus : Trillium, an imprint of The Ohio State University Press,
    [2017] | Includes bibliographical references.
Identifiers: LCCN 2016054826 | ISBN 9780814213377 (cloth ; alk. paper) | ISBN
    0814213375 (cloth ; alk. paper)
Subjects: LCSH: Thurber, James, 1894–1961. | Humorists, American—Homes and
    haunts—Ohio—Columbus—Biography. | Cartoonists—Homes and haunts—
    Ohio—Columbus—Biography. | Columbus (Ohio)—History—Biography. |
    Thurber, James, 1894–1961—Friends and associates.
Classification: LCC PS3539.H94 Z725 2017 | DDC 818/.5209 [B]—dc23
LC record available at https://lccn.loc.gov/2016054826

Cover design by Regina Starace
Text design by Juliet Williams
Type set in Adobe Sabon

Cover image: "Two thousand people were in full flight" by James Thurber, from the short story, "The Day the Dam Broke" from the Thurber book *My Life and Hard Times*.

9 8 7 6 5 4 3 2 1

CONTENTS

•

CHILDHOOD MATTERS

Homes, Haunts, Honeys, and Hangouts   87

UNIVERSITY MATTERS

Making It Through the Minefield   141

LITERARY MATTERS

Inspiration and Incubation in Thurberville   191

PREFACE

I grew up with James Thurber's *My Life and Hard Times*—because my brother borrowed it from the library when we were kids and failed to return it.

So I read it over and over again, never suspecting that I was preparing myself to live in Columbus, Ohio.

The long-overdue library book was a source of anxiety for my mother, who was the most law-abiding person I've ever known. (Once, on vacation to Niagara Falls, she self-reported to Canadian border authorities the presence of an apple in the car, nearly causing a crisis over the importation of agricultural pests.) The presence of the library book in her basement haunted her for years.

I kept telling her to just return the damn thing, but she felt too guilty and avoided the library, expecting to see herself on a Wanted poster.

Finally, one day in the 1990s, a good thirty years after the book was borrowed, I decided to take matters into my own hands. I anonymously returned the book to the library, with a note that said, "This book has been in my mother's basement since 1966. Please do not arrest her."

No criminal charges were filed and we never heard anything from library officials. And even if, upon my presenting the missing book, they'd demanded, say $500, I probably would have paid it. Because the insights that Thurber gave me into my adopted home would have been worth the money.

Thurber took a humorist's liberties with his hometown and the people who lived there. But underlying all that was a quirkiness that strikes me as authentic. Authentic to Columbus or authentic to humans in general? Probably the latter, but let's go with the former because I like the idea of living on an island of eccentricity. It's inspirational.

Long before I moved here from the Pittsburgh area (by no means quirk-free, but lacking a Thurber to distill those quirks into masterpieces), I knew that Columbus was prone to meteorological panic because I'd read *The Day the Dam Broke,* where the population flees a phantom disaster the same way they now rush to the grocery store to prepare for a light snow.

I also knew that Columbus took unusual interest in the academic performance of muscular teenagers because I'd read about Bolenciecwcz, the clueless football lineman who struggled to name a means of transportation despite hints from his professor in *University Days.*

And I knew that a certain insecurity gripped the town because it had been created out of thin air by the state legislature and, as Thurber said, "ever since then has had the hallucination that it is being followed."

Of course, Thurber was writing in the early twentieth century, and conditions do change. In the early twenty-first century, Columbus's main source of anxiety is that the rest of the world is unaware of its existence. So it has the hallucination that it's *not* being followed. The more important point is the anxiety, not what's causing it.

All of these insights have been useful in my job, which is writing a newspaper column for the *Columbus Dispatch.* Bob Hunter, author of this book, and I have both been writing for the Dispatch since the 1970s. Bob is a sports columnist, and he also has a keen interest in local history that I've made use a time or two.

I learned from one of his previous books the name of the man who received the first speeding ticket in Columbus and that John Wilkes Booth, Abraham Lincoln, and Dean Martin all had been on same block of State Street, although not at the same time. I often cite these facts when I feel a need to fascinate a group. Thanks, Bob.

Of course, both Bob and I are acutely aware that Thurber himself once worked at the *Dispatch.* I don't know about Bob, but I try not to think too deeply about Thurber as a *Dispatch* staffer because it's thoroughly intimidating, like having a distant cousin who won a Nobel Prize or was elected pope. But I've taken full advantage of his sense of what I call "Columbusness."

If forced to name a single Thurber story that best captures the comic essence of Columbus, I'd have to say *The Day the Dam Broke*. City officials ought to just hand out a copy to every new residents and say, "Read this. It will explain a lot."

Such as?

Well, first of all, it introduces a newcomer to the 1913 flood, a natural disaster that left its mark on Columbus for one hundred years. The town reacted to the flood by more or less imprisoning the Scioto River between walls of concrete and not releasing it until recently. The reprieve has resulted in a beautiful riverside park, but rest assured we're keeping an eye on the Scioto for parole violations.

Of course, what makes the dam story funny is that people living on the East Side panic over rumors of a broken dam, despite the fact that it's the low-lying West Side that's vulnerable to floods. Anyone living in Columbus would know that, but when the populace is determined to panic, facts rarely get in the way.

I can read the story right now and recognize, around Capital Square, the same kind of characters that Thurber described.

High Street is still a "canyon of trade," still characterized by "the placid hum of business and the buzzing of placid businessmen, arguing, computing, wheedling, offering, refusing, compromising."

There are still Darius Conningways, the lawyer described as telling the Public Utilities Commission "in the language of Julius Caesar that they might as well try to move the Northern star as to move him."

On any weekday, you'll find an assortment of lobbyists and lawyers striding importantly on the sidewalks surrounding the Statehouse, making their "little boasts" and "little gestures," just as Thurber observed.

They're easy to spot because even in the most frigid weather, they walk around outside in nothing but their dark power suits, a local form of male dominance display.

I arrived in Columbus in 1978 with a vague mental map of where things were located, based solely on the direction of the dam panic. I knew that the intersection of Town and Parsons is on the East Side, because that's where Thurber's delusional grandfather, stunned by a whack from an ironing board, regained consciousness during the great exodus to the east.

Clintonville, Reynoldsburg, Franklin Park, the statue of nineteenth-century heroes on the Statehouse grounds—those locations all sounded familiar. I have never been able to look at that statue—depicting Grant, Sherman, Garfield, and others standing in a circle—without picturing the woman who climbs above their heads in the story to escape the phantom floodwaters. (Thurber's accompanying cartoon, in which she seems to be naked and rather pleased with herself, makes it all the more memorable.)

In the story, someone begins to run and somehow that action escalates into a hectic mass scramble to escape what people have decided are raging floodwaters.

A television meteorologist can provoke similar reaction in today's Columbus with the word "snow" and a few sweeping arm gestures. Panicked residents will jump into their SUVs with a singular mission in mind: Get to the grocery store and stock up on toilet paper.

The next day—usually sunny with a glaze of snow too shallow to hide the grass tips—they'll act like nothing happened. Doesn't everyone keep a six-months' supply of toilet paper in the hall closet?

Thurber's *My Life and Hard Times* was published in 1933, about eight years after he left Columbus for good to become a reporter for the *Chicago Tribune* in Paris. After returning to the United States with his first wife, Althea, he was hired by the *New Yorker*, then a new magazine in 1927.

His first book, *Is Sex Necessary?* written with E. B. White, was published the next year. By 1930, his cartoons were beginning to appear in the magazine. Thurber seemed to think of them as mere doodles, but White is said to have fished them out of the trash and convinced the magazine to publish them. Soon Thurber cartoons were the subject of New York City art exhibits. He called it a "strange sort of acclaim."

The acclaim continued as he published books, plays, short stories, and fables. Among his best-known works were *The Secret Life of Walter Mitty,* a short story about the wild daydreams of a put-upon man; *The Male Animal* (cowritten with Elliott Nugent), which was performed on Broadway and was later made into a movie; *Fables for Our Time,* a collection of hilariously updated fairy tales; *The 13 Clocks,* a children's book; and *The Years With Ross,* his memoir about working at the *New Yorker* with editor Harold Ross.

Thurber's association with the *New Yorker* made him part of a literary all-star team, which included White, Dorothy Parker, and Wolcott Gibbs, among many others. His contemporaries were generous in their praise of his work. White said Thurber wrote "the way a child skips ropes, the way a mouse waltzes."

In 1952 he returned to the subject of Columbus with *The Thurber Album,* profiles of relatives, bosses, professors and friends who shaped him during his formative years. Thurber, who died in 1961 as a much-celebrated writer, cartoonist, and wit, often said Columbus was never far from his mind.

While working on a 2011 story about the fiftieth anniversary of Thurber's death, I interviewed his daughter, Rosemary. She grew up in Connecticut and knew Columbus only as the place where her father was from. But she said her father always had great, but not unconditional, affection for his hometown. He had mixed feelings, as most of us do about the places we know best.

Thurber's struggles to reconcile those feelings are, to me, the most fascinating parts of Harrison Kinney's enormous Thurber biography, *James Thurber: His Life and Times.*

He could be surprisingly considerate, even boosterish, toward Columbus when so moved.

Thurber's 1922 *Dispatch* story on the dedication of Ohio Stadium borders on worshipful: "Perhaps never again will the heart leap up quite so high and the breath come so swiftly," he writes of the marching band taking the field for the first time.

And yet he lampooned the university in Credos and Curios, his *Dispatch* column, for its football mania. And his play, *The Male Animal,* is a barely disguised satire of OSU sports madness. The less-than-brilliant lineman he calls Bolenciecwcz in *University Days* was in fact based on Buckeye running back Chic Harley, a town hero. Thurber changed the name (and position) so as not to offend Columbus, Kinney says.

Because of Thurber, I came to Columbus already aware that it was exquisitely sensitive about its football team. And yet not even Thurber can fully prepare a newcomer for the phenomenon. People schedule weddings—and probably births—around the Buckeyes' schedule. I'm sure some terminally ill fans have fended off death for a few extra hours just so they could watch the Michigan game.

No doubt the same sorts of things happen in the college towns of Lincoln, Nebraska, or Tuscaloosa, Alabama. But Thurber taught me to take in the whole picture—the football obsession combined with the insecurity, the weather panic and the self-aggrandizing gestures of the locally powerful. So of course the most famous football game in OSU history is a 9–3 loss to Michigan that occurred during a blizzard and was witnessed by a small crowd that has since grown exponentially—if the dubious claims of having been present at the signature event are to be believed. I know full well that most of those people, if they ventured outside at all that day, did so for the sole purpose of buying toilet paper.

In this book, Bob Hunter will take you to places where Thurber lived, the streets he walked, the classrooms he sat in during his years in Columbus.

It was a relatively compact place then, and Thurber's stories make it seem smaller and gentler than it was really was. Now its metropolitan population hovers around two million, and it sprawls across county lines and is forever reminding the uninformed that it's a major American city.

A lot of the landmarks from Thurber's days are gone, but many remain. The library where he attended story hours as a child still stands on Grant Street, but greatly enlarged and modernized. Ohio Stadium has bulked up like a sophomore tight end, and I imagine it would simultaneously impress the sports fan side of Thurber and appall the cynical observer in him. Union Station is gone, but there's an upscale replica of it nearby where you can get a latte or a filet mignon, but not a train.

Beneath the sprawl and glitter still lies something of the place Thurber knew and loved. Columbus retains some endearing small-town qualities: People getting off city buses in the morning thank the driver. The July 4th fireworks show (which is always on July 3rd) is a big deal. It's impolite, and in some cases dangerous, to wear the color blue.

Thurber left here in 1925 for grander places and bigger adventures, but I think if he were to come back today he would recognize the essential elements and idiosyncrasies of Columbus, Ohio. Especially if snow was in the forecast.

Joe Blundo

ACKNOWLEDGMENTS

The seeds for this book were planted more than fifteen years ago, when I first read Harrison Kinney's impressive biography *James Thurber, His Life and Times.* Kinney's fascinating twelve-hundred-page book chronicled every aspect of Thurber's life from birth to grave, but the chapters that dealt with his life in Columbus and his years at the *Columbus Dispatch* were especially intriguing to me as a longtime Columbus resident and *Dispatch* reporter and columnist.

In my later research for *Chic,* a biography of football star Chic Harley, who went to school with Thurber at both East High School and The Ohio State University, I found myself digging up more information on Thurber and his family and becoming more absorbed in their story. When that happened again during research for *A Historical Guidebook to Old Columbus,* it finally occurred to me that the people, places, and things that were both part of Thurber's life in Columbus and characters and subjects for his stories later might grow into a book.

This book couldn't have been written without the graciousness of Rosemary Thurber and her family. They allowed me to print her father's priceless descriptions of friends, neighbors, and family members and for use of some of the material and several of photos that are part of the Thurber Collection in the Rare Books and Manuscripts Library of The Ohio State University Libraries.

The collection is an incredible resource for Thurber scholars and includes many remarkable entries, including some of the early drafts of his stories with his own editing marks. Having a chance to "participate" in the writing process of a man who ranks among the greatest American humorists was an exhilarating experience that I will never forget.

The staff of the Rare Books and Manuscripts Library at the Thompson Library at OSU was always helpful and generous with its time. Rebecca Jewett, coordinator of public services and operations of special collections, was especially helpful. I also owe a debt of gratitude to Geoffrey Smith, now-retired curator of rare books and manuscripts, and his successor, Eric J. Johnson.

Interviews with many principals in this book that were done by the late Lewis C. Branscomb Jr., professor of Thurber studies at Ohio State and director of libraries at the school for almost twenty years, were invaluable and the transcripts of those interviews are part of the Thurber Collection. Rosemary O. Joyce also did extensive interviews with former Thurber friends, classmates, and family members for her 1984 book (with Michael J. Rosen and Donn Vickers) *Of Thurber & Columbustown,* which offered valuable insights.

A special note of thanks goes to Michelle Drobik, research archivist at the The Ohio State University Archives, who has always been more helpful than any visitor has a right to expect. She always ready to help despite her busy schedule and I am grateful for her assistance.

The *Columbus Dispatch* library has long been an invaluable resource for the newspaper, and Linda Deitch and Julie Fulton have always been especially helpful to me, both on this project and in my work for the newspaper. They refuse to accept defeat when a search comes up empty, and their persistence has paid off with valuable information or photos for me on more than once occasion. A thank you to them doesn't seem quite enough.

I would also like to thank Nick Taggart at the Columbus Metropolitan Library, who shares my interest in local history and is always happy to share his knowledge and expertise and use the library's resources to find an answer for difficult questions.

Thanks are also due to my friends at the Thurber House, especially now-retired executive director Susanne Jaffe, who offered her advice and assistance with this project early on. I also owe a debt of gratitude to my friend Jim Tootle, who is a regular contributor to the *Thurber House Organ* and who served with me on the board of trustees of the Columbus

Historical Society, and to Thurber House deputy director Anne Touvell. (To read more about James Thurber, go to www.ThurberHouse.org.)

I also want to extend my sincere thanks to Helen F. Bonte, adult services librarian of the Fairfield County District Library in Lancaster, Ohio; Kit Fluker, manuscript specialist at the Brooke Russell Astor Reading Room for Rare Books and Manuscripts of The New York Public Library; Kevlin Haire, assistant curator and assistant university archivist for The Ohio State Archives; Jamie W. Hasselbring of T. Marzetti Company; Lori Chien, Chief Librarian for Adult Services and Reference, Jervis Public Library, Rome, New York; and Professors Murray Beja and Clare Simmons of the Department of English at The Ohio State University.

Betsy Bringardner and Paige Gidney were also helpful in securing interviews with other members of the Fisher family, thus providing information that was invaluable to this work and much appreciated. Bringardner also furnished the photo of the 1898 Fisher reunion that appears at the front of this book.

Bob Hunter

Columbus as Thurberville

James Thurber's Columbus wasn't today's Columbus or even yesterday's. It was a Columbus he both knew and created, a place perched on the fringe of reality and the fringe of his imagination.

The Columbus he called home until his late twenties set the standard for average, a medium-sized city in the middle of America that probably veered toward the center of just about any kind of ranking in which it found itself. It sat near the geographic center of Ohio, which helped make it the state capital. It sat in the midst of miles of flat farmland, which helped make it a model of Midwestern monotony. It featured a state university that an average student could navigate and two small rivers that converged into one moderately sized river that average boats couldn't. It had a minor league baseball team, a minor league horse track, and, despite some major league attributes, a minor league mentality.

It also had Thurber, a chance occurrence destined to introduce a spectacularly average place to the world as the wacky, panties-on-his-head, joke-cracking life of every party. His Columbus is a wild and crazy place, a city full of peculiar characters, bizarre incidents, and unexpected events. There's a ghost in Thurber's house. Uncle Zenas dies of elm tree blight. Aunt Sarah Shoaf piles all of her valuables outside her bedroom door every night with a note advising would-be burglars to "take it, this is all I have." The city flees in terror over a rumor that the dam has broken. His grandfather still thinks he is fighting the Civil War. Sullivant Elementary is overrun by old students with muscles and moustaches. A servant mistakes Thurber's father for the Antichrist and comes after him while waving a bread knife.

The world came to know Thurber's Columbus and love it like an eccentric family member. The world became acquainted with his characters and never let go of them. It was the only Columbus many knew, and they became attached to it, regardless of how much or how little of it was real.

Playwright and screenwriter Donald Ogden Stewart grew up in the same Columbus Thurber did; he was nine days older. When he moved overseas in the 1950s to escape the arts-suspicious, Commie hunters of Senator Joseph McCarthy, he was surprised to find that people knew his hometown. "When I first came to live in London, I was amazed at the number of Englishmen who said 'Oh, yes, Columbus, of course. I know it very well, from Thurber's books, you know.'"[1]

But they didn't know Columbus as well as they knew Thurber's Columbus, which could be both different and the same. When Thurber wrote about the Get Ready Man, "a lank, unkempt, elderly gentleman with wild eyes and a deep voice who used to go about shouting at people through a megaphone to prepare for the end of the world,"[2] his subject was a living human who had caught the writer's attention and had taken residence in his mind. But whether the Get Ready Man interrupted Mantell's production of *King Lear* at the Colonial Theatre in the comic way Thurber described, stopping the performance with wails of "Get rea-dy!" and "The Worr-uld is coming to an end!" is anyone's guess.

Like any good humorist, Thurber could mentally store the seed from an amusing incident and have it germinate years later. This was the Columbus Thurber introduced to the world in his early days at the *New Yorker,* one that found his brother "Roy" gathering "a great many articles from the kitchen" and placing them in a "square of canvas" under the family car with a string attached to it, "so that at a twitch, the canvas would give way and steel and tin things would clatter to the street."[3]

As Thurber described it, "this was a little scheme of Roy's to frighten their father, who had always expected the car might explode," and it worked. When "Roy" released the utensils while his father was enjoying "a cool breeze," the clatter on the asphalt was tremendously effective. His father yelled at him to stop the car, and "Roy" told him that he couldn't because "the engine fell out."

By 1952, when Thurber's portrait of his father appeared in *The Thurber Album,* the fact that he was "plagued" by not only the mechanical but also the manufactured seems more humorous than clown like. At that point, Thurber's nostalgic images tapped into our longing for a simpler, more sensible age.

Thurber belonged to that age—and grew out of it. He was born in Columbus in 1894 to Charles and Mary Agnes "Mame" Thurber, the second of three sons. Young Jamie grew up with humor all around him, even while enduring the distress of vision problems. At age seven, Jamie had been hit in an eye accidentally by a blunt-tipped arrow shot by his brother.

He attended but did not graduate from Ohio State University, worked as a reporter at the *Columbus Dispatch,* and wrote, directed, and acted in plays during and after college before he left the city for good in 1925 in hopes of fulfilling larger ambitions as a writer. After he landed at relatively new magazine called the *New Yorker* in 1927, his career as a humorist took off, but it wouldn't be accurate to say that he never looked back. He often returned to his hometown in his writing.

Thurber's personal view of Columbus and his relationship with the city was all over the map. His mother and brothers looked to him for financial help for most of his life, so visits to the city and even correspondence with his family could be a challenge. He refused an honorary degree from Ohio State in 1951 after the school had imposed a ban on lecturers suspected of Marxist leanings, a sign he had been intellectually freed from the conservative culture of the city he called home.

When the Martha Kinney Ohioana Library Association decided to honor Thurber with an Ohio Sesquicentennial Medal in 1953, he couldn't attend because his second wife, Helen, was having serious eye trouble. He designated his brother, Robert, to accept the medal for him, and he gave his acceptance speech to former *Columbus Dispatch* colleague George Smallsreed, then the paper's editor, to read in his absence.

It proved to be a forceful denunciation of McCarthyism. But the speech ended with a surprising show of affection for his home state and hometown: "It is a great moment for an Ohio writer living far from home when he realizes that he has not been forgotten by the state he can't forget," he said, adding that his books "prove that that I am never very far from Ohio in my thoughts, and that the clocks that strike in my dreams are often the clocks of Columbus."[4]

In 1959, when Columbus was named an "All-American City" in a promotion by *Look* magazine, Thurber wrote a glowing appraisal to the mayor: "I have always waved banners and blown horns for 'Good Old Columbus Town,' in America as well as abroad, and such readers as I have collected through the years are all aware of where I was born and brought up, and they know that half of my books could not have been written if it had not been for the city of my birth."[5]

But as Robert Morsberger pointed out in his 1964 biography of Thurber, there were two distinctly different Columbuses in his writings: The crazy one he wrote about in *My Life and Hard Times* in the 1930s and in various pieces through the years, and the blissful, wholesome one he fondly recalled in *The Thurber Album* in 1952.

By the time that book appeared in print, the city's image as Thurberville had already been set in the minds of most of his fans. His *Album* homage to close family members, mentors, and local heroes still carried the ring of humor; it simply came with a measure of adulation and without some of the wackiness.

After Thurber died in 1961, the city made numerous, mostly half-hearted attempts to return the adulation. Several buildings, businesses, and parks in Columbus bear his last name, but the Thurber House on Jefferson Avenue is the only place with any direct connection to him.

There is a Thurber Park, a small area with a gazebo, walkways, and sculptures that had served merely as island in the middle of Jefferson when Thurber lived there. There is a Thurber Village, a 1960s re-make of a run-down area called Flytown that Thurber may never have visited. There is a Thurber Drive, Thurber Theatre in the Drake Performance and Event Center at Ohio State, Westminster-Thurber retirement center, Thurber Towers, Thurber Gate apartments, Thurber Square apartments, and Thurber's Bar, the latter of which is in the Westin Columbus Hotel. Thurber's mother lived in the hotel for many years when it was called the Great Southern, but the bar is a recent Westin creation.

Thurber House is devoted to his memory, annually handing out the Thurber Prize for American Humor, hosting writers in residence, and presenting writing workshops and other literary programs. But it is seems like an island of interest in an exploding city that often appears to have little in common with the place Thurber lived in and wrote about, and which sometimes acts blithely indifferent to his accomplishments.

Maybe this isn't surprising; the Columbus where Thurber grew up seems like a stranger to the trendy, white-collar, mostly recession-proof city that exists today. But Thurber's Columbus could also be a stranger to the one he had lived in, a kind of alternate reality that he could weave in and out of at the drop of an adjective.

Poet David McCord wrote in the *Saturday Review* that when he tried to review *The Thurber Album*, he found that it had been reviewing him. McCord admitted he hadn't been born in Ohio and had only been in Columbus once, between 2:00 and 4:00 a.m. at the railroad station. He bought an apple there that morning, but couldn't identify it the way Thurber's Grandpa Fisher knew one thousand varieties. McCord only knew it as red, polished.

> The world of Thurber, whether in Ohio, New York, or France, is a portable world which he carries around with him, probably in an old carpet bag. If you have not seen this world, if you can't remember Miss Malloy in the fifth grade in 1905, the Letters of James Thurber, the Pet Department, and irrelevant things like that, some of the present "Album" is going out of that window in your mind. And that would be a pity. Mr. Thurber, more than any writer I know of, living or dead, is able to pass within a single sentence from reality to unreality, from nonsense to the sublime.[6]

Because of that, Thurber likely would have found plenty of good material even had he grown up in Dubuque, Iowa; or Casper, Wyoming; or even, Detroit, Chicago, or Los Angeles. And then again, maybe all of those smile-inducing absurdities he wrote about were hiding in early-twentieth-century Columbus, waiting to be discovered by just the right humor detective. There is no denying that Thurber's family included a rich blend of colorful characters who would have provided their friends and neighbors with plenty of snickers and head-shakes and a lifetime of entertainment, even without a writer to chronicle and immortalize them.

Fortunately, they had a writer, and not just any writer. Thurber is ranked by most as no worse than the second greatest American humorist, probably the only one worthy to be mentioned in the same sentence with the immortal Mark Twain. And even Twain might have had difficulty introducing some of these oddballs to the world and bringing them to life as effectively as Thurber did.

Thurber published twenty-seven books during his lifetime. Nine more books that featured his writing, drawings and correspondence have been published since his death in 1961. He coauthored a famous play, *The Male Animal,* which is still popular in school productions, summer stock and amateur theater groups. He drew cartoons for the *New Yorker* that became as famous as his writing. Four biographies and two literary reviews have chronicled most of his life, and NBC even produced a short-lived television series ("My World and Welcome to It") about him with actor William Windom appearing as Thurber.

Since 2004 Thurber House has annually honored outstanding contributors to humor writing with the Thurber Prize for American Humor. It is announced in New York, gets a lot of press, and is a very big deal. In 2013 Twentieth Century Fox produced a remake of "The Secret Life of Walter Mitty," Thurber's classic short story about a hopeless daydreamer. The tale initially resulted in a popular 1947 movie starring Danny Kaye, but its attempt to showcase Kaye's talents strayed so far from Thurber's story that he sarcastically referred to it as "The Public Life of Danny Kaye."[7] Thurber probably wouldn't like the new one starring Ben Stiller as Mitty much more than the first one. But it does prove Thurber's staying power, given that his original story was written in 1939 and it remained movie-relevant in 2014.

More evidence of Thurber's endurance surfaced on June 12, 2014, when the *Wall Street Journal* ran a story on fantasy writer Neil Gaiman's favorite book, a stylish, twisted fairy-tale written by Thurber called *The 13 Clocks*. It was published on January 1, 1950, and Gaiman lavished it with praise to a national audience probably mostly unaware of its existence.

Wall Street Journal reporter Alexandra Alter noted that Gaiman had called it "the best book ever written." Even when she pressed him on that, Gaiman budged only slightly.

> Whether I would stand there at gunpoint and say, "This is the best book ever written," I don't know. But I would definitely stand at gunpoint and say, "There has never been anything like this before, and there will never be anything like this again." Thurber takes such joy in his language. I wonder if it's partly because he was losing his sight at that point. It's the first of his books that he couldn't illustrate himself. He couldn't see well enough. He takes such delight in the words. It's like it's written by somebody who wants to infect you with his love of words. There are poems hidden in the text. There are places where it wanders into rhyme and out again. There are all of the invented words. The story itself is nonsense in the finest possible way.

A lot of that fine "nonsense" was cultivated by experiences Thurber had in Columbus and in his dealings with family, friends, teachers, and acquaintances there. They are worth a revisit and, in some cases, an introduction.

Columbus is a star in his books, and not today's city that is approaching nine hundred thousand within its city limits and has exceeded two million in its metro area, but the compact city of one hundred eighty thousand he knew growing up. In "More Alarms at Night," a tale involving the misadventures of his father in the Jefferson Avenue home today called Thurber House, Thurber attempted to explain:

> In the early years of the nineteenth century, Columbus won out, as state capital, by only one vote over Lancaster, and ever since then has had the hallucination that it is being followed, a curious municipal state of mind which affects, in some way or other, all those who live there. Columbus is a town in which almost anything is likely to happen and in which almost everything has.[8]

THURBERVILLE

Charles and Mame Thurber in front of the house at 251 Parsons Avenue where James Thurber was born. The woman on the left is believed to be Mame's mother, Katherine Fisher. (James Thurber Papers, Rare Books & Manuscripts Library of The Ohio State University Libraries)

FAMILY MATTERS

The Fishers and the Thurbers

*T*here's nothing like being a humorist and having a hilarious cast of characters live in your house, attend the same family reunions and holiday celebrations, and practically audition for their parts in your future stories. Fate dealt Thurber a nasty blow by taking his eye in a childhood accident, but it repaid him by dropping him into the middle of television sitcom, decades before anyone knew what that was. As Thurber's career as a humorist unfolded, it became apparent to many of his friends that his family—the Fishers, the Thurbers, the Mathenys, and others—had provided a rich trove of material for his work.

Although not everybody in the family was knee-slapping funny, few of them would be described as average or even more important than that, boring. They were a fascinating lot that continually fed him material he could draw on later in his writing. And even if they hadn't provided such delectable fodder, the family genes gave him the sharp wit and creative vision to become one of America's best humorists.

Lifelong friend and fellow writer Joel Sayre recalled that there was always a "three-ring circus" going on at the Thurber household when he visited it as a boy, and he admitted he sometimes wondered 'Who couldn't be a successful comic writer with that kind of mother and family?'

The seeds of Thurber's creative genius were planted long began long before he was born in a two-story brick house at 251 Parsons Avenue to Charles and Mame Thurber. Great-great-grandfather Jacob Fisher displayed eccentricities that were made to order for a humorist in waiting, "throwing" people who didn't agree with him and then nursing them back to health. Step-great-grandfather Judge Stacy Taylor had so many children, stepchildren, and adopted children that, in Thurber's words, "nobody knows the exact number" of them.

The family outings to Uncle Jake Matheny's farm near Sugar Grove, Ohio, in the Hocking Hills southeast of Columbus, exposed Thurber to more intriguing characters, including Jake himself. He was a respected lawyer and businessman whom Thurber remembered walking around with a parrot on one shoulder and a tame raccoon on the other.

But mostly, Thurber's humor grew and matured in Columbus in the midst of a family that often seemed more than a little wacky: A madcap mother and a submissive, beleaguered father who served as her foil; brothers William and Robert who shared their mother's genes, but never found a way to channel their humor the way their brother did; William Fisher, a successful, egocentric grandfather who sometimes picked on young Jamie because of the way he played the fool; Fisher's loving, generous wife Kate who seemed determined to counterbalance that; and Aunt Margery Albright, a family nurse whom Thurber lived with for a time as boy and who could whip up a cure for all manner of illnesses with everything from tobacco to "sheep droppings."

This was both a dysfunctional family and the perfect family for a humorist in waiting. There is no doubt that Thurber would have been willing to accept such a tradeoff.

CHAPTER 1

The Original Thurber House

The original Thurber House is long gone. From all available evidence, there was no campaign to save the red brick house at 251 Parsons Avenue where James Grover Thurber was born in 1894, and it wouldn't have mattered if there had been.

Two blocks of homes on the west side of Parsons between Bryden Road and Main Street, including the two-story house Charles Thurber's family lived in from 1893 to 1898, were sacrificed for the construction of Interstate 71 decades ago. In their place is a narrow strip of grass and weeds; a chain link fence to keep people from accidentally taking a swan dive into the eight-lane freeway below it; and trees, bushes, and weeds that have somehow flourished in the wider, descending strip of ground on the other side of the fence.

Thurber doubtless would have seen the humor in having a weed patch memorialize his birthplace. He even poked a little fun at the house itself in a preface to *The Thurber Carnival* in 1944, "My Fifty Years with James Thurber:"

> The house, which is still standing, bears no tablet or plaque or any description and is never pointed out to visitors. Once Thurber's mother, walking past the place with an old lady from Fostoria, Ohio, said to her "My son James was born in that house," to which the old lady, who was

extremely deaf, replied, "Why, on the Tuesday morning train, unless my
sister is worse." Mrs. Thurber let it go at that.

Bill Arter, *Columbus Dispatch* writer and artist, wrote about some of
the houses where Thurber lived in his 1967 book *Columbus Vignettes II*
and noted that that "there was a plaque (or placard rather) at 251 when
I visited there recently. Its laconic inscription, 'For Sale.'"

Nothing is "for sale" on that block today, and if Mame Thurber were
alive, she couldn't point the house out to anybody. She might even have
difficulty finding the exact spot where it stood. There is nothing about this
two-block stretch that feels like a neighborhood, which robs the area of
any romance connected with the birth of one of Columbus's most famous
sons. When someone says that Thurber spent the earliest years of his life
here, we'll have to take their word for it.

Thurber didn't help matters by writing in that preface that he was
born on "a night of wild portent and high wind in the year 1894, at
147 Parsons Avenue, Columbus, Ohio."[1] Thurber frequently used wrong
addresses in writing about places in his hometown, so it's unclear whether
he purposely gave the wrong address for his first Columbus home or simply wasn't certain of the address. But in a letter to John O'Hara, Thurber
again got the address wrong, and there was no reason for him to disguise
it there:

> The night I was born, December 8, 1894, Cesar Franck's D-minor sym-
> phony had its world premiere in Paris. Fifty percent of the audience
> cheered at the end and the other booed, tore up auditorium seats, and
> fenced the other side with walking sticks. The piece is now known as "The
> keystone of modern symphonic music." At 245 Parsons Avenue that night,
> the score was 4–1 in favor of me.[2]

While the Thurbers definitely lived at 251 Parsons, it makes no difference whatsoever to a Thurber disciple intent on making a pilgrimage to
his birthplace. For two blocks there is a sameness to the landscape that is
difficult to penetrate. While we can make a reasonable guess about where
the house stood in relation to the former Ohio School for the Blind across
the street—south of the main entrance and north of the driveway that
leads to the main entrance—the difference between the "245" of Thurber's letter and the actual address of "251" on a block of trees and bushes
is problematic.

None of this diminishes the significance of the place, however. Mame Thurber's father, William Fisher, who lived just around the corner on Bryden Road, had the house built as a dowry for Mame. All three Thurber boys were born here: William (October 29, 1893); James (December, 8 1894); and Robert (December 15, 1896); which is amazing considering how many times the family moved while they were growing up.

Margery Albright, a nurse who had been so close to the family for so long that they called her "Aunt Margery," delivered all three boys, although there is a story that goes along with James's birth. Dr. John M. Dunham, one of Margery's "favorites" arrived at the house too late for the birth and Margery delivered Jamie (as the family called him) without assistance.

"You might have spared your horse," she snapped at the good doctor, when he finally arrived. "We managed all right without you."[3]

Photos of the house do exist, which gives us an image to plant among those trees and bushes, if little else. The place the Thurbers called home looked nearly identical to the other houses on the street, all of which occupied 25-foot-wide lots. A rectangular piece of thick, beveled glass decorated the heavy front door, lighting the front hall of the house. Large windows lit most rooms, with a bay window in the living room that gave the front of the house a good view of the blind school grounds across the street. The front porch was small, but large enough for the boys' rocking horse.

Thurber was only four when the family moved to 921 South Champion Avenue on the southeastern outskirts of the city, so his memories of the house on Parsons never made it into his memoirs.

"Not a great deal is known about his earliest years, beyond the fact that he could walk when he was only two years old, and was able to speak whole sentences by the time he was four," Thurber wrote.[4]

He has plenty of memories of the Ohio School for the Blind across the street, but most of those were made from his Grandpa Fisher's house on Bryden Road, which backed up to the blind school.

The family moved in 1898 because Charles Thurber had decided to seek the Republican nomination for Franklin County Clerk of Courts and he had to move from the Parsons Avenue address to establish residence in the proper political district. He had been working as a clerk in Ohio Governor Asa Bushnell's office.

"I think Grandfather Fisher bought the house for us," William Thurber said.[5]

Fisher was desperate to see his son-in-law succeed, and the move didn't accomplish that. Charles Thurber lost the election and Governor Bushnell retired from office in the same election, so he was without a job. He would work for a time as a free-lance stenographer and also sold Underwood typewriters, a job that helped Jamie learn how to type at an early age. The family would live on South Champion until Charles was chosen by a former Ohio congressman to serve as a stenographer for a U.S. Justice Department commission in Washington, DC, in 1901.

By then Thurber was old enough and the family had already lived on South Champion long enough to create the kind of lasting memories that he didn't have from the house on Parsons.

CHAPTER 2

A Good Man
Victimized by Humor

Charles L. Thurber lives on today mostly as the straight man/dupe of his son's humorous short stories. James repeatedly casts his father as a poor sap who is flummoxed by man and machine, a kind-hearted soul who is unwittingly victimized by the people, objects and events surrounding him.

Possibly because of this, Charles has been seen as a hapless daydreamer by many of Thurber's biographers, who regard him as a naïve political foot soldier who worked hard and was never rewarded for it.

Outside of Jamie's written remembrances of him, the only evidence of Charles's poor performance as a breadwinner for his family isn't even visible to most casual fans of his son's work today. The family moved so often—fourteen times between 1892 and 1918—that it might have left enough "Thurber houses" for their own bus tour if they had survived history's march of progress. Most didn't. The string of former addresses is the only real proof that Thurber's father might not have been the best of providers for his wife and three sons.

His wife, Mame, admitted in 1950, "I don't know why Charlie wanted to move so much."[1] But youngest son, Robert, said that it wasn't because of evictions. "My father never had a big salary," he said, "but he was never behind in the rent, though it was a struggle to keep making ends meet."[2]

While it's true that Charles failed to achieve the kind of financial success that others have belatedly demanded of him, this critical view of him seems a little harsh when viewed in the bright sun of the twenty-first century. Charles's image was crafted from his son's portrayal of him in exaggerated or fictional accounts that at times must have been a quest for funny storylines.

In *My Life and Hard Times,* Thurber's most famous book, he writes humorous but mostly fictional accounts of his family, and while he changed his brothers' names, he made no attempt to disguise his father.

So in *The Night the Bed Fell,* Charles is sleeping in the attic "to be away where he could think," and Mame is worried that the old bed will collapse and her husband will be killed when the bedstead falls on him. Instead, Thurber's Army cot overturns, and the crash sends the entire household into hysterics. Charles hears all the commotion and believes that the house must be on fire, and catches cold wandering around in his bare feet. It is all in harmless fun, but there is no way to appear brilliant when you are prowling around a drafty house in your bedclothes asking, "What in the name of God is going on here?"

In *More Alarms at Night,* "Roy" plays another practical joke on his father when he feigns temporary insanity by awakening him from a deep sleep and telling him, "Buck, your time has come!" Charles, who has never been called "Buck," leaps from his bed, rushes out of the room, and wakes up the household, who find "Roy" sleeping when they return to check. When "Roy" is awakened, he denies having roused his father, an explanation that Mame naturally accepts. Thurber impishly explains, "My father has been known to have nightmares, usually about Lillian Russell and Grover Cleveland, who chased him."

In *The Car We Had to Push,* Thurber's brother "Roy" assembles a canvas bag of kitchen utensils and hangs it under the family Reo, with the objects prepared to fall on the road at the tug of an attached string. The practical joke was naturally aimed at his poor father, who Thurber mischievously wrote always feared that the car might explode. The plan played out perfectly, with Charles shouting "Stop the car!" as the objects fell on the street and "Roy" saying "I can't. The engine fell out." Charles believed it, of course, until they drove back to "pick up the stuff and even father knew the difference between the works of an automobile and the equipment of a pantry."

Even father knew?

If unflattering, the accounts in *My Life and Hard Times* were all mostly fictional. Thurber tried to stick much closer to the facts in *The Thurber Album,* which was published much later, and younger brother

Robert was furious with the way his father was portrayed in "Gentleman from Indiana." He said that it should have been titled "Hoosier Half-Wit."

In it Thurber wrote—lovingly, he said—about true incidents involving his father, some of which were comical if not particularly flattering. It began with a day in 1900 when his "father was riding a lemon-yellow bicycle that went to pieces in a gleaming and tangled moment" while observers cried "Get a horse!" Thurber noted that he was "plagued by the mechanical," before adding, "He was also plagued by the manufactured, which takes in a good deal more ground."

> Knobs froze at his touch, doors stuck, lines fouled, the detachable would not detach, the adjustable would not adjust. He could rarely get the top off anything, and he was forever trying to unlock something with the key to something else. In 1908, trying to fix the snap lock of the door to his sons' rabbit pen, he succeeded only after getting inside the cage, where he was imprisoned three hours with six Belgian hares and thirteen guinea pigs.[3]

Thurber also chronicled how little athletic skill his father had, subsequently revealing that "he was addicted to contests of any kind." He told how he would "estimate the number of beans in an enormous jar, write essays, make up slogans, find the hidden figures in trick drawings, write the last line of an unfinished jingle or limerick, praise a produce in twenty-five words or fewer, get thousands of words out of a trade name, such as, for recent example, Planters Peanuts. . . . Over a period of fifty years, he won a trip to the St. Louis World's Fair, a diamond ring, a victrola, two thousand dollars worth of records, and many cash prizes, the largest, fifteen hundred dollars, as first prize in a proverb contest."[4]

This might not invoke the image of a distinguished statesman following in the footsteps of George Washington or Abraham Lincoln, but Charles did spend most of his life entering contests and Robert acknowledged that the bicycle and cage incidents were both true. What troubled him is that his brother wrote about them.

"Though Thurber had the genius to create a world of his own in which he safely prevailed," Harrison Kinney wrote, "Charles did not, and Thurber shows little mercy. Charles's record as a parent was increasingly subject to his son's recall and negative revision."[5]

There is no denying that Charles made a career out of being on the wrong side of elections, when he supported others and when he ran himself. At the age of 17, he strongly backed Republican James G. Blaine for

president against Grover Cleveland and wrongly predicted his election in
his letters to Mame; the loss seemed a harbinger of things to come. He was
an ardent supporter of Benjamin Harrison in the 1888 presidential election—he was made secretary of an Indianapolis civic club that promoted
Harrison's candidacy—and Harrison's win got him an appointment to a
clerical job in the Indiana secretary of state's office. He subsequently used
it to secure a corresponding position in the Ohio secretary of state's office
that emboldened him to the point that he proposed to Mame Fisher. Her
acceptance led him to spend the Christmas holidays with the Fisher family in 1889, which probably didn't thrill Mame's father, a rich, successful
businessman who thought his daughter could do better than a political
clerk with no real prospects for a big salary.

But given Charles's family background and lack of education, his
small successes could almost be considered remarkable. Three months
after he was born in Indianapolis, his father died when he was thrown off
a horse (or so the story goes; Thurber never believed it.) Charles's mother,
Sarah, struggled as a schoolteacher to support her son and a chronically
ill sister, and the strain eventually took its toll on her. Charles's ambitions
of either law school or a theatrical career ran into the brick wall of reality
in the eighth grade when his mom had to quit her job because of ill health
and he was forced to quit school to financially support her and his aunt.

When viewed from that context, Charles Thurber's career seems more
amazing than bland: He melded his interest in politics with writing ability
and penmanship to become a clerk to various politicians and eventually
became a staff aide to two Ohio governors, secretary to the state Republican executive committee, secretary to a Congressman, recording clerk to
the Ohio senate and secretary to the mayor of Columbus for nine years.

Even by the modest standards of the day, he wasn't paid particularly
well for any of these positions. But while earlier Thurber biographers
regard this as a sign of failure, today's Thurber scholars might see his
idealism in a more positive light: He worked hard to support those he
believed in, even those who seemed headed to certain defeat. Today, we
might say he was a man of conviction rather than a dreamer who wasn't
smart enough to hitch his wagon to the right candidate. Given enough
time—a couple of centuries, perhaps—the world might even see him as a
stunning success.

For better or worse, fate seemed to guide him. At age 11, young
Charles was sent by his mother to stay with Margery Dangler Albright at
185 South Fifth Street in Columbus for a school term; Aunt Margery, as
she was known to the Thurber family, may have been the sister of Sarah

Thurber's second husband, Tunis Dangler. The Fishers lived on the same street (the Fishers' impressive Bryden Road house was not built until 1884) and Charles Thurber and Mame Fisher attended the same school, which set the stage for their later courtship. Mame was 14 months older than Charles and a grade ahead of him in school, but she said that she fell in love with him "the first day I laid eyes on him. He came to live across the street from us with an aunt. I never cared for anybody else."[6]

By the time Charles felt that his finances were adequate enough to propose, Mame was 26. That was old for a first marriage in those days, and that coupled with her long standing desire to embark on an acting career probably made Charles a little more palatable for her father than he might normally have been. But William Fisher was never able to get past the notion that his son-in-law couldn't hold a steady job or make enough money. At one point, he even brought him into his wholesale fruit and produce business—the William M. Fisher Company—but the job he gave Charles was a menial one and Mame contended that her brother Willie ran him off.[7]

That wasn't what Charles wanted to do, anyway, so it probably didn't matter. His heart was in politics, even if politics didn't always return his affections.

In 1912, former president Theodore Roosevelt became disenchanted with the conservative administration of William Howard Taft that deviated from the progressive Republicanism that he favored and he formed the Progressive or Bull Moose Party and ran for president again on the third party's ticket. Charles, who to this point had been a loyal Republican, supported Roosevelt's candidacy—there's that idealistic dreamer again—and became the organizer and secretary for the Progressives' state campaign committee in Ohio. He did a lot of the groundwork for the Ohio campaign out of an office in the Harrison building on High Street on Statehouse Square; Roosevelt's candidacy split the Republican vote between Roosevelt and Taft and helped the Democrat, Woodrow Wilson, win. Charles stayed with the Progressives through the 1914 governor's race, coordinating the campaign of Clevelander James Garfield. The son of the former president lost, there was no money to pay Charles Thurber and the office was closed.

Thurber wrote later upon that upon his father's exit "the state organizer of the Bull Moose Party got six dozen yellow Mongol pencils, a few typewriter ribbons and several boxes of stationary."[8] While that little haul might yield hundreds of dollars in bids on eBay today, in those days it was all but worthless, the kind of payment that drove Mame's father mad.

But years later, Thurber's older brother William stoutly defended his father.

> He was secretary of (Theodore Roosevelt's) campaign in Ohio and the chairman of it was a graduate of Harvard Law school. And when he asked my father what college he went to why he almost fell out of his chair because my father wrote a lot of the speeches for some of the candidates. He couldn't believe it and almost fell out of his chair when he told him that he never went beyond the eighth grade. I think that our use of the English language and our (love of language) came from him. We never heard him make a grammatical mistake.[9]

After a sustained period of unemployment, Charles landed an appointment as cashier of the municipal court in 1916. It wasn't as heady a position as "secretary of the Progressive Party's state committee, but at least he got paid. He kept the job until 1923, showing stability he had never displayed before, and left only because he landed a much better position: secretary to the Columbus mayor James Thomas.

For the already humble Charles, the hiring process would have insured his humility. Mayor Thomas first tried to hire his son, James, who was then covering Statehouse Square for the *Columbus Evening Dispatch*. Thurber turned him down; he had been given a Sunday column, "Credos and Curios," and was probably as happy as he had been at any time during brief newspaper career.

The mayor met Charles during a lunch near City Hall shortly after that and asked him if he were related to the reporter who had turned down his offer to become secretary. Charles called James later—he was married and no longer living with his parents at that point—told him about the encounter and said that he was interested in the job himself. Thurber told his father he would put in a good word with Mayor Thomas the next day, but Thomas had supposedly been so impressed with Charles that he had already decided to hire him. Even if that's simply the story Thurber put out just to make his father seem a little more successful than he was, Charles enjoyed a good eight-year run as Thomas secretary and became a better known and more respected figure around town.

Joel Sayre, a friend to both Thurber and his brother Robert, always felt that their father deserved credit for living in a house full of zanies and believed that criticisms of him are misdirected.

These were all comedians. The Thurber house was an uproar. They were telling stories and there was this old man, Mr. Thurber, who was a sort of sad, very sweet old guy, would say "Oh, for goodness sake, let's have a little peace and quiet." And here is his wife and sons, they were just roaring away full throttle.

Mr. Thurber was in politics. . . . He was a sort of, well, Casper Milquetoast because he was a darling guy and didn't any have self-pity or anything, except he was worried about these zanies he was connected with. You know, Mr. Thurber was a pillar of probity. The cleanest living man in all of Ohio. He would be secretary to some politician who was carrying on with three or four women, you know. He would have to answer the phone and stall off the mayor's wife or something when the major was in the backroom laying one of the filing cabinet girls. Poor Mr. Thurber, he just hated all of this so much, he just had to take care of it.[10]

Charles was frequently in the news and sometimes stood in for the mayor on ceremonial occasions, gave after-dinner speeches and frequently greeted visiting dignitaries when they came to Columbus. He was popular with local reporters and photographers and sometimes appeared in their stories and pictures, which may explain why Thurber later referred to him in "Gentleman from Indiana" in *The Thurber Album* as "the most beloved man in City Hall."

When Thomas lost his bid for reelection and Charles lost his job, the *Dispatch* generously complimented him in print in 1932: "In spite of [his] long and varied public service, Thurber retains the energy and enthusiasm of his youthful days. His recent nine years in the mayor's office . . . was a supreme test of difficult, long-sustained service. He is still the same old efficient, cheerful and courteous 'Charlie' Thurber that he was at the beginning of his career."[11]

Those years in the mayor's office seems at odds with the depiction of him as a hopeless dreamer for whom success was always elusive. There's no denying that he lost elections—for the Republican nomination for clerk of courts in 1899, for the state legislature in 1932 and again at the age of 67 in 1934. Those failures didn't necessarily mean that he was a failure.

"He was easily the most honest man I have ever known," Thurber wrote.[12]

Charles began suffering from prostate issues in 1937 and gradually got worse. He died on Easter morning 1939. Funeral services conducted at the First Methodist Church—the family church that still stands under a different denomination at the corner of Bryden Road and Eighteenth Street—were crowded with people who came to pay their last respects; city officials, business leaders, judges, reporters, friends and neighbors took their turn pouring out their affection for him at the wake.

"After the eulogies faded," Thurber biographer Burton Bernstein wrote, "Charles Thurber went out as he came in—a good, honest man, easily forgotten."[13]

That may be true, although the display indicates that his contemporaries saw a different Charles than the hapless sap Thurber wrote about or the one some biographers condemn for not being able to adequately provide for his family.

Charles doesn't measure up to his son as a literary giant or to his father-in-law as a businessman. But he held responsible jobs in state or local government or the Republican Party for more than 40 years and passed qualities onto to his son that we can all be thankful for today.

When viewed from a distance of 75 years, that hardly defines him as a failure.

CHAPTER 3

The Funniest Thurber

If a professional athlete has a son or daughter who also excels in sports, it is rarely seen as some kind of remarkable coincidence. The community of outstanding athletes has never been a democracy. Genes can make a huge difference.

The offspring of professional athletes have a much better chance of becoming pro athletes than any of the rest of us. As much as we want to believe that kids who shoot basketball every day until their arms ache or don't stop taking batting practice until their hands bleed have a better chance of making it big than everyone else, it isn't true. Practice and hard work pays, but traits such as speed and hand-eye coordination are born not learned.

Although Thurber wasn't a terrific athlete, genetics served him well. Just as many a hard-throwing pitcher has gotten his sizzling fastball from his hard-throwing father, Thurber seems to have gotten his sense of humor, sharp wit and love of theatrics and mimicry from his mother. Mary Agnes "Mame" Fisher Thurber might be described as a comic genius; those who tired of her seemingly endless array of practical jokes and ceaseless chatter could also find her to be an annoying, attention-hogging pain in the rear.

Mame starred in school plays, performed for her family every chance she had and eventually longed to become a professional actress. She might just as well have told the Fisher clan that she planned to become an axe murderer.

"In 1884, when Mame Fisher got out of high school, she wanted to go on stage, but her unladylike and godless urge was discouraged by her family," Thurber wrote. "Aunt Melissa warned her that young actresses were in peril not only of hellfire but of lewd Shakespearean actors, skilled in the art of seduction, and pointed out that there was too much talk about talent in the world, and not enough about virtue. She predicted that God's wrath would be visited, in His own time, upon all theatres, beginning, like as not, with those in Paris, France. Mamie Fisher listened with what appeared to be rapt and contrite attention. Actually, she was studying Aunt Melissa's voice, so that she could learn to imitate it."[1]

Mame became the class clown, described by classmate Ruth White as "the livest wire of the old Rich Street and Mound Streets schools." The description probably also defined her performance at family gatherings.

"Mame would grab a shawl . . . a string of beads and begin to dramatize," White said. "She thought up all her own scripts, and with nothing to help her but her own keen wit and her own wild imagination, she would emote."[2]

As a teenager, she planned to run away from home with a friend who also coveted a career on the stage but her family caught wind of it and stopped her before she left town.

"I always planned for a life on the wicked stage," Mame said. "Being a comedienne was the life, was the way I looked at it. I don't know if I was funnier than the next guy, but I couldn't see myself swooning and dying onstage. I put off getting married, hoping to get on stage, and once I had all my clothes packed. Ray Brown, a schoolmate of mine, was going to run away with me to study dramatics—he finally did become an actor— but my folks caught me and made sure I stayed home after that. I was born too soon."[3]

Brown made it and eventually enjoyed a successful career as an actor, most notably as Madame (Helen) Modjeska's leading man. Mame became the star of her own little world, entertaining (and sometimes annoying) anyone who passed through it, including friends and family.

The theater's loss was literature's gain. On more than one occasion, Thurber gave his mother credit for the humor found in so many of his stories. He told Henry Brandon that "I owe practically everything to her because she is one of the finest comic talents I think I have ever known."[4] He told Alistair Cooke that "a great many things I've written were either inspired by her or deal with her."[5]

Mame Thurber would be a fascinating subject for any writer; she proved to be an inspiration for a son who inherited her sense of humor and love of theatrics. She also became widely known around Columbus for some of her antics, pranks that would have given her a small measure of local fame even if her son hadn't become a famous humorist.

While still living with her parents in their house on Bryden Road, she shocked a couple of her father's stately guests "by descending the front stairs in a dressing gown, her hair tumbling and her eyes staring, to announce that she had escaped from the attic, where she was kept because of her ardent and hapless love for Mr. Briscoe, the postman."[6]

On another occasion, she and a Cleveland newspaperman named George Marvin whom Thurber described as "a superior wag" attended a lecture at Memorial Hall given by a mental healer whom Mame thought was a fraud. During the lecture, she discovered an empty wheelchair sitting in the lobby, bundled herself up and had her companion roll her down the aisle after the woman "healer" had started her exhortations. At the peak of these, Mame leaped from the chair, cried that she had walked before and she could do it again, while the lecturer shouted "Hallelujah, sister!"

Some of the 200 or so in the audience doubtless recognized the healed cripple and realized that this was just another one Mame Thurber's gags, but the others didn't realize the miracle wasn't what it appeared until one of the patrons shouted "Hey, that's my wheelchair!" By then, Mame and her companion were headed toward the exit.[7]

She knew that a good gag can be adapted to fit occasion. Nephew Earl Fisher recalled the day that Mame and some friends were in a downtown store when they encountered a pitchman atop a makeshift stage, extolling the merits of a sure-fire cure for corns. Mame promptly removed her shoe and stocking and asked the salesman to apply his product to her corn. After she put her shoes back on, she eagerly told the gathered crowd how great her foot felt, then danced a jig on stage as a ringing endorsement of the wondrous anointment. The skeptics in the crowd thought the salesman had paid her for her performance. Those who knew her understood that this was just Mame Thurber being herself.[8]

She didn't calm down much when she got older. When she was in her 60s, she returned to Washington, DC, where the family had lived briefly years before to visit an old friend that she hadn't seen in years. She told her hostess that she would wear a red rose so she could identify her when the train arrived. When Mame got there first, she pinned the rose on a woman 20 years older sleeping on one of the terminal benches, then moved into the background to watch the "reunion."

Sure enough, her friend awakened the woman with "Why Mame Thurber, how are you? You're looking just fine," and had difficulty understanding why the stranger was less than thrilled to see her.[9]

"Have you ever seen *Auntie Mame?* It was a famous movie," said Suzanne Fisher Hutton, Mame's great niece. "She had the same personality as the main character (played by Rosalind Russell), the same kind of cuckoo, funny personality. If you saw it, you could get a sense of the way she was."[10]

The 1958 comedy depicts a free-spirited aunt who takes in an orphan, only to have the executor of his father's estate object to the aunt's zany lifestyle.

In January, 1946, Jim and second wife Helen came to Columbus for a delayed celebration of Mame's 80th birthday, which Thurber held at the Deshler-Wallick Hotel. He told his mother to come up with a list of guests she wanted; she came up with 150 names. Thurber, with Robert's help, cut the list to 55 relatives and close friends.

"Mame was equal to the hundred and fifty, but we weren't," Thurber told a *Columbus Dispatch* reporter. "Five years ago, she visited us in New York. We kept her up at a night club till 4:30 a.m. Two hours later we saw a light in her room. She was reading a detective magazine."[11]

Thurber added that she had been planning that party for a year and that she has "written me about 35,000 words in letters about it this year, and her letters are as humorous and alive as if she were 40 years old."

Somehow, that doesn't seem surprising. Not long before that birthday, Mame slipped off to the kitchen during a women's club meeting in one of her friends' homes in Columbus. She removed a dozen eggs from a cardboard container she found there and then returned to the meeting holding the box in the palm of her hand like a football. She shocked the prim gathering by announcing that "I've always wanted to throw a dozen eggs and now I'm going to do it!"

She launched the box before the horrified women had a chance to realize that this wild-eyed quarterback wannabe wasn't Eleanor Roosevelt but Mame Thurber. While the women shrieked, the empty box floated harmlessly to the floor.[12]

A lifetime of those gags can lead to an infamy of sorts. An old classmate named Mollie Harmon recalled running into Mame in the Lazarus department store one day and introducing her two granddaughters to her.

When they realized who she was, they hopped around excitedly and cried "Oh, Grandma, make her do something!"[13]

It wasn't all just gags, though, and not all of her manic behavior was met with a deep appreciation of it. Thurber biographer Charles S. Holmes quoted an unnamed Columbus resident who believed that Mame was "sadly affected with logomania," which Merriam-Webster defines as "abnormal talkativeness."

"I've known a lot of talkative women in my day," he said, "but none hold a candle to her as a compulsive talker from whom you would run. James inherited that trait (perhaps more endearingly) and harnessed it to his typewriter."[14]

Mame's embellishment of stories became familiar to all who knew her, so much that no one really knew how much of what she said was true. Thurber wrote about how his mother "set the oil-splashed bowl of a kerosene lamp on fire" while trying to light it and herded her three children out of the house at 921 South Champion Avenue while announcing that it was going to explode; he also noted the boys' disappointment when the spilled oil burned itself out and nothing happened. Mame's version of the story was even better.

"My mother claims that my brother William, who was seven at the time, kept crying 'Try it again, Mama, try it again,'" Thurber wrote, and then added, "but she is a famous hand at ornamenting a tale, and there is no way to tell whether he did that or not."[15]

There never was. Thurber's cousin, Clifford Fisher, told an interviewer about how his first wife had once included his Aunt Mame in a group of women who had been invited to their house and she "held the floor telling funny and outlandish stories. All the women said they had never had so much fun or laughed so hard.

> Aunt Mame would tell stories as if they were the gospel truth, and you couldn't budge her from that stand. For years, she had her boys believing a lot of things that were funny but just not true. She could read palms and tea leaves and bumps on your head—phrenology—and anything else she thought would entertain. She would keep the straightest face, but I had a feeling she was always laughing to herself.[16]

All of that wasn't just for entertainment purposes. Mame believed in astrology and numerology and wouldn't allow a doctor to treat her without first knowing the date and hour of their birth. When Thurber scheduled his second eye operation in October, 1940, she wrote two letters to his surgeon asking that he take the fullest advantage of the hour and planetary positions when he performed the operation. October 22 would be "a perfect time" and "after 1:30—Eastern Standard Time—would be ideal."[17]

This wasn't a joke to her. On another occasion, she had her husband Charles return a new set of car license plates because the numbers foretold ominous things from a numerology standpoint. The occult also interested her, as did any new paranormal theory or fad, which led to a lively correspondence with astrologer Evangeline Adams and a visit from French psychotherapist and lecturer Professor Emile Coue, who counseled his audiences to repeat the words "Every day in every way I am getting better and better."[18] She also sensed bad vibes in certain houses and certain rooms, although again, it was sometimes difficult to determine whether this was just another ruse.

All of this lunacy gave Thurber a terrific training ground for who he was to become.

"When I used to visit the Thurber home as a kid, there was a three-ring circus in progress all the time," writer Joel Sayre recalled. "Their mother had them all competing to be the funniest. Years later, when Jim began to ring the bell with his *New Yorker* pieces about his family life in Columbus, I'd think 'Who couldn't be a successful comic writer with that kind of mother and family?' He just had to write it straight."[19]

In the speech Thurber wrote for his acceptance of the Ohioana Award in 1953, Thurber gave his mother most of the credit for what he became.

"My only . . . regret is that my mother couldn't attend this meeting, for without her I never would have been able to write what I have managed to write," he said. "One of my friends who heard my mother tell stories one evening a few years ago when she visited me in Connecticut said 'Your humor is only a pale reflection of your mother's but if you keep at it you might be almost as good as she is some day.' This fond and wistful hope . . . is one of the things that keeps me going and will keep me going."[20]

CHAPTER 4

Aunt Pharmacy

If Margery Albright hadn't spent part of her life as James Thurber's second mother she would doubtless be lost to history, just like the vast majority of women of her generation. Once upon a distant time, most of us knew a woman like her, be it our great-grandmother, great aunt or one of those nebulous friends of the family kids accept into their lives without query. She lived as if she were a page out of a timeworn photo album, a remarkable lady whose values, work ethic, habits and cures were rooted in a time and place foreign to us.

"Aunt Margery," as Thurber knew her, had been midwife to him and both of his brothers. She had performed the same duties for Jamie's father, which was her introduction and induction into the family. She wasn't technically Jamie's aunt, although she may have been the sister of Charles Thurber's stepfather. It doesn't matter. Jamie spent a significant chunk of his youth in her care, particularly during times when the family was living with his maternal grandparents on Bryden Road.

An impatient Grandpa Fisher found Jamie the most disruptive of the boys, and in a house overcrowded with Thurbers, his parents often farmed him out to the widowed Aunt Margery for a few days or even a few weeks at a time.

Thurber may have spent a more important chunk of his time at Aunt Margery's rickety two-story frame house at 185 South Fifth Street than he did anywhere in Columbus, including the house on Jefferson that is

known as the Thurber House today. But in one those quirks of historical
preservation, there is nothing today to indicate he had ever been on the
street, let alone spent so much time there during his formative years.

To think that Thurber lived only in Thurber House, as some today
probably do, is to think that he and the family materialized there at some
point, lived there a few years and then disappeared. If you subscribe to
this curious line of thinking, the next thing you know Thurber materialized again in New York on the staff of *The New Yorker*.

The truth is that as a boy Jamie might have known Aunt Margery's
neighborhood better than any, because the family was constantly on the
move and Mrs. Albright wasn't. She moved into the old frame house in
1878 and was still living there when she died at the age of 87 in 1917.

"The old house was a fire trap, menaced by burning coal and by
lighted lamps carried by ladies of dimming vision," Thurber wrote, "but
those perils, like economic facts, are happily lost on the very young."[1]

Because Holy Cross Church and its accompanying parish buildings
occupied the block across the street, the east side of the South Fifth is
little changed from Mrs. Albright's day. The west side offers no clues the
area had ever been residential. She occupied the north side of a double on
what was the corner of Fifth and Walnut Alley. It takes some imagination
to see Aunt Margery's house or even the alley, which has been replaced
by a driveway to the parking lot in the rear of a two-story office building that has Mrs. Albright's address today. That building replaced a gas
station on the site in 1956. The modern building sits back from the street
far enough that it also occupies space that once served as Aunt Margery's
garden, which Thurber wrote about at age six in a kind of poem entitled "My Aunt Mrs. John T. Savage's Garden at 185 South Fifth Street,
Columbus, Ohio." That has been called his first piece of writing.

Thurber described the house "as one of the serene, substantial structures of my infancy and youth, for all of its flimsy shabbiness." He added
that "at the turn of the century. Fifth Street was paved with cobblestones,
and a genial City Council allowed a tall sycamore tree to stand squarely
in the middle of the brick sidewalk in front of Mrs. Albright's house,
dropping its puffballs in season."[2]

The eastern wall of Jim West's livery stable rose less than 15 feet from
her back stoop. ("Against that wall was a trellis of moonflowers." Thurber
wrote, ". . . and between the trellis and the stoop you could pull up water
from a cistern in the veritable oaken bucket of the song.") The three-story
Farmers Hotel, a popular spot for butchers and farmers who got up early
to prepare for their stands for a 6 a.m. opening at the Central Market on

Tuesdays, Thursdays and Saturdays, stood on the other side of that, and the market itself lay west of that, on the other side of South Fourth Street. That exemplifies the smaller Columbus of Aunt Margery's world. Even as an elderly woman, she could walk to the open-air market and buy fresh produce and meat from area farmers and butchers. She could walk to John Hance's grocery on Town Street, a half block to Town from her house and another half-block west his store. It would have been located in what is the Holiday Inn parking lot today.

Aunt Margery is one of the most interesting characters in a small army of them in the wacky world Thurber grew up in. She appears in Thurber's stories as herself, Mrs. Willoughby, Aunt Wilma Hudson, Aunt Ida and, even at age six, as Mrs. John T. Savage. His remembrance of her in "Daguerreotype of a Lady" in *The Thurber Album* ranks among his best work and is dripping with affection for her. It was one of only two profiles (his mother's was the other) in that book about his Columbus connections that he chose to include in a 1957 anthology of some of his best prose since 1942, *Alarms and Diversions*. That may have been in part due to the fine writing; he probably also saw it as a final tribute to his beloved Aunt Margery.

At various times during his life, Thurber liked to give his friends the impression that he had somehow succeeded despite a terrible childhood, and he sometimes earned this badge of honor by trashing Aunt Margery. It's difficult to believe that "that awful old woman" that he described to Ann Honeycutt in his *New Yorker* days was the same person he wrote about in "Daguerreotype of a Lady," but Honeycutt also described Thurber as "an exaggerator" to biographer Harrison Kinney and it seems clear that he wanted to make his friends believe that he had succeeded despite the abuse inflicted upon him by his family.[3] To fully illustrate his point he apparently thought he needed to inject a neglectful family and the Wicked Witch of Columbus into the tales he told them. But by the time he wrote the profiles for *The Thurber Album*, he may have wanted to set the record straight.

Thurber's older brother William told interviewer Lewis Branscomb that all three of the Thurber boys loved her, but that only Jamie lived there.

"When we were very young, why, they had an awful time with us because we used to fight among ourselves and Jamie was the peacemaker," William said. "Finally, my mother and father solved it. They sent Jamie down to this old aunt, nurse, not an aunt, we called her an aunt, and he stayed with her and Robbie stayed home and they sent me to my grandparents.

"She was a marvelous woman. She was a natural nurse and wonderful with children."[4]

"Aunt Margery" was born Margery Dangler in 1830, so when James came to know her she was close to 70 years old. The woman he described could have been any old woman as seen through the eyes of a small boy: She "was stout and round and, in the phrase of one of her friends, set close to the ground, like a cabbage. Her shortness was curiously exaggerated by the effect of an early injury. She had fractured her right kneecap in a fall on the ice when she was in her late teens, and the leg remained twisted, so that when she was standing, she bent over as if she were about to lean down and tie her shoelace, and her torso swayed side to side when she walked, like the slow pendulum of an ancient clock, arousing sympathy in the old and wonder in the young."[5]

As with any boy, the young Thurber would have been amazed to think she had once been young herself. She had been born in Long Branch, N. J., and came west with her family in a covered wagon during Martin Van Buren's presidency (1837–41). The family lived in Kokomo, Indiana, and Lebanon, Arcanum, and Greenville, Ohio. Her husband, Jonas, died in Greenville in 1865, and Margery apparently came to Columbus not long after that.

She first appears in a city directory in 1876 with a residence on Friend Street, the original name for Main, and she was in that house on South Fifth by 1878. She considered herself a nurse and often made house calls to the Thurber family, although nursing in those days didn't guarantee steady work. Thurber described her and her daughter Belle, also widowed at an early age, as "poor" and wrote that they took in laundry and ironing to help pay the $10 a month rent. At times, Mrs. Albright also worked as a housekeeper at the United States Hotel at the northwest corner of Town and High Streets (where a remodeled six-story building that once housed the F. R. Lazarus department store stands today) and the American House, exactly one block to the north on Statehouse Square. While working there, she remembered Stephen A. Douglas, the U.S. Senator from Illinois who opposed Abraham Lincoln in the 1860 presidential election, as "the tidiest lodger she ever had to deal with it," recalling that he sometimes even made his own bed. If true, she must have lived in the city sometime between 1858 and 1861, although there is no record of it. Douglas died in 1861 at the early age of 48 of typhoid fever.

If only Aunt Margery had been around at the time of his death, it's intriguing to wonder what she would have prescribed for him. Much of what Thurber wrote about her dealt with her cures for various ailments and afflictions, which clearly made an impression on him as a young boy.

> Shelves in Mrs. Albright's sitting room, where they were handy to get at, held alum for canker sores; cocoa butter, for the chest; paregoric, for colic and diarrhea; laudanum, for pain; balsam apples, for poultices; bismuth, for the bowels; magneeshy (carbonate of magnesium), a light, chalky substance, wrapped in a blue paper, that was an antacid and a gentle laxative; and calomel and blue mass, regarded by women of Aunt Margery's generation as infallible regulators of the liver. Blue mass came in the form of pills, and she made it by rubbing up metallic mercury with confection of roses . . .[6]

If this is starting to sound like your neighborhood Walgreen's, it is worth noting the differences. When her husband came down with a high fever one day in Darke County, Ohio, and it hadn't broken by the second day, Thurber said Margery knew what she must do:

> She went out into the pasture and gathered a pailful of sheep droppings, which she referred to in the flattest possible terms. Sheep droppings were not the only thing that Mrs. Albright looked for in the pasture and the barnyard to assist her ministrations as a natural nurse. Now and then, in the case of a stubborn pregnancy, she would cut a quill from a chicken feather, fill it with powdered tobacco, and blow the contents up the nostril of an expectant mother. This would induce a fit of sneezing that would dislodge the most reluctant baby . . .[7]

All of this seems a little crazy, but Thurber gave credit to Aunt Margery for saving not only his life but the life of his father. So as different as she was and as eccentric as she must have sometimes seemed, it's clear that Thurber loved and appreciated her and realized that at a time of his life when he really needed support, she gave it to him.

After she died, Thurber wished "that some closer student of Aunt Margery could have taken over those final rites. . . . Somebody should have told how she snatched up a pair of scissors one day and cut a hornet in two when it lighted on the head of a sleeping baby; and how she took an axe and chopped off the head of a savage outlaw cat that killed chickens, attacked children and, blackest sin of all, disturbed the sleep of a woman patient; and about the time she whipped off her calico blouse, put it over the eyes of a frightened horse, and led him out of a burning barn while the menfolks, at great distance, laughed at her corset cover and cheered her courage."[8]

Thurber knew and appreciated what Aunt Margery had meant to him. She may have been the first one to provide him with the support he needed to succeed as a writer. At the very least, she provided him material needed for his writing.

CHAPTER 5

The Man Thrower

Of all of James Thurber's individual profiles in *The Thurber Album,* his account of the life of his great-grandfather, Jacob Fisher, is the most fanciful.

Jacob Fisher was Hulk Hogan. He was Charles Atlas. He was Superman. He was Hercules. He was one of the strongest men in the region and maybe anywhere.

The Jacob Fisher who Thurber immortalized was also apparently a bit of myth, a muscular guy whose incredible feats of strength were probably mostly a nostalgic exaggeration of Thurber's step-great uncle. Mahlon Taylor was 85 years old when he recalled them for his nephew's *New Yorker* portrait "A Good Man" in 1942. After seeing that Jacob's obituary included the line "In his prime Jacob Fisher was the strongest man for many miles below the city," Thurber asked his uncle about it. By doing so, he inadvertently opened the floodgates of whimsical stories about the old farmer that stretch the bounds of imagination.

There is no doubting that Jake Fisher was a powerful man. Growing up on a farm in the first half of the nineteenth century demanded the kind of daily labor that would grow muscles on the meekest of men and he probably was stronger than most of his neighbors. But most of the tales of his great-grandfather that Thurber spun later in "Adam's Anvil"[1] sound like they sprung from the mind of an imaginative scriptwriter.

First, the facts: Jacob was born in 1808 in a log cabin that his father Michael built on the east bank of the Scioto River around 1800. The cabin stood on a farm that straddled the river in what is now the south side of Columbus. Jacob married Nancy Newell, who died shortly after they were married, in 1829, and then married Mary Briggs in 1830. Jake and Mary had nine children, including Thurber's grandfather, William Fisher.

He had a sawmill that had to be torn down when the Ohio Canal bisected his property and he built a stone house ("people used to go out from the town to watch him pick up a three-hundred pound granite sill and set it in place")[2] to replace his father's log cabin. The Chillicothe Road, which has the dual identity as U.S. 23 and South High Street today, also ran through his farm, which Thurber described as 10,000 acres. Because the Fisher farm, which ran from Williams Road on the south to Alcott Road on the north and Lockbourne Road on the east, seems to have been be 1,400 acres at its largest (when he also had property west of the river), this is probably a good place to gauge the validity of all of the fantastic claims about his strength. If Thurber was willing to go along with the notion the Fisher's farm was almost 10 times larger than it really was, then those fantastic tales Uncle Mahlon told—"He could throw a six-foot grown man as far as twenty-five feet when he was in a rage"[3]— are surely not to be believed.

Even if he were incredibly strong for his size, Mahlon Taylor described Jacob as "only a hair over five foot ten" and said he "weighed a hundred and ninety-eight pounds, most of it bone and muscle."[4] That might make for a scrappy fighter, but it doesn't explain how he always seemed to be beating up or "throwing" large groups of men in scenes that remind a twenty-first-century visitor of a hero in one of today's action movies.

Thurber's story is doubtless *based* on fact. When he writes that his great-grandfather could heft a bigger load of stone or iron than any other man for miles south of the city, or that he once picked up the old wheel of a locomotive and threw it 34 inches farther the next strongest man in the vicinity, it certainly seems plausible. It's when Jacob starts "whipping" people—Uncle Mahlon claimed that he "fought a thousand fights in his time" and "never lost a fight"—that the tale begins to feel fictional.

He supposedly fought men for swearing, saying "There's too goddam much blasphemin' goes on," a funny line that was remarkably similar to one Thurber attributed to his boss at the *New Yorker,* Harold Ross, in a another book.

Jake didn't like Andrew Jackson, supposedly because he heard a story of how the general ordered an execution of a young soldier who deserted in order to visit his dying mother. For that reason, "he licked every Jackson man he met."

The Chillicothe pike was originally a toll road, and Jake allowed the road contractor to use all the gravel he needed from a gravel pit on his property in exchange for toll-free travel after the road was finished. As these things always seem to happen, after the tollgate was put in place the agreement was quickly forgotten by everybody but Jake and the tollgate operators.

"He'd git out and beat up the tollgate keeper, and then raise the gate and drive on," Uncle Mahlon told Thurber. "They kept putting bigger and stronger men on the gate. Jake licked eight of 'em all told, and finally his patience gave out and he threatened to go over their heads to their bosses and lick them, and after that they didn't molest him. The gatekeeper would h'ist the gate when Jake's rig was still a quarter-mile away."[5]

The canal that ran through his property became the root of another story. In this one, the bargemen were using whips to lasso ducks and pull them up to the barge, ducks Jake believed were his property. It didn't take long for him to jump onto the boat and start throwing the thieves into the canal and onto the land. Uncle Mahlon reported that many bones were broken that day. It's a good bet none of them were Jake's.

Then there was the day that Jake shot an Indian who beat him in a foot race "over by the deer lick west of the river." Jake didn't like Indians, a common trait at a time when Indians raids that led to the Battle of Fallen Timbers were still a vivid memory for many living souls. But once Jake shot one—or for that matter, injured anybody—he would always take the victim home and nurse him back to health.

Maybe that explains this sentence in his obituary: "His education was not of the polished, modern sort, but a man of larger heart or one who delighted more in relieving distress, never lived."[6] Thankfully, it didn't say anything about his creating some of the distress before he relieved it.

Cooperheads, Peace Democrats who opposed the Civil War, were another one of his targets. When the war started, Jake was 53, Despite his repeated attempts to enlist, the Army wouldn't take him. So he fought his own war at home, taking on anybody who disagreed with Lincoln's policies.

"On market day Jake would lick as many as six, eight men," Uncle Mahlon told Thurber.

He ordered one of the critics off his horse, and while the poor guy was taking off his coat to fight, Jake "picked the animal up in his arms and moved it eight or ten feet away" because he said he didn't want the guy to hit the horse when he threw him. On another day during the war years, a friend told him that "five men, probably Copperheads were conspiring to beat Jake up." Thurber wrote that they were in the back room of "Frick's saloon"—John Frech had a well-known saloon that also sold imported wines, cigars and tobacco at 30–32 Town Street, just east of High Street—laying plans for a mass assault. Jake didn't wait for them. He rode a horse to Frech's and confronted them.

"He didn't knock those fellows down," Uncle Mahlon told Thurber. "He throwed 'em. Jake only fought with his fists over political or religious questions."[7]

All of these stories, exaggerated or not, were apparently well known within the family. Clifford Fisher, Thurber's cousin and another one of Jake's great-grandsons, told Alice Leighner that the tales weren't exaggerated.

> No, Jim's grandfather and mine, William Fisher, Jake's son, always admired his father and talked about him a lot, so what Jim wrote about Jake was well known to us all. Jake was always fighting somebody. Sometimes he'd beat up a guy and then take him home so he could nurse him back to health. After that he'd let the fellow go his own way with a warning not to do again whatever it was he'd done to cause the fight.
>
> But Jake, you might say, was a doctor of sorts, too, helping people out. He had a herb garden and he'd make concoctions to cure the ailment of liver, stomach, fevers and such. He called it his "physic" business. He felt people ought to go to church, and if somebody didn't have a good reason for not going, or if somebody beat his wife and Jake heard about it, he'd beat the guy up. If he thought it ought to be done, he'd just do it whether it was legal or not.[8]

Mary Briggs Fisher died in 1876, and shortly thereafter, Jake apparently moved into the city. He resided at the Farmers Hotel at the southeast corner of Town and Fourth Streets across from the Central Market and did some work at his son's produce company until his death at the age of 77 in 1885. He died at the home of his carpenter son, Milton, at 280 East Main Street, which seems odd given the size of William's house on Bryden Road and the number of family members who lived there at one time or another.

The 1885 obituary Thurber saw with the one-word headline "Memorial," actually reported that the deceased "was *one* of the strongest men for many miles below the city"—which takes him down another notch and brings him closer to mere mortal. That proves there is some basis for the stories, but also stands as one final piece of evidence that his physical feats were probably exaggerated.

If a modern relative wants to get close to old Jake today, probably the best place to do it is Walnut Hill Cemetery on Rathmell Road just west of Hamilton Township High School. Jacob, his wife, his parents and small army of Fishers are buried there, and Uncle Mahlon told Thurber that "about all the graves in the old Walnut Hill Cemetery were dug single-handed by Jake. He never allowed nobody to help him."[9]

He almost certainly dug his own while he was at it. It's the only ending to his story that would make any sense.

CHAPTER 6

Showing His Fisher

If a respectable businessman walked with a rose in his teeth from the Abramson & O'Connell law office at 695 Bryden Road to a building just east of the Columbus Commons today, he would probably elicit more than a few raised eyebrows and curious stares.

Yet Thurber's maternal grandfather, William M. Fisher, did just that every day. Fisher lived in the beautiful brick home at 695 Bryden and had a profitable produce business at 120 East Town Street. Town Street turns into Bryden Road at Parsons Ave., the corner where his property was located, and he walked eight blocks straight down Town to work. In the summer, he plucked a fresh red rose from his wife's garden and clamped it tightly in his teeth like a fine cigar. When her roses weren't in bloom, he would visit a florist to make sure he always had a red one to accent his black beard.

Fine Civil War era mansions lined both sides of Town Street in those days (some of which have survived) and all of his neighbors undoubtedly grew to expect that kind of behavior from Bill Fisher, even if it did seem a little odd. Thurber wrote that his Grandpa Fisher "had a compelling urge to stand out among men" and this was apparently only one of the ways he did that. He had all of his teeth capped with gold when he was a young man and enjoyed having people compliment him on his color scheme—rose, gold and black. He also loved having his picture taken, apparently to the point of obsession. A large "heavily-framed" photograph of him wearing his black derby hat and an overcoat and carrying a satchel occupied a prominent place in his living room, and a telegram had been inserted in the lower left corner, behind the glass, which read "Urgent. Do not go to Catawba tonight. Details follow." [1]

He happily explained the details to everyone who asked and Thurber also reported them in his portrait of his grandfather in *The Thurber Album*: ". . . he had been about to leave his hotel in Port Clinton, Ohio, where he had gone one summer in the eighteen-eighties to buy peaches, when the telegram arrived from his store. If it had come ten minutes later, he said, he would have been aboard a small excursion steamer for Catawba Island that sank with the loss of everyone aboard. Any other man, learning of the disaster and of his close escape, would have gone to the bar for a stiff drink. My grandfather hunted up the nearest photographer." [2]

It may seem like Thurber is guilty of going for a cheap laugh at grandfather's expense here. But the deeper you dig into William M. Fisher's story, the more his grandson's rise to prominence as a famous American humorist seems like a poetic justice. Fisher's financial success aside, he often comes off as an egotistical martinet with an obsession for toughness he believed had been inherited from his father and grandfather, one with the sensitivity of a wild boar.

Whenever one of his grandsons got hurt, he would offer them sympathy they might have received from a trainer in the corner of beleaguered professional boxer "Show your Fisher, boy!" he would yell. "Show your Fisher!"

Robert Thurber said his brother Jamie was unhappy during the period when the family lived with the Fishers on Bryden Road, and not just because the Thurbers were viewed as the poor relatives.

"The main cause of it was my grandfather," Robert said. "Sometimes he would be drinking a little and he'd like to be free with his hands, push us around. During those times, he went for Jamie first and would grab his wrist and squeeze until he heard Jamie cry out. He didn't like Jamie 'playing the fool,' as he called it. And, of course, Jamie never liked Grandfather." [3]

It's probably not surprising that Grandpa Fisher treated the comedic, one-eyed Jamie with some disdain. Fisher doubtless surmised that his soft grandson had been saddled with weak Thurber genes instead of the superior Fisher ones.

Thelma Roseboom, Jamie's second cousin, told interviewer Rosemary O. Joyce for *Of Thurber and Columbustown* that she had never forgotten how Jamie's grandfather treated him.

"When Jamie was on the stairway, Uncle Will would always yell at him commandingly '*Get out!*'" Roseboom said. "He didn't like him because he couldn't see. Isn't that unkind and cruel? I always hated Uncle Will for that. I still do, which will probably keep me out of the pearly gates, I'm sure."[4]

What William Fisher couldn't surmise was that his helpless victim would one day own a literary hammer considerably more effective than anything he could dish out with his hands and arms.

Thurber used his grandfather's tale about cheating death on Lake Erie as the model for "The Luck of Jad Peters," that short story set in Sugar Grove, Ohio. Peters is a fictional guy who "got so that he could figure out lucky escapes for himself in almost every disaster and calamity that happened in and around Sugar Grove." It's a funny story about a guy who is a bit of a kook, and as was often the case, Thurber must have delighted in his private joke as it applied to his grandfather. It's difficult to know exactly where all of the similarities between Jad Peters and his wife (Aunt Emma) and William and Kate Fisher begin and end. But Thurber loved his grandmother, a kindly lady who must have put up a lot with such a domineering husband, and Thurber took some shots here, saying that Peters "is remembered in his later years as a garrulous, boring old fellow," that some of Aunt Emma's "relatives said among themselves that it would be a blessing if Jad died in one of his frequent fits of nausea" and that "Aunt Emma never liked him very much . . . and she stayed married to him on account of the children and because her people always stayed married."[5]

For all of his flaws, there is no disputing Fisher's business acumen. He worked on his father's farm south of Columbus, and when William was 27, Jacob Fisher gave him 47½ acres of it in what was then Hamilton Township at what is now the northeast corner of Williams Road and South High Street. William's grandfather, Michael Fisher, was one of the state's earliest settlers; he came to Ohio before the turn of the nineteenth century and purchased a military tract of about 800 acres on the west side of the Scioto River four miles south of the heart of Columbus.[6] He sold part of it and bought 600 acres from John Dill on the east bank and lived in a log house there on the Chillicothe Road, which today is South High Street. His property appears to have extended from the river to Lockbourne Road on the east, a distance of about a mile, and from Williams Road on the south to a line approximately where Alcott Road crosses High today. The original log house and the structure that likely grew up around it is gone today, but it seems likely to have been in an area west of High across the road from the South Drive-In Theater, an area now well within the city limits but all farmland in those days.

William was one of eight children and the fifth of six boys of Jacob and Mary Briggs Fisher. He didn't take to farming; he also didn't make that decision until shortly after his father deeded the property to him, or two years after the Civil War. Regardless of whether this life-altering decision came to him naturally at that point, his timing proved remarkably convenient. He had paid another man to serve in the Army for him, an escape from duty made possible because he was doing work vital to the Union cause as a farmer.

He left the farm when he was 27 to work as a clerk in F. A. Sells's grocery store, and opened his own grocery with John Wagonseller at 114 South Fourth Street in Columbus shortly thereafter. The venture lasted only two years. Wagonseller apparently sold his part of the business to J. W. Leach and Fisher soon returned to his father's farm on South High Street. His appetite for the grocery business had been wetted, though. Before long, he went back to the city and started another grocery and added a wholesale fruit and produce house. He stopped commuting from his place in the country and moved into a house at 272 South Sixth Street.

An 1879 ad in the city directory describes the business as "Wholesale fruit and vegetable commission merchants, apples, berries, potatoes, eggs a specialty." Similar ads in the 1880 and 1882 directories had upgraded it this way: "Wholesale commission merchants and dealers in foreign and domestic fruits and farm products—poultry and game in season."

With his business flourishing, Fisher moved it into the Gwynne Block, an ornate three-story building at 120 East Town Street that had been constructed in 1854. The company grew until it occupied a larger part of it and Fisher bought the building in 1882. The company remained in business there as William M. Fisher and Sons Company until 1960, when it was sold. At the time, it was the oldest produce company in the nation still managed by the original family.

The early success of his business is evident in the fact that he bought the first three lots on the south side of Town Street east of Parsons Avenue; at the time, Parsons was regarded as the eastern edge of the still-small capital city. Fisher built a seven-bedroom, 3,962 square foot brick house with four porches there in 1884.

Construction of the house might have been another attempt by William Fisher to attract attention. Thurber wrote about how his grandfather

had witnessed his own father's feats of strength and "could not be dis-
suaded from the conviction that he could equal the great man's achieve-
ments. He thought of himself as a fighter up to the year he died and was
usually unable to argue with a man without letting go a right swing."

Again, the real punches Fisher threw couldn't match Thurber literary
jabs. He notes that "As far as we know, he never actually hit a man," a
subtle way of saying his gradnfather's physical feats more or less matched
his Civil War bravado. Union general (and later president) Ulysses S.
Grant was one of Fisher's idols. He named his second son after him and
displayed photos of the war hero in his house, which seems curious for
a man who avoided military service by paying another man to take his
place. Thurber obviously thought so, too.

"I don't know what old Jake Fisher, who kept trying to enlist in the
Union forces when he was in his fifties, thought of a son who had no han-
kering to fight with Grant's Army of the West," Thurber wrote, "but the
celebrated horse lifter probably complained about it from time to time
between Bull Run and Gettysburg."[7]

Even though Thurber obviously didn't hold his grandfather in high
regard, he acknowledged his good qualities when he profiled him in *The
Thurber Album*. He told of how his grandfather's interest in stories of
gold in Georgia led to only major business blunder of his life, the forma-
tion (with several friends) of the Dahlonega Gold Mining Company. He
sank $50,000 of his own money in the operation and induced friends and
relatives to buy a similar quantity of stock in the venture, of which he was
named president.

When the company went bust, Thurber wrote that he "couldn't sleep
until the last of his friends had been repaid." He was under no legal obli-
gation to do this, of course, but felt bound by his "word of honor," even
though he nearly went bankrupt while repaying those he had persuaded
to buy stock. During this period of financial distress, Thurber wrote that
"there is a legend that in the dark days he would chew right up to the
stem of the rose and start on the pedals."

After William Fisher died, his safe deposit box coughed up a clump of
letters from relieved investors he had repaid, including one from a regis-
tered nurse who had invested $1,000 in the ill-advised operation.

Thurber often softened his view when he wrote about identifiable
people, and Grandpa Fisher got the same break. And yet he was still a
frequent target over the years, starting with Thurber's characterization of
him in *My Life and Hard Times*.

It was all in good fun, or at least it was supposed to be. But Thurber had only one grandfather and in his "fictional" account titled "The Car We Had to Push" he portrayed him as a senile old man who couldn't differentiate between the death of the family car, a Reo, and a member of the family.

> He apparently gathered, from the talk and excitement and weeping, that somebody had died. He insisted, in fact, after almost a week in which we strove mightily to divert him, that it was a sin and a shame and a disgrace to put off the funeral any longer. "Nobody is dead! The automobile is smashed!" shouted my father, trying for the thirtieth time to explain the situation to the old man. "Was he drunk?" demanded grandfather, sternly. "Was who drunk?" asked father. "Zenas," said grandfather. He had a name for the corpse now; it was his brother Zenas, who, as it happened, *was* dead, but not from driving an automobile while intoxicated. Zenas had died in 1866.[8]

Thurber must have gotten tremendous enjoyment out of writing this:

> Now that grandfather knew, so to speak, who was dead, it became increasingly awkward to go on living in the same house with him as if nothing had happened. He would go into towering rages in which he threatened to write to the Board of Health unless the funeral were held at once.[9]

Later in *My Life and Hard Times,* Thurber again had fun at the expense of his fictitious grandfather in "Draft Board Nights." This time, his grandfather kept trying to enlist to fight in World War I even though he was an old man—a nice touch of irony considering that Thurber's *real* grandfather had paid another man to serve for him—and he was pictured reading the *Memoirs of U.S. Grant* at 7 one morning.

> One reason we didn't want grandfather to roam around at night was that he had said something once or twice about going over to Lancaster, his old home town, and putting his problem up to "Cump"—that is, General William Tecumseh Sherman, also an old Lancaster boy. We knew that his inability to find Sherman would be bad for him and we were afraid that he might try to get there in that little electric runabout that had been bought for my grandmother . . .[10]

Sherman was long since dead, of course, and hadn't lived in Lancaster since he was a teenager.

But the humorous tales of his fictional grandpa's problems with the electric runabout that followed also mimicked those that his real grandpa had with one.

His fictional grandfather approached the electric "as he might have approached a wild colt." When he wanted to drive, the family would take him to nearby Franklin Park, "where the roadways were wide and unfrequented, and spend an hour or so trying to explain the differences between driving a horse and carriage and driving an electric. He would keep muttering all the time. . . ." Once, when they found him driving in circles, he was "pulling too savagely on the guiding bars, trying to teach the electric a lesson . . . He had the notion that if you didn't hold her, she would throw you. And a man who (or so he often told us) had driven a four-horse McCormick reaper when he was five years old did not intend to be thrown by an electric runabout."[11]

Is this fiction? In "Man with a Rose" Thurber wrote of his real grandfather much the same way, saying that he approached the machine as if it were an unbroken colt.

> He would sit tensely erect, tightly gripping the guiding bar, and drive down the center of the street, occasionally talking to the thing as if it were alive, or shouting "Get out of the way!" at other drivers.

Both grandfathers—the "fictional" and the real—ended up crashing into a barbed wire fence. The fictional one had his accident on "Nelson Road, about four miles from the town of Shepard" and the real one had his "far from town," after Grandpa Fisher had paid the fifteen-year-old Thurber "a dollar to drive her out in the country and show him how" to back up. After it took the garage man an hour to free the car from the fence, Thurber wrote that his grandfather "said, in his bluffest manner, 'Drop in at the store and I'll give you a watermelon.' He was forever trying to cover up embarrassing situations by offering people watermelons."[12]

Fisher had senility issues late in life, which doubtless fed Thurber at least some of his material. Joel Sayre said that during World War I, Thurber's grandfather would often buy a ticket to the vaudeville shows at the B. F. Keith Theater on Gay Street and pace up and down the aisles during the performances. Because of Fisher's long standing in the community, the management of the theater tolerated this, warning the audience beforehand of his expected behavior.

But one afternoon, he went too far. He looked to the stage just as an actor playing Abraham Lincoln was getting roughed up in a cabinet meeting. He couldn't sit back while one of his heroes was mistreated and he leaped on stage and went after the antagonist, flailing away until the other actors subdued him[13].

Thurber never wrote about any of that in *The Thurber Album*, probably because he didn't want to generate an outcry from other members of the family. But that kind of behavior from his grandfather probably had a lot to do with Thurber's portrayals of him in some of his short stories, even if he "protected" him with a thin, easily recognized disguise.

It seems like a subtle way of paying back the old curmudgeon for squeezing and twisting his arm.

CHAPTER 7

•

Mother Katherine

James Thurber loved his grandmother. He leaves no doubt about that in the things he wrote about her. He also wrote so little about her that it is just as clear that he didn't know much beyond what he saw, heard and remembered of her as a boy and as a young man.

Katherine Matheny Fisher seemed almost the antithesis of her husband. While William Fisher was obsessed with his success, his pride and his possessions, Kate was sweet, kind-hearted lady concerned with those less fortunate than herself. She gave away so many baskets of her husband's produce to families in need that when William would find his wife gone upon his arrival at home he often responded with a not so charitable "Who's she looking after now?"[1]

Thurber appreciated those qualities in her even if her husband didn't. Being married to William Fisher must have had its trying moments, and she married him in 1862 when she was 16. Their family eventually grew to 11 children and she must have spent most of her time raising them while her husband worried about making money, playing the role of tough guy and getting his photo taken.

"I was just a child when she passed away," said ninety-two-year-old granddaughter Suzanne Fisher Hutton, by phone from Guelph, Ontario. "She was a wonderful, loving woman. Everybody loved her. She was a very kind person. It's typical. She had a strong husband who was the boss of every little thing they did and she was gentle and the opposite. She'd do what he said. You know, that was back in the age when Papa is boss. But she was dearly beloved by everyone."[2]

Thurber wrote that she was 39 when they moved to house on Bryden Road and had already become "Aunt Kate," source of advice, comfort or help to most members of the Fisher, Matheny and Taylor families.

> I have no memories of her sitting down—even at Sunday dinner she was forever up and fluttering around—and Whistler would have had his hands full trying to make her pose, even for an hour, relaxed and oblivious, while her world bustled around her. She moved about purposefully, swiftly and silently, as if she had small, oiled wheels on her shoes, lengthening the busy hours of her matriarchal days as the years went on, the fortune and responsibilities of her husband increased, and new rooms were added to the house on Bryden Road.[3]

The Fishers enjoyed having "a houseful of people," so relatives from all branches and all generations of their families visited their well-to-do kin on Bryden Road. The house was gathering place on special occasions, often serving as a meeting place before a family outing or picnic to Olentangy, Indianola, or Minerva parks, a day at the Ohio State Fair or even a trip to Sugar Grove for a family reunion. And through it all, "Aunt Kate" was the one everyone looked toward to bring order and purpose to the chaos.

Her charitable acts defined her. A dozen wicker market baskets were stored in her pantry, ready to be filled on Thanksgiving and Christmas with fruits and vegetables, canned goods, jams and jellies and even past issues of some of her favorite magazines—*Ainslee's, Pearson's, Munsey's, Everybody's,* and *County Life in America*—and possibly an envelope containing a check from her private bank account. The recipients of these might be friends or relatives or they might be total strangers, someone she had heard about who was suffering from health issues or was simply down on their luck.

When the Thurbers moved in with the Fishers, it seems to have been at Kate's insistence. In 1905, when Charles Thurber came down with a near-fatal illness that William Thurber later described as "brain disease," it was Grandma Fisher who convinced her husband to take the entire family in.[4] Even though the Fisher house on Bryden Road had plenty of space, her husband resented the fact his daughter had married a man who could be forced to move his family in with his in-laws at the first sign of a serious illness or job loss. But he relented and the family seems to have stayed there for most of the year. They moved into an apartment in the Norwich Hotel in 1906 when Charles Thurber's health improved and he was able to resume working in temporary clerical jobs, but the family was still struggling and apparently moved back in in 1907, again undoubtedly at Kate Fisher's insistence.

Thurber wrote that her grandchildren all remembered her "with great affection,"[5] which again seems in direct contrast to her husband, who could be generous and genial but could also be stern and cruel and must have been difficult for most of them to like. Some of this was doubtless a product of the age; the men of the day weren't expected to be sensitive, caring souls, which were seen as a woman's traits.

Grandma Fisher seemed to epitomize them, especially to her grandchildren, eleven of whom were still alive when Thurber wrote about her in *The Thurber Album*.

> She was always getting us out of the dilemmas of childhood, quietly, ingeniously, and without stern lectures, and buying the girls diavolos and woodburning sets, and the boys skates, fielder's gloves, games, or whatever else she had overheard us say we wanted. When her grandsons married, their wives got from her, in addition to a formal wedding present, some old cherished possession of hers, a piece of jewelry, a set of china, or anything else they had seen in her house and admired. If some familiar object could not be found, a search was never made for it until Grandma Fisher was asked if she had given it away. She usually had.[6]

When Thurber wrote "The Luck of Jad Peters" and more or less modeled the fictional characters after his grandmother and grandfather, the implication was that "Aunt Emma" probably spent the happiest years of her life after her husband died. It's difficult to say whether he intended to draw that correlation, although he obviously wrote about his grandmother with an affection that he didn't feel for her husband.

In the humorous fictional accounts of his family in *My Life and Hard Times*, Thurber's wacky grandfather is a character in five of the nine stories—"The Night the Bed Fell," "The Car We Had to Push," "The Day the Dam Broke," "The Night the Ghost Got In" and "Draft Board Nights." Thurber's grandmother is mentioned briefly and charmingly only in "Draft Board Nights" as having become "quite skillful in getting around in . . . the little electric runabout that had been bought for my grandfather." His grandfather was "astonished and a little indignant" about this, which of course leads to another story where he again plays the part of eccentric fool.

Long after Kate Fisher's death in 1925, Thurber's writing appears to deliver his own vengeful idea of poetic justice.

CHAPTER 8

A Frontiersman in the Family

Judge Stacy Taylor may have been the perfect leadoff hitter for *The Thurber Album,* a rare combination of Jim Bridger, Abraham Lincoln and Perry Mason who as chance would have it was Grandmother Kate Fisher's stepfather. Thurber relayed his tale in his opening chapter "Time Exposure" almost directly from an unpublished personal tale called "The Autobiography of Judge Stacy Taylor" that was loaned to him by that old master of exaggeration Mahon Taylor, who again happily filled in any holes that might have detracted from his father's legend.

Thurber's re-telling of the story seems to confirm that he had his doubts about some of it, if only because it stopped so abruptly when the judge's life was only half over. Indeed, when Taylor moved to Columbus at the age of 40 in 1846, his life of high adventure must have stopped suddenly and so did his "autobiography," which probably didn't have the same dramatic quality when he was representing thieves, drunks and brawlers in central Ohio courts.

Taylor stands as an excellent example of the different worlds some of Ohio's early settlers straddled when they reached old age. When he died in 1893 at the age of 88, he was nearing 50 years as a Columbus attorney—but one who harbored amazing memories of trapping and fur trading along the Wabash River in Indiana and of wild encounters with the Indians.

Taylor was born in Loudon County, Virginia, in 1806 and attended Locust Thicket Academy near Hillsboro, Va. In his writing, he tells about how he took his new wife, seventeen-year-old Mary Hollingsworth Taylor, to Alexandria, Va., to hear President John Quincy Adams speak on July 4, 1825. The nineteen-year-old Taylor not only shook hands with Adams afterwards, but also got to shake the hands of four former presidents, John Adams, Thomas Jefferson, James Madison and James Monroe.[1] Timing is everything; John Adams and Jefferson died one year later to the day, on July 4, 1826.

With no more former presidents to shake hands with—George Washington died in 1799—Taylor and his new wife moved West shortly after that. He took charge of a grade school in Clarksville, a tiny town near Wilmington in Clinton County, Ohio, in 1826. The move proved to be temporary. He started studying the law under Judge Halsey Crane in Dayton in 1827, and moved to St. Mary's, Ohio, in west central Ohio in 1828. Once there, he formed a fur trading partnership with George Johnson and for seven years the two of them wandered the Indiana forests near the Wabash, buying furs from tribes of Wyandot, Ottawa, Seneca and Shawnee Indians.

The Indians were friendly enough; an army led by Anthony Wayne had decisively beaten a confederation of hostile Indian tribes at the Battle of Fallen Timbers and forced them to sign terms of surrender at the Treaty of Greenville thirty-three years before. But Taylor's experiences with them still qualify as adventures. Thurber described the young trader as popular with the Indians because he dealt fairly and didn't drink or sell liquor. He still witnessed a dozen savage knife brawls among the natives, and graphically described a fight in which a number of Indians, including Captain Bright Horn, were killed in 1832.[2] Bright Horn had served under William Henry Harrison during the War of 1812 and commanded a company of Indians that had distinguished itself during the important Battle of Tippecanoe.

Taylor won election as associate judge of Mercer County the year of that fatal brawl. When St Mary's incorporated as a town in 1834, he was elected its first mayor. The following year he ran for the state legislature on the Whig ticket and won; he was re-elected in 1837. He represented 10 sparsely settled counties and rode horseback from county to country, informing his constituents of the issues, asking for their input and explaining his positions.

All the time he spent in Columbus as a legislator may have convinced him that he would be better off living in the state capital and practicing law. The chance to pull himself out of financial difficulty probably contributed to his decision as well. Thurber relayed that a section of his autobiography entitled "Financial Ruin" tells how Taylor squandered the small fortune he had amassed when "he made the mistake of going in for contracting on a large scale, building dams and other ambitious constructions." This led to him getting "stuck with a lot of checks of the unsound state treasury of Ohio" and having to sell them at a discount of sixty-three percent.

The death of his wife in 1845 may have cemented his decision to leave. The couple had produced eight children, four of whom were still living, and the widowed father now bore the sole responsibility of raising them. Whatever the reason, he moved to Columbus in 1846 and never left. The arrival of the Ohio and Erie Canal in 1831 and the National Road in 1833 opened up the little state capital to new avenues for growth, and its population grew from grew from 6,048 in the 1840 census to 17,882 in 1850.

All of these new citizens created plenty of opportunities for attorneys—and also provided a larger pool of potential mothers for his children. At some point, he married for a second time, at least according to the manuscript Thurber quoted, but the name of the bride and her fate apparently didn't make it into any of the family bibles. Taylor met and married Elizabeth Beall Matheny, Thurber's great grandmother, when he was forty-seven around 1853, and the couple had two more children, William and Mahlon.

"Judge Stacy Taylor was the father of four to six children by his first wife and the step-father to four," E. Stacy Matheny wrote. "But the unusual thing in their lives after their second marriages was the large number of children they took to raise. I have often heard them tell the story that they were the parents, step parents and foster parents to 38 to 40 children."[3]

When Thurber wrote "Nobody knows the exact number of his children, step children and adopted children" it proved an effective written way to raise his eyebrows over his great-grandfather's chaotic family life. It also served as a regretful admission of truth. While Thurber acknowledged that he didn't "know much" about Taylor's second wife, he confessed that he didn't even know much about his great-grandmother. After dutifully recording the marriage of Stacy Taylor and Elizabeth Beall Matheny, Thurber used the rest of his tale for recollections of Stacy Taylor's cousins, Dr. Thomas Beall and Mary Van York.

While Taylor became a familiar sight in the city's courtrooms, it seems clear he wasn't a star. He moved frequently during his almost half-century in Columbus and often changed partners and law firms. He had offices—and residences—up and down High Street, although in 1881 he shared an office with Thomas E. Taylor at the northeast corner of Broad and High, ground zero for the burgeoning city.

"He was an interesting character, widely known as a jurist and also as a temperance lecturer," E. Stacy Matheny wrote. "When he was old and in his dotage, he became so interested in the cause of temperance that he would forget everything else that he should have been interested in. When I was a boy visiting in their home, Grandma Taylor asked him to go to the grocery store for a dozen eggs. He started with them in a paper bag, the day was warm and he perspired, the sack was torn, but he put his large red handkerchief about it, holding it by the corners, continuing his walk to the house. But every few steps an egg dropped out on the sidewalk, and when he arrived as his residence, he was holding his handkerchief by one corner, but all the eggs and even the paper bag was missing. He unconsciously mopped his face with his handkerchief (and) walked into the home thinking only of the temperance lecture he was to deliver that night."[4]

In its description of him in 1880, *The History of Franklin and Pickaway Counties* made Taylor sound like a crafty old lawyer who knew how to work the courts to win cases over younger attorneys:

> Mr. Taylor is a veteran practitioner before justices courts, where he especially delighted in pricking up the young fledglings of the bar, making their debut before his favorite court, in which his opinions were wont to carry the weight of law. He is one of the few old pioneers left and is still in a good state of preservation in his seventy-third year.[5]

The fountain of youth must have found him. Even at 87, his death in 1893 wasn't seen as the natural order of things by his family.

"His son Mahlon, at ninety-four, bewails, now and then, his father's 'untimely' death, which he lays to an indiscreet diet," Thurber wrote. "'He could have lived to be an old man,' sighs Uncle Mahlon, 'but he ate himself into the grave.'"[6]

CHAPTER 9

Sugar Grove Days

When James Thurber received his first glimpse of Sugar Grove, Ohio, as a boy, the tiny southeastern Ohio town was home to approximately 350 residents. Over a century later, the 2010 census found 426 people living there. The village's west side profile seen in a 1900 postcard doesn't look much different from one viewed from the same vantage point today.

Some things don't change. Sugar Grove is still located 38 miles southeast of Broad and High streets in Columbus, within a short golf shot from U.S. Route 33. It is still seven miles south of Lancaster, on the doorstep of a weekend adventure in the Hocking Hills.

Some things do. In 1883, it had four dry-goods stores, a school, a general store, a hotel, three churches, three blacksmith shops, three shoe shops, a wagon shop, an undertaking establishment, two physicians, two tanneries and a grist-mill. In 2016, it had a small grocery store, a school, three churches and a bar.

Local farmers fueled the little town's economy, including many of those from the Matheny family that made up his Grandma Fisher's maternal side. The connection drew the Thurbers to Sugar Grove for reunions and holidays, gave a budding young writer vivid memories of visits to Uncle Jake Matheny's farm and a wealth of intriguing characters—eccentrics, family members and eccentric family members—for some of his later stories.

Distant relatives of Thurber still inhabit Sugar Grove and the surrounding hills, woods and farms, although Thurber would likely find the village's loss of isolation a little depressing. Every trip to Sugar Grove qualified as a genuine adventure for young Jamie Thurber. If today's traveler finds a drive from Columbus to Sugar Grove an adventure it's probably because he has always dreamed of a career as a NASCAR driver, bobbing in and out of a logjam of racing cars at high speeds. The little town on the edge of the Appalachian foothills seemed a world away from Columbus to Thurber and might not have been here at all if the state of Ohio hadn't decided to extend a feeder branch of the Ohio Erie Canal from Carroll, a small town 10 miles northwest of Lancaster, to Athens, 45 miles southeast of Lancaster, in the late 1830s.

"Sugar Grove and the canal came about the same time," Jim Stoner said. "I think Elizabeth Rudolph laid the town out. She got the land from her father—Abraham Ream—when he died. At the same time, the canal was starting down from Lancaster and I think she thought maybe she'd make some money."[1]

Stoner, Thurber's third cousin once removed, lives in Rudolph's two-story frame house in the 300-block of Main Street. The bearded, retired parochial school teacher said it is the oldest house in Sugar Grove.

"Her town started right here (the south edge of his house) on this side of the street up (to the north) and the canal went right behind our house," he said. "Her original plot, started here—it was the last lot in town—and went in that direction."[2]

He pointed north, up a tree-lined street that could have jumped off an old postcard.

"I figure she thought she'd make a buck off the canal," he said. "But there's no record that she ever made any money off the canal. The canal didn't really get going in Sugar Grove until about 1840 or 1841, and this house was built in 1842."[3]

When the Columbus and Hockey Valley Railroad was completed along the same general route in 1857, it took a chunk of the cargo business and the canal, which had never proved very profitable, finally closed in 1890. But parts of the old canal were around for years afterwards and certainly were in Thurber's day. It's remembered as Canal Street in Sugar Grove now.

Jake Matheny was Grandma Fisher's only brother and he served as postmaster of Sugar Grove in the eight years preceding his death in 1912. While Thurber saw his uncle through the eyes of a boy who loved to visit his farm, Jake was more than a farmer. Before the Civil War, he farmed in the summer and taught in the county schools in the winter, then became one of the first to enlist when the war broke out and participated in the first battle of Bull Run. After being honorably discharged, he re-enlisted and did six months duty during General John Hunt Morgan's raid in Ohio. After the Confederate raider was caught, Uncle Jake accompanied his Union troops to Kentucky to help stop other rebel bands.

After the war, Jake moved to Columbus, studied law and then practiced it in the state capital until 1878, when he decided to return home to Sugar Grove and resumed farming. Three years later, he took a position with the Boys Industrial School, located not far from his farm between Lancaster and Sugar Grove. He worked there for twelve years and later served on the local school board, most of which happened before Thurber was old enough to know about any of those things or care.

Thurber "and a hundred youngsters" knew Uncle Jake as a farmer with "white hair and a white beard," one who "could bark like dog to delight the children, and often walked about his lawn with a parrot on one shoulder and a tame raccoon on the other."[4]

Uncle Jake's wife, Christine Elizabeth Jackson Matheny, was affectionately known by nearly everyone in the family as Aunt Lizzie. She was the daughter of Colonel Ezra E. Jackson, a contractor, major landowner and one of the most important men in Fairfield County. With the giddiness of a ten-year-old boy, a grown-up Thurber happily recalled how that association became their ticket to the Jackson family reunions:

> One of the colonel's daughters, Lizzie, had married Jake Matheny, who served throughout the (Civil War) in Jackson's 58th Ohio Volunteer Infantry Regiment, and the fact that he was my grandmother's brother made my brothers and me, and our nine first cousins, eligible to guzzle the lemonade and dig into the layer cakes at the annual gatherings of the clan, and to take part in the baseball games, the foot races and other goings on that lasted all day. When the reunion was held on the Fourth of July, as often happened, it went on late into the night, and the sky rockets, aerial bombs, silver fountains, Roman candles, sparklers and pinwheels that light up Fairfield County for miles around were Grandpa Fisher's contribution to the celebrations. . . . Before the fireworks started, there was a banquet at noon, held outdoors unless it rained, and the food was supplied by all the aunts: fried chicken and turkey, potato salad and a dozen other salads, as many as forty layer cakes, and enough pies, blueberry, lemon, mince and cherry, for a half dozen Keystone comedies. There was always enough food for five hundred people, or more than twice as

many as came to the annual party from Columbus and a dozen other Ohio towns.[5]

Jackson's farm stood in the hilly region at the end of today's Bryan Road, approximately two miles southwest of town. Getting there requires a long climb through thick woods on a paved one-lane road that would make some modern cars groan; one can only imagine how difficult it was for horse drawn-carriages and Model T's.

Indeed, the original Matheny family homestead stood at the top of a different hill on the southeast branch of Bryan Road not far from the Jackson place, a hill that often created extra work for family members even after cars were common.

"When Model T's first came in, they would try to go up this hill and their gas tank was gravity fed," Stoner said. "If they didn't turn around and back up this hill, they couldn't make it. So they would end up being off the road, and they'd walk up to the house and Grandpa Jake ("Uncle" Jake's father) would hitch up a horse and come down and pull them up the hill."[6]

Thurber described the countryside around Sugar Grove "as deeply rural." When you invade those hills, two miles outside of town, it still feels that way now. The only difference is that the narrow roads are paved instead of gravel and some of the old houses have been replaced with luxurious summer homes for wealthy families from Columbus.

The farm where Uncle Jake and Aunt Lizzie lived and Thurber and his brothers often visited doesn't exist today, although it likely stood on what had been another chunk of Colonel Jackson's property straddling McGrery Road, just south of the 'Y' intersection with Blue Valley Road northwest of Sugar Grove. The property is just down the road from Blue Valley School that many of Uncle Jake's eight children attended.[7] When Thurber visited as a boy and Uncle Jake was the postmaster of Sugar Grove, the Mathenys also had a place in town at 30 Main Street. Today the addresses are designated as either North or South Main, and there are no house numbers below 100 today.

Jake Matheny's background as a lawyer, teacher, school board member and postmaster obviously impacted his children. Two of his daughters, Beall Matheny Smith and Alice Grace Matheny, became schoolteachers, and his youngest daughter, Elsie, followed in her father's footsteps and eventually became the postmistress of Sugar Grove.[8] His two sons, H. Grant and E. Stacy, both lived most of their adult lives in Columbus, Stacy as a prominent minister of several churches.

While his Uncle Jake may have been the most accomplished person a young Thurber knew in and around Sugar Grove, it would take more than a raccoon on his shoulder to make him the only star when the humorist decided to relate his Sugar Grove stories later. Thurber's great-grandfather, John Matheny, fell into Rush Creek and drowned in November, 1852, at the age of 34. How it happened isn't clear, but the tragedy occurred where the Hocking River tributary ran behind what was then City Hall. The victim, a father of four including a daughter named Kate who married William Fisher and became Thurber's grandmother, worked as an auditor in the building, and the wooded bank behind the building is precariously steep.

The old City Hall building that stood at the eastern end of Third Street has been gone for years and has been replaced by a white frame house. The bank remains steep, though, and could treat a modern visitor as rudely as it treated John Matheny if he weren't careful.

"The creek is pretty deep right there," Stoner said. "It's shallow in some places, but not there."[9]

John Matheny is buried in a graveyard in the tiny settlement of Horn's Mill, two miles north of town, and the rectangular slab charged with illuminating his life can't begin to address the unspeakable tragedy his family must have felt when the accident occurred. But that was too long ago for Thurber to mourn him. He devotes much more of his writing to his great-grandmother's second husband, Judge Stacy Taylor, even though Thurber shared a physical bond with John Matheny.

Thurber associated Sugar Grove and the heavily wooded hills that framed it with the people he remembered from his trips here, including Uncle Jake and Aunt Lizzie and a small army of aunts, who not only furnished the food for the family gatherings but also furnished him with material for his written musings: Aunt Molly—Mary Ann Mollie Jackson—whom Thurber described as "jolliest of all." She was the daughter of Colonel E. P. Jackson and married Joseph Henry Cook. They had six children and she died in Lancaster in 1921.

Aunt Lou—Rebecca Louise "Lula" Matheny—"who wrote poetry and believed that everything was for the best." The youngest daughter of John and Elizabeth Matheny, she married J. Henry Swartz and lived in the northeast Columbus suburb of Westerville.

Aunt Melissa—Melissa Matheny—"who knew the Bible by heart and was convinced that Man's day was done." She married James Bailey, lived at 1194 East Rich Street in Columbus, worked in various missions and devoted herself to helping the poor in the city's slums.

Aunt Sarah, "who had the most beautiful face I ever saw." Sarah Sunderman Matheny is the only Sarah in the family, although pictures posted of her at various genealogical websites aren't at all flattering. This may have been Thurber the practical joker, enjoying an inside joke that only he knew. Or maybe another hard-to-track Sarah is sitting out there in some genealogical cul-de-sac, hiding from Thurber researchers.

Two of the more "interesting" aunts, at least from Thurber's descriptions of them, are even harder to locate in his family tree: Aunt Fanny, "plagued in her old age by recurring dreams in which she gave birth to Indian, Mexican, Chinese and African twins." Fanny is normally used as a nickname for Frances or Veronica, and there are no close relatives in this generation whom fit this description.

Aunt Florence, "who once tried to fix a broken cream separator on her farm near Sugar Grove and suddenly cried 'Why doesn't somebody take this goddam thing away from me?' This may describe Flora May Smyth, daughter of Mary Ellen Matheny and George Smyth of Zanesville, Ohio, and wife of Sherman Shiplett, but maybe not. Thurber sometimes changed the names of those he thought might take exception to his memory of them. He may have also taken some poetic license here and embellished stories that he thought needed it.

Some of Thurber's more compelling tales involved Sugar Grove neighbors and friends who weren't members of the family. The first time Thurber saw Biddleman Blazer he was "dressed in a clean shirt, overalls, and shined up boots, calling the tunes of a square dance in Uncle Jake's barn and playing on the harmonica, over and over, the only tune he knew, 'Turkey in the Straw.' Biddleman had only a few teeth, and a mere fringe of hair, but although he lacked the fatal charm of, say, Aaron Burr, he considered himself an irresistible beau, and plagued the young Matheny and Taylor ladies with his attention."[10]

The lifelong bachelor's name is every bit as strange as he must have been. Thurber recalled how Blazer wasn't named when he was born and after a few months "various members of his family wrote names on slips of paper, put them in a hat, and let the infant select one. To their astonishment, he grabbed them all, and thus became Biddleman Bistam Bastam George Washington Finche Blazer, the 'Bistam' and 'Bastam' having been, I suppose, a waggish uncle's notion of the comical." Thurber added that he didn't know "when Biddleman B. B. G. W. F. Blazer died. For a long time he was the most evident of men, and then suddenly he was gone, and now there is no longer the faintest rumor, in and around Sugar Grove, of the fellow who played 'Turkey in the Straw' more than ten thousand times, at square dances, and walking along the roads, and alone in his room."

If this sounds like a made-up tale about a fictitious individual, rest assured that it isn't. A Biddleman Blazer appears in the 1904 Lancaster city directory as a "shoeworker" who boarded at 307 Wheat Street, a two-story frame house that still stands a few blocks south of Main Street. What happened to him after that is anybody's guess, although Thurber's "guess" obviously has him playing "Turkey in the Straw" somewhere for the enjoyment of somebody, even if it were only himself.

Effie Young and her husband Lewis were two of Thurber's Sugar Grove favorites. The Young's 64-acre farm was located on the west side of McGrery Road, next to and across the road from Jake Matheny's place. Thurber wrote about them because of their "notorious absent-mindedness," and cited the day that Lewis "sat on a high limb of a tree and sawed at it, jabbering away, without realizing that the blade was between him and the trunk of the tree. He came down with a mighty crash, amid the guffaws of his friends who were lucky enough to be on hand." Effie tried to make it seem like a reasonable mistake, explaining that the problem was that "Louie is left-handed and was sitting on the offside of the tree." No one bought it.[11]

Effie also had her moments. Thurber recalled "the day on Jake Matheny's lawn when Effie, chattering without pause, set about putting a sunbonnet on her small daughter's head and absently adjusted it to the somewhat larger head of little Grant Matheny. She was tying it under his chin when someone called her attention to what she was doing. 'Smartest lawyer in Lancaster could have made the same mistake!' snapped Effie."

Thurber recounted another time when a neighbor came to her to get a recipe and Effie looked for it in a Bible instead of a cookbook, talking the whole time. When the woman finally politely told her of her mistake, Effie scolded her. "A man could lose his farm bettin' Effie Young don't know where things is."

Modern conveniences could be a mystery to her, and "she had a stern contempt for tony folks who enjoyed the effete comforts of modern sanitary engineering." She once returned from a visit to a relative in Columbus and announced "She's turned finicky since she left Sugar Grove. Got an electric toilet." As Thurber noted, "to Effie Young, all mechanical things were electrical."

His best Effie Young story concerned the death of her husband, Lewis, in April, 1929. Thurber told of how the undertaker called from Lancaster to find out whether the funeral services would be conducted in the family home, as they usually were in those days.

"You will want to bring him back home, of course," the undertaker asked.

"Merciful heavens, no!" Effie cried. "What in the world would I want with a dead man?"[12]

Effie went to live in Columbus after her husband's death and was living with their son Ralph at 1680 Manchester Avenue on the city's north side when she died in 1937.

Not all of the people whom Thurber wrote about in Sugar Grove were real. *The Luck of Jad Peters,* a story that is set in Sugar Grove and first appeared in the *New Yorker* on December 8, 1934, looks to be a work of pure fiction.

The tale opens with Aunt Emma Peters preserving a table of husband Jad's lucky souvenirs that include a large rock that weighs 20 pounds. All were reminiscences of something fortunate that had happened to him; the older he got, the more adept he became at finding and identifying these strokes of good fortune when no sensible connection existed.

Old Jad got so that he could figure out lucky escapes for himself in almost every disaster and calamity that happened in and around Sugar Grove. Once, for example, a tent blew down during a wind storm at the Fairfield County Fair, killing two people and injuring a dozen others. Jad hadn't gone to the fair that year for the first time in nine or ten years. Something told him, he would say, to stay away from the fair that year. The fact that he always went to the fair, when he did go, on a Thursday and that the tent blew down on a Saturday didn't make any difference to Jad. He hadn't been there and the tent blew down and two people were killed. After the accident, he went to the fair grounds and cut a piece of canvas from the tent and put it on the parlor table. . . . Lucky Jad Peters![13]

The story of the rock ends this wacky tale. In August, 1920, engineers were supposedly widening the channel of the nearby Hocking River, apparently with dynamite. Jad was walking along Main Street one day with an old crony. After they parted, Jad stopped, turned and called back to his friend. He had taken six steps in his direction when a rock dislodged by the blast flew over the four-story Jackson Building and struck Peters squarely in the chest, killing him.

The fact that Emma kept the rock with Jad's other "lucky" souvenirs may have been her way of making a statement about how living with this goofball had made her life miserable; the rock may have been more her souvenir than his. But it's clear this isn't a historical incident; it's just Thurber being Thurber.

"There has never been a four-story building in Sugar Grove," Stoner said.

Or for that matter a "Jad" Peters. None of the characters and events corresponds to real people, although some of them doubtless are modeled after them. Thurber used local names that made them seem like living persons, even if they weren't.

A James Peters lived near Sugar Grove in those days with his wife Loretta and his niece Emma. He died long before the fictitious Jad was "suddenly flung up against Matheny's harness store like a sack of salt."

Whether any of the Mathenys ever had a harness store isn't the point. The Mathenys were as much as part of Sugar Grove as the old canal. They had to be in the story somewhere.

"When I taught school to the kids here, I'd read that story and it really grabbed their attention," said David Shiltz, who retired from a teaching career that including eight years at Sugar Grove's Berne Union school in 1991. "He used all those local names. Being specific like that makes a story come to life."[14]

It's a device Thurber used in other places. In *The Secret Life of Walter Mitty,* Mrs. Mitty says to her husband "It's one of your days. I wish you'd let Dr. Renshaw look you over." Again, the work is fiction, but Renshaw had obviously been stuck in some remote corner of Thurber's mind since young Jamie visited Sugar Grove long ago; in Thurber's youth, Dr. Samuel Renshaw was the village doctor.

That Dr. Renshaw died in 1912, but his son of the same name also became a physician and practiced in Columbus. He resided in the city's suburb of Upper Arlington when he died in 1981, one of many examples where the families of characters Thurber wrote about from Sugar Grove ended up in Columbus and its suburbs.

Just as there are many more "Irish" in America today than there are in Ireland, there are now many more descendants of the Mathenys in Columbus than there are in Sugar Grove. But the little town where they once lived is frozen in Thurber's writings forever.

CHAPTER 10

The Real Walter Mitty

On July 31, 1958, the *Columbus Citizen* published a story about the demolition of one of the innumerable Thurber houses in the city, accompanied by a large, three-column photo of Thurber's smiling older brother, William, perched like a bird on a pile of rubble.

A headline over the photo cutline reads "Humorist's Brother Inspects 'Damp' House," when in fact he was a little late. It appears that the only part of the house still standing was a partial rear wall bearing a large sign with the number "568," the latter possibly placed there by the photographer to help the reader make sense of the picture.

The house William supposedly "inspected" had stood at 568 Oak Street. It died to create a parking lot for the 1,000-seat First Baptist Church on East Broad Street. The parking lot is still there today but the church isn't, having vacated the premises for a smaller building on the east side in 2005 because of a dwindling congregation. The old church building houses the Bluestone concert and event venue today.

The house's claim to fame is its place in the popular Thurber tale "File and Forget," a hilarious series of letters purportedly between the author, then living in Connecticut, and his publisher concerning mix-ups and missed communications over the delivery of a shipment of books.

William had scant memories of the house, where the family lived in 1908–09. He recalled it only as a "damp" house where their father tried to fix a lock on the rabbit hutch behind the house and, as Thurber wrote, "succeeded only after getting inside the cage, where he was imprisoned for three hours with six Belgian hares and 13 guinea pigs."

William lived at 212 East Frambes Avenue northeast of the Ohio State campus at the time, so it seems a little odd that a sixty-five-year-old man who still held a full-time job as a city inspector would make a four-mile trip across town to tell a reporter "I don't remember too much about it" and climb on a pile of rubble to have his photo taken. But William enjoyed basking in his younger brother's fame, always believing that with a subtle twist of fate that fame could have easily been his.

William could have been a real life model for Walter Mitty. He thought that some of the wacky stories about his family that Jamie wrote belonged to him, and believed he had the same talent, wit and imagination that carried his brother to international fame.

William didn't begrudge his brother his success. He might be described as an average guy who fantasized about success and never really achieved it. He held down a series of ordinary jobs that required little or no talent and chased a succession of get-rich-quick schemes that didn't make him rich, slowly or quickly. Still, he always had his own dubious claim on the success Jamie achieved.

It's a sweet delusion with no evidence to support it. William Thurber worked for the city of Columbus in the Division of Weights and Measures for twenty-five years. He sold pens for the Waterman Pen Company, worked for the United Fruit Company and spent a significant chunk of his life without any job at all. In his eighty years on earth, he rarely rose above the ordinary, seldom confronted reality and when he did, probably didn't recognize it.

From the cheap seats, he looks like just another dreamer whose delusions of grandeur far outstripped his expectations. He may have had the talent, wit, or creativity to become a famous writer, but the only sign of it were his own claims to that effect. Like Mitty, most of William Thurber's successes were in his head.

It must have confounded him that his brother could take seemingly ordinary incidents in their lives and turn them into successful stories, especially when he apparently believed that he could have done the same thing if he had gotten there first. It also apparently bothered him that Jamie sometimes co-opted his role in those stories. In "The Night the Bed Fell," a 1933 tale that launched Thurber's *My Life and Hard Times* series in the *New Yorker,* Thurber is sleeping on an Army cot, which he tips over in the middle of the night. The loud crash awakens his mother, who believes that the big wooden bed in the attic had fallen on her husband

Charles. Thus begins a chain of humorous incidents, which might have seemed a lot funnier to William if Thurber had written what really happened: it had been William who had fallen out of the Army cot and not Jamie. It had been William—whom Thurber cast as "Herman" in these stories—whose loud whoop had awakened his mother. Thurber had been on the fringe of this story and was not the central character, even though he wrote it that way.

Thurber's 1935 *New Yorker* casual "Snapshot of a Dog" perturbed him even more because Rex, the dog Thurber wrote about, was *William's* dog. Thurber wrote about how the three brothers had named him, how Rex had "three masters" and how they had all been distraught over his death. But as the oldest brother, William had been the first to work and have money to pay for a dog. It had been him who had paid for Rex, so as far as he was concerned he had dibs on mourning his death.[1]

Even his brother's "art" must have seemed like a cruel joke on him; when they were boys, their parents considered William the family artist. He sketched lifelike reproductions of photographs when he was a boy and could draw literal reproductions of real people that were more accurate than anything his younger brother could produce. Robert believed William's drawing encouraged Thurber to draw; while that be partially true, Thurber's scrawls seemed more like doodling when compared to William's meticulous reproduction. Even after Thurber had achieved some success as a cartoonist, his parents were still convinced that their oldest son was the real artist and William undoubtedly agreed. It must have befuddled him that Jamie's "art" achieved such popularity, unaware that it was Thurber's creativity, and not his ability to draw, that separated him from the crowd.

Sad as it is to say, William's most significant contribution—an odd use of the word, for sure—probably came when he was eight years old and he accidentally shot his younger brother in the eye with an arrow while the family was living in Falls Church, Virginia. It was a horrible accident—the loss of an eye because of the negligence of seven- and eight-year-old kids playing with bows and arrows couldn't be considered anything else. But because it nudged his one-eyed brother away from sports and most physical activity and toward more sedentary pursuits such as reading and writing, a case can be made that Thurber might never have become Thurber if it hadn't happened.

In the days before everyone from politicians to public relations executives to Little League coaches have learned how to spin a negative story into a positive one, William mastered the art. He liked to tell interviewers that the accident that took his younger brother's eye may have actually been a *good* thing.

"They say if a person loses one of his senses, like his eyesight, other things develop to compensate for it," William said. "I look at all Jamie got done and figure maybe it was a blessing in disguise."[2]

This is remarkable attempt at rationalization, an attempt to turn the culpable party—William, in this case—into a hero. William always used this explanation to make himself look good, which isn't easy to do when you were responsible, even accidentally, for your brother losing an eye.

"I suffered more from it than he did because that's something I never got over," William said.[3] Thurber never blamed William for indulging in such foolishness or for the accident. He always recognized that that was all it was.

"We were taking turns with the bow and arrow that day," he said. "I could have shot *his* eye out by mistake."[4]

He could have, but he didn't. In fact, the remark sounds like it may his own attempt to spin the tragic events in something better, a way to publicly absolve William of any blame.

Thurber's second wife, Helen, lived with him long enough to know that her husband didn't harbor any hard feelings toward his older brother because of the incident. However, she did admit that William sometimes irritated him.

> Jamie only got mad when William would boast about his twenty-twenty vision years later. "Why does he have to keep talking about his damned eyesight?" Jamie would say. Now that I think about it, Jamie never invited William to his house, although he supported him for most of his life. I guess Jamie couldn't bear having William around too much, as a kind of constant reminder.[5]

All we are left with are their own memories of the unfortunate accident, which make it clear that William's errant arrow was indeed an accident. But things are much fuzzier when it comes to the lifelong relationship between the two, and don't really support their mother's later contention to *Time* that "William is twice as crazy as James, but he just couldn't put it down," or for that matter, William's contention that he *could*.

"That's just one of her nifties, I call them," William said. "She just had a whimsical sense of humor and she just told them that. And the truth is that I might have been twice as crazy but I could put it down if

I wanted to because I used to write letters to my friends all the time and they always looked forward to my letters on the wit and humor . . . A lot of my friends thought that I did it and he got the credit for it."[6]

It's almost possible to see Mitty sitting down at his typewriter and banging out a classic piece of humor here, a Mitty who bears a strong resemblance to Thurber's older brother. There is no doubting that all of the Thurber boys inherited some of their mother's wit, but the idea that William or his brother Robert could have written all of those marvelous stories that Thurber did or drawn his wacky images if they had had the chance isn't worth debating.

William may have been "twice as crazy as Jamie" but that wasn't necessarily a positive thing. In the early 1930s, Mame wrote Thurber a hysterical letter about William, saying that he was unemployed, stayed in bed most of the day and laughed insanely for much of the night. Thurber shared parts of his mother's letter to him with Ann Honeycutt, his close friend at *The New Yorker*:

> William has no job and simply worries the life out of us because he hasn't—it has almost finished us the way he gets his spells and wants to run a 'machine gun' on all of us and relieve us or our misery—then end his own life. Last Sat.—week ago—he got one of his mean insane spells and tore around here raising his voice—and with no excuse for it—Just goes nite after nite without sleep and isn't really responsible for his actions— My heart aches for that boy who has so many fine qualities and when he is *making* money he is so good to us and everybody and happy, but even *then* is never well—has these awful thots constantly running thru his mind, as he puts it, and the worst feature about it all is the way he laughs to himself all nite.[7]

That doesn't paint a picture of a guy who just needed a little luck to become a literary giant.

William often seemed forgetful and distracted. Family members remembered how he sometimes absent-mindedly left the door open when he got out of a car. When he and Thurber were having lunch at Uncle Kirt Fisher's house as boys, William dreamily put butter in his coffee.

"For God's sake, Bessie," Kirt said. "Hide the eggs."[8]

When Thurber and his wife Helen were vacationing in 1936, they let William use their New York City apartment. As might have been expected, he lost his key, tried to climb through a window and was spotted by the woman next door, who called the police.

"I told them I was James Thurber's brother," William said. "The police-man said 'Sure, and I'm (New York mayor) Jimmy Walker's cousin.'"[9]

A thyrotoxic goiter—Graves disease—caused him to drop out of high school during his third year, and because of that, he didn't work for several years. Possibly because of the thyroid troubles, he always had difficulty concentrating, which again doesn't make his claims that he could written all of those marvelous stories believable.

"I could hold my own with most of these college graduates," he said.[10]

He claimed to have attended "night school," which was, in fact, one evening course on agriculture at Ohio State. He tried to make the case that he didn't need to go to college because he had "done a lot of reading."

Thurber saw his brother for who and what he was; he got along with him, but didn't spend a lot of time with him. He was amused by his get-rich schemes, even though they sometimes cost him money, and took advantage of the fact that William's gullibility made him a perfect foil for some of his practical jokes.

On a business trip to New York in 1927, William stayed at the 34-story Shelton Hotel, which was later called the Halloran House and has been the Marriott East Side since 2007. A mental hospital was located nearby, and patients sometimes wandered away and were caught by the hotel's detectives. William made the mistake of relaying that information to his brother, who chanced to drop by for a visit one day while William was down the hall taking a bath. Thurber slipped into the room and locked William out. When William tried the door, Thurber disguised his voice and told his brother over the transom that he had escaped from the hospital and couldn't return until he killed someone. After setting the hook, Thurber proceeded to slowly unlock the door, the only action necessary to cause William to flee the building in his robe and slippers.[11]

William claimed the three boys all "inherited our sense of humor from my mother" and "we were all great mimics," but the available evidence indicates that Thurber got the better of his siblings, particularly the more pedestrian William.

In 1934, Thurber made a surprise visit to Columbus and telephoned upon his arrival, asking for William and pretending to be a foreign-born Jewish tailor with a shop in downtown Columbus. William admitted that his brother had him fooled:

> At the time, I was selling real estate and I thought this man was a prospect and I wanted to be pleasant to him. . . . And he said "Mr. Thurber, this is Abe Schlotzheimer, man's tailor." And I thought "Well, here's a good

prospect." . . . He says "On the 18th of January, you came into my store and I took for you the measurements of an English broadcloth suit. Here comes February, March, April. For why does nobody come?" So I said "Say, when I want to buy a suit of clothes, I don't go to a man like you. I've got my own special stores that I go to and I'm sure I wouldn't go to buy a suit from a man like you." Then I said "What are you trying to do, blackmail me?" And he said "You call it blackmail, Mr. Thurber, and here I am caught with the garment! I give you two choices, either you pay your $50 and I deliver to you this suit or I take it to court, you pay your $50 and you have no suit!"

And by this time, it was too much for my mother. So she said "Will you let me talk to him?" And I said "All right, my mother wants to talk to you." He said "You call your mother. You call your mother!" My mother grabbed the phone and said "You're so smart, what does my son look like?" And he hesitated a moment and he said "A great mother! A great mother that doesn't know what her own son looks like!" And then she hung up on him and later on he called up and disclosed who he was. But my mother was still mad! . . . She didn't get over it for a while.[12]

William thought the bit was funny enough to try it out on one of his friends—remember, he believed he was as good at mimicry as his younger brother—but it didn't work the way it had for Thurber. He said that his friend "got as mad as a wet hen. He hasn't spoken to me since, and it's been sixteen years."[13]

Unlike Robert, William dated women occasionally, but never seriously. He didn't marry until he was seventy years old and living in Clemson, South Carolina, where he gone in search of better weather and a lower cost of living in 1962, two years after he retired with the city of Columbus. Because he had always been a bit of a loner, his abrupt marriage—into a prominent local family—was a bit of a shock to his family. Thurber had advised his older brother against marriage after his ill-fated union with Althea Adams, but he had been dead two years when William suddenly took the plunge.

When William got involved in a real estate venture in Greensboro, N.C., he invited Robert to live with them, using William Sydney Porter as the lure. Greensboro was O. Henry's hometown and he had always been one of Robert's favorite authors, as he had been with Thurber. But the experiment lasted only two months before Robert returned to his personal comfort zone in Columbus.

William often had been apart from his family. He lived with his parents in their rented house at 330 East Gay Street at times during the 1930s, but after his father died in 1939, Mame and Robert moved into the Great Southern Hotel and lived in a two-bedroom apartment there for fourteen years. For at least six of those years, William also lived there in an apartment of his own. He contacted Thurber sporadically, sometimes to ask for help with one of his moneymaking ideas. His famous, wealthy brother seemed to find these requests more amusing than annoying, as indicated by this 1940 letter to William in response to a request for financial help for a business venture in Puerto Rico:

> You think of more remarkable things than Walter Mitty. I'd love to hear you match your nervous Ohio accent with a West Indian's broken English. Why not try selling wood-burning sets to Eskimos, or Adler elevator shoes to the Pygmies?[14]

In 1948, Thurber outlined for Elliott Nugent a version of a play he was writing about the *New Yorker* that was eventually called *Make My Bed*. In it, he offers a hint of what he really thinks of his older brother:

> I am using real names with the exception of Ross and one or two others. Managing editor No. 33 is just quitting and No. 34 starting in. At the end of the play we see the advent of No. 35, Ross—Walter Bruce—has many problems this day including the descent of Tim's mother and brother Williard from Illinois. Willard is my brother William who thinks he is "shelled," who has never been able to work, and who thinks that that he could have been better at anything than anybody. I have always wanted to put William on stage, since he would make wonderful comedy and now fits into my plot.[15]

Thurber never finished the play, probably a fitting way to honor his oldest brother.

CHAPTER 11

The Star-Crossed Thurber

The team photo of the 1913 East High School baseball team finds a handsome Robert Thurber with his arms crossed in the middle of the front row, staring into the camera with a confident, almost defiant expression.

He was the captain of a city championship team that he remembered losing only one game, and was so good with the bat that long-time *Columbus Dispatch* columnist Johnny Jones, an East graduate, called him "the best hitter they ever had."[1] He was an even better pitcher than hitter and may have been good enough to pitch professionally if he hadn't broken his arm while trying to crank the family Reo. That turned out to be the first in a series of injuries and illnesses that hijacked a promising life, health issues that ultimately led him to a solitary existence as a poor semi-invalid who lived his last twenty years in an aging apartment building on East Town Street.

The transformation of that strong, cocky youth into an insecure shut-in who depended upon his famous brother for support, never felt healthy enough to court women and lived with his mother until her death is a sad tale, especially for those who knew Robert as a boy.

"There must be some kind of strange law about disasters piling up on certain people," Thurber wrote. "Take my brother, Robert. He not only had goiter, but pleurisy, t.b., eye trouble, soft teeth, permanent rheum, and a dozen other things, including duodenal ulcer which he seems to have been born with; also, he broke his right arm in two places, his left in three, sprung out the spool pins of one ankle, fell out of a bus on his head as a child, was run over by a milk wagon, and so on. I got shot in the eye at six years old and they called it a day."[2]

Joel Sayre had vivid memories of all the Thurber boys when he was 9½-year-old volunteer water boy for the Blinky baseball team, the sandlot squad of employees of the Ohio State School for the Blind that Thurber later wrote about in "The Tree on the Diamond." But it was Robert who made the biggest impression on him.

"Robert was the flash Thurber brother as this time; handsome, a juggler and future baseball captain at East High," Sayre said. "Among us kids, he had the reputation of being a terrific fighter and a demon player of duckpins. William was only a so-so athlete, but a pretty good fighter. Jim could do nothing athletically. . . . He was known, however, as a rabid fan and sports critic and a rapid-fire comedian."[3]

At 16, Robert seemed to have the most potential of the Thurber siblings, which is why his fate seems so tragic. He was energetic and assertive and by his own admission, "instigated" fights with brothers, despite being the youngest of the three. He was the first to drive in the family. He drove the Reo that Thurber sometimes wrote about and taught both of his brothers to drive.

"Father and Mother never learned to drive," Robert said. "I tried to teach them once. Mother ran up a hill in Franklin Park and damn near killed us. I never tried again to teach them."[4]

He enrolled at Ohio State in the fall of 1915 and was forced to drop out in March for a goiter operation. An emergency appendectomy followed, and after Robert enlisted in the Army during World War I, he was given a medical discharge after only five months. He contracted pulmonary tuberculosis in 1919, was confined to his bed and under doctor's care all spring and summer.

In the meantime, Jamie, who couldn't enlist in the Army because of his vision problems, received an appointment as a code clerk in Paris, in part because of his father's political connections. Stuck at home, Robert delighted his brother by reconstructing Columbus events with newspaper clippings, theater programs, popular songs and detailed reports, which Thurber called "Robert's Weekly Journal and Log Book of Ohio."

As his younger brother prepared to undergo yet another operation, the ever-magnanimous Thurber sent him a ten-dollar check. "I understand you are about to have six or eight more cuttings," Thurber wrote to him. "William is able to work and you ain't just yet."[5]

The $10 check he sent to Robert dated March 18, 1919 may have been the first of a lifetime of checks the famous humorist wrote to various members of the Thurber family. In later years, when all of the William Fisher and Sons stock had been sold, Thurber became the family's primary means of support in much the same way Mark Twain supported his family.

When he returned from Paris in 1920, Thurber moved back into the house the family rented at 330 Gay Street. His father's financial struggles as an underpaid Municipal Court clerk persisted as Robert's medical bills piled up and devoured the family's stock. Thurber met and married Althea Adams during this period; as much as he loved her, the family didn't care much for her and she didn't care much for the family. She considered William a laughable failure and she bluntly told the chronically ill Robert that he was a hypochondriac.

That may explain in part why Robert always harbored resentful feelings toward Althea, sentiments he willingly shared with those who interviewed him later in life. He said the family never expected Jamie to leave Columbus or to be anything more than a newspaper writer and editor. When Jamie quit his job at the *Dispatch* and went to France in 1925, Robert felt certain that the idea was Althea's and not his brother's, almost as if her belief that his writing talents would take him beyond Columbus were a bad thing.

Her feelings toward the Thurbers are also understandable. With the obvious exception of her husband, they must have seemed like a family of misfits to an outsider. Years later, Rosemary Thurber—James and Althea's daughter and Thurber's only child—pretty much described them just that way in an interview with Burton Bernstein:

> I don't remember my grandfather at all. Robert was like a little old lady, wiping off the silverware and all that, and William was actually a letdown after seeing my father's imitations of him. They were a different family from a different world.[6]

After James Thomas lost his bid for re-election as Columbus mayor in 1931 and Charles found himself out of work, he and Robert tried to sell their ideas for contests, puzzles and pamphlets of quotations or historical facts to newspapers. They went to New York on just such a sales trip in December, 1933, and dropped by the *New Yorker* offices to see Thurber without calling ahead to let him know they were coming. After a secretary directed them to the editorial floor and they found that Jamie wasn't there, they wandered the halls until Katherine White saw them and sharply asked who they were and what they wanted.

"We felt as if we'd been caught robbing the place," Robert said. "My father explained we were Jim's brother and dad. The *New Yorker* had just been publishing Jim's pieces about his family that came out in *My Life and Hard Times,* and Mrs. White was a nice as she could be. It occurred to me later maybe she thought we'd sneaked in to blow up the place for revenge, and was trying to humor us until she could find Jim."[7]

In February, 1934, the family's apartment at 303 East Gay Street burned; it caught fire when stacks of newspaper clippings and publications that Charles and Robert had accumulated for their newspaper promotions were left too close to a hot chimney pipe. The damage forced the family to move into temporary quarters and Thurber thought it would be a good time to invite Robert to stay with him at the Algonquin in New York. Robert remained for several weeks, which provided him with a wonderful opportunity to meet the rich and famous. It also must have been an eye-opening experience for him; he didn't drink and he admitted that everyone around him seemed to be drinking all the time.

> I never could figure out how all those people could drink all that stuff and stay so sharp. When Jim had things to do, as he put it, he'd buy me a ticket to the theater while he took off. The tickets were always for the third and fourth row orchestra seat, just about the best in the house. Ordinarily I'd go to bed at 10:30 or 11 p.m., but Jim would sometimes come into my room at four or five in the morning to sleep, and on Wednesday mornings, when he had a Talk meeting at the *New Yorker,* he sometimes wouldn't go to bed at all. . . . I couldn't keep up with Jim and never understood where he got all the energy."[8]

The puzzles and contest business wasn't all it was cracked up to be, especially during the Depression., and in 1935 or '36, Robert and his father opened the Big Ten Magazine and Book Shop at 1544 North High Street. The store, located a few doors south of Tenth Avenue near the southern edge of the Ohio State campus, may have been his father's attempt to find a meaningful mission for the sickly Robert and it seemed to buoy his spirits. But Charles was almost 70 and he started suffering from prostate issues shortly they started the business. His health gradually deteriorated and the shop was finally closed; Charles Thurber died on Easter morning in 1939.

Understandably, Robert's forced idleness had brought him closer to his parents than the other boys and he was devastated by the death.

"Robert and his father were in the bookstore business together for the last four years and they were *pals* too," Mame wrote, in a letter to Minnette Fritts, "and it has surely crushed him and not being well anyway—has made it so much worse."[9]

Upon Charles's death, the family—Mame and grown-up sons William and Robert—moved out of their Gay Street apartment. Counting the twelve years they lived in the house at 330 Gay, they had been in the same neighborhood for over twenty years. They briefly moved into an old frame duplex at 1054 Franklin Avenue before moving into an apartment in the Southern Hotel. Robert tried to revive his business, shifting his emphasis to rare books and occupying space at 22 East Rich Street, one block from the hotel. That venture also didn't last, although he used his business in part to collect books, newspaper clippings and magazine articles that documented his brother's life story. Some of that material is now part of the Thurber Collection at Ohio State and the rest is at the Thurber House.

"I started (collecting) in 1931, because of interest in my brother," Robert told the *Dispatch* in 1987, five months before his death. "I wanted to keep everything about my brother, oh golly yes." He called Jamie "a once-in-a-million brother."[10]

But the two came into serious conflict when Thurber wrote his profiles of family and friends for *The Thurber Album*, which was published in 1952. Thurber hadn't run into any problems when he fictionalized the family into comical characters for *My Life and Hard Times* eighteen years before, so he didn't anticipate problems when he depicted family members as relatively normal, likable people. Thurber had even enlisted Robert for some paid research on *Ohio State Journal* editor Robert O. Ryder—Thurber did that occasionally both for his own needs and to help give his brother a sense of purpose—and sent copies of some of the pieces back to Columbus so the family could see what he was doing.

It stunned him when his profile of their father, titled "Gentleman from Indiana," sent Robert into orbit. Unknown to Thurber, Robert had gradually become convinced that his older brother had no use for their father. He wanted him to stop defaming his memory for the sake of a few more laughs in his writing.

An exasperated Thurber described his brother's reaction to the piece in a letter to E. B. White:

I called my family in Columbus Saturday and my brother Robert answered
the phone and began to bawl hell out of me for the piece on my father. He
was so nasty that I hung up on him. It turned out that a letter from him
was at the Algonquin desk and we got it and read it. It is a savage and
relentless attack on almost everything I said and he seems to have persuaded my mother to react in the same way, except not violently. He says
the piece should have been called "Hoosier Half-wit," claims I must have
had a deep resentment of my father, and categorically denounces almost
every paragraph. . . . It is a rather shocking situation.[11]

Robert probably wouldn't have been pleased with anything that
Thurber wrote about their father at that point, in part because he didn't
understand why his brother had to write about the family again.

"Jamie was irritable, not friendly or sociable," Robert said. "It was
in 1951 I first noticed his hot temper. He talked poorly to me and my
mother over the telephone, and unless we agreed with him on everything,
he would fly off the handle. I didn't know what to say or not to say to
him. I took issue with things he wrote and said about my father. I couldn't
understand why William Fisher—who wasn't ever nice to Jamie—was
glorified in the book and my father wasn't. I still think it should be the
other way around. Maybe our grandfather was a more interesting character, although I thought the world of my father. Other people have told me
since that there was nothing offensive in *The Thurber Album* stories, so it
could be I just imagined the whole thing."[12]

Robert obviously missed the subtle shots Thurber took at their Grandfather Fisher in his *Album* profile, but again, this seems to have been more
about his perception of Jamie's feelings toward their father than what
Thurber actually wrote. The two brothers didn't talk for months; much
to Thurber's consternation, Robert and his mother didn't even acknowledge the checks he sent to support them. Thurber tried repeatedly to make
up with them and kept getting rebuffed, and his frustration grew. He let
some of this loose in a July 1951 letter to White.

"Nothing much can be done about him, I'm afraid, since he has
become a unique hermit in the past 40 years," Thurber wrote, "out of
touch with everybody and everything, except his mother . . ."[13]

Sad as that seems, it was probably true, at least in part.

Thurber telephoned Robert, and they finally made up just before
Christmas that year, but there was no denying that the rift had strained
his relationship with his family. Helen, Thurber's second wife, said he
"refused to go to Columbus to visit them for years" after that.

Things did improve, though. When the Martha Kinney Cooper Ohio-ana Library Association awarded Thurber its Sesquicentennial Medal on October 24, 1953, and he couldn't attend because of Helen's illness, Robert accepted the medal for him.

When Mame was dying in 1955, she and Robert lived in an apartment at the Seneca Hotel. Nurses were on twelve-hour duty there. On November 23, Mame suffered a stroke and was moved to University Hospital. Thurber and Helen took a train to Columbus immediately and stayed at the Deshler-Wallick Hotel for the entire month until she died on December 20.

Mame's death depressed Robert. Thurber had promised Mame that he would look after his brothers after she died, and because William had a job and lived on his own, Robert drew most of her concern. She must have anticipated the loss of both parents would be a considerable blow to a son who had rarely lived away from them and her fears proved to be right. Almost a year later, a lonely Robert continued to mourn and he pondered a move away from Columbus, for either Cincinnati or Florida, to escape the city's painful memories. A Thurber letter to his brother William in 1956 showed how much he cared about his younger brother:

> I didn't intend to be rough on Robert and I know he cannot work, but I was afraid he was sinking into hopelessness. Probably he does go to the library and read the papers and have other activities. Inactivity to me is death or worse; he never writes about his routine and I was alarmed when he said he "rested more and wrote less." He did some good research for me on the Ryder stuff in 1952, and I had some hope of something else like that. An hour a week or two weeks . . .
>
> I promised Mamma to look after him while I lived, and it seemed to me that Cincinnati in the winter would be out of the refrigerator into the snow. . . . I suggest that you go with him to Cincinnati some Sunday and look over the situation and find a place. I want to send him an extra $25.00 each month and am sending it to him for November. His diet must be built up, and I wish he could see a good doctor in Cincinnati. I know he is utterly miserable, and it is miraculous that he can go on. I will be glad to send him to Florida, but seems not strong enough, and you should both talk to your travel expert about it. The dangers and rackets there are famous for travelers. Try to explain the situation to him and say I did not intend to hurt his feelings and that we must not get into another period of drawn-out difficulty.[14]

Robert decided to stay in Columbus, and eventually moved into Townley Court, a three-story, yellow brick apartment building at 580 East Town Street. It had been built in 1927 and stands only a long block from his Grandpa Fisher's house where he spent so much time as a boy. Robert lived there by himself for the last eighteen years of his life, all but the last one in apartment 310.

Even though he was in poor health, he never tired of sharing stories about his famous brother and their family. Donn Vickers, the first executive director of Thurber House, said Robert's help proved critical in the house's restoration; he gave restorers invaluable details about the rooms where family members slept, where the furniture stood, and even where the dog napped, down to the patterns of wallpaper.

Robert came to view Vickers as a trusted friend and named him as executor of his estate. As family members and friends died or moved away, Robert found himself increasingly isolated and increasingly reliant upon Vickers. Vickers told of the day Robert pointed to a closet in his apartment and asked him to retrieve a big box on the top shelf. Vickers described the box as one you would use to give somebody a bathrobe for Christmas.

"It was heavy," Vickers said. "So I brought it over and he took the lid off, and there were letters, letters, letters. And he said 'All right now, you know where that incinerator is out here?' I said 'Yep.' And he said 'I want you to take this and dump it all in the incinerator.' I said 'What is this, anyway?' He said 'These are letters from my brother, some of them to me and some of them to my mother. And there's some stuff I don't want anyone ever to see, because I got upset with him when he did *The Thurber Album* and the way he talked about our father.'"[15]

Vickers knew what he must do: stall. He said there were "80 to 100" letters in the box and asked Robert how many were upsetting to him. When Robert told him "maybe two," he offered to find them and get rid of them.

"I said 'Ohio State would love to have these letters,'" Vickers said. "I know Bob Tibbetts and I'll tell them we found these and see what they will pay you for them, because they'll pay for this." As a one-time rare book dealer, Robert should have known that but it apparently had never occurred to him. Tibbetts, curator of special collections at The Ohio State University Library, took a little time to look over what Vickers brought him and then offered $12,000 for the letters, the same ones Robert had sentenced to death by incinerator.

"So I went to Robert and said 'They want them and they will give you $12,000,'" Vickers said. "And he said "Je-sus *Christ!* Twelve thousand dollars! Je-sus *Christ!*' And I said 'You know what, that's their first offer, I think we can get them to fifteen, and he said 'Don't you do that! You'll screw up the deal.' I said 'Robert, that's not gonna happen.'

"So I just went up to Bob and I said 'That's great, Bob. But he needs to have fifteen,' and he 'All right.' I probably could have gotten twenty out of them.' But Robert, oh my God, he felt like he'd died and gone to heaven. So that was (his) high point right there, that he'd kept all that stuff and he put it to the university and got 15 grand for it, which was about $200 a letter. Some of the letters were like 'Hi, hope you're doing well.'"[16]

Robert tried to give his friend half the money, but Vickers refused it. The money Robert made off the sale of the letters became virtually all the assets of his estate when he died. His generosity with the money and who he left it to not only says a lot about him, but also the sad life he led after beginning it with so much promise.

Robert left $500 to a maintenance man at the apartment building where he lived, a guy who was nice to him.

"He said 'I don't know where he lives, but I know where he hangs out.' And he gave me the name and address of this bar—a crummy bar—on Parsons Avenue," Vickers said. "So when he died, I took a check down there and I'd go in and say 'I need to see Ralph.' And they'd say 'He's not here today. But he's usually here about.' . . . And then I'd come back and he wouldn't be there again. So I finally tracked him down and gave him the check."[17]

Robert wanted to give the biggest part of his estate to a woman who had been waitress at Marzetti's restaurant at 16 East Broad Street.

"Thurber continued to go there (to Marzetti's) when he used to come back to visit his mother and Robert at the Southern," Vickers said. "There was a server there who they admired so much, and it wasn't a flirtatious thing. She was really a good woman. Robert used to talk about her a lot.

"He told me 'She lives in Chicago and she's still working, and her husband is incapacitated in a wheelchair.' And that was the big number. He wanted to give her $10,000, which was 75 percent of his estate. So I got an airplane and flew to Chicago to track her down, and I had it in my pocket. I saw the restaurant on the way to the house. It was in the neighborhood—I couldn't tell you now where it was—and they were lower-middle-class apartments.

"I went in there; it was hot as hell and all cooped up. I introduced myself to her and I said I have something for you from Robert. I pulled out this check and gave it to her, and man, she went bananas. She just fell apart. 'Look at all the zeroes on that! Oh, my *God!*' and she and her husband, they both sat there and wept about this. Amazing. It was a joyful thing for me to be that messenger."[18]

Charles and Mame Thurber with their three young boys. From left: Robert, William, and James. (James Thurber Papers, Rare Books & Manuscripts Library of The Ohio State University Libraries)

CHILDHOOD MATTERS

Homes, Haunts, Honeys, and Hangouts

*I*f Thurber came back for one of those Thurber tours that local history groups occasionally conduct of his hometown, he might be surprised how little of his childhood is on it. It is not an oversight. A tour of all of the places where the nomadic Thurber family lived, the schools he attended, and the places he played as boy would leave a lot to the imagination.

The house where he was born on at Parsons Avenue is gone. So is a house at 921 South Champion Avenue where Mame Thurber pranked both family and neighbors; a less memorable one on Oak Street; and the Park Hotel, where the family lived when they returned from Washington, DC, in 1903. An unremarkable house on South Seventeenth Street and the Norwich Hotel, where the family also lived briefly, remain, the latter as a remodeled office building. A small park occupies the Town Street location of William Fisher and Sons, the produce commission house that fed his grandfather's fortune and Thurber's imagination. The Fisher house on Bryden Road is still there, converted into law offices and without the porches and the idyllic setting Thurber knew when he spent time with his grandparents. Ohio Avenue School, where Thurber attended first grade, has been beautifully restored, but Sullivant School, which he often wrote about, has been reduced to a cornerstone. The ball field behind the Ohio School for the Blind is a parking lot. Old East High School on Franklin

Avenue is a vacant lot. The plot where Aunt Margery Albright's home stood sits beneath a small office building.

Such is the price of progress in an exploding city that dwarfs that he one he grew up in, although Thurber could probably visualize all of those places and revisit some of the memories of them that follow in these chapters. He fell so hard for Eva Prout when he was a student at Sullivant, that he still carried a torch for her after she left town for several years to star on Vaudeville. He picked up with her after he left Ohio State and stayed in contact with her after he moved to New York and she married someone else.

Griggs Dam, the unnamed star of his tale 'The Day the Dam Broke,' is still around. It may not hold any personal memories for Thurber as a location, but the day thousands in Columbus ran to avoid an imaginary disaster was imprinted in his memory and the incident was immortalized in his writing.

Thurber said in the 1950s that that the clocks that strike in his dreams are the clocks of Columbus, and he almost certainly had the tower clock of Holy Cross Church in mind. It stood across the street from Aunt Margery's house on South Fifth Street.

Although the clock still marks the passage of time, it does it for downtown business people and hipsters who seem to reside on a different planet from those who once lived in the working-class neighborhood only a block removed from the bustling Central Market House. The old market has been gone since 1966.

CHAPTER 12

·

The Edge of Civilization

The empty lot at 921 South Champion Avenue wears the forlorn look of a child lost in a crowded amusement park. The 2½-story red brick house that once stood there was torn down in the 1980s, leaving all of the surrounding houses to mourn their most famous neighbor.

When Charles Thurber's family lived here in 1898 and 1899, they occupied the southernmost house on the street and Champion Avenue narrowed into little more than a cow path that disappeared into the woods to the south. Woods also stood off to the distance on the other eastern side of the street opposite the Thurbers' house, which made the family feel like they were perched in a remote outpost on the edge of civilization.

James was four years old when the family moved there. He wrote, their "nearest neighbor on the north was fifty yards away, and across from us was a country meadow that ticked with crickets in the summer time and turned yellow with goldenrod in the fall."[1]

It's all very difficult to imagine now. The Thurber lot sits in the middle of a block of large brick homes that stretch as far as the eye can see in both directions, a crowded mixture of restored and run-down that could place this in any inner city neighborhood in any large Midwestern city. Some of the homes stand as fine examples of historical restoration and others have the weary look of an abandoned soul, the boards on the windows hinting at an impending visit from a gang of crackheads or a hostile bulldozer. This is a different kind of solitude than that which Thurber described in his writing. Somehow, the loneliness of desertion seems more depressing than that of a creeping city that still hadn't arrived.

The relative isolation of the house at turn of the twentieth century doesn't mean the family avoided its normal lunacy. It was in this house that Mame Thurber coaxed sixteen dogs from the neighborhood into the cellar, and kept them there until Aunt Mary Van York, a notorious dog hater, innocently opened the cellar door and was knocked down by a pack of freedom-loving yelping animals.

"Great God almighty," a flustered Mary said, in a moment Thurber captured in "Lavender With a Difference." "It's a dog factory!"[2]

William Thurber told a back storyabout Aunt Mary that his brother didn't write about.

> She started smoking a pipe when she was about eight or nine years old. She started smoking a pipe from almost the time she was born and I used to visit her. In her early life she had been used to luxury and having everything she wanted and then in later years of her life she had to live in a little flat and I used to go there and see her and I would always bring her Star Tobacco. And she would also look forward to my visits.
>
> To the time of her death, she was over ninety years old, they wouldn't let her smoke and she waited until the nurse got out of her room and she saw I had a cigar and she grabbed ahold of it and crumbled it and ate it. They wouldn't let her smoke.[3]

But that was years after Aunt Mary served as a foil for one of Mame's jokes on South Champion Avenue.

"The thing that puzzled me more than anything else was all those dogs kept from fighting each other," William said.

On another day of her life here, Mame "bought" a neighbor's house. Harry and Laura Simmons had been trying to sell their "cold, blocky house" for so long that it became a standing joke among the Frioleras, a club to which both families belonged.

This provided the perfect setup for Thurber's jokester mother. She waited for a day when Laura wasn't home and disguised herself as an "avid purchaser . . . wearing dark glasses, her hair and eyebrows whitened with flour, her cheeks lightly shadowed with charcoal to make them look hollow, and her upper front teeth covered with the serrated edge of a soda cracker." She brought along giggling cousin named Belle Cook who was unknown to the Simmons. Little Jamie Thurber played the role of Belle's son.[4]

The added texture to this story shows just how small a city Columbus was: Laura's father, Ebenezer Poe, had been the state auditor. At the time of his death in 1895, he had been living next door to Thurber's grandfather, William Fisher, at 691 Bryden Road.

Thurber's description of Harry Simmons' gullibility in his 1951 story seems unfathomable to us today:

> Harry Simmons, opening his front door on that dark evening in the age of innocence, when trust flowered as readily as suspicion does today, was completely taken in by the sudden appearance of an eccentric elderly woman who babbled of her recently inherited fortune and said she had passed his house the day before and fallen in love with it.[5]

"Suspicion" in 1951 couldn't approach the distrust of today, although we can certainly appreciate Simmons' naiveté in either case. That he bought Mame's tearful account of "the sad death of her husband, a millionaire oil man," that she upped his asking price by several thousand dollars and offered to buy his furniture and also upped his price on that seems like something from another age, which of course, it is. That she took some of the items with her, gift-wrapped them, and sent them back to Harry inscribed "To Harry Simmons from Mame Thurber with love;" seems almost cruel, but no less so than a grown-up Thurber immortalizing him for his gullibility in his story. But by then, Harry was no longer part of the neighborhood that apparently enjoyed retelling the stories for years afterwards. And their name really wasn't Simmons, as Thurber wrote, but Simons. Harry E. Simons and his wife Laura eventually moved to Benton Harbor, Michigan, where she died in 1909 at the age of thirty-eight, and he moved to Detroit and remarried. Harry would have been eighty-two in 1951, so it's possible he never knew Thurber wrote about him.

The house on South Champion is also where twenty-three-year-old Belinda Woolf came to live and work as a cook for the Thurbers. James memorialized her for the night in 1899 when she "suddenly flung open a window of her bedroom and fired two shots from a .32 caliber revolver at the shadowy figure of a man skulking about in our backyard."[6]

Thurber wrote that from that day forward he "stood in awe, but not in fear, of a lady who kept a revolver under her pillow." His favorite memory of Belinda was a call she made to his mother while Mame was living at the Southern Hotel, fifty years after they had last talked. Belinda apologized for not calling her sooner and said she had thought of her "every day since I worked for you on Champion Avenue," but something always seemed to turn up to keep her from calling.

When Belinda called in 1948, she was living with husband Joe Barlow, the master carpenter of the Neil House, at 1153 South Ohio Avenue, six blocks from the Thurbers' old house on South Champion.

In an odd twist of fate, both the Simons' "cold, blocky house" at 664 Oakwood Avenue and Barlow's home on South Ohio survive in 2016, long after the house at 921 South Champion has gone.

CHAPTER 13

The Great, Dark House on
Bryden Road

From the outside, the house at 695 Bryden Road doesn't look much different than probably five hundred other brick, two-story, nineteenth-century survivors in the city. It is sandwiched between a modern two-story brick medical building pretending to be as old as its neighbors and an ancient 2½-story brick house with a peaked roof and a pair of fat, two-story pillars that seem a couple of sizes too large.

Once inside, it doesn't take a visitor long to realize that the outside doesn't do the interior justice. This is partially because there is no way to judge the house's extensive depth from the street and partially because Lawrence Abramson and Thomas O'Connell, partners of the law firm that has occupied it since 2000, have done a fine job returning it to its old glory.

As soon as he stepped outside of his house, William Fisher wouldn't recognize much of anything around him; he would be a stranger in a strange land today. The huge, two-story brick mansion across the street that had been built by George McClellan Parsons, a place where Kate Chase (daughter of former Ohio governor and Lincoln secretary of treasure Salmon P. Chase) came to a party as the new bride Rhode Island governor William Sprague during the Civil War, was torn down in the 1950s and replaced by an office building. Parsons' mansion faced the street once called East Public Lane because it served as the city's unofficial eastern boundary, a street that would eventually take his name. At the time it was built in 1847, Parsons' lot was a half-mile deep and one thousand feet wide,

Thurber wrote about a tall oak tree that stood in the way of Town Street's eastern progress at the intersection with Parsons Avenue, and how the street "suddenly took a jog to the right, as if to avoid the old tree,"[1] but there is no sign of the tree or the jog today. Neighboring buildings have long encroached on Fisher's once-impressive yard, and the whizzing traffic on Parsons, and two freeways—Interstate 71 west of Parsons and Interstate 70 a few blocks to the south—have robbed the area of its once-bucolic setting.

The Bryden Road address didn't even come into existence until four years after Thurber was born; for the first fourteen years of its existence, the deep, two-story house that still sits there lived as 589 East Town Street. When Thurber's grandfather had this house built in 1884, it was the only house east of Parsons Avenue on Town Street; in the late 1890s, Town became Bryden where it crossed Parsons. Fisher owned the first three lots on the east side of the street so he maintained an extensive yard. Even with the Parsons' mansion occupying those expansive grounds on the other side of Town in 1884, the Fisher house must have seemed like an unwelcome intruder on the east side of Parsons Avenue.

As hard as it is to imagine the Fisher house without its crowding neighbors, it's easy to envision Charles Thurber's family moving in here when it fell on hard times, and just as easy to understand Thurber's fascination with the place long after he had moved away from Columbus.

The fourteen-room house William Fisher occupied—now called a ten-room house by the Franklin County's auditor's office—was small when compared to the Parsons place across the street and uncommonly large to most of us. It sprawls to almost four thousand square feet. Although a modern legal firm and a nineteenth-century family don't necessarily require the same kind of space, the modifications that had to be done by Abramson & O'Connell and the others before them didn't destroy the character of the building.

When the law firm acquired it, the Ohio Humanities Council had been the previous occupant, and Abrahamson believes the rooming house Thurber mentioned in his profile of his grandfather probably occupied the building before that.

"We fixed it up several years ago and brought it back with the wood floors," Abramson said. "There had been stuff like asbestos tile glued on to the floors. So we had to get down to the wood. There was nothing that was really here, except we found these things."[2]

He pointed to three items on a shelf in his second floor office.

"Found this bottle, found this old nail, and found this railroad spike."

The small empty bottle, nail, and spike could have belonged to almost anyone. After Grandma Fisher died in 1925, building inspector Charles Werlin, his wife Mary, and their two children moved into the house. The Werlins occupied it for the next nineteen years. When they sold it in 1944, it was the first of ten ownership changes in the next forty-four years. A street that had once been home to some of the city's wealthiest citizens fell into a fast decline.

"The last I heard, my grandfather's house had been cut up into apartments," Thurber wrote, "and it is hard to picture the rambling coolness of the old place quartered and confined."[3]

It is hard to imagine it that way even today. Since the last renovation, the house's layout doesn't suggest more than one occupant at a time. Two of the largest first floor rooms make it clear that this is a business and not a residence, but that doesn't carry over to the rest of the house. When a visitor is buzzed through the heavy, wooden front door, he finds himself opposite a beautiful staircase and next to a well-appointed conference room that must have served as a sitting room in the days when former Ohio governor William McKinley was in the White House.

A framed photo of the house in the Fishers' days hangs on a wall in this room, and it takes a second look to be certain it is the same place; an odd shaped porch on the front and porches on the side identified it as the house Thurber described:

> The house was darkened by four porches—front, back, kitchen, and living-room—and by an ancient oak tree that dropped leaves on the roof in autumn. When you closed the front door behind you in the midsummer weather, shutting out the clip-clop of carriage horses on the asphalt street and the lazy splash of the fountain sprinkler repeating its sparkling patterns in some shady corner of the lawn, you were in a wide hallway ten degrees cooler than the world outside. Just inside, against one wall, stood an incredible piece of furniture, a monstrous oak bench whose high back supported an ornate mirror and whose seat could be lifted, revealing a gloomy chest jammed with gloves, overshoes, skates, ball bats, games and whatnot.[4]

That wall is now occupied by a couple of plaques honoring the Abramson & O'Connell law firm and plaque bearing a copy of a 1998 *Columbus Dispatch* story about a medical negligence lawsuit the firm

handled for four-month-old Alexis Hayes. In that case, the jury returned a
verdict against the primary anesthesiologist and her professional corporation for a record $17.854 million in damages, the largest award in a case
of that type in Franklin County history.

Thurber did such a good job of describing the house and its contents
in his grandfather's day that it's impossible not to look for the old house
in the new one. On the wall above "that monstrous oak bench," which
presumably would be above the law firm's plaques, "hung an elaborately
framed lithograph of six hunting dogs with strong muzzles, long ears and
melancholy eyes." At the landing at the top of the steps hung a copy
of Ross Bonheur's "The Horse Fair," which Thurber wrote was "hard to
make out unless the gas mantle on the wall was lit." He noted that the
upstairs hallway started here "and zigzagged to the sewing room at the
rear, in and out of shadows of light. There were seven bedrooms, some
of them with closets as large as bathrooms, and the place seemed to us
grandchildren designed for games of hide-and-seek."[5]

The parlor, which Thurber described as "the brightest room" in the
house, must have been the room on the other of the first floor wall behind
the staircase; that room, which now contains several desks and is occupied by secretaries and paralegals, is lit by three large windows.

When the Fishers lived there, "it was lighted on festive occasions by
a rococo crystal chandelier that threw gleams on family portraits and on
the enormous framed presence of the late James Grover, Methodist minister and first librarian of the city of Columbus, who was shown sitting in
a great chair holding a Bible in his lap."

Thurber got his middle name from Grover, which gave him a made-to-
order joke: "I often thank our Heavenly Father that it was the Reverend
James Grover, and not another friend of the family, the Reverend Noah
Good, to whom the Fishers were so deeply devoted."[6]

That crystal chandelier Thurber wrote about is another casualty of
time. Even if it survived the Werlin years, it probably didn't stand much
of a chance during days when families were more concerned with finding
a way to put food on the table than impressing their rich neighbors on
Town Street.

But some things survive. Thurber described a trapdoor in the ironing
room at the rear of the first floor that led to storage space underneath, "as
if some jolly carpenter had put it there for the sake of the grandchildren
who assembled on Saturdays and Sundays and invented games suitable
for a house that was full of ramble and surprises."

As soon as a "trapdoor" was mentioned to Abramson, he smiled and acted as if he were going to have to search for it. He took a dozen steps toward the rear, pointed at the floor and grinned.

"You mean this one?"

It is an affirmation that this is the same place Thurber wrote about, without the four porches, the oak bench, the lithograph of the hunting dogs, "The Horse Fair" lithograph, and the photo of Grover the librarian. *That* place, the place Thurber remembers, must have been without ghosts, which was one of Thurber's later obsessions gained from his experiences at 77 Jefferson Avenue.

The ghosts that occupy the Fisher house would seem to be those of people Thurber knew or of his relatives. Abramson readily relayed the experiences of one of the law firm's tenants, Elliot Boxerbaum, before he died of Lou Gehrig's disease on June 10, 2014.

> Elliot had a company called Security Risk Management Inc., which was on the first floor. We were the landlords and our office was upstairs. I came in one morning and he said to me, "Larry, look at the clocks." They were antique windup type clocks, nineteenth-century clocks that were on the mantels of my paralegal's office and the room across the hall. Both have fireplaces. And I looked at the clocks and initially I didn't see anything that impressed me about them . . . but both clocks were stopped at midnight. The hands were at midnight and he pointed that out to me and he said "I want to tell you, Larry, I've had these clocks for a while and I take very good care of them and I make sure that they are wound because you don't want them unwound. You want to keep them running." So both clocks, for lack of explanation, were stuck at midnight. This confounded us and it became office legend.
>
> So I was reading portions of a biography of James Thurber and I noticed that one of the chapters that dealt with the Thurber family and the extended family that lived in this house, that there was a reference to a nephew (it was actually one of William Fisher's sons) that I believe suffered from some kind of mental, bipolar disorder and had sought refuge in the house because he had apparently fallen on hard times. According to the biography, this nephew's only job was to keep the clocks running. So that's the story.[7]

He laughed.

There was another occasion where Elliot had received a Federal Express
package from a client. Elliot was very careful about correspondence and
business matters; he was fastidious, a compulsive kind of guy. He had
received a package from a client containing documents, and being a security risk management company, he was very interested in maintaining
good client relationships, strong communications, and the trust of the clients, and for some reason this Federal Express package that had been in
his office on his desk had disappeared. And there was a very small group
of people who worked with him, and he asked those people if they had
seen it and nobody had, and it was a rather limited operation. Of course
Elliot did everything he could to locate this package and couldn't find it
anywhere. He turned the place upside down. He didn't want to call the
client because he didn't want the client to think he wasn't paying attention to his mail, and as he was going to pick up the phone to call him
a couple of days later after searching all over, he looks on his desk and
there's the package.

He grinned.

"Those are two of the better ones. There are some other anecdotal
reports of feeling icy cold breezes and wind on a warm day up on the
stairs. I don't know. James Thurber spent some years of his youth here."[8]

Thurber spent a lot of time here, but he actually did his best to avoid
the place because his grandfather tended to bully him. He also loved it
because it served as the domain of Grandma Kate Fisher, who "was up
at dawn every morning, even in her late seventies, setting the big house
in motion, putting in phone calls, looking after her flowers in season—
roses, lilacs, phlox, larkspur, hydrangeas, and her prized peonies, which
she called 'pinies.'"[9]

Thurber recalled Sundays as long days in the house because breakfast often lasted until ten and "noon dinner" was never served until two
o'clock.

"There were few Sunday dinners when a minister was not present to
say grace," Thurber wrote. And there was often a crowd of people at the
dining room table, "which seated ten and could be leafed out to make
room for a half a dozen more."[10]

Thurber fondly recalled that his grandparents "liked a houseful of
people,' which explains why so many relatives found their way here so
often. These included the Fishers' adult children, of which William Jr.,
the clock winder, was one. Harrison Kinney wrote that Thurber's mother,

Mame, was so impatient with her Uncle Willie's middle-aged indolence, that she threw dishes at him.

"(He) sank into a deepening lethargy over the years," Kinney wrote, "seemingly finally inclined to do little else than keep the clocks in the house wound and sun himself in the backyard."[11]

There isn't a backyard to speak of now. In the crowded confines of the twenty-first century, a small parking lot for the attorneys and their clients has devoured the final remnants of the yard where Grandma Fisher tended her flowers and Uncle Willie tended his tan.

Thurber wrote that with Grandma Fisher's passing, "the great, dark house on Bryden Road, which her intense vitality had lighted, seemed suddenly gaunt and cold. It was closed up and the things she hadn't given away were divided among her children and grandchildren. I got the lithograph of the hunting dogs and enormous photograph of the Reverend James Grover. . . . I gave the picture of Rev. Grover to the Columbus Public Library, where I think the likeness of the city's first librarian properly belongs. I hope it looks benignly down from the wall of some serene and sunny room."[12]

The Columbus Metropolitan Library on Grant Avenue has many sunny rooms since its impressive 2016 renovation, but the Grover photo doesn't hang on the walls of any of them. The Carnegie Room on the second floor of the original building would seem to be a likely location for a man who was the city librarian from 1873 to 1896; portraits of Andrew Carnegie, whose $200,000 funded the library's construction; John W. Andrews, one of the library's founders and its first president; and John Pugh, longtime head librarian, hang there.

The Grover portrait Thurber wrote about can be found in the library's digital collection. But the accompanying description of it doesn't mention its history, offering only "source unknown."

CHAPTER 14

•

The Clock in Thurber's Dreams

When James Thurber wrote "the clocks that strike in my dreams are often the clocks of Columbus" for a speech for his acceptance of the Ohioana Sesquicentennial Medal in 1953, it is likely he had one clock in particular in mind.

Any boy who lived in the city and grew up with one footed planted in the nineteenth century and the other in the twentieth as Thurber did probably passed a dozen or more churches in his daily treks to school, the playground, the library, and his friends' houses. But Thurber spent a significant chunk of his childhood at Aunt Margery Albright's house a few doors north and across South Fifth Street from Holy Cross Catholic Church, and he must have checked the time on its clock and heard its church bells toll hundreds if not thousands of times.

"On the opposite side of the street, the deep-toned clock in the steeple of Holy Cross Church marked, in quarter hours, the passing of the four decades (Aunt Margery Albright) lived there," Thurber wrote. "It was a quiet part of town in those days."[1]

Neither Thurber's family nor his aunt or her widowed daughter attended the church, so it is doubtful if he had any appreciation for its history or what it represented. But from Aunt Margery's porch, Thurber had a clear view of the clock on the church's bell tower, the rectory next to the church, and the small vacant lot next to that, which was the site of the first Roman Catholic Church in Columbus in 1838.

Nathaniel Medbery and Otis and Samuel Crosby made a gift of that lot to the Dominican fathers of Somerset, Ohio, in May, 1833, on the condition that a church be erected on it within five years. Medbery was destined for less spiritual pursuits; he became the first warden of the new Ohio Penitentiary the following year. There weren't many Catholics in the city at the time and they struggled to meet the deadline but finally did, opening a little stone church, fifty by thirty feet, called St. Remigius in April, 1838. The tiny church hosted services while still unplastered, unpainted, and without seats, and Father Henry Jamien Juncker said the first High Mass in Columbus there.

By 1843 when the first resident pastor, Father William Schonat, arrived, the small church was too small to accommodate the growing number of Catholics moving to Columbus and the decision to build the present church was made. Schonat had recently come from Silesia, a region of central Europe now located mostly in Poland with parts also in the Czech Republic and Germany, and he preached in German. It was a good fit. At the time, most of the church's parishioners were German.

Archbishop John Baptist Purcell, namesake of Cincinnati's Purcell Marian High School, dedicated the present structure, on Sunday, January 19, 1848, and the little stone church became a school until a new one was completed behind it in 1870.

Reverend Casper Henry Borgess, the future Bishop of Detroit, succeeded Father Schonat in 1848 and during his ten years there, the tower and spire were added to the church, which was again becoming a busy place. In 1857, when Columbus had eighteen thousand residents, Holy Cross had three thousand members.[2] By then, the parish was mostly split between members who spoke German and English, with Irish dominating the latter group.

More space was needed to accommodate the Holy Cross congregation and the parish's Irish members helped establish St. Patrick Church in 1851. Holy Cross parishioners donated $1200 toward the construction of the new church in an area on the north end of the small town where most of the Irish immigrants settled. The Holy Cross choir provided the vocal music at St. Patrick's dedication at the northeast corner of Grant Ave. and Naghten Street, which was nicknamed Irish Broadway, in 1853.

In fewer than ten years, Holy Cross found itself in the same position it was in when before St. Patrick's was built: overcrowded and looking for another outlet for its members. That led parishioners to purchase land at

694 South Third Street, just under a mile to the south, for what proved to be the beginnings of the present St. Mary Church. A committee made up of Holy Cross members made plans the construction of a school, which opened in 1865, and the church, which was dedicated three years later.

A young Thurber doubtless didn't know any of this, of course. There were eight Catholic churches in the city when he was born in 1894. The church, rectory, and school that lay just to the southeast of his aunt's house were merely part of the neighborhood to him. Although he knew that the area south of his Aunt Margery's house was predominantly German and that a tablet bearing the German inscription *Heilige Kreuz Schule* was situated at one end of the Holy Cross school building, it's doubtful he knew anything about Holy Cross's status as the "mother church" of the Columbus archdiocese or the fact that city's Catholic heritage had been born in that little vacant lot across from his aunt's house.

Thurber wasn't Catholic, but the time he spent at Aunt Margery's made a lasting impression on him, and the church was part of his childhood. The clock still had a place in Thurber's mind a half-century later, and Holy Cross is probably one of the few places in the city that would appear exactly as he remembered it if he returned for a visit today.

CHAPTER 15

•

Fighting for an Education

The cornerstone of Sullivant School sits benignly in the front of the Columbus Board of Education building on State Street, like a regal, gray-haired gent of some distinction.

It reminds you of the barroom-brawler whom time has robbed of both his fire and his belligerence, an elderly, grandfatherly figure who seems like a wonderful guy now that he no longer has the strength to break an offending human's nose or the brass to pitch another annoying interloper through a plate glass window.

Thurber remembered the "tough" downtown elementary school in "I Went to Sullivant," a combination memoir and guidebook on how not to run a school. It is ironic that when Sullivant closed in 1923, the city's board of education moved its offices into the red-brick, circa-1871 structure, remained there until 1961 and still administers the city's education business in a modern building on the site today.

When parents and teachers remember education's good old days with minimal regulation, they doubtless aren't thinking of schools such as Sullivant, which seems to have endured all of the problems today's inner city schools encounter and then some. Thurber makes it clear that while the Sullivant he attended from 1900 to 1908 was a conglomeration of classes, it was a tough place.

The boys of Sullivant came mostly from the region around Central Market, a poorish district with many colored families and many white families of the laboring class. The school district also included a number of homes of the upper classes because, at the turn of the century, one or two old residential streets still lingered near the shouting and rumbling of the market, reluctant to surrender their fine old houses to the encroaching rabble of commerce, and become (as, alas, they now have) mere vulgar business streets.[1]

Future artist George Bellows came from a upper-middle-class family when he attended Sullivant from 1889 to 1897; his father, also named George Bellows, was an architect. Thurber probably purposely left his own family status to the reader's imagination; suffice it to say that he didn't come from one of those "fine old houses" of the upper class. But he did represent a different kind of boy than many of his classmates. In the "tough" atmosphere he recalled there was at least one fight after school daily and "sometimes there were as many as five or six raging between the corner of Oak and Sixth Streets and the corner of Rich and Fourth Streets, four blocks away," Thurber described himself as "one of the ten or fifteen male pupils in Sullivant School who always, or most always, knew their lessons."[2]

He wrote about how his survival of his elementary school years came courtesy of one of his biggest, oldest schoolmates, a black "student" named Floyd: "Nobody knew—not even the Board of Education, which once tried to find out—whether Floyd was Floyd's first name or his last name."

Floyd supposedly was "charmed" by the fact Thurber somehow knew how to pronounce "Duquesne," and "after that, word got around that Floyd would beat the tar out of anybody that messed with me."[3]

Whether there really was a Floyd and whether the studious, nonathletic Thurber needed a protector to make it through his elementary school days is open to speculation, but others have also have memories of the school's tough environment. Helen Thurber recalled that playwright Donald Ogden Stewart once told her husband in London that he became a Marxist when he was beaten up by a bully at Sullivant and suddenly realized what it was like to be persecuted. Thurber supposedly replied, "But Don, you won that fight."[4]

Stewart didn't mention that incident in his 1975 autobiography, but he did have other equally painful memories of Sullivant:

My first conscious memories begin with the three and one-half years I stayed in Sullivant School until I was eight and a half. It was here that grandfather John Ogden addressed our little class one morning—to my horrible embarrassment, when everyone looked at me as he and my mother were introduced to us by the principal of the school.

Another moment which sticks because of the embarrassment was when, in the second grade, I wrote "I love you" on my slate and passed it forward to a very pretty girl named Jennifer Baldwin. This spontaneous if somewhat premature Casanova-like gesture did not, I think, have anything to do with sex; if it did, it certainly had a most negative effect, not only on the beautiful Josephine but particularly on me, because of the cruel teasing which I got from my schoolmates. I dimly remember them trying one day to force me to kiss a girl, and later three older Negro girls in my class chased me down Fifth Street, caught me hiding in a doorway and screamed with laughter as they kissed me. I was terrified—and I have been afraid of girls ever since. And, for a long time, I was afraid of sex.[5]

Thurber spent the biggest part of *I Went to Sullivant* writing about the school's baseball team, and the teenaged students who helped make it successful:

Most grammar school teams are made up of boys in the seventh and eighth grades, or they were in my day, but with Sullivant it was different. Several of its best players were in the fourth grade, known to the teachers of the school as the Terrible Fourth. In that grade you first encountered fractions and long division, and many pupils lodged there for years, like logs in a brook. Some of the more able baseball players had been in the fourth grade for seven or eight years. . . . One or two of these fourth-graders were seventeen or eighteen years old, but the dean of the squad was a tall, husky man of twenty-two who was in the fifth grade (the teachers of the third and fourth grade had got tired of having him around as the years rolled along and had pushed him on.) His name was Dana Waney and he had a mustache.[6]

Dick Peterson, another "old" black student, was the team's star player, and "Floyd" was another one of the better ones. Thurber claimed that the Sullivant team defeated several high school teams in the city and claimed the state high school championship, a title which Thurber agreed it had no "technical right" to own.

Thurber's personal triumphs weren't quite so impressive. It was in the fourth grade that a teacher, Miss Cora Ballinger, told him that he had a flair for art. The moment was one of mixed emotions for Thurber, who described it in a 1959 letter Mrs. Rachel Rowe Macklin of Columbus:

> My teacher in the 4th grade at Sullivant School once brought a white rabbit to class and held it in her arms while we drew pictures of it in pencil. She thought mine was the best but made the mistake of asking me to stay after school the next day and draw it again, with just her and me and the rabbit in the room. The results were nervous and deplorable. I never drew after that with a woman or a rabbit in the room.[7]

Thurber fell into his mad schoolboy crush on third grader and future vaudeville star Eva Prout at Sullivant and didn't shake it for years.

> Once in the 5th grade at Sullivant School, Miss (Mary) Farrell [*sic*], (the) teacher, had an Xmas concert and Eva Prout, my girl, sang "Slumber Boat" and "Sing Me to Sleep" and others sang similar songs: "Silent Night" etc. . . . in the end Miss Farrell called on a tall yella gal whose name I remember after all these 32 years was Almeda, and she asked Almeda to sing—so Almeda gave us "In the Shade of the Old Apple Tree" with something of that plaintive, sure, easy individuality . . . that simple song was therefore a touch of that black shining glory that never quite illumines the brow of the lovely white race. So I've never forgotten Almeda. She probably died years ago in a Long Street cuttin' scrape.[8]

Stewart's parents apparently decided that they had had enough of Sullivant.

"When I was eight I transferred from Sullivant to Douglas School," Stewart wrote. "The Douglas School was way out on 17th Street near Broad Street in the fashionable East End and necessitated a walk of over a mile each way. Why I changed was never clear to me. It was, I imagine, my parents' idea that Douglas was a 'better' school, in a 'better' district. This may have been the beginning in me of a sense of class distinction which gradually came to be connected with 'security.'"[9]

Thurber also ended up at Douglas for the seventh and eighth grade, although his transfer came with his parents' move out of the Norwich Hotel and into the Fisher residence on Bryden Road.

Thurber liked Douglas, but he maintained a certain affection for Sullivant, in spite of all of its issues. He was still bragging on that 1905 Sullivant baseball team almost a half-century later.

"All of us boys were sure our team could have beaten Ohio State University that year," Thurber wrote, "but they wouldn't play us; they were scared."[10]

Thurber didn't say whether the OSU players were "scared" because of the Sullivant's baseball prowess or scared of the players themselves. But he did note that when Peterson was in the sixth grade, he got into a saloon brawl and was killed.

It sounds like a joke, but it might not be. Franklin County has a death certificate for a black man named Richard Peterson who died on September 17, 1917, from a bullet wound to the neck. He was twenty-three.

CHAPTER 16

Parking Lot of Dreams

The old ballfield that once occupied the grounds behind the Columbus Public Health building on Parsons Avenue is lost to time, but it lives in Thurber's writing.

The ancient chestnut tree immortalized by him in "The Tree on the Diamond" is gone, long since replaced by Columbus's favorite nod to progress, the parking lot. An interesting character pops out of a car occasionally, but he or she is gone within seconds, having disappeared inside the modern doors of an ancient building that once served as the Ohio School for the Blind.

The athletic field Thurber wrote about once drew neighborhood boys like ants at a Fourth of July picnic. It was a fascinating place to watch a team of blind school employees the boys called the Blinkies play a curious game that passed for baseball. Today the action is limited. A person in need of a birth certificate or flu shot can find a comfortable place to leave his car for a few minutes or a few hours on some of the finest asphalt in the state and nothing else. The only games are played by people in cars with smart phones.

The space was never really much an athletic field anyway, even in its heyday. Wedged behind and between the intruding wings of the four-story sandstone building with a mansard roof that opened here in October of 1874, the playing field mostly served as the best use of available space.

A makeshift baseball diamond appeared at some point . . . with that "gigantic tree between first and second" that Thurber described as "a hazard out of Lewis Carroll."[1] In the modern, travel-team culture of $100 shoes and $150 aluminum bats, this baseball obstacle course wouldn't fly with today's youth. But at the dawn of the twentieth century, it was part of life—and the Blinkies' home field advantage.

Thurber's humorous tribute to the team and its player-manager Frank James focused on the way the Blinkies used all of the field's unusual features to beat teams from around the city that played on more, uh, conventional fields.

James' players were the only ones who knew how to play balls in and out the giant tree "that made pop flies out of triples and base hits out of pop flies." The tree's gnarled and sinewy roots were also known to trip unsuspecting visiting runners when they were rounding first. The home team also knew how to play the field's other hazards: One wing of the building lurked 50 feet behind the second baseman and the other peered menacingly over the shoulder of the center-fielder. There was thirty feet of paved courtyard in left field—the one part of the field that hasn't changed much to this day—near the school's stables; Thurber described the visiting outfielder there as "an easy victim of ricocheting balls, frightened horses and stablemen with pitchforks."[2]

If Thurber's story sounds as if it were embellished for comic effect, boyhood friend Joel Sayre offered a description of it in his memoirs that makes it clear he had the same memories of the place as Thurber.

Sayre was six years younger than Jamie and four years younger than Robert, but he loved to watch the Blinkies play as much as they did.

> They could not be beaten on their home ground. And Thurber was very funny about that. The ground had trees. Right in the near outfield were great big elm trees. So if you hit a ball up there it often got stuck in the branches. Somebody would get a home run by just knocking the ball in. When the ball wouldn't come down, they had to throw rocks up at it and knock it down.
>
> Another feature was that if you hit a ball into right field, there were huge stretches of cement sidewalks. So the ball would land on the cement sidewalk and roll 100 yards out to Parsons Avenue. Also, just beyond shortstop there were very high weeds and the blind asylum shortstop used to play in the weeds so sometimes the visiting team would rap a liner over short and this arm would come up out of the weeds and catch it. It was very strange. It was surrealistic.[3]

Thurber knew even more about this place than most of his friends did. He lived across Parsons Avenue from the spacious front lawn of the blind school until he was four, and he spent a lot of time later at his Grandfather William Fisher's house near the corner of Bryden Road and Parsons, which backed up to the north side of the property within sight of part of the ballfield.

Because it was the only ball field in that area of town, most of the city's youth played here at one time or another. In the winter it even turned into a football field with one goal post.

Although Thurber didn't play much baseball or football here because of his lost eye, both of his brothers did. Future artist George Bellows lived around the corner on Monroe Avenue and he often played here before becoming an Ohio State baseball and basketball player. Actor/playwright Donald Ogden Stewart played football here, as did William Burnett, who wrote the classic crime-novel-turned-movie *Little Caesar*, and Sayre, who became an author and screenwriter.

"I was not much of a ballplayer," Sayre said. "I used to go up to the Blinkies for the baseball. One season, I remember, I was the waterboy. I would go get a big bucket of water in the boiler room at the blind asylum, as it was known."[4]

The boiler room was James's domain, at least for a while. In the 1910 census, he lived at the blind school and listed his marital status as single, his occupation as "elevator," and his race as Mulatto, which Thurber either didn't know or deliberately didn't mention in his writing. James was thirty-seven that year, and as he got older his occupation changed to "houseman" and then to "teacher." The latter may have referred to his instruction on broom making. In the eyes of the neighborhood kids, nothing could have compared to the way he taught his troops to beat the team from the State Asylum for the Insane or teams of local firemen.

There is no record of any of the Blinkies going on to greater glory, but that old ball field produced some impressive athletes before it settled into its new life as a parking lot. The Avondale Avenue baseball team from the West Side, captained by future major league player and manager Billy Southworth, played here in 1908. Hank Gowdy, who enjoyed a seventeen-year major league career that included hero's status in the 1914 World Series, played here as a boy. So did Billy Purtell, who was destined to play third base for the Chicago White Sox.

Chic Harley, the little East High star who was Ohio State's first three-time football All-American and the catalyst for the construction of Ohio Stadium, played baseball and football here. Raymond (Fike) Eichenlaub, the fullback for the famous Notre Dame team of Knute Rockne and Gus Dorais, which beat Army in 1913, practiced on this makeshift gridiron, as did Johnny Thurman, future all-American tackle at Penn.⁵

It's a roll call of real athletes that would hard to duplicate in many places, one that a driver who parks his Ford there on the way to the Columbus Health's dental clinic would never suspect. This not-so-picturesque parking lot seems like the last place Thurber might have immortalized with a story read all over the world. But the games that were played here were as real as any of the Fords, Nissans, Hondas, and Chevrolets that rest their weary tires here today.

Can't you just imagine how Frank James could utilize those cars if his Blinkies were playing there now?

CHAPTER 17

The One Girl

An Internet search for Eva Prout finds her as a teenager in the silent movie era, a young actress who appeared in thirty-three shorts from 1911 to 1915 for Essanay Studios. Her brief biography on the Internet Movie Database (IMDb) is a flat, one-dimensional view of her life, a dry recital of film credits and vital statistics that does nothing to explain the quest that would have brought 98 percent of searchers here in the first place: The cherubic, little warbler was James Thurber's first "love."

Thurber fell for Prout in Miss Mary Ferrell's third-grade class at Sullivant School. She was petite, pretty, and talented, and when Thurber wasn't busy taking spelling tests or learning long division, he focused his attention on the girl he just knew was the one for him.

"Jim sat across the aisle from me," Prout said. "We were always seated in the front row because of my being very small and Jim's eyesight."[1]

From Thurber's perspective, there was more to this than classroom proximity. Karl Hoenig, a German choirmaster and organist at Trinity Episcopal Church, had been drawn to Eva's deep contralto voice when she was in the first grade, and he arranged Sunday evening mezzanine concerts for her in the Neil House, the Chittenden Hotel, and the Great Southern. That exposure paid off with a week's booking at B. F. Keith's Theater on East Gay Street, which caught the attention of a booking agent for the Caille and Kunsky circuit (Arthur Caille and John Kunsky owned a chain of theaters in Detroit) and her vaudeville career had begun. Eva was nine years old when she took her show on the road every summer after school let out, with her mother and older sister as traveling companions.[2]

Mary Ferrell must have known Eva even before she became one of her students. Belle Prout and daughters Marie and Eva boarded in a three-story house once owned by Civil War general Samuel Thomas on Statehouse Square next to Trinity Episcopal church at 12 South Third Street, a half-block north of the Ferrell family's residence. Eva's father had died when she was eighteen months old, and her mother ran a boarding house just around the corner from the Ferrells at 132 East State Street. Mary Ferrell would sometimes have little Eva sit on the teacher's desk and sing a cappella to the class, and it's not hard to imagine a moon-eyed Thurber dreamily staring at her.[3]

Most boys find a pretty girl to worship in grade school, a true "love" who can make a young heart ache in ways its unsuspecting owner never knew possible. Eva was that girl for Thurber. They shared the same classroom through the eighth grade, the first four years at Sullivant and the last two at Douglas. She became his first kiss during a birthday party game when he was thirteen, which only reinforced his belief that he would love her forever.

Some of his friends and classmates undoubtedly felt similar feelings for other girls. But for Thurber, always a little behind the curve when it came to the opposite sex, this infatuation with Eva existed well into adulthood. This might not seem quite so bizarre if she hadn't left school after the eighth grade to sing and act professionally. Thurber didn't see her again for 11 years.

Even after his thoughts had turned to college girls, even after he had gone to Paris as a code clerk during the war and gotten his first taste of sex, Thurber still carried a torch for her. When he wrote to her and finally saw her again in 1920, he convinced himself that nothing had changed and poured his feelings out in a letter to Elliott Nugent:

> Eva, the Girl of Dreams . . . The Girl heroine of movie stories, and "Prince Chap" plays and pipe dreams, the girl one's heart yearns for and the devil take Joey Taylor's neat philosophy and H. James' cool churches! The girl of Browning gondolas, of Lee Robert's songs, of Douglas Fairbanks' fifth reels and of Harold McGrath's novels. The one, after all, we marry.
>
> I can deal with her fairly, too. Letters and thoughts since seeing her have done wonders. I love her, always have, always will. I loved her when

I saw her. There were the 'rapid heart beats' and all. I sat and stared at her
as I never sat and stared at anyone . . .

I don't know what it is, or was to begin with, but there was the same
sensation after eleven years that I had when, as a kid, I told her good-bye,
pulled my cap to pieces, and felt an ache and an urge in my heart too old
for my years, but too eternal and atavistically strong ever to be classified as
"puppy love" or any other thing. She was the One Girl. And I felt it again,
that unexplainable thing. When sitting opposite her, after dinner in her
home, we were for the first time solidly alone. I wanted her. That's all's.[4]

All of this seems a little crazy from almost one hundred years away,
but it was very real to Thurber. He continued to write long letters to
Nugent detailing his quandary in having to choose between college prey
Minnette Fritts and grade school infatuation Eva, an emotional stew
which seems odd to those reading the letters from afar.

A lot had happened to Eva since she had last seen Thurber as an eighth
grader. Her summer vaudeville bookings got her a deal with Chicago-
based Essanay Studios, famous for a series of Charlie Chaplin pictures
including *The Tramp*. It cast her in various children's roles, most notably
Little Red Riding Hood and *An Orphan's Plight* in 1911 and *Margaret's
Awakening* in 1912. In 1916, at the age of twenty, she appeared in a revue
at New York's Winter Garden for one season and in a couple of Shubert
revues of unrelated acts after that. But her film career was just about finished and theater business was slowing down.

"When the war began, the theaters began closing around the country,
and mother thought we should go home, which by then was Zanesville,
where my sister lived," she said. "I'd been acting and singing for nearly
eight years."[5]

That was 1917. She had heard from Thurber "in 1914 or '15" when
he was a student at Ohio State "for the first time after we had left school."
Gleason McCarthy, a friend of Thurber's who was infatuated with the
stage, told him that Eva was still acting and singing. It was all the Eva
news Thurber needed. She said Thurber "found me through one of the
papers like the *Billboard* or the *Variety*. I was playing in Denver and there
is (where I received) the letter."[6]

Still, it wasn't until 1920, after Thurber returned from Paris, that he
was able to arrange that meeting with her in Zanesville that he gushed
about to Nugent.

At first Thurber was convinced that Eva was still the one, even though
he had spent almost no time with her. Once he did, he quickly realized

that the Eva he had been obsessed with no longer existed, that his infatuation was a beautiful memory that didn't reflect 1920 reality.

After telling Nugent that Eva was "the girl of my dreams," ten days
later he confessed that "this Eva girl is *not* the girl of all of my dreams,
that I really did manage through the years to build up a glittering image
based upon a pretty little bob-haired girl, an image which was so wonderful that she couldn't, I suppose, live up to it."[7]

He kept after her, anyway, probably in part because he discovered
that she was also interested in Ernest Bailey Geiger, a Zanesville man she
eventually married. Thurber took the Columbus, Newark, and Zanesville
interurban railroad cars to visit Eva at her mom and stepfather's home
at 431 Fairmont Avenue in Zanesville—a distance of fifty-three miles—
nearly every weekend during this period, still convinced that he would
marry her. She said he asked her and she couldn't give him a "yes."

> We talked it over and I remember the very spot where we became engaged,
> not what we would call "officially," but we became engaged in a way. We
> had walked across the golf course, we lived very close to it, and it was
> one Sunday when he down to Zanesville. And we'd walked across the golf
> course to the yard of the MacIntyre Children's Home. They have these
> beautiful big trees and we were strolling along. We stopped under this
> tree. . . . And that was when he asked me if I would become engaged and
> I said, well, I didn't think so then. And he asked me if I would wear his
> (Pi Kappa Psi) pin. He had sent me his pin and I had never worn it. And
> I said "No." But if I decided to marry him we would wait—and he was
> willing to wait—and if I did, he would know because I would have the
> pin on my dress.[8]

She never wore the pin. They kept dating for a while, with what Eva
called an "open" proposal from Thurber.

"I think that I returned his love to a great extent because I think that I
really was in love with Jim," she said. "But I realized that Jim had a great
future ahead of him and that possibly it would be better if, well, that I
just wasn't for him. I might hold him back."[9]

Thurber convinced her to go to a May dance for his fraternity at the
Columbus Country Club, even though she worried that she would be out
of place in a college environment. She stayed overnight with the Thurbers
at 330 East Gay Street and she had a good time. But Thurber reacted with
jealousy when he found her looking at the stars with Elliott Nugent at the
club, and his fit of pique over such a random moment bothered her. The
sudden intensity of his interest worried her a little.

Mame Thurber went to Zanesville at one point and told Eva that she was making a mistake by turning down Thurber's marriage proposal. Eve didn't know what to think. Geiger, who danced and played the piano, had been inching his way into the picture. Meanwhile, as it became more and more clear to Thurber that Eva might end up picking Ernest, he started to think that college friend Minnette Fritts might actually be the one. These feelings intensified as school let out and Minnette was about to leave for Chicago, when Thurber confessed to Nugent that the "most contented marriage in all history failed when Minnette and I missed out."[10]

It was too late for Minnette and may have been for Eva, although he continued to see her for a while at the same time she was seeing Ernest. He eventually met and married Althea Adams during this period, and Eva married Ernest two years after that. That should have been the end of it, and, of course, it wasn't.

With Ernest playing the piano and Eva singing, the Geigers went into show business. In 1928, when Thurber and Althea were estranged, Ernest and Eva played New York. They got in touch with Thurber and three of them went out nearly every night while they were there. But when the Geigers moved on to Toronto, that was the last they saw of each other until 1935, when a confused and somewhat agitated Thurber was on the eve of his second marriage to Helen Wismer.

The Geigers had long since left the stage, and Thurber and a colleague of his from the *New Yorker* showed up at their house in Zanesville on the way to Columbus. Eva hadn't heard anything from Thurber—no card, letter, or phone call—since they had seen each other in 1928. Ernest wasn't there, and Thurber's friend left the two of them alone.

"He had come to see if Ernest and I were even still living together, because I hadn't seen him for . . . perhaps close to seven years," she said. "He asked me if I was happy, and I said, well, yes, I was. Well, then I was going to remain with Ernest? And I said, 'Well, of course.' Well, what can you say?

"That was it. He said he was going to remarry. But the impression, my impression, was that he first wanted to know if I was going to remain with my husband."[11]

After they had "a wonderful, wonderful long talk about old friends, old times and so forth," Thurber and his friend left for Columbus. The Geigers moved to Miami two years later and managed a music store there. Thurber sent them a couple of Christmas cards around 1940, but never saw Eva again.

Eva and Ernest divorced in 1946.

CHAPTER 18

Scorpions, Spiders, and Boas— Oh, My!

The solemn girl cast in bronze is holding a fireman's hat, flanked by both a firefighter and a policeman as part of the showpiece memorial in the Ohio Police and Fire Memorial Park in downtown Columbus. The small, neatly manicured park is an oasis of tranquility in a bustling city, its polished granite benches beckoning passing pedestrians and eliciting little if any response.

The landscaping is beautiful. For historical value, it could be improved with the addition of a few fruit trees. Before the park occupied the space at the northeast corner of Third and Town Streets, the three-story Gwynne Block stood here for more than one hundred years, and for almost eighty of them the produce commission house that William M. Fisher started occupied a significant part of the site.

Many of the today's Fishers have memories of the family produce business that aren't a lot different than those of James Thurber. William M. Fisher and Sons, which was founded by and flourished under Thurber's grandfather, was sold in 1960 and is still fresh in the minds of those who visited there.

The ornate three-story building initially called the Gwynne Block went up in 1854, was purchased by Fisher in 1882 and was torn down in 1965. The serene park that occupies the space today doesn't even hint at its previous life, which doubtless would have made the same impressions on that little girl in artist Ron Dewey's bronze sculpture that it did on all of the children in the Fisher family.

Suzanne Ford Hutton, Fisher's great-granddaughter and daughter of Thurber's cousin and good friend Earl Fisher, remembered it as an exotic spot, a place she enjoyed visiting when she was growing up.

"We loved it," Hutton said, in a phone interview from her home in southern Ontario. "They had things from all over the world, produce, and stuff. People would come in and buy—you could come in and buy something if you wanted to—but they also sold to hotels and all that. . . . My uncle Clifford, after grandfather passed away, he was the president. He was a very quiet personality, but he was funny. He had smart remarks, witty I guess is the word I'm looking for. And my father was an outgoing personality in sales.

"We used to go down there and the building smelled wonderful. You could smell potatoes in huge rooms. You could smell fruit. You could smell bananas. And there was a funny elevator, because there were three stories, and I don't know if I have ever seen that kind of elevator. It was open so you could get lots of things in it. You could operate it yourself. I don't know how to describe it, but we loved to go to the store.

"Because of that, my father would bring home all these different kinds of fruits that people hadn't even heard of in Ohio . . . like persimmons."

She thought about that for a moment, and laughed.

"There were tarantulas there," she said, "and we were terrified of the darned things."[1]

It's funny what people remember, eh?

"The old produce house. I have strong memories of that. I can still smell the fresh fruits and vegetables," William Miller Fisher II said, by phone from Stratham, New Hampshire. "I remember going there as a young boy with my dad—he was also Bill Fisher—in the morning. There was a guy named Henry, I called him Henry the banana man, downstairs. He was quite an interesting fellow. They used get their bananas from Guatemala. Every Saturday morning, my dad and I would go down to the train station, pick up the bananas and haul them back to the produce store, and interesting things would occur. Tarantulas would be found, and baby boa constrictors and so forth."[2]

Fisher was born in 1949 and Thurber died in 1961, so their lives overlap only slightly. But the tarantulas are a shared memory of all of the Fisher children—and of Thurber.

All of us grandchildren were enchanted by the store when we were young. You walked into a dark, cool place smelling richly of fruits and vegetables. In one room were enormous wooden bins filled with a million nuts, and kegs of grapes from Spain. Two or three black cats prowled softly about looking for mice, and occasionally we saw the darting figure of a ferret that had been installed in the store to fight off rats. In another and colder room, lighted by flaring gas jets in the years of my earliest memories, bunches of bananas hung from the ceiling, most of them green, a few turning yellow. We were always breathless and a little scared in this room, because big, hairy tarantulas were occasionally found among the bananas, which came from Honduras and Guatemala. The men in charge of the banana storeroom captured a tarantula alive now and then, and it was put on display in the front room of the store on a table, under an upturned glass tumbler. Scorpions were sometimes found in the bananas, too, and less frequently, a baby boa constrictor.[3]

Apparently the quality control on banana shipment didn't improve much through the generations. But if importing fruit from Central America can be a tricky business, it could also be quite lucrative, especially in the days before chain grocery stores and mammoth supermarkets. When he was twenty-seven, Thurber's grandfather, old William M., decided to leave the farm on what is today's south side of Columbus and go to work as a clerk in F. A. Sells' grocery store. It wasn't long before he wanted open his own grocery with a partner, John Wagoneseller, a decision that didn't separate him from the masses; there were dozens of small groceries in Columbus at the time.[4] After two years, the two men decided they had had enough and sold out, and Fisher returned to his father's farm on South High Street. He raised grain and stock, making extensive grain shipments over the Hocking Valley Railroad, but couldn't let go of his grocery dream. He went back to the city in 1870 and went into the grocery business on his own for eighteen months. At that point, he decided to add a wholesale fruit and produce house, which quickly became the primary business. The little company was located on Fourth Street near Town when it started, but moved to the Gwynne building when it required larger quarters in 1882.

As odd as it might seem to modern Columbus residents used to the sight of towering office towers, the three-story building was seen as a local landmark at the time of its construction. It stood immediately south of the Central Presbyterian Church (which still stands on South Third Street) and was so solid and large that it kept the winter sun from warming the stone walls of the church. Large stone slabs from the local Marble Cliff Quarry comprised the sidewalks in front of the building, which had a sheet metal canopy to the curb line.[5]

At the age of forty-two, William M. Fisher was about to become one of the community's leading businessmen. Once his commission house moved into the east end of the three-story building at 120 East Town Street, his business took off like a rocket.

"Basically they were suppliers for small mom and pop grocery stores throughout Ohio, and especially in southern Ohio," William Miller Fisher II said. "They would basically provide all the produce, from bananas to oranges, apples, potatoes from Idaho."[6]

In the days before supermarkets, there were many potential customers, and Fisher knew his business. Long after its passing, Ben Hayes wrote of the company, those memorable bananas, and the mess they made in the street that ran past the loading docks on the east side of the building.

"Lazelle would get clogged with stripped and darkened banana stalks," Hayes wrote. "For Fisher had a control room that did a perfect job of banana ripening. People still talk about the bananas, and would even if James Thurber hadn't written about his grandfather's commission house."[7]

Fisher developed an extensive knowledge of fruits and vegetables, in part because of his upbringing on his father's farm. Many of today's shoppers believe that the variation between apple varieties and their usage is a new thing, but Fisher had honed in on the differences more than a century ago. Thurber wrote about how "he was an authority on applies and could identify nearly a thousand varieties.

"He liked to take his grandsons around the place," Thurber wrote, "pointing out Yellow Transparents, Duchesses, Early Harvests, Wealthies, Grimes Goldens, Jonathans, Stayman Winesaps, and McIntosh Reds, and, later in the season, Baldwins, Rome Beauties, York Imperials, old-fashioned Winesaps, and Ben Davises."[8]

Fisher's knowledge extended beyond fruit to business. He served on the board of directors of Ohio National Bank and the American Savings Bank, and he was both vice-president of the Columbus Board of Trade and president of the Central Market Board of Trade. His receiving house earned a local reputation for being equipped with facilities for receiving, storing, and shipping goods, all important elements given how many clients the company came to have.[9]

The founder died in 1918. His son, William G. Fisher, had been listed as the vice-president of the company for several years, but *his* son, Clifford Fisher, took over the company as president. He remained in that position until it was sold in 1961. Earl Fisher, Thurber's cousin and one of his pals in his youth, became vice-president on William G.'s death in 1939.

William M. Fisher II visited the building with his father often enough to have a vivid picture of the building's layout:

> The building had three floors. The first floor had all the produce with loading docks located on the eastern side of the building. There was a small billing office inside on the left just after you walk into building through the front entry.
>
> The second floor was used for business offices. The third floor was empty and unused. It was large open dirty room with a couple broken windows. It was a wonderful birdhouse for pigeons. The basement was dark like a dungeon. The basement is where they stored and packed bananas for shipping.
>
> There were rickety old stairs going to each floor, but as a kid we enjoyed taking the old freight elevator. The old elevator had gated doors. You closed the elevator gates by pulling one gate down from the top and one pulled up from the bottom. It was controlled with two ropes located on the left inside the elevator. You pulled the rope up to go up and then pulled the other down to go down. We love this as kids. It was so much fun to ride.[10]

Working there was much harder. Some family members believe that Clifford and Earl were close to retirement and tired of running the business when the opportunity came to sell. William Miller Fisher II said his father, William Morgan Fisher, was working with the family business and was willing to take it over, but Clifford and Earl Fisher knew the business was changing for the worst and they decided that they just wanted to sell.

"It was probably in the 1950s, the supermarket chains came in and pretty much drove middle man guys, like Fisher and Sons, out of business," William Miller Fisher II said. "Birdseye came in and offered to have Fisher and Sons become a distributor of their products in Ohio. My great-grandfather, William M., was the entrepreneur, and he probably would have gone with the idea. But my grandfather, unfortunately, was not that way."

He laughed.

"He said, 'Frozen foods will never last.'"

CHAPTER 19

The Dam That Didn't Break

The dam that didn't break in "The Day the Dam Broke" is a real dam on the Scioto River seven miles northwest of downtown Columbus near the suburb of Upper Arlington. Griggs Dam, built in 1904, is five hundred feet long and thirty-five feet high.

It is the star of one of Thurber's most famous stories, a fictional tale that like so many of his stories isn't as fictional as it appears to be. During the devastating 1913 flood that submerged much of the city's West Side, claimed ninety-three lives, destroyed four bridges and left the entire city without power for twenty-four hours, the dam didn't break, as Thurber dutifully reported. But many on the higher East Side did run for high ground when word spread that the massive concrete structure had ruptured. That part of the story truly seems like fiction, especially through the prism of more than one hundred years.

Who were these gullible creatures who broke into a dead run away from the river toward the east as soon as they heard shouts that the dam had broken?

Thousands of people from all walks of life, apparently. Viewed in the context of the times, it doesn't seem quite so remarkable. Most of the city's West Side was covered by fifteen to twenty feet of water, and most of the homes in a four-block stretch of Glenwood Avenue had been swept away. With disaster only a few blocks away and no one sure exactly how high the water would rise and what might happen next, the idea of a crumbling dam that released another torrent of water must have been frightening to people who didn't have a smart phone to help them decipher what was going on.

"Later when the panic had died down and people had gone rather sheepishly back to their homes and offices, minimizing the distances they had run and offering various reasons for running, city engineers pointed out that even if the dam had broken, the water level would not have risen more than two additional inches in the West Side," Thurber wrote. "Only a rise of some ninety-five feet could have caused the flood waters to flow over High Street—the thoroughfare that divided the east side of town from the west—and engulf the East Side."[1]

The local news accounts didn't report anything about the frantic "run" when it happened, in part because the panicked joggers included some of those who worked on the local newspapers.

George Smallsreed, a *Dispatch* reporter at the time who eventually became the managing editor, admitted that the press didn't report "the run" for a year after it occurred, both because of embarrassment to the city and to staffers who had panicked.

"There was a silent agreement among us on the paper that the panic run was best forgotten," he said. "It wouldn't have done much for Columbus. It was a year before we broke that part of the story."[2]

The story the newspaper "broke" then was that a bootblack at the Neil House thought he saw the rampaging river rising faster than it was, made what to him must have seemed a logical assumption and became the first one to shout "The dam's busted!" The *Dispatch* reported that his call was taken up by a modern Paul Revere, a guy on horseback who spread the alarm. That's all it apparently took to empty stores, shops and stables and start the stampede to the east.

In the days before jogging became popular, some of the runners got winded by the time they reached Grant Avenue, a half-mile to the east, but some reportedly made it all the way to Franklin Park, a distance of two miles. Thurber had some running all the way distant Reynoldsburg, twelve miles away, but that probably should be consigned to the fictional part of the tale, exaggerated for comic effect.

Smallsreed, Bill McKinnon, and nineteen-year-old Norman "Gus" Kuehner (future city editor, Thurber antagonist and the subject of another chapter) were covering the flood on the city's West Side that day and as they returned to higher east side of the river water was overflowing the Town Street bridge and lapping at the hubcaps on their car. When they parked the car, they heard shouts of "The dam has broken!" and "Go East!" and instantly became part of the retreat. At one point they hesitated long enough to release horses from a livery stable, an act of goodwill that for some reason the owners of the horses later failed to appreciate.

"The last I saw of Kuehner that day," Smallsreed said, "he was running up the hill on Town Street between two white horses, all going like furies."[3]

Smallsreed didn't say how far he got, but McKinnon, later the newspaper's sports editor, got a ride from some city detectives he knew to Parsons Avenue, a mile to the east, where he waited for floodwaters that never came.

It wasn't just the paper's reporters who got caught up in the hysteria. Longtime *Dispatch* printer Carlton C. Berry recalled the day as one "of great excitement in which several *Dispatch* printers had a part. Extra editions? Sure, big news for several days. It is said that Claude Hubbell . . . one of the composing room proof readers, was seen running at top speed out East Broad Street in order to reach 'high ground' to escape the 'onrushing waters.' On that fateful day in the downtown district, police officials were shouting 'The dam has burst, make for high ground.' Don't laugh at Claude, he was just obeying orders.

"Big Tom Hatfield, stereotype, ran full speed to the roof of the *Dispatch* building, not waiting for the elevator. He said 'I wasn't going to get caught like a mouse in a trap.' Yes, this is very funny now, but there was no humor in it on that day of the 1913 flood."[4]

It became a lot funnier after Thurber wrote about it. He beautifully depicted the absurdity of the scene, thousands running from a monster that wasn't chasing them, desperately trying to get away from a threat that really didn't exist.

"The fact that we were all as safe as kittens under a cook stove did not, however, assuage in the least the fine despair and grotesque desperation which seized upon the residents of the East Side when the cry spread like a grass fire that the dam had given way,"[5] he wrote.

Thurber even drew one of his classic cartoons, where a massive number of Thurber people and dogs are all running in the same direction, past buildings where a frantic Thurber man in the window is waving his arms in his distress over the flood—or not having found a way to join the great run.

Thurber also found a way to again make his grandfather the butt of his jokes, writing that grandfather's reactions to the flood "were based upon a profound misconception, namely, that Nathan Bedford Forest's cavalry was the menace we were called upon to face.

> The only possible means of escape for us was to flee the house, a step which grandfather sternly forbade, brandishing his old army sabre in his hand. "Let the sons———come!" he roared. Meanwhile hundreds of people were streaming by our house in wild panic, screaming "Go East! Go East!" We had to stun grandfather with an ironing board. Impeded as we were by the inert form of the old gentleman—he was taller than six feet and weighed almost a hundred and seventy pounds—we were passed, in the first half-mile, by practically everybody else in the city. Had grandfather not come to, at the corner of Parsons Avenue and Town Street, we would unquestionably have been overtaken and engulfed by the roaring waters—that is, if there had *been* any roaring waters.[6]

The irony is that Griggs Dam's rupture wouldn't have threatened the city at all; the dam was already overflowing with water, so a "break" wouldn't have created the torrent of water that just about everyone apparently feared.

"I do not believe anyone can really, wholly appreciate Thurber who didn't participate in the Great Run on the day the Scioto River dam didn't break," Neil Martin wrote in the *Columbus Citizen Magazine*. "I was one of several thousand who joined in the run and I have reason to think that none of us ever after was able to take himself too seriously."[7]

Local community leaders found the gullibility of their panicked citizens humiliating and worried that outsiders would never again look at Columbus the same way. It must have relieved them that when Thurber finally wrote about it, it sounded like a wild tale cooked up in that creative mind of his rather than an actual news event.

"I lived in the same part of town that Thurber lived in," Joel Sayre said. "People had just been reading about the big flood in Dayton. My brother and I and some other kids were playing ball in the street and suddenly a lot of grown-ups came striding by, some of them doing a dog trot. We said 'What's the matter?' They said 'The dam broke.' We thought they were drunk or crazy. But a neighbor of ours, a Mrs. Sangly, got very alarmed, took all her groceries with her up to her attic and stayed there about three weeks. It's really true that there was a stampede. Thousands of people did run."[8]

CHAPTER 20

·

Wool-Stocking School

Most everyone who has ever lived in Columbus knows East High School. It sits like a royal monarch on the north side of East Broad Street about a mile east of downtown, an impressive two-story structure of Indiana limestone that looks the part of "silk-stocking school" that *Columbus Dispatch* cartoonist Billy Ireland dubbed it shortly after it opened.

Mansions flanked the 120-foot wide boulevard at the time. While the large houses snuggled on the side streets on both sides of Broad didn't drip quite so much opulence, Ireland's implications that the new school catered to the wealthy seemed a snug fit. The only people who didn't know that apparently worked for the architectural firm of Howell and Thomas, an outfit that had been born in Columbus in 1908 but had since moved to the affluent Cleveland suburb of Shaker Heights. The architects didn't leave room for a parking lot near the school, so well-heeled students didn't have anywhere to park their cars.

In those days, East flaunted its reputation as the best high school in the growing city. Its entrance was flanked by six fat columns that might have adorned an important government structure in Washington, DC. It boasted of a capacity of fifteen hundred students, an auditorium that seated one thousand ninety and cost a whopping $727,000 in construction costs, all of which makes it a seem like a suitable launching pad for a literary figure of James Thurber's stature.

The problem is that isn't the East High that Thurber attended. The East everyone knows today opened in 1922. Thurber entered a smaller, less impressive East at 1390 Franklin Avenue in 1909. The three-story East that Thurber attended opened in 1899 and was hemmed in by two- and three-story homes, most made of brick, that were less than twenty years old. The school had been born a little over year after Thurber in 1896, in eight rooms of the Ohio Avenue School on the city's southeast side. Some called for a new school building then, but not everyone was convinced of the need.

The penny-pinchers were like the little boy with his finger in the dyke. The city had grown from 18,554 in 1860 to 125,560 in 1900, pushing Central, the city's lone public high school at the southeast corner of Sixth and Broad downtown, beyond its capacity. Many people living on the far-flung east side also found that location inconvenient. A building boom had been chewing up farmland for almost two decades and planting houses to the east of what had been East Public Lane; the street now called Parsons Avenue runs on the eastern edge downtown and Interstate 71 today. The expansion had begun to accelerate, so much so that the Ohio Avenue School, at the southeast corner of Fulton and Ohio, needed to take back two of the rooms it had loaned the new high school the following year.

The new high school received some additional rooms at the new Felton Avenue School, fifteen blocks to the north, which raised capacity at the expense of convenience. School officials first called the school "South." Then they called it "East." The confusion over the name further dramatized the need for a new high school. Freshmen and sophomores attended Felton and juniors and seniors attended Ohio. Sixteen teachers made the trek back and forth between the two. With the "school" straddling the east side in two buildings fifteen blocks apart, approval for a new high school building came quickly the second time.

The new building of Columbus brick and terra cotta trimmed with sandstone was dedicated in April, 1899, and called "one of the most complete high school buildings in the state." Open land still existed a few blocks to the east of the new three-story school, but not for long. It was already getting crowded by the time Thurber arrived there—its original enrollment of 400 had doubled to 800—and would be replaced by the new East only twenty-three years after it opened. The old building became Franklin Junior High School then and was torn down in 1928 and replaced by a new Franklin across the street from it. The spot where

Thurber attended school is a vacant lot today, five blocks southwest of the East High everyone knows.

The old East was actually good enough for Thurber. He began to blossom there. He had always been a teacher's pet and that seemed even more obvious at East, where his love of reading paid off, particularly among women teachers.

Thurber's lifelong friend and former East classmate Thomas Meek said it was Thurber's writing that drew his teachers' affection.

"(He was) a studious and sometimes withdrawn type, a kind of loner," Meek said. "But he wrote much better than the rest of us and that made the teachers love him. He was, without a doubt, their favorite. He was constantly drawing and then throwing the drawings away, as if he had no further use for them. I believe it was his family that made him different, more than his half-blindness."[1]

Outside of his popularity with his teachers, his high school years seem remarkably ordinary. He is notably absent from extracurricular activities, including the staff of the *X-Rays,* the school publication. To be fair, there wasn't a lot to participate in outside of proms, class plays, and sports and James was the least athletic of the three Thurber boys, even without his vision difficulties.

Like most East students, he became a huge fan of the school's athletic teams and especially of Chic Harley, who excelled in football, basketball, baseball, and track as a sophomore when Thurber was a senior. Thurber's brother, Robert, starred on the East baseball team that had Harley as the shortstop.

James held down various part-time jobs, so it's difficult to know how much he lingered after school, but a short retail district on Oak Street two blocks north and west of the school drew a lot of East students. That section of Oak is devoid of life today, a pock-marked row of vacant lots and rundown buildings. A student during Thurber's days as a high school student knew it as a bustling, busy stretch of businesses: Hahn's Confectionary, a popular ice cream shop and bakery owned by Joe and Grace Hahn that occupied a small brick building at 1256 Oak, served as an after-school hangout for students. The Hahns sold ice cream and ices, fine chocolate cakes, bread, rolls, and an assortment of other goodies; they were good enough at it to have another place on East Long Street. A dry cleaner (Kossman Dye Co.) stood on one side of Hahn's and the Oak Theater on the other, and a hardware store (Segwick Hardware) and a meat market (J. Yaekle and Son) shared the same block. Harley, a good enough pool player that he later beat the legendary Willie Hoppe in a billiards match in The Clock restaurant on High Street, honed in his skills in Ned Mason's pool room near the corner of Oak and Wilson.[2]

Thurber's friend, Karl Finn, the athletic editor of the *X-Rays*, wrote about all of Harley's exploits. Thurber didn't. The first story of Thurber's to be published—a western potboiler called "The Third Bullet" that sounded like a lot of the nickel novels he read—was published in the *X-Rays* in May, 1913, a month before he graduated.

In a 1951 *Time* cover story about his life, Thurber made it sound like his lack of participation on the *X-Rays* wasn't his own idea.

"Was greatly disappointed not to be made editor-in-chief of the high school magazine the *X-Rays*," he said. "Found out some years later that my mother asked principal John D. Harlor not to give me this post because of my eyesight."[3]

This may have been revisionist history, a practice he frequently employed in his later years. Unlike Finn, who later worked on the *Ohio State Lantern* with him and helped get him a job at the *Columbus Dispatch* after graduation, there is no indication that the teenaged Thurber had any real interest in the publication.

He did have an interest in running for class president as a senior, which shows that the "somewhat withdrawn type" had come out of his shell. He ran against his cousin, Earl Fisher, and the son of a prominent Columbus attorney; Robert Thurber said that one of the reasons James decided to run was because he was told he had no chance.[4]

He won, a sign that his popularity grew as he lost shyness and his humor leaked out. Thurber graduated with honor and he gave the President's Address on Class Day, no easy feat for high school senior who never felt comfortable speaking in front of a large group even after he had achieved international fame.

East High School, even the smaller one on Franklin Avenue no one remembers today, apparently provided a good launching pad for those who needed one.

CHAPTER 21

The House the Ghost Got In

Thurber House was born on a day of wild portent and high wind in 1984. It stands as compelling proof of the existence of reincarnation.

The house where Charles and Mame Thurber and their family lived from 1913 to 1917 while James was a student at Ohio State was built long before that, probably in 1873 when its first owner got a $1,600 loan from the Home Building and Loan Association. It rose on land where a syndicate created a high-end development called East Park Place, a thirty-acre tract that had previously been the site of the Ohio Lunatic Asylum.

The house had intriguing stories to tell before the Thurbers moved in. It also had a parade of owners after they left and gradually slid down the city's social strata until it was condemned and ticketed for demolition in the late 1970s. Its history might have ended in a pile of rubble like many of the other Thurber residences in the city were it not for the vision of Donn Vickers, then director of the Metropolitan Learning Community.

Vickers was working with attorney Arthur Vorys to create a block on Jefferson Avenue devoted to educational and arts organizations and other non-profit groups. In the beginning, he didn't even know that the boarded-up house at 77 Jefferson had once been home to the Thurbers.

"I didn't know when I took the job at the Jefferson Center," Vickers said. "I came there to create a learning community of non-profit organizations, where we could work with one another in a helpful ways. The

Vorys family did that, they're the ones who bought all that property. So my office when I first came here was in the Vorys law firm. The buildings on the block, including the Thurber House, were all boarded up except for two, where there were multiple families who lived in them. So there was no place for me to have an office. They gave me an office at Vorys, Sater for about a year and then we started little by little fixing those places up.

"Somewhere along there I heard that was Thurber's house. I didn't know it when I first came, and I don't think half the people on the board knew it. But once I understood that, I thought we could save that for a while because that's going to be easy to get done and some of these other things are harder. So we did in effect. We put it off for three years. And then I decided that we ought to get going on it."[1]

He set up a meeting with *Columbus Dispatch* editor Luke Feck and Walter Bunge, director of the Ohio State University School of Journalism, to discuss their interest in saving and restoring the property, figuring that Thurber's connection to both as a former *Dispatch* reporter and an OSU student might strike a positive chord.

His vision wasn't as easy to share then as it would be today. The place was a wreck. During one early inspection, Feck recalled the rickety floor suddenly giving way when he walked into the alcove area off the dining room. A foot and leg plunged all the way through the rotted floorboards; fortunately, he didn't end up making an unexpected visit to the basement.

"I remember that day," Feck said. "We had a photographer from the *Dispatch* with me to kind of document it and he took a picture of me in the doorway, and it was a real shambles." He laughed. "It was just awful. All of the doors in the house upstairs were painted an institutional kind of green and the doors had numbers on them. It had been a flop house. It was really bad. And then I went down to the parlor and then the dining room, and off the dining room there is a little cove where the Thurbers' dog, I think its name was Muggsy, used to lie and that's where I went through a board up to my knee. I wasn't smart enough to figure out what I was falling into. You don't necessarily expect to do that when you're walking into a house."[2]

The trio pressed ahead undaunted. Vickers recruited others for his Steering Committee—Norm Spain of Phil Kappa Psi, Thurber's college fraternity; Lewis Branscomb, curator of the OSU Library's Thurber Collection; Judith Kitchen of the Ohio Historical Society; and construction expert Dave Timmons. The group identified twin goals of getting the house listed on the National Register of Historic Places to halt demolition proceedings and raising the necessary funds needed to restore the house and provide the programs to fulfill its mission. Costs were estimated at $250,000.

"I said right from the outset, and it's true, that it's going to cost more to restore it than it would to tear it down and build a replica," Timmons said. "Nonetheless you wanted to be authentic about it. Judy Kitchen was involved, she being the architectural preservation person for the (Ohio Historical Society), so we had to comply with all the guidelines on restoration.

"Much of the interior woodwork, even though it had been painted over and that sort of stuff, much of the interior detail was still intact. The balusters and the staircases and that were still pretty much unmolested. One of the main restorations was the fireplaces, which had been covered over. We had to find to new parts material and tile for those. The walls all needed to be redone, but at least it hadn't been cobbled up or the original details obliterated to the point that they couldn't have been restored. Those pine floors, the restoration of those was a real challenge. The temptation as to replace them, but again we wanted to be (authentic)."[3]

Maintaining an old house's history costs a lot of money, and local businesses and individuals responded in ways that surprised most of them.

"I think we raised a quarter of a million dollars, something like that, with a fledgling organization that was just starting, and that was hard; that was really hard," Feck said. "I played golf with (Wendy's founder) Dave Thomas and I had said if you are of mind, we could use some money for this project. And on the first tee, he gave me a check for $5000 and he said 'Is that enough?' And I said 'That's more than enough, Dave. Thank you, thank you, thank you.'"[4]

Curtis Moody's local architectural firm took charge of the restoration, with focus on returning the house to its appearance during the Thurber era. Thurber had been dead for twenty years, but younger brother Robert had vivid memories of how the place looked when he lived there. One day he watched while workers peeled away several layers of old wallpaper and suddenly shouted "That's it!" when he recognized the pattern from the Thurbers' day.

The house formally opened on Sunday, December 10, 1984, with a museum of Thurber materials and journalist and novelist William O'Rourke as its first writer-in-residence. A fund-raising $100-a-plate dinner the night before celebrated Thurber's ninetieth birthday and attracted actor and director Burgess Meredith, one of Thurber's old New York

drinking buddies, and John Courtright, one of Thurber's college fraternity brothers.

It proved a good start to a remarkable thirty years, one that has a witnessed the creation of the Thurber Prize for literary humor, writers' workshops, and two literary events series, Evenings with Authors and Summer
Literary Picnics.

"One of things we did, which I think was right, was immediately con-
nect to the family," Vickers said. "They were living up in Connecticut—his
widow. And his daughter was over in St. Louis and then Michigan, so I
used to arrange to fly to New York City and take the limo up to Connecticut and stay in the house where his widow lived. Rosie Thurber,
his daughter, would arrange to stay there at the same time, because she
wanted to visit her stepmother.

"You know, it's funny. I felt they made far too much of me, that I was
like a stand-in for Thurber. They used to have these fancy dinner parties,
with Peter DeVries and all these writers—you know, the place up there
is littered with artists and writers—so I was having a great time. It was
wonderful stuff. And they were very supportive of Thurber House, financially and also with permission of use. Those were heady days."[5]

Thurberphiles well know Thurber House as the home that served as
the base for his famous short story "The Night the Ghost Got In," a
humorous account of the family's reaction to what he described as an
inexplicable "rhythmic, quick-cadence walking around the dining room
table" and steps "up the stairs" two at a time—when no one living there
had made those sounds. The wild tale still draws laugher from those who
read it, although in Thurber's mind it was always more than a fictional
ghost story. He lived it, and to his dying day he believed the ghost experience was real.

"The ghost that got into our house on the night of November 17,
1915, raised such a hullabaloo of misunderstandings that I am sorry I
didn't just let it keep on walking, and go to bed," wrote Thurber, to begin
his tale. "Its advent caused my mother to throw a shoe through the window of the house next door and ended up with my grandfather shooting a
patrolman. I am sorry, therefore, as I have said, that I ever paid attention
to the footsteps."[6]

His mother may have thrown a shoe through the window next door—
Thurber's brother Robert later said that his mischievous mother would
often throw a shoe down the stairs to add to the confusion in similar
circumstances[7]—but his trigger-happy grandfather was never there. The
story is probably mostly fictional, but Thurber and his brother believed

they heard steps on the stairs, and for the rest of his life Thurber steadfastly believed that the house was haunted.

In the story, his reporting of the address as 77 Lexington Avenue was
done with a purpose, as he explained in a letter to *Dispatch* reporter and
artist Bill Arter in 1957:

> I deliberately changed the address for the simple reason that there *was* a
> ghost in the house. I often wonder if it is still heard there or if it has finally
> been laid to rest. The family who lived in the house ahead of us moved
> out because of the strange sounds (we) found out later. The corner drug-
> gist to whom I related my own experience, described the walking and the
> running upstairs before I could describe it myself. They were undeniably
> the steps of a man. It was quite an experience to hear him running up
> the steps toward us, my brother and me, and to see nothing whatsoever.
> A Columbus jeweler is said to have shot himself after running up those
> steps. This is the only authentic ghost I have ever encountered. I didn't
> want to alarm whoever might be living there when I wrote the story. I
> think it was a music school for girls.[8]

Thurber apparently had done some research on the subject. In the
1920s Wallace Collegiate School and Conservatory of Music was located
in the house. The building later housed a beauty shop and then a boarding house. Based on the reports of later residents, it is unlikely he would
have alarmed anyone.

In 1987 a man named O'Bear Thompson, who had once been one of
the boarders, played a game of Trivial Pursuit with his family. When he
came upon question about Thurber's ghostly account of the house at 77
Jefferson, he recalled hearing footsteps going up and down the stairs and
stopping at his door. Although he couldn't explain it, he said he didn't
believe it was a ghost.[9]

According to a 1988 copy of the *Thurber House Organ,* when the
house was owned by Anna Bancroft, a state employee named Esther Reich
rented an upstairs suite of rooms and she often heard footsteps running
up the back stairs from the dining room. She thought they were coming
from the neighboring house until she met William Thurber at a dance and
he explained to her that the house was haunted. Reich eventually moved,
but she later returned for a visit with her former landlord and spent the
night in the alcove of the living room. She awoke to see a hunched-over
figure in a nearby rocking chair, with his elbow on his knee. She lay back

in bed and closed her eyes and when she sat up and looked again, the figure was gone.

She may have been dreaming . . . or maybe not.[10]

The story Thurber told about the jeweler contained enough truth to at least add to the mystery. Prominent Columbus jeweler Thomas Tracey Tress did indeed kill himself in the house in 1904, although the news accounts of the day differ from those in Thurber's story. Reports describe the thirty-nine-year-old jeweler's death as a horrible accident and it may have been just that. Still, the story begs for examination.

Tress, his wife, and another woman the *Dispatch* identified as Miss Tina Ackerman were in an upstairs bedroom when they were called to dinner. Thomas decided to change his collar, got into the nightstand, and came upon his gun, which he proceeded to wave around and even point at the women. His wife asked him to stop doing that. He told his wife the gun was harmless and that it wasn't loaded, at which point he pointed it at his breast and fired, presumably to show her how silly she was to worry about it. The gun was loaded, of course. The wounded Tress, who was carried downstairs for some reason, was dead within the hour.[11]

"We don't know which room upstairs that it happened in, but we know that he was in the front parlor, and he was almost gone when the police got there and then he died," Thurber House deputy director Anne Touvell said. "In the mirror in the front parlor, people have seen behind them a man dressed in a Victorian-era collar. So every once in a while I allow a ghost hunters group to come in and spend the night. I do it infrequently because I have to spend the night with them. But I let one group come in and they asked Thomas Tracy Tress 'Did you accidentally kill yourself in this house?' And the EVP (Electronic Voice Phenomena recording) came back and said 'Ask her.' There is another woman mentioned in the newspaper article named Miss Atkinson. We don't know anything about her. So when it came back with 'ask her,' I was like 'Oh my God, what if they killed him? What if they killed him and he didn't get it to out anybody before he died?' So who knows? But it's fascinating."[12]

Skeptics abound, as with any ghost story. But Thurber believed it, and so did many members of his family.

"It was the only time the boys ever actually heard the ghost, but it was true they did, even though Jamie wrote it so funny," Mame Thurber told a *Time* magazine reporter in 1950. Thurber's brother Robert also confirmed that he and his father were in Indianapolis that night, as James wrote, and that they really did call the police.

Mame, known to embellish tales at every opportunity, frequently told of how the jeweler had telephoned his girlfriend and was told that their relationship was over. He rushed home, growing more hysterical by the moment, ran up the back stairs and shot himself.

Thurber's cousin, Earl Fisher, believed that Mame was responsible for planting the story in her sons' brains.

> She could convince the boys that they had heard a ghost, whether they had or not. She was an actress and a convincing one. Her children would believe whatever she'd tell them. She was apt to move the furniture around and tell them, "Why, look, it must have been a ghost. Why that clock was here last night and now it's over there." Sometimes she'd turn to Uncle Charlie and say "Isn't that so, Charlie?" He'd just smile. He never contradicted her.[13]

It is a compelling argument, but it doesn't explain why those who work in the house at 77 Jefferson Avenue are still experiencing strange phenomena there.

"I think everybody gets tested when they start working here," Touvell said. "For me, I had the office that was on the first floor, and I'm sitting there, and I'm the only one in the building, Susanne (Jaffe) was off doing the Thurber Prize and we had just come off the John Stewart event and everybody had the day off. It was my first week, so I was there. And the chair in her office was rolling back and forth across the floor. I swear it was. And I just sat there like 'I don't hear anything. The back door is right here, I can run if I have to. Nothing's happening.'"[14]

Patricia DiPerna, a writer-in-residence in 1988, told Harrison Kinney she often heard inexplicable clattering in the kitchen cupboards. She also claimed to have seen a ghost as she stepped out of a car in the back parking lot.

"I happened to look up to the (attic) apartment and the ghost—a hefty, somewhat stooped, black torso shadow, apparently dressed in a raincoat with the collar turned up, moving at a silhouette's pace—made a single pass through the hallway lights just as my eyes traveled up the building wall, as if waiting there, set in motion by my glance," she said.[15]

Patty Geiger, a public relations professional who worked for Thurber House for three years, said she had several experiences there, including hearing those now-famous footsteps and having a shelf of books inexplicably fall behind her as she walked by. But her best story is about a photo of Chic Harley, an Ohio State football hero who attended East High School with Thurber and who was occasionally a topic of his writing.

> I was working in the upstairs office and there was another woman, Jennifer McNally, who was in the office with me. She and I were the last ones to leave that day, and when we came back the next morning, she was the first one back, and when I walked into the office, she was just standing there staring at the floor. And I said, "Jennifer, what's wrong?" And she pointed to a pile of glass on the floor that had all been swept into a very neat little pile.
>
> I was dumbfounded. And then she said "Now, look at the mantle." And the photograph of Chic Harley was right where it had always been, but it was now minus the glass. Nobody had been in the house since we left the night before. There were no resident authors. The cleaning crew was not there. We set the alarm when we left, and she dismantled it when she came in, so absolutely nobody had been there. We even double-checked. Nobody had been in the house. So apparently the ghost knocked the picture off the shelf and felt kind of bad about it, swept the broken glass up into a neat pile, and put the picture back up on the mantle.

There have been so many stories that Touvell has kept a log of them and offered some of them up when *Ghost Hunters,* a show on Sci-Fi channel, featured Thurber House.

> We got some stories from the cleaning people. They don't come at night anymore because stuff was happening to them. I know one night, I think it was Sheila, was there with two helpers—I think it was her son and daughter—and they were upstairs where she was and she heard the piano start to play. And she thought it was one of her kids (and yelled), "Get up here! Stop, stop, stop!" and they were already upstairs. They came around the corner—"Why? What's goin' on?" And the piano was playing. And right when the piano stopped, all the computers in the office they were in started flashing on and off.
>
> Another time she was cleaning. She was done downstairs, she went upstairs and was coming back down to leave and all the chairs were pulled out from the table in the room where we have lunch. There is a table with four chairs, and they were all pulled out, like really far away from the table. So she fixed them and they went on with their work. A light was left on and they were getting ready to leave, and one of them made a comment, "Oh, have James turn off the light"—and let me be

clear, it is not James Thurber that haunts Thurber House—and when she said that, we have a curio in our alcove that is full of china, and it started rattling back and forth, and they just ran out. They didn't turn off the light. They just left.[16]

Thurber would be gratified to hear this because he had a difficult time getting anyone to take his claims seriously. One night in the final year of his life in 1961, at the home of Rose Algent, a French teacher in a private school in Connecticut, Thurber related the *real* story about "The Night the Ghost Got In" with more passion than ever. Thurber and Mark Van Doren—a poet, critic, Columbia University professor, and Thurber's friend and neighbor for over twenty years—had exchanged letters debating the ghost's existence, but this time it didn't end well.

"I thought Jim was putting it on a little thick, so I questioned the ghost story in a kidding way," Van Doren told Burton Bernstein. "It turned out he wasn't just talking this time. He was very serious about that damned ghost. I should have realized he was sick and therefore offended by my kidding, but it was too late. He was a wild man, shouting and threatening. I had to leave. It was awful. There were no formal apologies exchanged, and we didn't see each other much after that. It was never the same between us."[17]

If Touvell is right, "The Night the Ghost Got In" might be an appropriate title because the ghost really does get in. Because other houses on Jefferson have experienced similar hauntings, she believes that the "ghosts" may be related to the mental hospital that once covered the entire area and thinks that the spirits may travel from one house to the next.

It sounds crazy . . . but maybe not. The state bought thirty acres at this location in 1836 for the site of Ohio's first "lunatic asylum." It seems odd today that a spot only about a mile from ground zero in the city—Broad and High streets—was considered "remote enough" for a mental hospital, but the state capital was still a small town with only about five thousand residents. A Greek Revival building to house the mental patients rose within two years, and by 1847, three additions had finished a quadrangle of four hundred forty rooms.

It was one of the largest structures in town when it caught fire and was destroyed on November 18, 1868, with the loss of seven women's lives. Six women died in the fire and one died later from the injuries she suffered in it.[18]

"The lunatic asylum, when it burned, six women were killed," Touvell said. "And people have also had experiences in the Thurber Center, which is next door to the Thurber House. It's a modern building, but Joe, one of our cleaning people, he went in and saw a woman in white trying to open the door to the girls' bathroom. And he said something because he thought it was an actual person . . . and she was gone.

"So one of the theories is that the six women aren't seeing through modern eyes, they're seeing through their eyes and still walking the halls, because the whole neighborhood experiences this . . . some of the other buildings always have strong smell of wood burning or just fire."[19]

Whether you believe the tales or not, it makes for a fascinating story. And Thurber *always* believed.

In a letter to Edmund Wilson, Thurber wrote, "In his play 'The Potting Shed,' Graham Greene had a character say 'No one who has ever experienced a ghost can be argued out of believing he did.' After laughing off my own ghost in my story 'The Night the Ghost Got In,' I now share with Greene the conviction that it was a supernatural phenomenon"[20]

With or without the ghost, Thurber House has become one of the city's treasured landmarks, which, in a ridiculous twist of fate, is probably the only reason some central Ohio residents have heard of James Thurber. It's hard to imagine today that this living monument to Thurber and good writing grew from the run-down, boarded-up old house that was just days from demolition when the project started.

"I think Donn Vickers and Susanne Jaffe should have a real sense of accomplishment because there would not have been a Thurber House without either one of those people," Feck said. "Donn got it started and Susanne navigated it through some really difficult financial times. The 2000 recession, it was touch and go whether we were going to make it, and (Jaffe) made us make it.

"When Donn retired in 2000, we had a going concern. We had established a foothold in the arts community and in the community itself. People were really happy with the Thurber House. Right at 2000, GCAC changed the accounting rules on how you keep the books at art institutions, and a place like the Thurber House, we had been keeping them one way, and now we had to do it a new way, and it was tough. It was really, really tough. And Susanne, to her everlasting credit, pulled it off. So Donn started it, made it work, made it thrive, Susanne pulled it out of a financial pit, and it has thrived. It's in a different place now than it was in 2000. She's done a great job with it. We're lucky in both cases to have them there. They both brought what we needed at that time."[21]

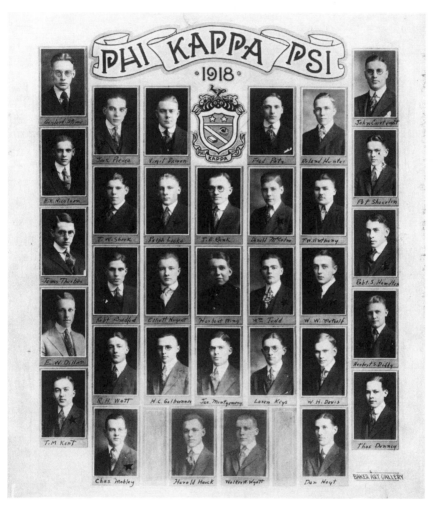

The members of Phi Kappa Psi fraternity, including Thurber and Elliot Nugent, from Ohio State's 1918 *Makio* yearbook. (The Ohio State University Archives)

UNIVERSITY MATTERS

Making It Through the Minefield

A lot of college graduates could probably relate to Thurber's college experience. He started school as a tentative, insecure freshman at Ohio State who wanted to be there but wasn't sure he belonged. The fact that he lived at home contributed to his isolation—the family lived 3½ miles from campus at 77 Jefferson Avenue in today's Thurber House during his college years—and it didn't help that when he went through the fraternity rush process with one of his high-school buddies, his friend received an invitation to join and Thurber didn't.

Thurber struggled with class and struggled with the university's required military training from Captain George L. "Commy" Converse, a powerful university figure who essentially treated Thurber as a despicable, one-eyed klutz. Because of all of this, Thurber dropped out of school even though he didn't tell his family about it. He didn't feel comfortable there and didn't seem to fit in.

When he decided to return to school, his outlook gradually brightened. He met Elliott Nugent in an American literature course and Minnette Fritts in one of his journalism classes, and they both recognized his talent and humor and offered him encouragement. Nugent, a handsome, popular student who had appeared on the Vaudeville stage with his actor parents, helped get him into his fraternity, Phi Kappa Psi, and

Fritts helped give him confidence with the ladies. Although she played the field, Thurber won small victories for her attention over some of his college friends.

One of those was Karl Finn, a friend from East High school who was also a journalism student. Finn covered East-High-turned-Ohio-State star Chic Harley for the student newspaper. Both Finn and Thurber had known and admired Harley since their East days, and he had turned into the most celebrated athlete OSU had ever had, igniting an explosion of football interest in the city with his play. Although Thurber would be a lifelong fan of Harley's, that didn't stop him from poking fun at him by disguising him as a dumb lineman in one of his later stories.

Thurber's primary interest was in writing, which is reflected in fawning admiration for his favorite professors, Joseph Taylor and Joseph Denney, both of whom worked in the OSU English Department. When he wrote profiles of many members of his friends and family in *The Thurber Album* in 1951, he profiled both of them and included one on a third OSU English professor, Billy Graves. Thurber was no fan of Graves and didn't agree with his teaching methods; he seems to have included Graves because of his enormous popularity with other students, which would have made his absence noticeable in a book where Thurber wrote about the others.

Thurber didn't graduate from Ohio State, but his college days made an impression on both him and Columbus. Nugent would become a lifelong friend, later collaborating with him on *The Male Animal*. The Broadway play was based on life at football-crazed Midwestern University, a thinly disguised duplicate of Ohio State. Thurber would also use memories of those days for some of his best stories, turning Converse into General Littlefield in "University Days" and a ghostly visitor on Jefferson Avenue into "The Night the Ghost Got In."

It has helped make Thurber House one of the city's most popular landmarks.

CHAPTER 22

Dear Old Nugey

A case can be made that Elliott Nugent discovered James Thurber. A case can even be made that without Nugent, there may not have been a Thurber—or at least the Thurber we know—to discover.

When the two young men met in an American literature course at Ohio State, Thurber was a lank, rumpled student with thick, steel-rimmed glasses and unfashionable clothes, a diffident townie who was making his fourth run at higher education.

Thurber was smart and talented, but he lacked initiative and direction. He certainly isn't the first college student to exhibit those characteristics, and it's plausible that if Nugent hadn't noticed him and brought him out of his shell, that mission would have picked up by someone else. Thurber's talent did catch the attention of others, including journalism classmate Minnette Fritts and at least three of his OSU professors, so Nugent or no Nugent, his life may have turned out just the same. But there is no denying that Nugent took an interest in Thurber, infused him with confidence, and helped put him on a path to success.

At that point, Nugent was just about everything that Thurber wasn't, which is to say "handsome, athletic and popular." He was born and raised in Dover, Ohio, and had performed on the vaudeville stage as a boy. His father, J. C. Nugent, was an actor and playwright, and his mother, Grace Fertig, was a vaudeville performer.

Nugent planned to make college a brief stop on the way to fame and fortune as an actor and playwright, and it pretty much worked according to plan. Nugent made his Broadway debut in 1921, and he appeared in several productions, some of which he wrote, before acting in his first feature film in 1925. He eventually appeared in eighteen movies and directed more than thirty, and wrote a novel and several screenplays.

None of those successes would have surprised him when he came to Columbus in the fall of 1915 and rented a big room with two of his Dover friends, Art and Pete Reese, above Hennick's, a popular campus restaurant and hangout at the northeast corner of Fifteenth Avenue and High Street. Nugent knew where he wanted to go and he believed it was only a matter of time before he got there.

And really, why wouldn't he?

Nugent had excellent grades; he likely would have gone to either Yale or Princeton if his mother hadn't become seriously ill toward the end of his high-school years. (Doctors diagnosed her with a serious kidney condition, high blood pressure, and hardening of the arteries. They gave her two years to live, but she actually lived until 1930.) Elliott was an excellent writer, an aspiring actor, and captain of his high school track and football teams. He had met a member of the Phi Kappa Psi fraternity through a friend in Dover before he ever got to campus, and when he arrived in Columbus, a "small committee" from the fraternity greeted him. They took him to the Neil House for lunch and then to the chapter house to meet the other Phi Psis. He and his two Dover buddies were also rushed hard by two other fraternities, but they pledged Phi Kappa Psi. In Nugent, the Phi Psis had snagged a whopper.

The three Dover boys continued to live in the room above Hennick's among a cluster of rooms called the Bachelor Apartments. Nugent went out for the freshman football team and quickly discovered he wasn't cut out for college ball. Chic Harley, an East High grad who would become a three-time All-American and the talk of the town, was.one of the players he met during his brief college career.

"My own collegiate football career actually lasted about two weeks," Nugent wrote in his 1965 autobiography. "The very first time I was put in as left end to scrimmage the varsity, I tried to tackle a 200-pound human locomotive. I hit him, bounced off and found that I could not lift my right arm. After that, I ate with my left hand for some time, and before long the football season was over."[1]

As it turned out, Harley lived in one of the other apartments above Hennick's and Nugent dropped in on him one evening to chat.

"I soon learned that books and words were not of much interest to Harley," Nugent wrote. "How the professors managed to keep him eligible for athletics was later classically explained in a story by James Thurber called "University Days," in which someone resembling Harley appears as Bolenciecwcz, who has trouble naming any means of transportation."[2]

Fellow East grad Thurber would have been interested to know that Harley lived across the hall from Nugent, but the paths of Nugent and Thurber still hadn't crossed.

"I think it was Professor (Edwin) Beck's class that I first became conscious of Jim Thurber's existence," Nugent wrote. "The professor read aloud a piece Jim had written, and I was impressed. After class I spoke to him on the steps of the building and we exchanged compliments. Before long, I was also meeting him in a journalism class. Jack Pierce, a handsome Phi Psi, was one of the student editors of the *Lantern,* and we two began a campaign to get this lanky Columbus boy with the artificial eye out of his private shell and into Phil Kappa Psi."[3]

As Nugent got to know Thurber, he learned the story behind his glass eye and his struggles when he first came to campus.

"He had been rushed by a fraternity in which he had a friend, but he had not been asked to join," Nugent wrote. "This experience made him a bit of a hermit and a loner around the campus, and this feeling may have deepened after a bout of bad health forced him to drop out of college for nearly a year. When he returned, he was with a younger group that included very few of his acquaintances or friends."[4]

Nugent became one of his best friends and did a lot to restore his confidence. He got him a haircut and a new blue suit to help him get into the fraternity, which took a bit of a sales job. The members couldn't see what Nugent saw in him.

One of Nugent's Phi Psi brothers, Dr. Virgil "Duke" Damon, said that "Nugent cleaned Jim up a bit" and lobbied hard for him. Nugent could see through Thurber's rough façade to his talent, and he had learned how funny and entertaining he could be.

"Jim was considered an oddball by the brothers, but Elliott, even though he was an actor from a theatrical family, was considered one of the boys," Damon said. "To be truthful, Elliott had a problem getting Jim into the fraternity. None of us knew much about his background or his folks. We were never invited to his home, for instance. It was like he pretended he didn't have a family. But Elliott went to bat for Jim as a great genius and got him in."[5]

That proved to be the beginning of a radical transformation in Thurber, who immediately started to blossom as a fully engaged college student. He and Nugent both worked as reporters on the *Lantern* during the 1916–17 school year, and both were made issue editors of the paper the following year. Thurber took charge of the Wednesday edition and Nugent had the same responsibility on Thursdays.

Following Nugent's example, Thurber began to take full advantages of the opportunities offered to him. He started contributing to the *Sundial,* the school's monthly humor and literary magazine, and eventually became its editor. He followed Nugent to the Strollers, the school's dramatic society. He got involved with Bucket and Dipper, a junior class honorary, and La Boheme, a literary group of students and faculty members which met for dinner and pressing intellectual discussions. As a senior, he and Nugent were both "linked" for Sphinx, a posh society reserved for the biggest men on campus.

Nugent's personal road found few potholes outside of those in his immediate family. With his mother's health deteriorating, Nugent's father moved the family into a rented house at the corner of Twelfth Street and Neil Avenue for Elliott's sophomore year; during most of this time, his father played the Orpheum circuit in the west. Elliott lived close enough to walk to classes from there, and his sister, Ruth, attended the Columbus School for Girls, which she gradually grew to accept after a rough start. But his mother and sister both missed Dover, so it proved to be a rough transition. The family gave up the house on Neil in the spring of 1917 when the school year was nearly over and moved into a suite in the Great Southern Hotel downtown; J. C. had decided that Ruth was old enough to take care of her mother. That meant they could move back to Dover, where they were both much happier, and Elliott could move into the Phi Psi house and sample parts of college life he had been missing.

World War I interrupted all of this and separated Nugent and Thurber. Nugent went home to Dover to await a call from the Navy, and Thurber, unable to serve in the military because of his eye, went to Washington and eventually Paris, France, as a code clerk, a position that had been secured for him by his father. The end of the war brought Nugent back to OSU in 1919 for the one semester he needed to graduate. Meanwhile, when Thurber's stint as a code clerk ended, he decided that he wasn't going to return to school. After five years of studies, he still had only eight-seven credit hours out of the one hundred twenty he needed to graduate, and he was twenty-three, an age that told him it was time to move on. A few days after his graduation, Nugent did that literally, moving to New York to join his father and pursue his acting career.

Actors went on strike that summer seeking recognition of a new union and shut down most of the New York theaters; because Elliott could do such a good imitation of an Amish accent—his eastern Ohio background paid off there—he landed a part in *Tillie, A Mennonite Maid,* playing outside the city. He sold a short story to the *Smart Set.* Nugent had also sold an option on a play that was never produced, so a Paris-bound Thurber couldn't help but be both happy and envious of his close friend.

By 1921 Nugent was playing the juvenile in *Dulcy,* the first Marc Connolly and George S. Kaufman collaboration, and he had fallen in love with Norma Lee, the ingénue, before the play was four months old and gotten engaged. When they were married on October 15, 1921, at the Chapel Notre Dame in Morningside Heights, New York, Thurber came in by train from Columbus to be the best man.

The distance might have ended the Thurber-Nugent friendship, but it had little effect on it; they exchanged long letters with each other that detailed the joys and frustrations of their social and professional lives. They often begin with "Dear Old Nugey" or "Dear Old Thurber," as if they had been away from campus for decades. In them, one finds a Thurber who always seems to be lagging behind his friend's professional, artistic, and romantic success.

As close as they were, it must have been difficult for Thurber to see his pal succeed so splendidly in pursuits where he had yet to make his mark. By 1928 Thurber had landed at the *New Yorker* and had begun producing some of his classic prose. But when he returned to Columbus in the fall, Nugent was in town playing in *The Poor Nut,* a play he had written based on their Ohio State days. Opening night was attended by the governor, the mayor, and the OSU president. The school presented Nugent with a scarlet sweater with an O monogram, like those given to varsity athletes. Timing is everything. While Thurber would eventually overtake Nugent and far outstrip him in fame or popularity, the prospect of that happening seemed remote in the 1920s. Nugent was a successful young actor and playwright, and Thurber was a local guy and former Columbus newspaperman who worked at a relatively new magazine in New York.

The irony is that today Nugent is remembered mostly for coauthoring *The Male Animal* with Thurber in the late 1930s, even though he enjoyed impressive career as a Hollywood actor and director. The play about college life at football-crazed Midwestern University, easily recognized as Ohio State, didn't appeal to Nugent when Thurber first proposed it to him, and he told his friend that he was too busy to work on a play. But Thurber kept the heat on and Nugent missed the theater. When Thurber wrote to him in January 1939, and enclosed a couple of scenes from the proposed play and a brief outline, Nugent agreed to do it, and the Nugents eventually met the Thurbers at the Algonquin Hotel in New York. The two college friends spent two weeks there plotting the play, and Nugent's father, who was still involved with the theater in New York, offered suggestions. Thurber's initially saw it as a comedy about married life in the college community titled "Homecoming Game." Nugent insisted that they add some "social significance" to the plot. They hit upon the idea making a battle over academic freedom part of the storyline, centering it on a college professor who faces dismissal for his defense of free speech. Thurber didn't care about this as much as Nugent did, but the change seemed to finally assure that the pair would successfully collaborate on a theatrical project, as they had always said they would in college.

It wasn't smooth sailing. Thurber and his wife, Helen, went to California so that Nugent could continue his work there while they worked on the play; he had contracted to direct Bob Hope and Paulette Goddard in *The Cat and the Canary*. The Thurbers booked passage on the SS President Garfield so they could take their Ford with them, and it didn't go well. The ship went by way of Havana, Cuba, and the Panama Canal, the heat was horrendous, and Thurber suffered an attack of blindness, which may have been caused by it. All of this sent Thurber into a state of high dudgeon, and after their arrival, the southern California sun didn't help his disposition.

The Thurbers stayed for four months, first at the Nugents' Bel-Air home and later in a rented place in Beverly Hills. They frequently argued. Once, while the Thurbers were still living with the Nugents, Thurber stormed out of the house and vowed never to return; Nugent found him sleeping in the car in the garage.

They worked during the day and socialized in the evening. Thurber was treated like royalty both by the movie crowd and the press, which flocked to Nugent's house to interview him. His answers could surprise. When he was asked what he thought of the beautiful southern California weather, he replied "Monotonous. The sunny skies look as though they had been done by the Pittsburgh Plate Glass Company."

At one of Nugent's parties, a man told Thurber that he didn't think his cartoons were funny.

"Will you tell me what's funny about them, Mr. Thurber?" he said.

Thurber finished getting his glass refilled, before replying: "When I was younger and more patient, I might have said that I don't think they're so funny myself. But right now my eyes are troubling me and I don't have time to talk to dumb sons-of-bitches."[6]

Despite their numerous disagreements, their strengths complemented each other. Thurber's creativity took him all over the place. He often didn't know where the plot would lead him when he sat down to write, which was probably what kept him from completing his own play; Nugent knew structure, which offered needed direction. When they finally finished a rough draft, they edited each other's work and that led to more arguments. The play was finally ready for a tryout production late in the summer of 1939.

That meant that it was time to resolve another one of their disagreements: Thurber wanted Nugent to play Tommy Turner in the production, but Nugent didn't want to commit that much time to a role that would take away from his movie direction. Myron McCormick was cast in the role, and when he dropped out early on, Nugent reluctantly took over and eventually starred with Gene Tierney in the play, which is still popular in stock and amateur productions. Nugent also directed the 1942 Warner Brothers film version of *The Male Animal,* starring Henry Fonda and Olivia de Havilland.

Thurber and Nugent remained friends after that, frequently seeing each other despite the health issues that both suffered. In 1949 Nugent suffered from severe symptoms of bipolar disorder; because Thurber had recently suffered some mental health issues of his own, he was particularly sensitive to Nugent's problems.

Thurber continued to hold Nugent's opinion in high esteem. In 1959, when Haila Stoddard, a soap opera star and Thurber fan who dreamed of being a Broadway producer, came up with the idea of a revue based on short dramatizations of his work, she took her outline to Nugent first. He liked the idea, and his enthusiasm for it helped convince Thurber that *A Thurber Carnival* was worthwhile project. Thurber became the writer and general consultant for the revue, which opened in the Hartman Theater in Columbus on January 7, 1960. It played in six cities before it landed on Broadway. Thurber eventually played himself in the revue, a kind of last hurrah for a writer and artist who always wanted to be an actor.

Thurber began to experience health problems shortly after the revue's Broadway run closed on November 26, 1960. His last year was a difficult one and was marked by several awkward incidents that may have stemmed from a series of small strokes. After he collapsed a final time on

October 4, 1961, he was taken to Doctors Hospital on East End Avenue in Manhattan, where he stayed until he died on November 2. During that month, Elliott Nugent was one of his most frequent visitors.

When Thurber's ashes were buried in Green Lawn Cemetery in Columbus on November 9, "Dear Old Nugey" was one of those who attended the graveside service.

CHAPTER 23

Captain Coldheart

The General Littlefield we meet in "University Days" is a comic figure. The inept commander of the school's cadet corps almost seems more suited for clown shoes and a laugh track than a military uniform, an approach that revealed James Thurber at his devious, vengeful best. The real Littlefield was Captain George L. Converse, a grim-faced man with a thick, whisk-broom moustache and a stern, military-bearing who wasn't as funny or as forgetful as Thurber made him appear.

Converse lost an eye fighting Indians at the Battle of Big Dry Wash in the Arizona Territory in 1882, the last major battle between United States troops and the Apaches. The injury effectively ended his active military career, eventually leading him to his position as an Ohio State instructor who helped establish the Reserve Officer Training Corps at the school.[1]

Converse may have been a military hero. He was definitely no hero to Thurber. He made Thurber's life miserable in the military science and tactics classes that all male freshmen and sophomores at the university were required to attend, particularly when the gangly, one-eyed student had to march during close-order drills. Even though Thurber hated Converse, a martinet not so affectionately known as "Commy" to Ohio State students—behind his back, of course—he never tried to assign all of the blame to him.

"As a soldier, I was never any good at all," Thurber wrote. "Most of the cadets were glumly indifferent soldiers, but I was no good at all."[2]

It's not difficult to imagine a clumsy, uncoordinated Thurber having a tough time impressing his strict, military-minded teacher. But good or bad, it's difficult to whip up much sympathy for Converse, who apparently wouldn't have felt any compunction if he had stopped Thurber from becoming an internationally known humorist because he didn't excel at military drills. As ridiculous as it seems when it is put that way, it may explain why Thurber seemed to take such great delight in making fun of Converse in his story. The stone-faced captain helped turn Thurber into an insecure, troubled student, and General Littlefield escaped from the writer's imagination as a satisfying answer to that torture.

Converse's lost eye might have served as common ground between him and Thurber. It didn't. Thurber's military difficulties at OSU, which he practically celebrated in his writing but suffered painfully in real life, seemed especially galling to the Army officer who some said was the third most powerful person on campus behind the school president and the athletic director.

"You are the main trouble with this university," Converse said to Thurber, when he was having trouble with the drills he was supervising.

"I think he meant that my type was the main trouble with the university but he may have meant me individually," Thurber wrote. "I was mediocre at the drill, certainly—that is until my senior year. By that time I had drilled longer than anybody in the Western Conference, having failed at military at the end of each preceding year so that I had to do it all over again. I was the only senior still in uniform."[3]

It seems clear that Thurber despised Converse. He often cut his classes, resentful that he had to take them when he knew his eye would disqualify him for military service. He often entertained family, friends and fraternity brothers, donning an eye patch to offer unflattering imitations of him.

In February 1916, before the second semester was to begin, Thurber received a letter from President Thompson's office, saying that his registration for school was being protested because of his "continued absence from military drill." The registering offices had been instructed not to register him except on written authority from the president, which apparently wouldn't happen unless he brought a note from Converse withdrawing his protest. The choice was clear: Thurber could plead with Converse to give him another chance or drop out of school.

For Thurber, it was no choice really. He quit. With the help of a friend, he got a job folding circulars and addressing and sealing envelopes with the Ohio Department of Agriculture, which quickly convinced him that he needed to get back in school. So at the end of the summer he made an appointment with President Thompson, who sympathized with him and decided to reinstate him without any letter from Captain Converse. Thurber drew incompletes in military science in 1914, 1915, 1916, and 1917, and because of Thompson's largess, or maybe because the school president understood Converse better than anyone, Thurber managed to stay in school.[4]

Even so, it begs the question: Who *was* this despicable guy who might have driven Thurber into clerical work?

For the university's perspective, we give you James E. Pollard, a contemporary of Thurber as an OSU student who later became director of the school of journalism and wrote numerous books, including a history of Ohio State that was published in 1952.

In it, he reports on Converse's hiring as professor of military science and tactics in 1900 and wrote that he "became a campus figure of importance and influence. When it came to spotting a cadet out of step, or with the wrong kind of shoes or a soiled collar, he could see more and farther than most men with normal vision. He was strict but he was fair."[5]

Fair is in the eye of the beholder, obviously, and it is doubtful Thurber felt Converse was fair.

Harrison Kinney summed it succinctly in a sentence about the rush of students signing up for the armed services after the United States declared war in April, 1917.

"It was almost worth a world war to Thurber," Kinney wrote, "to see his nemeses, Captain Converse, called to Army service the following year."[6]

Commy was one of four Ohio State men responsible for including the Ohio Plan for Reserve Officers in the National Defense Act of 1916. (President William Oxley Thompson, Dean Edward Orton Jr., and Ralph D. Mershon, a 1890 OSU grad and former head of the alumni association who had become a New York engineer, were the others.) It established the Reserve Officer Training Corps (ROTC) throughout the nation. During World War I, Converse was appointed inspector for the sixth district of student army training units and later became the recruiting officer at Indianapolis. He was promoted twice and retired in 1920 with the rank of colonel.[7]

Converse wasn't totally to blame for the writer's failings, as even Thurber himself acknowledged. He doubtless deserves better than he got in "University Days"—Littlefield is busy swatting flies when Thurber shows up, barks at Thurber for "startling" one he was about to swat, and then forgets why he even summoned him there—and wouldn't have been a Thurber favorite even if he had breezed through the drills. Dogs and cats have more in common than they did.

George L. Converse Jr. was born in 1857 not far from his longtime home at 1463 Neil Avenue, on land owned by his father, a prominent local attorney and three-term Democratic Congressman. As soon as he was old enough, he rode a horse to Lancaster, Ohio, to take the entrance exam to West Point, an opportunity doubtless secured for him by his father. He graduated from the academy about 1880 and was serving in the Third Cavalry in Wyoming when it was ordered to Arizona to help the Sixth Cavalry quell an Apache uprising. He had only been in active service for two years when that bullet took out his right eye. Converse recalled in a 1944 article that the bullet was fired from a Winchester and that the soldiers were equipped with inferior Springfields. The bullet was never removed.

"There were about 25,000 men in the Army when I joined," an eighty-six-year-old Converse said. "If there were three or four troops at a post, it was considered a big post."[8]

By comparison, Ohio State became a huge "post" for him. During his time there his ROTC program grew from three hundred students to nearly three thousand. When he died in 1946 at the age of eighty-nine, a news release prepared by the Ohio State University News Bureau noted, "He not only taught the cadets of his day the intricacies of squads right, but along with them he taught, by precept and practice, the lessons of promptness, of orderliness, of obedience, of alertness, of discipline, and of self-reliance. His Thursday morning talks to freshmen men were as much a part of university life as were the Wednesday convocations of those days at which President Emeritus Thompson spoke."

Converse's Thursday morning talks with the freshmen may have included one at least one disgruntled senior.

CHAPTER 24

The Girl Who
"Discovered" Thurber

Every life has its share of either/or moments, fortuitous times where an unforeseen event or a chance meeting with someone can send an unsuspecting subject in one direction or another. Elliott Nugent was obviously one of those catalysts for Thurber. Minnette Fritts was another.

When Thurber took a seat in Joseph (Chief) Myers' first year journalism class at Ohio State in the fall of 1916, there was no way for him to know that Fritts, the pretty sophomore who was seated at the typewriter next to him, would have a significant impact on his life. Fritts was a native of Mount Sterling, a town of fifteen hundred about twenty-five miles south of Columbus, an education major with a minor in journalism. She had attended a prep school in Illinois and taught school for two years before entering OSU as a freshman in 1915.

The Thurber she found in that journalism class was a gangly, poorly dressed townie who lacked self-confidence, but one who had genius hiding beneath that tentative exterior. She watched him write quickly to complete an assignment and then begin writing anew on another sheet of paper before crumpling it up and discarding in the trash can.

After Fritts saw him do that a few times, she stuck around after he left, rescued the wadded up sheets from the trash, and shared them with Myers. Both were astounded at how good Thurber's garbage was.

"I really was the one who discovered him," Fritts said. "Because he was so shy and backward, he didn't turn anything in. so I would pull everything he wrote out of the waste basket and take it to our journalism professor. I just wanted to see if they were good. I'd wait until Jim left and then I would pull them out, everything he wrote; and I thought 'Oh the wit!' It was just really clever."[1]

Those fascinating moments, which unfolded on the second floor of the Shops Building (later called Welding Engineering Laboratories), just south of Woodruff Avenue where the School of Earth Sciences is today, were the kind rarely recognized for what they are at the time. Student and professor received a sneak peek at a genius before anyone knew of him; unfortunately, neither of them had any way of knowing where Thurber would go from there. Myers, an OSU alum and a former Pittsburgh news-paperman, realized Thurber had talent. Fritts liked him and took a spe-cial interest in him. Nugent also saw Thurber's ability, and it wasn't long before the two of them were talking about trying to get him into Nugent's fraternity, Phi Kappa Psi.

At first, this was a lot like trying to convince a family of lions to adopt a rhinoceros.

"There was the matter of Jim's looks and attitude," Fritts said. "He still had very little self-assurance, and that showed. He was awkward and poorly dressed. I remember the difficulty Elliott was having persuading his fraternity to offer Jim a bid."[2]

Fritts fed Thurber's self-confidence by praising his writing and embrac-ing him as a friend. Nugent helped him spiff up his act with new clothes and frequently brought him to the frat house and gave the others a chance to see how funny and entertaining he could be. The Phi Psis' eventual acceptance of Thurber provided him with a huge confidence boost, and the recognition of his ability added to it. He started working on the cam-pus newspaper, the *Lantern,* and landed a job as the editor of the *Sundial,* the campus humor magazine. His sudden makeover proved so dramatic that by 1917, he began pursuing Fritts as a prospective suitor.

Minnette played the field while in school and Thurber joined the crowd. Among the j-school regulars, Thurber, Maurice Mullay, Karl Finn, and Tom Meek all were on her date list, often at the same time.

Finn loved sports but, like Thurber, couldn't participate. He had had part of a leg amputated as a youth, and satisfied his love in other ways. He served as manager of many of the school's sports teams, served as campus sports correspondent for the *Columbus Dispatch,* and took Min-nette to many of the games. Meek was an excellent dancer and frequently took her to dances. She loved books and worked at the library. Thurber engaged in countless hours of discussions with her there, literary and otherwise.

"Tom was the editor of the yearbook and also editor of the newspaper; Tom and Jim were together a great deal," Fritts said. "They were always coming over at midnight and throwing stones at my window, getting me to come down to get something to eat at midnight. That's one of my most fond memories. I was a serious student, but those times were so much fun."[3]

Thurber and Meek usually made those treks to Fritts's window after putting the *Lantern* to bed. Offices for the school newspaper were also located on the second floor of the Shops building. For at least part of this time, Fritts lived at 206 West Tenth Avenue, which was four blocks to the south and only a couple of blocks from Marzetti's, their late-night stop on High Street.

By the time the Phi Psis prepared to host their annual May dance, Thurber and Fritts had shared so many library talks and campus walks that he asked her on a formal date. Her acceptance marked it both as a big moment and a scary one. Thurber couldn't dance, so he did what any desperate American male would do as the absolute last resort when trying to impress a girl: he took dance lessons. Unfortunately, Fritts' memories of it weren't those of a young woman who had somehow landed a date with the future Fred Astaire.

"Jim walked over me pretty much of the time," Fritts said. "He was not much of a dancer."[4]

The ham-footed Thurber thought he had blown it. He didn't ask her on any more formal dates in the months after that, believing that she would find all of his journalism department rivals more attractive than him.

As he prepared to leave for Washington for his training as a code clerk in June, 1918, twenty-five thousand men, women, and children marched in a Columbus-win-the-war parade and he and Fritts spotted one another through the crowds on the sidewalk. He asked her to go with him to see Marguerite Clark in *Prunella,* a romantic fantasy film based on the 1906 play, and she accepted. He borrowed the family Reo for the date and took her to Marzetti's for a late-night meal after the show. Two moonlit nights later, they were back in the Reo, this time in secluded spot on the banks of the Scioto, where they engaged in a long necking session. Thurber reacted by overreacting.

Mullay had asked Minnette if she would wear his fraternity pin, and she had responded with an encouraging "perhaps." Sensing opportunity,

Mullay had asked his buddies, including Thurber, to stop competing for her affections and give him a chance to seal the deal. Thurber had agreed, thinking he and Minnette had no future, but now he changed his mind. Mullie had left for the Navy, and Thurber not only renounced his pledge to Mullie in a conversation with Minnette, but also made it clear to her that she and only she was the object of his fancy.

Even if he believed that in his moment of passion, it wasn't true. Eva Prout had come back to Zanesville from the road. Although he didn't get a chance to see her before he left for Washington, his affections were clearly divided between the two women.

In a letter to Nugent from Washington dated July 16, 1918, he told his friend about moonlight parking with Minnette along the Scioto, and joked about his problem:

> Oh, well, hell, Nugent, it's gone pretty damn far and I only wish I could hope for a repetition of the Minnette engagement history. But a little hunch informs me I'm in. . . . At any rate, I'll never be able to get back home with the suitcase I brought here, on account of Minnette's loving letters taking up so darn much space. And Nugey, like a damn fool, I can't retrench or nothin! I haven't the heart to appear less amorous than I was during the moonlight madness of those few dates. I like Minnette very much, more than any girl at school by far. . . . I think that we are engaged. Go ahead, you blond Don Juan, and laugh your head off! Now I could learn to love the kid, and I'm sure that as married couples go, we would be domestically out there. But Nugey, the blow that cools James is the Hope that Spouts eternal about the One Girl, somewhere I'll find her. I've quite an O. Henry philosophy and Faith. Oh, quite, I'm positive that me and the Eva are Hero and Leonidas, or Heroine and Alexander or whoever it was, those eternal destined lovers, that swam the Halcyon.[5]

So he was still stuck on Eva, or at least he thought he was. He went to Washington for training and then went on to Paris. He wrote to both of them from there, without being sure exactly how he felt.

"I'm sure I had a letter every day," Fritts said. "I'm sure of that because I had stacks and stacks of letters from Washington and Paris. They were beautiful."[6]

Mame Thurber loved Minnette and continued to invite her over for dinner. Mame urged her son to forget Eva, whom both she and Charles saw as tainted by the theater, and stay with Minnette. Eva remained his "One Girl," but when Minnette dropped out of school and left town for

Red Cross training, Thurber complained to Nugent that he hadn't heard from her for twelve days, and "as time goes on, I admire her, and yes, damn it, love her more."[7]

She returned to school in the fall of 1919 and they continued to write to one another regularly while Thurber was in Paris. Over the Christmas holidays, she went to Chicago for a dental appointment. She had corresponded with an old friend of hers she "had known since childhood"—Oscar (Ossie) Proctor—and he had an internship as a doctor in Chicago. She dated him and surprised herself by accepting his sudden proposal for marriage.

When she wrote to Thurber early in 1920 and explained she had "unexpectedly" married, he was crushed, even though his real fixation was on Eva.

"The last communication from Jim was a cable from Paris," Fritts said. "Three words—'What the hell!'"[8]

Fritts returned to school after her marriage, and she and Thurber maintained their friendship when he returned from Europe. She even introduced him to first wife Althea Adams; Althea badly wanted to meet him, and Fritts reluctantly arranged it, even though both she and Tom Meek thought they were wrong for each other.

Minnette's eventual move to Seattle with her husband put more distance between herself and Thurber, but it didn't kill their friendship or his infatuation with her. She said he always said he sent her copies of his books when they were published, "autographed in some clever way."[9]

Whenever Thurber experienced trouble in his marriage, he usually fell back on his old loves, Eva and Minnette. In 1934, with marriage with Althea breaking apart, Fritts said that "he was phoning me several times a week. I realized he was mentally and emotionally disturbed. He insisted on coming out to Seattle, which my husband would not have understood at all. I knew I could not help him."[10]

Thurber never visited Fritts in Seattle, and a half-dozen years passed before she wrote to him again. He didn't answer her letter for almost a year, and then she waited a year to answer that one. Finally, in 1945, they met in New York, the first time in almost twenty-five years. He reserved a room for her at the Algonquin Hotel and arranged for tickets for them to attend a play, meet the Nugents afterwards, and then go to a matinee the next day. Helen Thurber decided to stand aside and let him revisit his old romance on his own terms. He was nearly blind by then, which made for an awkward moment when Minnette had forgotten her reading glasses and realized that neither of them could read the menu; the waiter rescued her by lending her his. It was a nice visit, including a stop at the offices of the *New Yorker* to allow her a desired introduction to E. B. White, but it was also a dose of reality for Thurber. The flirty, pretty darling of the journalism crowd had . . . grown older.

She invited him to come to Seattle the following year and received a rather stiff rejection from him, and another visit from Minnette in 1948 on the way to Europe also didn't impress him.

"In college, I mysteriously identified her with one of Henry James's worldly and intelligent women, which gives you some idea of my perspicacity about the opposite sex in those days," Thurber wrote to Katherine White. "She has managed somehow in the intervening years to unhook her own intelligence like a telephone receiver. Her transmitter works, but the connection is bad."[11]

What seems more likely is that his infatuation with the young woman from Chief Myers' journalism had dimmed as she turned into a middle-aged woman and his marriage to Helen matured.

"One of his last typewritten letters was signed 'Jim' on the typewriter, and I don't know why I was so childish when I answered it," Fritts told Branscomb. "I said 'Why don't you at least sign your name? If you can't write long hand, why don't you sign your name, anyway?

"And oh, the letter that followed was most amusing because he said he wasn't allowed to have any ink in his office because he spilled it on everything and he would go on signing his letters with a typewriter. But underneath I think there were about a twelve signatures in all different shapes and forms."[12]

They exchanged letters one last time in 1951, and there is no indication of any contact between them after that. Minnette and Oscar Proctor divorced in the 1940s, and she eventually married again at the age of sixty-three, to Kennyth Ewart, another former OSU classmate who had been infatuated with her during her college days. Ewart hired a detective to find her after his wife died.[13] They lived in Cuyahoga Falls, Ohio, until he died in 1966; after that, she moved back to the Seattle area.

When she died in 1992 at the age of ninety-seven near Olympia, Washington, she was buried near her son David Storrs Proctor and his wife in Elmwood Cemetery in Brighton, Colorado.

A simple quote above her name—Minnette Fritts Proctor Ewart—on the gravestone summed up her long journey:

"I enjoyed life."

CHAPTER 25

Thurber's Favorite Player

Chic Harley was almost three months older than James Thurber and graduated from East High School in 1915, two years after him. They knew many of the same people, shared many of the same teachers and went to many of the same places. They weren't at all alike.

Harley's life revolved around athletics. He stood out in games played among boys on neighborhood sandlots on the east side of Columbus, and eventually starred in football, basketball, baseball, and track in high school before becoming Ohio State's first real football star. Thurber couldn't participate in sports because of his lost eye and became a familiar face in the reading room at the library.

Thurber loved books. Harley acted as if he were allergic to them. His academic struggles at Ohio State served as a model for a humorous classroom incident Thurber wrote about later, and it's clear from some of the jokes about him in copies of *The X-Rays,* East High School's student newspaper, that the struggles began much earlier:

> MISS FERRELL (IN THIRD PERIOD ENGLISH): "Harley, how many lines
>   are there in a sonnet?"
> HARLEY: "Five feet."[1]

As different as Thurber and Harley were, they are also forever linked. Like many people who lived in Columbus during the years before, during, and after World War I, Thurber idolized Harley, whose fame and popularity soared during that era. He wrote a poem about Harley during his days at the *Columbus Dispatch* in 1922, and was still writing about him later, long after Thurber had left Columbus.

It would have been odd if he hadn't. In Ohio State football circles, Harley is the Messiah, the player who all but created the religion that has millions of followers. Venerable Ohio Stadium, the old concrete horseshoe that opened in 1922 with an eye-popping total of sixty-four thousand seats and is at or near capacity with one hundred seven thousand fans at every home game today, is called "The House that Harley Built," and it is no exaggeration.

The dedication of the new stadium provided Thurber with the opportunity to write the poem *When Chic Harley Got Away* and publish it in the *Dispatch*:[2]

> The years of football reach back a long, long way,
> And the heroes are a hundred who have worn red and gray;
> You can name the brilliant players from the year the game began,
> You can rave how this one punted and praise how that one ran;
> You can say that someone's playing was the best you ever saw—You can
> claim the boys now playing stage a game without a flaw—But admit there
> was no splendor in all the bright array
> Like the glory of the going when Chic Harley got away. . . .

With or without Thurber to chronicle it, Harley's story is an amazing one.

When Chic first reported to East as a smallish, 5-foot-6, 125-pound sophomore in 1912, the idea of sharing a football field with the school's brawny upperclassmen intimidated him. Friends who had played with him on the sandlots on the east side of Columbus knew he would be successful, but Harley experienced the same anxieties that plague most young students when they attend high school for the first time.

Thurber could appreciate that sentiment. The confidence and popularity he enjoyed at Douglas didn't make the crosstown trip to East, although he was a senior destined for the class presidency when Harley showed up for his first high school classes on Franklin Avenue.

"[Harley's] modesty was evident when he entered East High School and had to be pressured to try out for the football team," former neighbor Paul Gingher wrote. "He is quoted as having said to his young friends 'You fellows think I'm good, but look at the size of those guys.'"[3]

The incredible hulks who intimidated Harley weren't big by modern standards, but neither was he. Brothers Howard and Harold "Hap" Courtney, a senior and junior who played the two tackle spots, would both star at Ohio State in a few years. At a respective 170 and 160 pounds, they were two of the biggest players on the team. Senior captain Husky Thurman also weighed in at 170 pounds and senior Howard "Bugs" Schory checked in at 168. They all looked like trouble to the pint-sized sophomore.

He worried for nothing. The other players were bigger, but they were also slower, and they had to find a way to catch and tackle him. Harley could probably run faster than all of his east side contemporaries, and when that speed was coupled with his athleticism, it gave *him* the advantage. He flitted around East's practices in nearly Franklin Park like a firefly, changing speeds and directions so quickly that his new teammates found themselves lunging for a body that was no longer there.

Joe Murphy, who had been East's starting quarterback the previous season, didn't report on time for some reason, and after four days of practice, East coach Frank Gullum (who was Thurber's chemistry teacher) made Harley the first team quarterback in the team's first intra-squad scrimmage. The *Dispatch* picked up on the fast promotion, calling Harley "a youngster who seems to be the most promising quarterback Mr. Gullum has had on the field since the passing of Ike Carroll,"[4] and its sources must have been good ones. Harley started the team's season opener against Mt. Vernon at Recreation Park ahead of Murphy and East won 16–0 with Harley throwing a "splendid" pass to Ed Gochenbach for a touchdown.

None of this could have escaped the notice of Thurber, who was a huge fan of East's athletic teams, even though his vision problems kept him from playing. His brother Robert, an excellent athlete, captained the East baseball team that had Harley as its star shortstop and undoubtedly played with him and against him in pickup games while they were growing up. So when Chic arrived at East, Thurber already knew plenty about him; like everybody else, he just had no way of knowing how good Harley would be.

Over the course of his sophomore season, Harley's reputation grew. In a game in Athens, he scored touchdowns on runs of sixty, forty, and sixty yards in a 40–6 win over a team quarterbacked by future Ohio University star Ross Finsterwald, whose son, Dow, would become a well-known professional golfer. But the team also tied Springfield 7–7 and lost to Newark, and it wasn't until East beat rival North, which had dominated the series in its thirteen meetings, that Harley's reputation began to spread.

The East-North games were played at Ohio Field on North High Street, the OSU field where Harley would gain national fame on the college gridiron. At the time, the East-North games drew more fans than many Ohio State games did, so the fact that Harley scored two touchdowns to seal a 20–3 East victory, one on a fumble recovery and the other on an interception, made an impression on local people who hadn't been that aware of him.

None of this meant he was destined for greatness, of course. In those days, the city only had four high school football teams—East, North, South, and Aquinas—and they didn't have a history of producing outstanding college football players. (West High School was open but had yet to start a football program, and the High School of Commerce, before and after called Central, had been unable to find enough players to suit a team.) Even in that small world, he still wasn't the biggest star. The *Dispatch* named the little sophomore only second-team all-city behind South senior quarterback Hal Gaulke,[5] who ended up playing for five seasons with the Columbus Panhandles, a legendary local professional team that was one of the charter members of the NFL.

But this is where the story starts to feel like a ride with a stunt pilot. His family had moved from Chicago to Columbus in 1907 when Chic was twelve. His father got a job offer there and decided to move back before his junior season. Chic didn't want to go, and the wealthy family of team captain and future congressman John Vorys offered to let him move in with them. Chic's parents didn't like the idea, but he finally won them over, and he stayed and led East to an unbeaten season that included an easy win over North. The situation grew more complicated. John Vorys' older brother, Webb, would be home from college at Christmas and he needed his old room back, so there was talk of Chic moving to Chicago to rejoin his family. The Notre Dame coaches may have sensed this impending crisis, and they tried to recruit Harley for Notre Dame's prep school, presumably so it could easily move him over to the university squad. Logistically, Harley's move to South Bend, Indiana, which was closer to Chicago, would have made sense.

But Harley didn't want to go and his football teammates and East classmates didn't want him to leave. East principal John Harlor stepped in and offered to let him live with his family in their big frame house on Franklin Avenue across from the high school, and a happy Harley stayed and played basketball and baseball and ran track for East, all the while adding to his local reputation.

Chic lived with his parents in Chicago over the summer, then returned to East for his senior season. This time, he stayed with a bachelor named William Walker who lived with his widowed mother in a house at 1418 Oak Street behind the school. The East football team wasn't quite as good as it had been, but only because many of his best teammates had graduated. East remained unbeaten until the North game and fifteen hundred people showed up at Ohio Field, many to see Harley, for what turned out to be a 14–0 East loss. Even though Thurber was an Ohio State student at the time, he doubtless attended the game. Like many in that era, he rarely missed an East-North game even after he graduated from high school and sometimes talked and spoke of the East-North rivalry with the same reverence as an Ohio State-Michigan game.

"We went to the North-East game a week ago," Thurber wrote in the *Dispatch* in November, 1921. "It was like opening an old school book in which your name is written with a girl's above it and letters are mystically crossed out. You may have forgotten the girl in between, but she will come back as radiant as firelight on snow."

Thurber must have been thrilled when Ohio State's Phi Gamma Delta fraternity recruited Harley in the spring of his senior year and he eventually decided to go there. But no one, including Chic, knew whether he would be successful at a school that had taken a huge step up from the Ohio schools that it had been playing and joined the Western Conference—today's Big Ten—only two years before.

Even though Harley enjoyed some shining moments playing for the OSU freshmen team in 1915, when the 1916 season dawned, the *Chicago Tribune* printed what many thought as he took his talents to the varsity: "Ohio coach Wilce is happy to welcome the local boy, Chas. Harley, who might find the going too much when he starts playing with the big boys."

If this assessment seems a bit harsh, it is worth noting that Ohio State had no real standing in the college football world when Harley reached the varsity. Since playing its first official game of football in 1890, OSU had enjoyed only modest success while playing a schedule heavy with Ohio schools. Kenyon College had been its early rival, and the games had been competitive. In fifteen meetings since 1897, OSU had never beaten Michigan. It rarely drew more than three thousand or four thousand fans to a game at the field on North High Street, which had been expanded again and again and still held only nine thousand.

The impending changes effected by Harley and his teammates would hit Ohio State and Columbus like a major earthquake. There was no buzz before the 1916 season started. The word OSU coach Jack Wilce used to describe his 1916 team's prospects was "fair." Even the most devout optimists believed that prospects for the team were murky at best. The 16–0 win in the season opener against Ohio Wesleyan drew 4,889, celebrated as one of the biggest crowds ever to see an OSU season opener. Harley, as a local hero, filled some of those seats.

"I have not seen an Ohio State game in two years," a seventy-year-old man told the *Dispatch.* "But I saw Harley play in high school games and I want to see what he will do."[6]

Harley did okay; he was the team's leading ground gainer with eighty-seven yards. But Ohio Wesleyan was a remnant from the old schedule; it ranked a few notches below teams from the Western Conference. Ohio State beat Oberlin, another holdover from the old schedule, by the ridiculous score of 128–0. Most of the starters, including Harley, played little. The test would come with the following week at Illinois.

No one suspected that a miserable, rainy day in Champaign, Illinois, would produce a game that amounted to the Big Bang of OSU football. Illinois was becoming a conference power under Coach Bob Zuppke. Fans back in Columbus hoped for the best and expected the worst. Only 4,388 showed up at Illinois Field to watch runners on both sides slip and slide in the mud; the conditions neutralized Harley's speed to the outside. Illinois led 6–0 with two minutes to go when the sophomore began chewing up big chunks of yardage inside. With 1:10 left and OSU in a fourth and three situation somewhere between the 13 and 20 yard lines—the rain had erased all the markings—Harley faked a pass to the right and ran left, straight-armed one tackler, eluded another and then another, and finally made a desperate dive for the end zone from about three yards out and scored.

As unfathomable as the 6–6 score was to the Illini and their fans, what happened next was even more stunning. Under the complicated extra-point rule of the day, the scoring team had to kick the ball out of the end zone and if a teammate fielded it cleanly, the team was given the chance to kick the extra point from there. Harley booted the ball to teammate Fred Norton, who caught it near the 22-yard line. It wasn't a good spot, especially on a muddy field, but Harley would have a chance to win the game.

He looked at his shoe, which the rain had caked with mud, and called time out. He walked over to the team's trainer, Doc Gurney, and uttered words that every OSU football fan of that generation would remember forever.

"Gimme a shoe," he said.

Gurney gave him a clean one, and while everyone watched, Harley calmly changed shoes, sauntered over to the spot and kicked the game-winning extra point in his third college game. Ohio State had won 7–6. Football in Columbus would never be the same.

News of the upset shook the city. Interest in the team exploded. By Monday, school officials were already making plans for a home game against Wisconsin in two weeks and newspapers were reporting that the crowd would exceed the school record of 8,200 that had attended the 1902 Michigan game. OSU athletic director Lynn St. John announced the school would add more seats to Ohio Field to increase capacity to 12,000. Then, when the Buckeyes beat Wisconsin 14–13 in another huge upset, this time on an 80-yard run from scrimmage by Harley, interest exploded again.

The rest of the season played out like a wonderful dream. The Buckeyes won game after game, usually with Harley as the star, and finally ended it by beating Northwestern 23–3 to finish off an unbeaten season before a crowd of 11,979 that the newspapers actually called "disappointing." Harley kicked a field goal and had touchdown runs of 61 and 16 yards in that game, and the local fans celebrated as if they had won the World Series.

The *Chicago Tribune's* Walter Eckersall, one of nation's leading college football authorities, announced that Harley had been named to his All-America team and called him "as great as Willie Heston." It was remarkable statement. Heston, who starred for Fielding Yost's famous point-a-minute Michigan teams from 1901 to 1904, was considered the best player in Western Conference history.

With Harley's stature continuing to grow, Ohio State went undefeated again in 1917. The crowds were down slightly, probably in part because of the emotional drag of World War I. Just about all of the players, including Harley, were in the armed forces in 1918. But Harley came back and had another incredible season in 1919, which included a first-ever OSU win over Michigan. The team was unbeaten again until the final game against Illinois, when St .John again tried to expand the seating to accommodate all of the fans.

An estimated 20,000 attended the game, not counting the dozens that perched in trees surrounding Ohio Field, to see what felt like a devastating 9–7 loss; St. John claimed afterwards that he could have sold

60,000 tickets, a sales pitch that helped sell the public on the construction of Ohio Stadium. Harley, who played in the game even though he was injured, broke down on the field afterwards and couldn't stop crying. He had to be helped to the locker room, where he reportedly continued to show signs of despondency many hours later.

No one knew it at the time, but it was probably the first public sign of mental illness that plagued him for the rest of his life. Two years later, Harley would exhibit similar symptoms after he was injured while playing pro football for the Decatur Staleys team that became the Chicago Bears. He was diagnosed with dementia praecox—a chronic, deteriorating condition with no cure that was later described by some doctors as schizophrenia—and committed to a sanitarium to treat his problem.

In September, 1922, with the dedication game for the new stadium only about a month away, Thurber wrote of Harley's condition to his friend Elliott Nugent:

> On football, I wonder if you have heard of the truly sad condition of Chic Harley. He has been in a bad way since last winter and is variously reported as hopeless, his case being diagnosed as dementia precox [*sic*] by a number of examiners, although the Harley mind, unless known of old, might bother any medical man. At any rate, he has dropped out of life, and is now in a Dayton sanitarium.[7]

Harley was in and out of mental hospitals for the next fifteen years. Friends proved ferociously loyal to him, even when he got out and exhibited unruly behavior that didn't befit the old Chic. A Harley Fund was even set up by the university to help defray the costs of his medical treatment. Thurber continued to revere him, although that didn't stop him from using him as a model for a character in "University Days," one of his fictional accounts account about his hometown and his family in the 1933 book *My Life and Hard Times*. In it, he disguised the academically challenged Harley as a dim-witted tackle named Bolenciecwcz, who was one of the stars of one of the best football teams in the county, but "in order for him to play it was necessary for him to keep up in his studies, a very difficult matter, for while he was not dumber than an ox he was not any smarter." Thurber went on to describe the professor's difficulty in getting Harley—er, Bolenciecwcz—"to name one means of transportation," which included both the prof and his students imitating a train in every conceivable manner including "Choo, choo, choo" while the clueless player drew a blank.

As a story topic Harley was no more immune from Thurber's quest for good material than any member of his family, even though he remained one of the humorist's athletic heroes and became a tragic figure after he left Ohio State.

In 1938 Harley entered the Veterans Administration hospital in Danville, Illinois, and except for occasional stays with his family, he remained there for the rest of his life. The development of insulin shock treatments in 1940s substantially improved his condition, and in 1948 he returned to Columbus for an Ohio State–Michigan game that became a remarkable homecoming for him. A crowd estimated at 75,000 cheered him as he rode in an open convertible down High Street in a ticker tape parade held in his honor; the crowd size was amazing given that the city's population was only 375,000 at the time. The parade consisted of 21 floats and the OSU marching band, and the governor and mayor were there to greet him at the Statehouse when it ended.

Ohio State Journal sports editor Bob Hooey wrote a column about Harley to mark the occasion. In it, he "borrowed" a description of Harley that Thurber had written in 1941 for the New York newspaper *PM*. Hooey printed it as his own, causing many to mistakenly attribute it to him:

> If you never saw him run with the football, we can't describe it to you. It wasn't like [Jim] Thorpe or [Red] Grange or [Tom] Harmon on anybody else. It was kind of a cross between music and canon fire, and it brought your heart up under your ears.[8]

At the time Thurber wrote that, talk about naming Ohio Stadium for Harley often made the rounds in Ohio newspapers. It went nowhere because it was accepted practice not to affix the names of living people to public buildings. As beloved as Harley was, it was widely assumed that he would eventually have his day. But by the time he died at the age of 78 in 1974, he had outlived many of his friends and admirers including Thurber, and the talk of such a memorial went to the grave with them.

CHAPTER 26

·

Literary Tour Guide

It seems crazy to consider the impact Joseph Russell Taylor made on hundreds of students over his forty-three years as an English professor at Ohio State against the true source of his immortality, yet it is impossible to avoid it: Taylor was the subject of one his famous student's profiles in *The Thurber Album* and the subject of a portrait done by another student who became one of America's most famous artists.

Maybe as much as anyone, Taylor is living proof that it's not always what you do but when you do it, and how it is presented to the public. He is a salient example of the value of good marketing.

By all accounts, Taylor earned his reputation as a fine professor. He represented the first encounter with intellectual thought for many of his students, which doubtless contributed to his popularity. The wit and eloquence of his lectures sparked the interest of even some of his most resistant students in the poetry of A. E. Housman and the fiction of Henry James. He introduced many of them to a literary world they didn't know existed, a defining moment in their education that stayed with them for a lifetime.

"To have come into Joe Taylor's classes from a Columbus high school in my day was like coming into a lovely city the first time from a cave in a hill," Thurber wrote in a long, affectionate tribute to Taylor in the October, 1933, *Ohio State Alumni Monthly.*

The much-beloved professor became "Joey" to several generations of students, and they mourned his passing that year at the age of sixty-four from the after effects of arteriosclerosis that resulted from shock he suffered when his parked car was rear-ended in an accident on a campus street a year before. He had been a member of the university's teaching staff for forty-four years and had been a professor of English there since 1908. But he has achieved a measure of fame because of two students, James Thurber and George Bellows, who breathed eternal life into him the way only a writer or artist can.

Taylor shaped Thurber's literary tastes more than anyone and the evidence of it exists in his published writing; through the years, his letters and speeches frequently mentioned his favorite professor. Taylor specialized in nineteenth-century writing, and Thurber took the first half of his poetry course (Wordsworth, Shelley, Keats, and their contemporaries) in the fall of 1916, and the second half (Tennyson, Browning, Arnold, Swinburne, and Taylor's favorite, Housman) in the spring of 1918. He took Taylor's course in the novel (first semester, Richardson to Scott; second semester, Dickens to Meredith) in 1917–18, and he always looked upon that course as the highlight of his college career.[1]

I will always remember my first view of Joseph Russell Taylor, in one of his English classes at Ohio State, more than thirty-five years ago. He was round of face and body, with yellow hair, pink cheeks, and fine blue eyes. He usually wore a brown suit, and he always brought to class the light of the enchanted artistic world he lived in, of whose wonders he once said "It is possible that all things are beautiful." He was a poet and painter as well as a teacher, and he believed that the materials of art were in all the activities of men. His classes were popular from the beginning, and in the nineteen-twenties as many as a hundred and twenty-five men and women crowded into his lecture room. On the opening day of one of his classes in 1914, he began by saying to us, "I do not expect you to take notes in this class." Forty of the fifty young men and women present wrote that down in their brand-new notebooks with their brand-new fountain pens. Standing at the lectern, possibly lost in contemplating two of his favorite fictional heroines, Henry James's Mme. De Vionnet and George Meredith's Diana—for whom he had named his own daughter Diana—he seemed oblivious of the aimless scratching in the notebooks. I don't know what experiment he was trying, but it didn't work. He should have known that the things he had to say were always worth recording. Some of his former students, after thirty years and more, still have at hand the notes they took in his courses, including that one in 1914.[2]

Thurber may have been referring to himself; it's unlikely any of the professor's students ever had the appreciation for the literature and the written word—or for that matter, Taylor himself—that he did. But Taylor's students had lots of reasons for appreciating him beyond the English courses he taught.

Taylor often said "We are not here to teach you how to make a living, but how to live,"[3] and Bellows would doubtless have agreed with that. As a boy growing up on the east side of Columbus, his constant drawing of odd figures—prizefighters without faces, for example—was regarded as a waste of time by his parents.

But when Bellows arrived at Ohio State, thirteen years ahead of Thurber, he found an encouraging voice in Taylor, who taught drawing before he taught English at OSU and was a painter himself. Taylor may have been even been responsible for introducing Bellows to Robert Henri, his first influential art teacher.

Bellows painted an oil portrait of Taylor sitting in a chair and holding a pipe in his hand. It hung in Taylor's house and eventually made the walls of the Columbus Museum of Art. Thurber wrote that when Taylor first saw it, he said, "That is a painting of Joseph Russell Taylor by a young artist, but it will one day be known as Bellows' 'Man with a Pipe.'"[4]

When Taylor died, the portrait graced the north wall of the OSU Faculty Club lounge during a tribute to him held there on the morning of the homecoming football game (Thurber came from New York at his own expense to serve as one of three speakers that morning); watercolors depicting Columbus scenes done by Taylor hung on surrounding walls that day.

Taylor had spent most of his life in Central Ohio. He was born July 10, 1868, in Circleville, Ohio, twenty-nine miles south of Columbus, and graduated from Ohio State in 1887. He became a member of the faculty in charge of drawing and painting in 1889 and started in the English Department in 1894. Other than 1896–97, when he achieved his master's degree at Columbia University, he remained there until his death.

The professor might have stepped out of one of James's novels. He was a product of the genteel tradition, sought beauty in the late Victorian fashion, worshipped women, and was a devoted feminist. He believed in elegance and precision in style.

He wrote a small textbook on the art of writing entitled *Composition in Narration*; four books of poetry; a long, unpublished study of Tristram legend; and *Taylor on James,* an unpublished study of the novelist. Even though Thurber practically worshipped him, the famous humorist came to recognize Taylor's limitations as a writer; after his death Thurber read both essays and described the work on Tristram work as "remarkable" and the James' piece disappointing.

"He never could get it down on paper," he wrote, in a letter to James Fullington.[5]

Taylor did, however, create a literary framework that Thurber never lost. Thurber kept his infatuation with Henry James for the rest of his life, and he never forgot some of the professor's remarks in his classes.

"You can't get passion into a story with exclamation points," was one. "Nothing genuine need fear the test of laughter" was another. "A straight line can also be the dullest distance between two points" was yet another.[6]

From 1910 to 1927, the Taylors lived in a ten-room, two-story brick house with a big porch and an attic at 155 East Thirteenth Avenue that Thurber sometimes visited to engage the professor in intellectual discussions.

"Jim Thurber came to our house frequently," Joe Taylor's son, Stafford, told Kinney. "Sometimes, he'd be invited; other times, he'd just drop in for a chat with father. He had an elfish humor, but more often than not he was serious on those occasions. The dinner conversation might cover everything from literature to the newspaper comics. Thurber didn't strike me as a studious student—not Phi Beta Kappa material. But he liked to hear my father's thoughts on everything."[7]

When Taylor died in 1933, Thurber hadn't seen him in a couple of years. In 1927, Taylor and his wife, Esther, had moved to an impressive home at 1080 Lincoln Road in Grandview, a relatively new Columbus suburb west of campus. Not long after his death, Esther brought some of Joe's poems to New York and asked Thurber if he could help her find a publisher for them.

Thurber did his best to do right by his friend and mentor. He made the rounds of poetry editors and came up empty. But E. B. White, Thurber's pal at the *New Yorker,* was blunt in his assessment of the material. "These verses do not sing," he said.[8]

Thurber's affection for Taylor never wavered. On a visit to campus in January, 1944, he complained to the *Sundial* that OSU had failed to give the distinguished professor the proper recognition, calling Taylor, "a really great man, but few people realized it."

Thurber's affection is the most visible in the letter he wrote to the *Ohio State Alumni Monthly* following his former professor's death.

"I encounter Ohio State people in far places, on ships, in France, in small American towns, whose hearts leap up when you mention Joe Taylor's name," Thurber wrote. "In their friendship, their respect, their gratitude, and their love he has something that lives on after him which any man might envy and most men despair of. 'My heart is not made of the stuff that breaks,' is a line of Meredith's he was fond of repeating. This stuff that went to make up hearts was his specialty. The formula from which his own heart was made was lost, I'm afraid, when he died. There will never be another Joe Taylor."[9]

CHAPTER 27

•

Professor Courageous

Of all of the people who inhabited the place we call Thurberville, the one with the most impressive monument in twenty-first century Columbus is Joseph Villiers Denney, one of Thurber's favorite English professors.

Denney Hall, a modern, five-story structure of glass and brick that honors the former head of Ohio State English department and dean of the College of Art, Philosophy and Science, sits at 164 Annie and John Glenn Avenue near the heart of the OSU campus. Thurber served as the primary speaker at the building's dedication on April, 1960, a task he had said he would fulfill even "if I had to crawl out here."[1]

He practically did. A fading Thurber had written the speech even though he had been sick in bed for over a month, and after he made a few introductory remarks, he allowed his wife, Helen, to read his words. This would be his last trip to Columbus—Thurber died the following year—and his mere presence there is another indication of his high regard for Denney. He had expressed that in vivid detail a decade before when he honored Denney as one of three English professors with a separate chapter in *The Thurber Album*. Thurber entitled that piece "Length and Shadow" after a line that appeared in Denney's 1935 obituary in the *Columbus Dispatch*: "Ohio State is, in large part, the length and shadow of Joseph Villiers Denney."

In his dedication speech, Thurber second-guessed his choice of titles.

"I realized in having the piece re-read to me twice the other day—I am pretty fond of it still—that I cannot associate the word shadow with Joe Denney, but prefer the word 'light,'" Thurber wrote. "He cast a light, and still does—the light of learning, of scholarship, of laughter, of wisdom, and that special and precious light reflected by a man forever armored in courage."[2]

Thurber first showed how much he believed this when he cowrote the play *The Male Animal* with Elliott Nugent in 1940 and patterned a character named Dr. Damon, the dean of the English department, after Denney. The play dealt with academic freedom at a narrow-minded, football-crazed Midwestern University, which they modeled after Ohio State.

"In that play he stood staunchly," Thurber said, "and Elliott and I stood proudly beside him, as defender of the rights, obligations and dedication of the university professor to the ideal and principle of the inviolability of the university faculty in conducting the affairs of an institution of higher learning. Joe Denney was afraid of nobody; that is, of no individual person, and of no body; that is, of no group or organization."[3]

While Denney was a first rate scholar, his stands against censorship in support of academic freedom made a strong impression on Thurber, who kept a wary eye on his former school all of his life. During his days as a student, the university stressed agriculture and shortchanged the arts, which led to a Denney quote often cited by Thurber: "Millions for manure, but not one cent for literature." It wasn't original and Denney always made certain to credit it; it had originally been uttered by Ellis Parker Butler after the Iowa state legislature appropriated $20 million to the Iowa State University department of agriculture. But the thought resonated with idealistic, like-minded students.

When Ohio State instituted a ban on "controversial" speakers during the McCarthy Era—"the trustees decided that nobody could speak on the campus until he had been intellectually seized and searched to see if his political opinions contained anything that might corrupt the minds of students"[4]—Thurber found himself wishing that Denney were still alive and able to stand up to the fools who proposed it.

"Joseph Villiers Denney, through all this, must have turned restlessly in his grave," Thurber wrote. "Ohio State, trapped somewhere between Armageddon and Waterloo, needed him and his strategy of reason and his tactics of friendliness, and all the armament of his intellect and humor. But he wasn't there, and there was nobody to take his place."[5]

Denney stood his intellectual ground at OSU for forty-two years. Born and raised in Aurora, Illinois, he graduated from the University of Michigan in 1885 and worked two years as a journalist, first as an editor of the *Aurora (Illinois) Beacon* and then as a freelancer for the *Chicago Tribune,* before going back home to Aurora and spending two years as a high school principal. He returned to Michigan for a year to teach and take advanced study, then went to Ohio State as an associate professor of rhetoric in 1891.[6] There were vast differences between that OSU and the massive university with 60,000 students on the main campus we know today. When Denney started, the school had an enrollment of 465 and consisted of six buildings, not counting the old North and South dormitories. Classes for the law school were held in the Franklin County Courthouse. Including assistant professors, the faculty numbered 30.

Denney quickly demonstrated the leadership skills that would mark his long career at OSU. He taught the first journalism courses—Rapid Writing I and II—that the school offered, and he made full professor of rhetoric and English in 1894. From 1893 to 1901, he served as the faculty secretary; in 1901 he became the dean of the College of Arts, Philosophy, and Science and in 1904 he became the head of the English department. Early in 1909, when William Oxley Thompson suffered from a serious illness, he served as acting president of the university.

He coauthored a popular series of English textbooks with University of Michigan professor Fred Newton Scott (notably one called *Paragraph Writing* and another entitled *Composition-literature*) and earned recognition as an authority on Shakespeare.

It's not hard to see why Thurber had so much respect for him or why the building which houses the school's English department carries his name today. He was the first member of the Ohio State faculty to be listed in *Who's Who in America* and served as president of the American Association of University Professors. Thurber wrote that he also proved to be the source of amusing anecdotes to several generations of students at the university:

> The Denney legend may have got its start one day about 1905, when he ran out of blackboard space during an examination and, without hesitation, quietly wrote the last two questions on a bare, kind of chalk-colored wall. Another professor, after a reasonable interval, might have erased the first two questions or dictated the final ones to his class, but the young Dean—he was then forty-three—was not a man of hackneyed or conventional solutions. "Braque," said a painter, hearing of the writing on the wall, "would have done the same thing." That small, impulsive gesture of nearly fifty years ago has not been forgotten at Ohio State; several gentlemen, well into their sixties, learning that I was exploring the Denney yesterdays, wrote me that they were in his class that unusual morning.[7]

Thurber carried a strong devotion to Joseph Taylor and the words he spoke and wrote about Denney indicate he felt a higher level of respect for him. Taylor made bigger impact on both Thurber's writing and his love of literature, but Thurber also recognized his limitations. Denney's standing, both within the university and beyond, was unassailable.

Thurber's personal experience with Denney consisted mostly of a class on Shakespeare that he had taken from him, so he found his *Album* piece on him difficult to write and had to rely on research on him provided by others. He exchanged numerous letters with Professor James Fullington, who knew both Denney and William Graves, another English professor Thurber wrote about in the *Album,* and found himself writing and rewriting those two chapters for over a year.[8]

Fortunately, Denney's distinguished career furnished a wealth of stories, a few of which he used and some of which he didn't, possibly because the distinguished dean tended toward absentmindedness that didn't fit Thurber's intention to eulogize him.

A story he used in *The Thurber Album* had Denney taking a street car home from the Kit Kat Club one evening and dropping a strip of six tickets into the box when he only needed one for passage. The conductor immediately called him on his error, whereby the distinguished professor tried to turn his mistake into an ordered plan.

"It is my considered intention to—ah—lie down," he said.

Another story Thurber didn't use had Denney's wife, Jane, finding his trousers still hung over the back of a chair after the distinguished professor had left for class. She didn't realize he had purchased a new pair of pants the day before and she ran to the classroom clutching the old pair, knowing that such an oversight would be entirely in character for her brilliant but forgetful husband.

Denney retired in 1933. Thurber wrote about how there were "no awkward or sorrowful moments" on his last day, as he said good-bye to his friends.

"He came, last of all, to the late Herman Miller, one of the younger professors with whom he was fond of engaging in banter," Thurber wrote. "He took Miller's hand, gave him the famous over-the-glasses peer, and said 'Herman, after forty-two years of teaching I have come to the conclusion that the human species is—ah—ineducable.' Then he winked, poked his young friend in the ribs, made a little sucking sound, and left the campus forever."[9]

CHAPTER 28

•

"Gentle, Lovable Billy Graves"

The second page of William Lucius Graves' file in the Ohio State University Archives is titled "Former students of Prof. William Graves who have achieved literary fame." It comprises less than one-half typed page.

Seven names are listed—Elliott Nugent, James Chalfant, Frank Presnell, Gardner Rea, Daphe Alloway McVicker, Dorothy Reed Miller, and Bernard Raymond—with a brief description of all of them but Nugent, who ironically may be the only one who might not need an introduction to modern readers.

But it is the typed line beneath the list that catches the eye: "James Thurber and Dorothy Canfield Fisher were NOT in any of his classes."

The capital letters for the word "not" make it clear this is intended to be the final word on the topic, an absurdly ambitious plan for a sheet of paper in a forgotten folder amidst hundreds of similar folders in a university archives building. Yet its discovery launches a provocative, if relatively minor mystery. Thurber himself claimed to have taken Graves's short story class in 1916, and biographer Harrison Kinney wrote that Thurber was mistaken, that in fact he had taken the course in the spring of 1917.[1] The *Ohio State Alumni Monthly* takes no sides in the Kinney-Thurber debate, but sides with both against the anonymous author of that note in Graves's biographical file; in a four-paragraph piece the celebrates Graves's wedding, it notes, "Many distinguished writers in America today are former students in his short story writing classes, Dorothy Canfield Fisher, '99, James Thurber, *w*'17, Elliott Nugent '19, Alberta Pierson Hannum '27, and others."[2]

Why anyone would go out their way to contradict those sources is open to conjecture. It seems plausible that it was done by one of Graves's former students unhappy with the way Thurber dealt with the former English professor and his teaching methods in his profile in *The Thurber Album,* one who saw the opportunity to discredit his opinions and seized it.

If that is what happened, it almost makes sense that the perpetrator would include Fisher's name in front of that accusatory "not." While it is uncertain whether Fisher took a class from Graves, this isn't: Thurber enlisted her aid in researching some of the subjects Thurber profiled in the *Album,* profiles that probably included that of Graves. For that reason, it is possible that Fisher also was targeted by an anonymous librarian seeking justice for the ever-popular "Billy" Graves.

The unsolved mystery merely adds to an already fascinating story. Graves stands as one of the most intriguing figures in Thurberville for a variety of reasons, not the least of which is Thurber's decision to immortalize him in a profile in *The Thurber Album* despite his relatively low opinion of him.

The Ohio State English professor may or may not have been "the most popular professor in school history," as Thurber called him in that profile, but he clearly qualified as a local celebrity and man-about-town. The handsome, longtime bachelor played the piano at parties and excelled as a conversationalist who knew art, music, and literature. As dashing as he must have seemed to those who shared a party with him, his personal life didn't quite measure up to that: For much of his adult life he lived with his older brother, Joseph Howard Graves, and his wife, Wilmetta, at 28 Northmoor Place in the Clintonville section of the city, which is just north of campus. (When Thurber took his class—or didn't—Graves was living in a house at 1313 Forsythe Avenue off Neil Avenue south of OSU, his home for nineteen years.)

For years he attended university events and other functions with former classmate and friend Edith Cockins, registrar and secretary of the faculty; that led to rumors of a romantic attachment between the two but apparently didn't really lead to anything.[3] Possibly because of his gentle manner and long period of bachelorhood, some assumed he was gay.

Graves's starred at local cocktail parties and could "fill-in awkward drawing room pauses with his piano-playing,"[4] often with a ragtime theme. He proved to be the ideal extra man to invite to these gatherings, and he often found himself in high demand by faculty hostesses and downtown wives, many of whom were former students.

In 1900 Graves began writing a weekly column in the *Lantern,* the Ohio State student newspaper, at the request of the editor, and he continued to do it for over forty years. For many years he also wrote a piece called "The Crow's Nest" for the *Ohio State Alumni Monthly,* and the combination of the two doubtless made him the faculty's most prolific writer. He even read prose and poetry on WOSU (on the AM dial at 570 at the time) and was supposed to appear on the campus station on the day that he died.

All of this doubtless contributed to his enormous popularity. Then in the late 1930s, he used his *Lantern* columns—"The Idler's Chronicle and Comment"—to denounce the British for having instigated World War II and delivered sharp criticisms of America's pro-British Congress.

Some attributed his late-in-life, pro-Nazi stance, to his marriage to a much younger Annie Colburn, a former OSU graduate student who had taken four courses under him. His criticisms of England, which started in 1940 and continued until Pearl Harbor, shocked friends who had known him for years and drew some sharp rebuttals from other members of the faculty.

Speaking to a campus student group shortly after that firestorm, Graves refused to back off: "I suppose I am a heretic because I am not a supporter of England in this conflict. I feel sincerely that the policies of the British government were as much to blame for the conflict as any other factor."[5]

The criticism caused Graves to announce that he would no longer discuss controversial topics in his "Idler" column in the future:

It is becoming increasingly evident through conversation, letters and hints from various sources that my opinions on international affairs as expressed in this column are irritating to some of my friends and readers as well who lie outside that category. . . so fearing chiefly that [I] might embarrass the department of journalism and the sponsors of the *Lantern,* though no hint of disapproval has come from those sources, will now abandon those controversial fields.[6]

Some lamented Graves's decision to muzzle himself—this occurred in a university environment where passionate debate is encouraged, after all—but Thurber was living on the East Coast and didn't know about it at the time and mostly steered clear of it later. Thurber never held Graves in particularly high regard as a professor, and he may have written about him out of respect of his long tenure and remarkable popularity. There is also the suspicion that he might have done an *Album* profile on Graves simply because not doing one would have generated a lot of uncomfortable questions from former students who revered him.

Thurber didn't originally intend to write a chapter about him in the *Album*. He told Dorothy Miller that "I have now decided to devote one whole piece to Joe (Taylor) and to deal with Denney and a few others in the second piece. The last half of the piece will be devoted to the best of them all, Herman Allen Miller."[7]

He never wrote about Miller, which is probably just as well given his close friendship with him. But he wrote an extensive piece on Graves, despite the fact that he never felt the same admiration for him as Denney, Taylor, and Miller. Kinney wrote that Thurber, Elliott Nugent, and Ralph McCombs sat in the back row of Graves's class in 1917 and snickered over the things the prof said and did.

The negative feelings Thurber felt toward Graves didn't change with time. Syndicated columnist Earl Wilson made that clear when Thurber visited campus shortly after Graves death.

"Asked to say a few words of regret about a very revered professor," Wilson wrote, "Thurber told reporters I was never one of his great admirers."[8]

Graves is a fascinating character, regardless of Thurber's opinion. He was so obsessed with his fraternity, Beta Theta Pi, that one of his fraternity brothers estimated that he visited the old chapter house at 165 East 15th Avenue five thousand times between his graduation from the university in 1893 and his death in 1943. It explains why Thurber used the name of the fraternity as the title for his *Album* piece on Graves.

Thurber's "tribute" to Graves seems to be more of the back-handed salute than a sincere one:

Joe Denney, like Joe Taylor, was loved and admired by the appreciative few, but Billy Graves was known for more than forty years as the friend of the freshmen, the confidant of the seniors, and the chum of the alumni. Every night before going to bed, he wrote at least one personal letter, and most of his personal correspondence was with former students, literally hundreds of them. They recognized the tall, well-groomed bachelor, forever young in heart, as a mere visitor in the intellectual world, like themselves, and not one of its awesome, withdrawn first citizens. They liked him because he never missed an issue of the *Cosmopolitan* magazine, and he made no bones about it, and because he sometimes openly confessed his inability to understand certain so-called masterpieces of writing that had set his colleagues to twittering.[9]

It's not difficult to sense Thurber's disapproval here, although he carried on with a description of a man he found to be a nice, if somewhat vacuous individual. He took particular offense at the way Billy taught his short story course.

"He stubbornly insisted on outlining ready-made plots for his students to follow in writing their 'original' short stories,"[10] which didn't set well with Thurber. In fact, it so irritated him that he took a "deferred pass" in the course, which meant that he didn't turn in enough themes. (Could *this* be the basis for that emphatic "NOT" about Thurber and Fisher in Graves's file? Well, maybe.)

Regardless of whether Thurber's criticisms of Graves's teaching methods were justified, he was clearly swimming against the strong current of popular opinion. Graves' classes usually filled up as soon as they were offered, and affection for him was sometimes handed down from father or mother to son or daughter. Graves's popularity was not open for debate around campus and in the city for decades.

His pre–World War II turn against the British, whom he had always admired for their literature, caught even his most ardent admirers by surprise. He praised Charles Lindbergh for his outspoken advocacy of keeping the United States out of the war and claimed that this is "why Lindbergh will never again be the great American hero to the American masses. He knows too much. He is too intelligent, too fair-minded, he has too much accurate information, he has had too many contacts of the sort that demagogues avoid and would not, in their ignorance, want to make anyway."[11]

Philosophy Professor Joseph A. Leighton responded in the *Lantern* with what Thurber called "an indignant, well-considered reply," and Graves never responded, although he continued to repeat his views so vociferously on campus that many of his friends and colleagues began to avoid him. His late-in-life marriage also seemed out of character; the typed biography of him in his file at the OSU archives strikes a tone that expresses disapproval with the marriage:

In 1941, he married Annie Colburn of Quaker City, M.A., 1928. Their budding romance, it was said at the time, was on the stormy side, and he died suddenly September 7, 1943, after thirty months of marriage.[12]

Thurber wasn't a regular reader of the *Lantern,* so this was news to him when he started researching his former professors for the *Album* profiles.

"I was astonished to discover that Billy was a vehement pro-Nazi in his late sixties, a hater of Britain and France, and a violent admirer of Lindbergh," Thurber wrote to Elliott Nugent. "He got married about the same time to a woman of identical views [and] lost a lot of friends when he wrote his political views in the *Lantern.*"[13]

Living in Connecticut and working in New York, Thurber felt detached from subjects such as Graves that he didn't know well. Because of his researchers, Thurber had plenty of material for his *Album* profiles; he just found writing the ones on Graves and Joe Denney—and he greatly admired Denney—to be difficult. He rewrote both chapters over a dozen times in a span of over a year.[14]

Thurber considered OSU English professor James Fullington a good friend, and he exchanged long letters with him about both men. In one letter Thurber expressed frustration over the end result of his profiles on both of them.

"You are right about personality being hard to get down on paper," Thurber wrote. "After more than three years on the book, I have come to the conclusion that nobody is simple and that everybody is complex, each in his own way. I have found keys to people but for some reason they don't open the doors, or all of the doors, anyway."[15]

Thurber seemed to have no difficulty writing about the men he knew well and respected, which was clearly not the case with Billy Graves. For that reason, his difficulty writing a lengthy, laudatory piece about him for the *Album* probably isn't surprising.

Many others felt a tremendous affection for Graves, though, including the editors at the *Columbus Citizen,* who penned these words when the former professor collapsed in a chair and died of a heart attack at the age of seventy-one: "Billy Graves is dead, gentle, lovable Billy Graves."

Again, Thurber preferred to throw cold water on the tribute, noting that the *Citizen's* obituary made no mention of his "dark sabbatical." In his final paragraph in the *Album* piece, Thurber surmised that "the well-remembered charm and affability of Ohio State's professor-plus has obliterated, like a ramble of morning glories, his flaws and frailties."

It is fun to imagine the struggles Thurber encountered in writing this. It seems likely that if he had a chance to take a second stab at *The Thurber Album,* Thurber would probably leave Graves out.

CHAPTER 29

•

A Place Not to Call Home

James Thurber never lived in the Phi Kappa Psi house, so it probably shouldn't be too surprising that his spirit doesn't live there now. The beautiful old mansion at 124 East Fourteenth Avenue east of the Ohio State campus has a large room current fraternity members call the Thurber Dome, but it doesn't seem to have much to do with Thurber.

"It's a triple, the largest triple in the house," said Cody Griffiths, one of the room's most recent residents. "The main attraction to the room is it is a social gathering place. Everyone hangs out there, and you get to see everything that is going on. This is my last semester, so that's why I wanted it. Usually seniors get it. I wanted it because of the social aspect, not because of Thurber."[1]

Griffiths couldn't think of anything anywhere in the house that related to Thurber. Chapter advisor Kyle Andrews said that might be because everything was removed during a renovation four years ago.

"We took out all the composites and a lot of the other historical type stuff," Andrews said. "We have a lot in the archives. Some of that will come back at some point and be in the house."[2]

The house doesn't look a lot different than it did when Thurber was a member of the fraternity. The three-story brick mansion with massive white columns in the front and smaller white columns on the east side was built for real estate man Alfred Linton in 1908 and seems almost unchanged from early photos of it.

In 2014 Coed.com ranked the OSU Phi Kappa Psi house number 4 in the "20 Most Impressive Fraternity Houses in the Midwest," noting that "when you're modeling a fraternity house to look like the governor's mansion of South Carolina, you're doing something right. Phi Kappa Psi is one of the most classic-looking fraternity houses in the country."

A Phi Psi time traveler from Thurber's day might be shocked to find the same house they left almost one hundred years ago. If the old mansion looks as new as the day it was opened, it isn't because it is sitting atop the fountain of youth: The Ohio Delta Chapter has a lot of alumni with money.

"We did the exterior in the summer of 2010 and the interior in the summer of 2011," Andrews said. "We paid for that with donations from alumni, and some of them contributed quite a bit. The renovation cost about $3 million, so the house should look good."[3]

Even though Thurber never lived in the house, he spent a lot of time there. Longtime Thurber House board member Dave Timmons, a Phi Psi in the late 1940s, couldn't recall how Thurber's name got attached to a room in the fraternity house.

"I'm trying to think when we started identifying it [that way]," Timmons said. "In fact, we still refer to it as the Thurber room; the second floor, southeast room we called the Thurber room, and I'm trying to figure why, because he didn't live there. He always being a town man; he lived at home. It may have been the room that Elliott Nugent had.

"It's bigger now that it was originally. We've remodeled drastically in the last five years. It's configuration now is different from what it was originally."[4]

Several of his fraternity brothers described him and Elliott Nugent in Nugent's room, with papers strewn about as they went about the task of frantically writing scripts that may or may not take them somewhere. And then again, they might have been writing about just about anything.

"I had a funny experience with them," Wendell Postle said. "I was taking freshman English and I must have looked kind of down or discouraged or something because Nugent or Thurber, one of them said, 'What's the matter with you? You look like you're all down.' I said, 'Well, I'm supposed to have a theme ready, a 100-word theme for tomorrow morning at eight and I don't have it.' Thurber said to Nugent, 'Why don't we write him one? We can write him a 100-word theme real quick.' He said, 'What do you want to write it on?' Oh, it's supposed to be a narrative of some kind. He asked, 'Have you ever been up in an airplane?' No, I haven't. 'Well, you're going to take a ride in an airplane.' So they wrote a theme, and the title of it was 'My First Airplane Ride.' I flew from Columbus to Dayton and back. They typed it even, they had the typewriter there and everything, and I took it over and handed it in the next morning. I got an A. The teacher handed it back and said, 'That's a wonderful theme! I want to talk to you after class.' So I stopped and she said, 'That's a wonderful experience you had!' Well, of course, I hadn't had the experience. She said, 'I want you to tell the class tomorrow morning all about that trip.' So I had to fake it. I got by with it all right because, of course, not many had had airplane rides so they didn't know the difference. I've always been sorry because I didn't know at that time that those two fellows were going to become famous, so I didn't keep the theme."[5]

As a freshman, Postle was impressed with Thurber—he described the two seniors as "egoists" who "had no idea of failure," which shows how far that insecure townie from the city's east side had come in a couple of years. Without Nugent's intense lobbying, Thurber would never have become a Phi Psi.

"It took a year to get Thurber into the fraternity," said Virgil (Duke) Damon, chapter president as the time. "The Phi Psis and the Phi Gams were the two leading fraternities on campus then. They took college boys with money. It cost $50 a month for room and board and you were expected to have $4.50 a week spending money. Thurber simply didn't fit the picture. He had no money at all, it seemed. Nobody knew much about him. He was a towner, but never mentioned his family, or invited anyone home to meet them. He seemed to have come from nowhere and some of the fellows thought that strange. I remember the big debate over whether Thurber should be taken in. The question was: would he be socially amenable, contribute to the esprit de corps? Thurber was such an improbable fellow, older than most of the boys, and not all that popular with the majority, so the vote was to postpone the decision for a year."[6]

Nugent wouldn't accept that and made sure Thurber was around enough for the other members to realize what an entertaining guy he was. The fact that fraternities put on skits at each other's houses helped convince some of the holdouts that he could contributed in ways that would help the chapter, and during the winter of 1916–17, Damon finally asked him to join.

It thrilled Thurber to be issued the invitation, and Nugent wrote in his autobiography that he "cheerfully submitted to the semicomic tortures of 'Hell Week' and soon endeared himself to everyone. . . . I do not believe that he had any false ideas about the importance of fraternities, but he really liked most of the fellows and began to take more interest in social life."[7]

Not surprisingly, Thurber's reminiscences of his days in frat house in 1937 for the local chapter's newsletter focused on a humorous incident in 1917 involving Nugent and another brother called "Love" Houk there.

"It happened this way," Thurber wrote. "Houk was in his room at the old fraternity house, studying a note book in which were a lot of names, addresses and telephone numbers. A young Ohio brother by the name of Elliott, or Elmer, Nugent—I have forgotten which—took to annoying Houk by throwing things over the transom into his room; erasers, vases, cats, insults and the like; Houk finally announced that if Nugent (or was it Newman?) bothered him further, he would throw a bottle of ink back through the transom. Nugent, not a brother to be easily intimidated, continued to bother Houk, whereupon Houk threw the ink. It was a good shot and ruined Houk's overcoat, which Nugent had put on for the occasion. Houk was distressed, but Nugent said 'That's all right, old man, it didn't fit me very well anyway.' They later became great friends. Much later."[8]

Thurber obviously had some good times. But he never forgot the fraternity's initial failure to accept him and his earlier experience with Chi Phi when his close friend Ed Morris was accepted and he was rejected. His overall experience kept him from fully embracing the fraternity system, and he never returned to the Phi Psi house in later years with the same enthusiasm felt by many of his brothers.

Thurber had a difficult time getting into the fraternity, but later generations of Phi Psis are glad he did. In a mocking twist of irony, the kid who might not have become a Phi Psi has become the Ohio Delta chapter's most famous member and the fraternity has tried to honor his memory. When Donn Vickers was recruiting members of a steering committee to lead the saving and restoration of Thurber House in the early 1980s, Norm Spain, president of the local chapter of Phi Kappa Psi alumni, signed on early. It was the beginning of a long involvement of the fraternity with Thurber House.

"Thurber House had the support of Phi Kappa Psi right from the start," Spain wrote. "In the early 80s, I was president of the Columbus Alumni Association and for that reason was invited to join a small steering committee formed to decide what to do with the dilapidated old house on Jefferson Avenue. One of the early financial contributions to a fund to restore the house came from the Endowment fund of Phi Kappa Psi.

"In the ensuing 20 years, three Phi Kappa Psi alums have served terms on the Thurber House board of trustees: Dave Timmons, Ohio Delta '49; Win Logan, Ohio Delta '66, who also served as board president; and me. In addition, scores of Ohio Delta undergraduates have volunteered throughout these twenty years for Saturday work sessions at Thurber House, washing windows, floors and woodwork, trimming shrubbery, raking leaves, and providing other needed assistance."[9]

A composite photo of the members of Phi Kappa Psi in 1918 hangs in Thurber's bedroom at the Thurber House. Directly below the composite is a frame holding five photos of the Phi Psi house, an exterior shot in the middle and two interior shots on each side, old pictures of the place that might have been taken today.

Times have changed dramatically, but there's a good chance that if Thurber were alive, the Phi Psi house wouldn't seem a lot different to him. It wouldn't seem like home, however. It never did.

A young Charles Thurber at work on a typewriter. (James Thurber Papers, Rare Books & Manuscripts Library of The Ohio State University Libraries)

LITERARY MATTERS

Inspiration and Incubation in Thurberville

hurber's infatuation with good writing started early. When Jamie was a young boy he knew author O. Henry had been a prisoner in the Ohio Penitentiary, and the thought of the famous short story writer as a "resident" of his hometown must have fascinated him. In Thurber's later letters to family and friends, he often makes reference to O. Henry stories and his style.

Thurber became even more intrigued with O. Henry later in life when he learned the details of his imprisonment. A prison physician named Dr. John Thomas had mailed O. Henry's manuscripts to a third party in New Orleans so that the submissions wouldn't appear to have come from behind bars. Thomas was also involved—with popular *Columbus Dispatch* editorial cartoonist Billy Ireland—in an incident where a stack of O. Henry manuscripts had been lost. Thurber knew and admired Ireland, and he later wrote about the mystery.

Robert O. Ryder, the managing editor of the *Ohio State Journal*, was another early influence on Thurber. Ryder excelled at the art of "paragraphing"—short, witty, newspaper commentary that was popular during those days—and Thurber later imitated his idol during his newspaper days at the *Dispatch*. It always bothered Thurber that Ryder didn't achieve the fame of men he believed had lesser talent, and he was still writing about that long after Ryder was gone.

Thurber's three years at the *Dispatch* (1921–24) comprise what may be his most intriguing time period in Columbus. The newspaper office was located in a different location than it is today in a building that still stands; the old newsroom now serves as the headquarters for the Franklin County Republican party. It was here that Thurber ran across a tough, caustic city editor named Norman "Gus" Kuehner who didn't like college boys and didn't like Thurber's flowery writing. During this time Thurber also became close friends with *Ohio State Journal* reporter John McNulty, possibly during morning sessions in Marzetti's restaurant on Gay Street, where competing reporters from the city's three major papers often congregated. McNulty was a talented writer who had been fired from nearly every newspaper in New York for drinking, and he added a few Columbus newspapers to his resume. He stayed in Columbus longer than Thurber did and ended up with him at the *New Yorker,* achieving national fame as an author of several books.

Thurber's childhood in Columbus also served as the foundation of a lifelong friendship for two writers who achieved success on a national scale. Donald Ogden Stewart was a grade ahead of Thurber at both Sullivant and Douglas schools, and he wanted to become a humorist. Instead he became a successful playwright and actor, and ended up with a successful career in Hollywood. Sayre was six years younger than Thurber and got to know him at the ball field behind the Ohio School for the Blind. They worked on competing Columbus newspapers at the same time and both ended up in New York with stints at the *New Yorker.* Sayre eventually became a successful screenwriter and drifted to Hollywood for a time, but they shared a lasting friendship and a love a good writing until the end.

All are part of the city's underrated literary legacy.

CHAPTER 30

The Mystery of the Missing Manuscripts

History will never forget Dr. John M. Thomas. He will always own a small measure of fame as the prison physician who was asked by prisoner William Sydney Porter—O. Henry—to give his handwritten manuscripts a first read before sending them to a go-between who in turn sent them to prospective publishers, thus disguising their origin behind the massive stone walls of the Ohio Penitentiary.

That alone would have been enough to give Thomas a special place in the heart of James Thurber, an O. Henry fan from the time he was a boy. But Thurber came to have a deeper understanding of the Thomas-Porter connection. He knew Thomas put Porter in the position to mine rich tales from the other prisoners that were the basis of many of his best stories, and that he also became part of an enduring mystery, one involving some of the celebrated writer's missing manuscripts. The latter tale so intrigued Thurber that he wrote about it in "Loose Leaves" at the end of *The Thurber Album*.

Thomas is a fascinating story topic on his own without Thurber and without having a mystery attached to his name. He was just out of medical school when a young state representative from Marion, Ohio—Warren G. Harding—helped secure his appointment at the old penitentiary on the north edge of downtown Columbus. Porter arrived there in 1898 to serve a five-year term for embezzlement while working as teller and book-keeper at the First National Bank in Austin, Texas; when Thomas learned that he had gotten his pharmacy license while working at his uncle's drug store in Greensboro, North Carolina, he immediately put him to work in the prison hospital. Porter always claimed innocence of the crime—the bank was loosely run and customers often helped themselves to "loans" they never paid back—and Dr. Thomas steadfastly believed him.

"Porter was a graduate pharmacist," Dr. Thomas said, in a 1916 news story. "And I put him at once to work under me. He became the night doctor. That gave him a chance to go to the cells of the prisoners, and remain there as long as he wished talking to them. Then he would return to his cell and write those inimitable short stories which have delighted the world. In the morning he would leave them on my desk. I would read them. There was always a market for his stories."[1]

While in prison, Porter wrote fourteen of his best known stories, at least three of which were published while he was incarcerated. He may have written countless others; there are many accounts of his prolific output. Thomas told Porter biographer C. Alphonso Smith that O. Henry could turn out a story "in from one to three hours."[2] While living in New York in 1904 and 1905, Porter produced an incredible one hundred fifteen short stories.

"He was an unusually good pharmacist and for this reason was permitted to look after the minor ills of prisoners at night," Thomas wrote, in a letter to Smith for his biography. "He would spend two to three hours on the range or tiers of cells every night and knew most of the prisoners and their life stories. 'The Gentle Grafter' portrays the stories told him on his night rounds. I remember having heard him recount many of them."[3]

The penitentiary's night physician, Dr. George W. Willard, remembered reading O. Henry's description of safe cracker Jimmy Valentine in the popular story "A Retrieved Reformation" and thinking "that's Jimmy Connors through and through." Connors served as one of the day drug clerks in the prison hospital, befriended Porter, and shared many of his experiences with him.

Thomas said that Porter never went by his serial number while in prison but was always known as "Dr. Porter." He said that outside of his "patients," Porter didn't associate much with anyone during his imprisonment except for Thomas and the "western prisoners, those from Arizona, Texas, and Indian Territory. [He] got stories from them and retold them in the office."

Porter, called "Bill" by some prisoners, seems to have taken the "O. Henry" pseudonym while in the Ohio Pen, and may have gotten the idea for it from Orrin Henry, the captain of the guard. Porter was always cryptic about where he got the name, not surprising since he kept his prison background secret. Even his daughter, Margaret, didn't find out that he had been in prison until after he died.

He knew he had a good situation there, working under Dr. Thomas and three other doctors. On May 18, 1898, shortly after he was imprisoned, he wrote to G. P. Roach, his late wife's stepfather, that "all of the men stationed in the hospital live a hundred percent better than the rest of the 2500 men here" and that "we have good food, well-cooked and in unlimited abundance, and large, clean sleeping apartments."[4]

But his letter to Roach also made it clear he wasn't happy, and it isn't hard to see why he might have "reached the limit of endurance.

> The doctor goes to bed about ten o'clock and from then on during the night I prescribe for the patients myself and go out and attend calls that come in. If I find anyone seriously ill I have them brought to the hospital and attended by a doctor. I never imagined human life was held as cheap as it is here. The men are regarded as animals without soul or feeling. They carry on all kinds of work here; there are foundries and all kinds of manufacturing is done, and everybody works and works twice as hard as men in the same employment outside do. They work 13 hours a day and each man must do a certain amount of work or be punished. Some few strong ones stand the work, but it is simply slow death to the majority. If a man gets sick and can't work they take him into a cellar and turn a powerful stream of water on him from a hose that knocks the breath out of him. Then a doctor revives him and they hang him up by his hands with his feet off the floor for an hour or two. This generally makes him go to work again, and when he gives out and can't stand up they bring him on a stretcher to the hospital to get well or die as the case may be. The hospital wards have from one hundred to two hundred patients in them all the time.[5]

In another letter to his wife's mother, he went into even more excruciating detail:

> We sometimes have a death every night for a week or so. Very little time is wasted on such an occasion. One of the nurses will come from a ward and say—"Well, So and So has croaked." Ten minutes later, they tramp out with So and So on a stretcher and take him to the dead house. If he has no friends to claim him—which is generally the case—the next day the doctors will have a dissecting bee and that ends it. Suicides are as common

as pie here. Every few nights, the doctor and I have to strike out at a trot to see some unfortunate who has tried to get rid of his troubles. They cut their throats and hang themselves and stop up their cells and turn the gas on and try all kinds of way. Most of them plan it well enough to succeed.[6]

Even as well as he was treated, it's not difficult to see why Porter would want out. And with Thomas's recommendation, Porter received a promotion to bookkeeper in the office of the prison steward in October, 1900, nine months before his release. The office was in a two-story building across the street from the entrance of the prison near the Scioto riverbank, and during his time there, Porter felt as free as any normal bookkeeper. He ate and slept in the office building; after working hours, he was free to do whatever he liked. He often took long walks by the river at night and sometimes just wandered the streets of Columbus, meeting people who had no clue that he was an inmate of the penitentiary. The prison stood just south of where Nationwide Arena is today, so O. Henry probably wandered the same streets now crowded with concertgoers and Columbus Blue Jackets hockey fans.

The mystery has its roots before that, probably in 1899. According to Thurber, Dr. Thomas took a great many of Porter's manuscripts home one evening; Porter liked to have the good doctor give him feedback on the stories he produced before sending them off for possible publication.

At the time, Thomas was single and lived in a boarding house at 383 Oak Street. A young *Columbus Dispatch* cartoonist named Billy Ireland also lived there. Thomas supposedly gave "a great many manuscripts," which Thurber described as "10 inches high," to Ireland to read. They subsequently disappeared and no one knows what happened to them.[7]

One story has Ireland putting the manuscripts on a table in his room and a maid who may have wanted to dust move it to a washstand where it somehow disappeared. Another story has Ireland not even reading them because he didn't have time, and by the time he got around to it, they were gone. Another had the landlady taking the pile of manuscripts out and burning them because she was tired of seeing them lying around. And still another has Ireland reading the manuscripts and recognizing their value but disposing of them because Thomas told him, or he *thought* he told him, that Porter said that he didn't want them back.

Given the legendary literary status O. Henry achieved after he left Columbus, the idea of a trove of lost stories of his that might never have been published is intriguing. What if the manuscripts didn't find their way to the dump? What if they were moved to a place that couldn't be reached by an aggressive dust cloth or an angry landlady and then moved again and again like a restless nomad with a proclivity for wandering? They might now innocently reside on a Columbus shelf somewhere like a stack of old billheads, waiting for some unsuspecting soul to stumble across a ten-inch stack of papers that might fetch more in an auction than a winning a lottery ticket.

It seems significant that Thurber worked with Ireland at the *Dispatch* in the early 1920s and never heard Ireland talk about the missing manuscripts; he mused that maybe by then the celebrated cartoonist had tired of talking about them. It also seems odd that Thurber never asked Ireland about them, although it's possible Thurber didn't hear about this mystery himself until many years later after all of the principals were dead. *The Thurber Album* was published in 1952, more than a half-century after the manuscripts disappeared.

It's possible the stories were among rejects Porter had received and he was simply looking for a final opinion on them, in which case, maybe he didn't care if they were discarded. It's also possible that he rewrote the stories from memory later; the first eleven stories in his book *The Gentle Grafter*, which wasn't published until 1908, had never appeared in print before that and are among those that Porter is thought to have penned in prison. More speculation: Those eleven stories may have been lost and Porter may have taken his good old time re-writing them.

Porter always had very little to say about himself, so the fact that he never offered his own version of what happened isn't surprising.

"He had a genius for taciturnity and a profound admiration for silence," biographers Robert H. Davis and Arthur B. Maurice wrote in *The Caliph of Bagdad*, a 1931 study of Porter.

Porter also didn't live a long life following his release from the penitentiary in 1901, two years early because of good behavior. He moved first to Pittsburgh, where his late wife's parents lived and he was reunited with Margaret, his eleven-year-old daughter, who was never told of her father's incarceration.

He quickly discovered that a place doesn't need stone walls to make you miserable. He hated his new city. He wrote to Al Jennings, a convict he had met in Honduras while on the run. Jennings was still confined in the Columbus penitentiary:

> I want to say that Pittsburgh is the "low-downdest" hole on the surface of the earth. The people here are the most ignorant, ill-bred, contemptible, boorish, degraded, insulting, sordid, vile, foul-mouthed, indecent, pro-

fane, drunken, dirty, mean, depraved curs that I ever imagined could exist. Columbus people are models of chivalry compared to them. I shall linger here no longer than necessary.[8]

Porter moved to New York in 1902 to be near his publishers. He married Sarah Coleman, a woman he had known in Greensboro, North Carolina, while growing up. But Porter was a heavy drinker, and his health began to deteriorate in 1908. He died in 1910 at the age of forty-seven of various ailments associated with alcoholism—cirrhosis of the liver, diabetes, and an enlarged heart.

Thomas would never have signed that death certificate. He knew what really killed the former prison pharmacist.

"The memory that he was a convict and the probable result should this information become public eventually killed Porter," Thomas said.[9]

If not for Thurber, the life span of the mystery wouldn't have been long, either. Although Ireland was much younger than Porter, he also didn't live to a ripe old age. He died of a heart attack on May 25, 1935, at the age of fifty-five, long before Thurber wrote about his role in the missing manuscripts.

If anyone could have cleared up the mystery, it would have been Dr. Thomas. He left his position at the penitentiary in 1908 and later served as chief of staff at Grant Hospital. He practiced medicine for more than fifty years in a little pillbox house that still stands just north of his former home at 1126 Neil Avenue, about ten blocks from the old pen. He started to practice there about the time Porter's prison term ended.

The good doctor remained active to the end. He played handball at the Athletic Club of Columbus on April 6, 1951, saw patients on April 7 and suffered a heart attack at the age of seventy-five as he closed up his office that afternoon. He died at home the next morning, apparently without the missing manuscripts in his possession.

One thing we know for sure: The missing papers aren't still sitting on a shelf in that old boarding house on Oak Street. That building has long since been torn down and replaced by a row of red brick apartment buildings that never knew either Thomas or Ireland.

"I leave the mystery of the missing manuscripts of O. Henry to a younger and more active researcher," Thurber wrote, "but I warn him that the task is hard, and that it may even be impossible."[10]

CHAPTER 31

A Paragrapher for the Ages

Only a few days after reading James Thurber's tribute to Robert O. Ryder, the talented *Ohio State Journal* editor who served as one of his early idols, I found myself not twenty feet from Ryder's old office.

My employer owned the five-story building at 62 East Broad Street on Statehouse Square in Columbus and maintained some departments there. On this day, I had a bulky cellphone that required replacement, and the twenty-something guy whose tech duties included handling the company's cellphones kept a makeshift office on the second floor. While my associate called to get a replacement set up, the empty office that overlooked the Statehouse drew me to it like a powerful magnet.

When the technician pulled his cell away from his mouth and asked me if something was wrong, it suddenly occurred to me that I must have looked strange standing there gaping at an empty room.

"No, it's just kind of weird." I treaded cautiously, aware that this might be squishy ground. "This used to be the *Ohio State Journal* building, and the newsroom was on this floor. Bob Ryder, who was the paper's editor, had an office that overlooked the Statehouse, so this has to be it."

The guy's expression looked as blank as a clean sheet of typing paper. I kept going, a little more tentatively now, like a boy gingerly crossing a frozen river, waiting for the ice to break.

"I was just reading James Thurber's profile of Ryder—he was Thurber's hero—a few days ago, and he mentioned that office. Ryder probably wrote dozens of columns in there, so it's just kind of weird to be here after I just read about it."

He looked as though he wanted to do the right thing and respond. He had nothing to say. He wore the uncomfortable look of someone who stumbled in on two teenagers kissing and wanted to get out of there without making a scene. He saw the escape hatch and took it.

"I have your phone ready," he said.

One of the houses where Thurber lived in Columbus is a brick-and-mortar monument to him called Thurber House. Ryder, the writer who inspired Thurber, also has a house in Columbus. It is called 1041 Franklin Avenue.

The *Ohio State Journal* editor moved into the house when it was built in 1907 and lived there for twenty-two years. During that time, Ryder served as the paper's managing editor and excelled as a "paragrapher"—the lost art of writing short, witty commentary or "paragraphs" mostly for newspapers—and often wrote about the people on his street and his neighborhood. His work was reprinted at numerous papers around the nation and often in the *New York Morning World.*

But Ryder's 2½-story house in the Olde Town East neighborhood on the city's near east side, a mixed frame and masonry home where he composed many of his witticisms, has been offered for sale four times since 2007 and he doesn't rate a mention in the real estate ads. It has been offered as an "Arts and Crafts masterpiece." It has been offered as a "spectacular renovation." It hasn't been offered as the former home of a talented but mostly forgotten writer and editor.

None of this would have surprised Thurber. Without his adulation, Ryder would probably be completely forgotten today. He was apparently already a distant memory in 1951 when Thurber wrote a lengthy tribute to Ryder in *The Thurber Album* called "Franklin Avenue, U. S. A." In "Loose Leaves," a final chapter of that same book which Thurber described as "A department of annotation, amplification and afterthought," he punctuated a brief tribute to his journalistic hero with a paragraph that both acknowledged and ridiculed Ryder's relative lack of fame:

> The death of Bob Ryder, March 16, 1936, got only one sentence in the *New York Times,* but that paper printed nearly two thousand words about the passing of Ed Howe, October 3, 1937. The Kansan was, after all, the author of twenty-eight books, and he had always spurned the Ryder cult of invisibility. When he was eighty-two, he said, for everybody to hear, "Give me two years and I'll write the greatest book in the world." He had

written his best book long before that, "Story of a Country Town," which ran into fifty editions. It was praised by William Dean Howells, who probably never heard of Bob Ryder, although Howells was once a reporter and editorial writer for, of all American newspapers, the *Ohio State Journal.*[1]

Howells probably had at least heard of Ryder. The celebrated editor of the *Atlantic* and author of numerous books lived until 1920, which was certainly long enough to take notice of a writer and editor of Ryder's talents at his former paper.

Ryder created a good literary reputation for himself without Thurber's fawning approval; his fame just didn't stick. Ryder's "paragraphing" fell out of favor almost a century ago, and if Thurber hadn't become famous and immortalized Ryder in *The Thurber Album,* his humor would be known only to the research gophers who inadvertently stumble across it while mining newspaper microfilms for other information.

Thurber grew up reading Ryder in the *Ohio State Journal,* and he thought he was as good a paragrapher as any, which at the time meant something. Thurber put Ryder at the top of his class partially by eliminating others on technicalities; he said part-time paragrapher Will Rogers's "stuff appeared in a fancy box off the editorial page, so he can't be included among the elite," and also eliminated "the dialect boys like Abe Martin, or the column conductors, such as Franklin Pierce Adams and Bert Leston Taylor, who printed poetry, of all things, and stuff from contributors."[2]

There is no doubting that Ryder wrote some good stuff, but whether he deserves the pedestal Thurber created for him is debatable. While Ryder wrote lots of clever quips, if he remembered for anything, it should probably be for his profound influence on Thurber. Thurber often said that Ryder's humor inspired him and served as an early model for his light writing style. If that's true, the modest, unassuming Ryder had a much greater impact on American humor than he possibly could have known.

Both because of his lost eye and his early college struggles, Thurber struggled to find his identity, and his imitation of his literary hero's writing style helped him find his way. As Harrison Kinney wrote, "The 'lost' school year of 1914–15 proved to be one of transition for Thurber. If he couldn't command recognition or find personal resolve in ordinary social competition, he would, like Ryder, develop a literary personality. Ryder was the proof that it could be done even in Columbus, drawing on material from the very environment Thurber inhabited."[3]

Thurber never denied it. In 1949 Thurber wrote of his appreciation for Ryder in a letter to Harvey Breit, a poet, editor, and playwright who at the time reviewed books for the *New York Times Book Review*:

> The man who first inspired me to write humor and whose memory I greatly revere will probably not be known to you. He was the late Robert O. Ryder, the really great paragrapher of the *Ohio State Journal,* who died in the 1930s. He is often mentioned by other great admirers of his, including John McNulty, Frank Sullivan, Joel Sayre, and Donald Ogden Stewart. . . . I rate him among the great American humorists from Twain to Andy White.[4]

Regardless of whether Ryder deserved that kind of royal treatment, he is a fascinating character and certainly worthy of remembrance. He was the son of the Reverend William Henry Ryder, a professor of Greek language and literature at Oberlin (Ohio) College. The family eventually moved to Ann Arbor, Michigan—home of the University of Michigan—where his father became pastor of the First Congregational Church. His upbringing by a college professor in a college atmosphere probably explains in part why Robert became such a good student; he attended Phillips Academy in Andover, Massachusetts, Williams College and eventually graduated from Yale.

Brother Jack, a Williams College grad, came to Columbus to teach at the Columbus Latin School, then under the management of two Williams graduates, and he got his younger brother a teaching job there upon his college graduation.

Jack had played football at Williams and that experience was valued at Ohio State, where a football team had been started in 1890, and he was hired to coach the team. From 1892 to 1896, he served as the Buckeyes' second football coach—former Princeton player Alexander Lilley had been the first—at a salary of $300 a season. Bob, then living in The Normandie residential hotel on East Long Street, often accompanied him when he turned in results of his various sports teams to the *Ohio State Journal* and got to know some of the staffers. When Jack went off to fight the Spanish-American War, his kid brother used his connections to land a job as a reporter there.

Bob's career advanced quickly. He wrote features and local beats and it wasn't long before he was covering the state legislature, where his sense of humor proved to be an asset. Once he wrote a story about two legislators who got into a fight and kept calling each other "liar" and ended his piece with "Both gentlemen were correct."⁵

Ryder was named city editor of the newspaper in 1901 and moved into a large, two-story yellow brick double at 1231 Fair Avenue five blocks from his future home on Franklin. He was promoted to managing editor and then editor in 1903—he was not yet thirty—when brothers Robert F. and Harry P. Wolfe, bought the paper. Their purchase was problematic in those distant days and eyebrow-raising for a different reason today.

The *Ohio State Journal* had been a Republican newspaper and the Wolfes—whose family is known today for its staunch conservative Republican support—were loyal Democrats. Ryder was also a Democrat, a fact that alarmed local Republicans who despaired over the likelihood of a paper that had been the next thing to a Republican party organ suddenly switching sides.

To the Wolfe brothers' credit, they realized that if this happened it promised to set the local political world spinning off its axis and doubtless also understood that a political switch probably wouldn't be good for circulation. So when Ryder proposed a tenable solution, they jumped at it.

Why not make Ryder's father-in-law—conservative newspaper publisher Colonel E. S. Wilson of the *Ironton Register* in southeastern Ohio—the "editor" of the paper, even though Ryder would still run it as managing editor.

"Colonel Wilson wrote glowing editorials in praise of the Grand Old Party, cherry pie, sunsets, and other glories of God and Man, presided at banquets, addressed meetings, joined clubs, and in general acted as the *Journal*'s official, and unquestionably, Republican spokesman," Thurber wrote. "As the gregarious gentleman from Ironton became a prominent and familiar public figure, his shy son-in-law gradually began to withdraw from the company of men."⁶

Wilson's most recent duty had been his appointment by President William McKinley as United States marshal of Puerto Rico, a position he declined when President Theodore Roosevelt tried to reappoint him. He had an illustrious past, having enlisted as a private in Ohio's 58th volunteer regiment and risen to the rank of first lieutenant and earned the brevet rank of captain during the Civil War. He was "promoted" to colonel by his friends after the war and the nickname stuck with him until his death in 1919.⁷ When he first moved to Columbus in 1904, he lived two doors from Republican party king-maker Harry Daugherty—the man credited with making Warren Harding president—at 485 Town Street, but

he had a 2400-square-foot house built at 1043 Franklin for him and his
wife George Anna shortly thereafter, and he built a house on the neighboring lot for their daughter Florence and son-in-law Bob.

Bob Ryder was ahead of his time. He owned a black Cadillac with
Ohio license plate 844, but Thurber wrote that he preferred to drive to
the *Ohio State Journal* building in his electric runabout.

> He gave up the old electric in the early twenties after it had become one of
> the last in town because he thought it was beginning to attract attention,
> and he disliked nothing so much as being conspicuous, or even noticed.
> A tall man, almost six feet two, with red hair, blue eyes, and a pleasant
> smile, he was recognized by everybody in Columbus when he rode in the
> electric, a straight-stemmed pipe between his teeth, his knees almost as
> high as the steering bar, but he had the delusion that almost nobody knew
> him by sight. When passersby stopped to stare at him as he unsnarled
> himself and stepped out of the car in front of the Journal Building, he
> would feel furtively for his black bow tie, to see if the ends were dangling,
> or if he had forgotten to put one on. He always wore, conceivably as pro-
> tective coloration, a blue serge suit, white shirt, and one of a dozen black
> ties he owned, but he was much too striking a figure to manage the invis-
> ibility and anonymity that he craved.[8]

It was especially hard to do while penning memorable prose in an
era when the newspaper served all of the purposes that television, radio
and the internet do now. Over the twenty-two-year period that Ryder
contributed his quips on a regular basis, a researcher could find hundreds of good examples of his work, including many that make fun of the
"neighbor women." Several of his "paragraphs" can serve as representative samples:

> The night has a thousand eyes, and the neighbor women as least twice
> that many ears.

> A careful scientific experiment reveals the fact that an unfertilized field
> produces only 198 crates of spinach to the acre, whereas a fertilized one
> produces 507, and the Anti-Fertilizer Club of the Franklin Avenue Protec-
> tive Association will be organized to a large and enthusiastic meeting this
> evening.

Another depressing reminder of the decadence of the times is that they have named a new salad after Col. Lindbergh, instead of a good five-cent cigar.

What will probably always puzzle us, as we don't dare ask anybody in a position to know, is what becomes of the five inches that the so-called stylish stout corset gets rid of.

A vociferant candidate always seems to find it easier to explain to thoughtful audiences why his opponent should not be elected than why he himself should be.

A woman is either hearing burglars or smelling something.

Whoever named near beer was a poor judge of distance.[9]

Ryder also created a feature with *Ohio State Journal* cartoonist Harry J. Westerman called "The Young Lady Across the Way," which might be described as an early-twentieth-century version of the "blonde" joke. Ryder wrote a gag that could be applied to any pretty girl with an empty head and Westerman penned a drawing to accompany it.

A few examples:

We asked the young lady across the way if she didn't think the party spirit was carried too far in this country and she said you didn't have to accept all your invitations if you didn't want to, did you?

The young lady across the way says she saw in the paper that the railroads' operating expenses were unusually heavy and for her part she thought it was perfectly right that they should have to pay the surgeons' bills when they hurt so many people.

The young lady across the way says she overheard her father say he guessed he'd have to try to raise something on his real estate to give his bankers and wasn't it funny how every city man thought he could be a success as a farmer?[10]

The feature proved so popular that it was syndicated and picked up by many newspapers and in 1913 a small volume of the best quips titled *The Young Lady Across the Way* was published by John W. Luce and

Company in Boston. Thurber wrote that Ryder agreed to both syndication and the book "in order to promote the fame of his collaborator" and
not his own.[11] This seems entirely plausible: despite Westerman's obvious
talent, he was overshadowed by *Columbus Dispatch* editorial cartoonist
Billy Ireland locally, and Ryder doubtless wanted to give his own man a
much-deserved boost.

That may explain, in part, why his editorial staff "adored" Ryder, a
verb that Thurber said he "spent some time looking for . . . and that's it."

As John McNulty wrote to Thurber: "To imagine such a man as Bob
Ryder coming over to my desk, almost sheepishly, and leaning over and
saying, in manner as if he were being very bold, 'That was a good story
you had this morning, John,' is to imagine the unbelievably happy jolt."[12]

Ryder wrote many of his paragraphs at his home on Franklin Avenue—longhand, as he never used a typewriter—and when he got to the
Ohio State Journal office, he would stuff them in the pneumatic tube that
led downstairs to the composing room. "Only one of two of the *State
Journal's* printers could decipher it."[13] His "elegantly appointed office," as
he called it, overlooked the Statehouse and still does, although it is now
just another room on another floor in a building that has become home
to the *Columbus Dispatch* editorial offices since the newspaper's sale to
Gatehouse Media in June 2015.

In Ryder's day, the office didn't have a desk or a typewriter; the editor
wrote out all of his copy longhand with a pencil and "he sat at one of two
long tables placed side by side, with lamps in the center. For the visitors,
there were several comfortable leather chairs that had come from the old
Neil House on High Street, so that the room looked more like the lobby
of a small hotel than the office of a working newspaper editor."[14]

Ryder often wrote editorials that seemed contrary to his newspaper's
position, making him something of a spy in the enemy camp. While the
Journal quite naturally endorsed Republican Herbert Hoover in the 1928
presidential election, Ryder wrote editorials that were favorable to the
Democratic candidate, New York governor Al Smith. After Hoover's election, Ryder wrote three positive editorials about the defeated candidate,
the final one adding "It would be a tragedy if the country should hear no
more from the clear-headed, honest-minded, frank spoken, liberal leader
of the useful minority."[15]

Ryder must have enjoyed this inside joke, although the election and
its aftermath seemed to take something out of him. For a respite, he and
his wife settled on a vacation in Montreal in the summer of 1929, but
when he got off the train in Canada, he looked pale and weak. When he

couldn't sign the hotel register, the Ryders returned to Columbus, where he was diagnosed with a slight cerebral hemorrhage. He spent three weeks recovering, but at the age of fifty-four, his thirty-one-year newspaper career was over.

The Ryders moved to Berkeley, California, near his brother Arthur, who taught Sanskrit (the primary liturgical language of Hinduism) at the University of California in 1930 and "settled down in a house on a winding street" overlooking San Francisco Bay. He intended to return to writing and couldn't; "he found that he couldn't hold a pencil in his hand more than a few minutes at a time."[16] Instead he spent his time reading books he had never had time to read and enjoying the Bay Area weather. He died in his sleep in 1936, a half-continent away from his Franklin Avenue neighborhood that proved to be the source of so many memorable paragraphs.

He also died without knowing that he had had such a major impact on one of America's literary giants. Thurber met Ryder only once, when he was a junior at East High School. He had done a little paragraphing of his own for the school newspaper "in callow imitation of the master" and had sent them to him. Thurber claimed that Ryder used one of them in the newspaper. He was introduced to Ryder by his father, and as Thurber wrote, "I still remember that great day."

It seems odd that Thurber didn't meet Ryder again while employed at the *Dispatch* in the early 1920s. Thurber's friend Joel Sayre worked as a reporter at the *Ohio State Journal* at the time and he must have spoken glowingly about him.

"Bob Ryder was a wonderful man, wonderful journalist," Sayre said. "He was a great friend of my brother-in-law, Billy Ireland, the cartoonist and our two families saw a lot of the Ryders and liked him immensely. It's a pity Bob wasn't in a larger city, although his work was reproduced in papers all over the country from the *New York Times* to the *Booville Bugel*. Those little paragraphs he wrote were very good . . . but he could also do anything on a newspaper. He had many offers to come East and work on New York papers, as did Billy Ireland."[17]

At that point in life, Thurber probably didn't acknowledge how much he idolized Ryder. But he wasn't shy about imitating him when he started writing his "Credos and Curios" column in the *Dispatch,* just as he had in both high school and college.

In addition to all of the positive literary attributes Ryder bestowed on Thurber, he also must have reinforced the dim view of women his young disciple carried with him for the rest of his life.

In "Credos and Curios," Thurber drafted first wife Althea for his version of Ryder's "Young Lady Across the Way."

An example: "A woman will ask you a question from the next room just as you turn on the water in the bath tub and feel that you are beginning to neglect her when you ask her to repeat it."[18]

Thus begins Thurber's literary mockery of women, a prejudice that would he would take with him to the grave.

Whether Ryder deserves the blame for this is debatable, but it is worth noting that Thurber's attitude didn't change much over the years, long after his hero's death and after others began to promote a more respectful role for women.

In 1960 Thurber took some shots at women in an interview with Harvey Taylor of the *Detroit Times,* comments that would bring down the wrath of today's feminists and might even embarrass Ryder, if he were still alive. They also sound as if Thurber could have been talking about "the young woman across the way":

Women are taking over the world because they are blandly unconcerned about its history. I once sat next to a woman who asked why we had to purchase Louisiana when we got all the other states for free. I explained to her that Louisiana was owned by two women, Louise and Anna Wilmott and that they sold it to General Winfield Scott provided that they name it after them. That was called the Wilmott [*sic*] Proviso, and his closing of the deal was the Dredd [*sic*] Scott decision.

She answered, "Never mind the details. Why did we let them talk us into it at all?"

I don't believe the canard that some women thought that Pearl Harbor was a movie actress. But one woman, asked to name the martyred presidents, said "Yes, but how do you know what torture they inflicted on their wives?"[19]

CHAPTER 32

The News Was Served Here

A search for the scene of Thurber's first real job as a newspaper reporter leads to the second floor of the white-gray cut stone building on the northeast corner of Gay and High Streets, known to today's downtown denizens as the home of Café Brioso.

The downtown coffee, breakfast and sandwich shop has occupied the ground floor of the narrow, five-story building for fourteen years, or one year less than the afternoon newspaper that constructed the building to replace one that was gutted by fire in 1907. This building housed the *Columbus Dispatch* from 1910 to 1925, so it's not surprising that neither the patrons nor the coffee shop workers had any clue that the space where they were serving coffee and drinking it had served as the newspaper's business office—advertising departments, telephone want ad counter, cashiers, bookkeeping, and the offices of the business manager and company president—long before most of them were born.

"Seriously?" a twenty-something guy working behind the Brioso counter asked, after that startling information was replayed to him. "I heard that it used to be a Hallmark."

The comment drew a sympathetic smile. Café Brioso had probably occupied this space for over half of the clerk's life, so a greeting card store from the 1990s might have seemed like eons ago to him. And then again, he might have just been a direct descendent to one of those clueless Columbus characters Thurber wrote about.

When the confused clerk was told that the newspaper had moved out in 1925 to the larger, five-story building on at 34 South Third Street that it occupied until 2016, his eyes glassed over. Mention that James Thurber worked as a reporter at the *Dispatch* when it occupied this building didn't penetrate the target, either. The clerk apparently assigned Thurber, Abraham Lincoln, and Julius Cesar to the same category: ancient history.

The quality of the conversation improved upstairs, reached by an elevator at the rear of the first floor. The Franklin County Republican party occupies the second floor space that once served as the *Dispatch* news room, and Brian Metzbower, the local party's executive director, knew that this had been a newspaper building and seemed genuinely intrigued by it.

"I love the art work [on the building]," he said. "I love to point those out to people. Those are all literary references, the globe and the owl and everything. Once you put it into context that a newspaper was here, it's kind of cool, I think."

It transcends "cool" when you see the open space on the second floor that looks like it *could* house a newsroom, albeit a smaller one than newspapers in a city the size of Columbus would occupy today.

"Someone else told me the length of the building, the reason that it is so uniquely long, is to accommodate printing presses [in the basement]," Metzger said. "I heard that those [iron covers] on the sidewalk outside the building are there because that's where they used to bring the papers up and load them."

Thurber immortalized those covers in "Newspaperman—Head and Shoulders" in *The Thurber Album* by telling the story of how city editor Norman (Gus) Kuehner once snatched a shoe dangling from a female reporter's foot and tossed it out the window. When she went down to the street, one shoe on, one shoe off, to retrieve it, she discovered that "the slipper had fallen through the open iron cover of a sidewalk elevator shaft and dropped into a second sub-basement." She finally returned and told Kuehner what had happened and he gruffly replied "Good shot" without looking up at her.

It's easy to look at this space and visualize incidents such as that one, in part because the room is relatively open with the exception of a few offices at its western end. It doesn't take much imagination to see the room bustling with activity, crowded with reporters' desks, clacking wire service machines and cigar-chomping editors or even picture cartoonist Billy Ireland sketching out "The Passing Show" in one of those offices.

As much fun as that mental journey is for the modern time traveler, grizzled, objective-obsessed newspapermen such as Kuehner and Thurber probably wouldn't be pleased to take a similar trip into the future and see how partisan their old work space has become. A table next to one of the windows is crowded with neat stacks of political propaganda for various candidates. Two elephant paintings hang on the walls—symbols of the Republican Party and not friends from the Columbus Zoo. Photos of former President George W. Bush and his vice-president, Dick Cheney, have their own space, with accompanying autographs underneath, probably a thank-you for what Ohio did for their careers. The walls also hold photos of former President George H. W. Bush and his vice-president, Dan Quayle, and a drawing of former president Benjamin Harrison and Levi Morton, the vice-president Harrison dumped from the ticket when he ran for a second term and lost.

A large portrait of Theodore Roosevelt that hangs in one corner would seem to be misplaced, if only because the former president ran on the Progressive or Bull Moose party ticket for president against Republican incumbent president William Howard Taft in 1912, probably enabling Democrat Woodrow Wilson to win. Maybe the local Republican Party has been infiltrated by an old holdover from Bull Moose days, but that seems doubtful. Roosevelt *was* a Republican, so this is probably a case of forgive and forget.

Even Robert F. and Harry W. Wolfe, the brothers who owned the *Dispatch* in those days, would probably have conflicted feelings about what it means to have Republicans plotting strategy in a place that once served as their old newsroom. Although most of the brothers' descendants strongly supported the Republican party right up to the day that publisher John F. Wolfe engineered a sale of the newspaper to Gatehouse Media in June, 2015, Robert and Harry were staunch Democrats in those days. Family members say that Harry switched political parties in the 1930s in response to President Franklin Delano Roosevelt's banking policies during the Depression. Robert died in 1928, so he was a Democrat until the end. It seems safe to say that at least he probably wouldn't be pleased to see the old news space in the hands of Republican political operatives.

But then the old building went through a lot to get to this point. After the *Dispatch* moved to its larger digs on South Third Street in 1925, the long, rectangular space on the first floor held a women's clothing store (Roberts Women's Wear) and shoe store (R. L. Taylor Shoes), for more than thirty years, and a music store (Summers & Son) for at least ten years after that, so the tables occupied by today's coffee-swilling customers fill a space that has doubtless been remodeled numerous times.

The location led an eventful life even before the current building arrived on the scene. In 1820, eight years after the new state capital was laid out and the little town's first residents arrived, Wilson's Tanyard occupied this site. It was the first building on the east side of High Street north of Broad Street; the only structure north of that was a vacant log cabin at the corner of High and Spring Streets. A swamp north of Spring may have scared a few would-be buyers away, early proof of the that familiar real estate maxim: "Location. Location. Location."

The *Dispatch* moved into a six-story building on that spot in 1895. The newspaper had been located a half-block to the south since its founding by ten printers with $900 in capital in a small, rented four-story building, and was first published on July 1, 1871. The new location at High and Gay burned in a massive fire in the early morning hours of April 9, 1907, and the newspaper moved into a temporary location in the vacated Beggs department store building at 38 North High while the old *Dispatch* building was torn down and this structure replaced it. The *Dispatch* moved back to High and Gay Streets in 1910, eleven years before Thurber applied for a job there at the suggestion of one of his Ohio State pals, Karl Finn, who was already a reporter there.

The new structure looked like a newspaper building although it was only 23 feet wide and 118 feet long. The lower basement, which held the pressroom, mail room, stereotype department and boiler room, is 17 feet wider. Size considerations explain why the paper remained here only 15 years.

Thurber worked at the *Dispatch* for almost three years, from August, 1921, until the spring of 1924. He just missed, by a year, the move to the new building. He had never planned a long career as a newspaperman; he saw it only a step toward more serious—or more humorous—writing.

Besides, most of what was churned out of that second floor newsroom didn't have the kind of flair or color that Thurber preferred, and the editors intended to make sure it stayed that way.

"He was sensitive, keen, and he wrote elegantly, but he wasn't appreciated by either the editor or the managing editor," Thurber colleague and later *Dispatch* editor George Smallsreed wrote in a letter to Kinney. "They liked their news straight with no trimmings. Thurber simply wasn't cut out for newspaper work. He wasn't brash enough, if that's the word."[1]

Nelson Budd, a competitor of Thurber's on the *Columbus Citizen,* had similar recollections in a piece on his old friend for the *Ohio State*

Monthly. He recalled Thurber being upset over one of his *Dispatch* co-workers "relentlessly and callously pressing" the family of a murder victim for a photo and "outraged" over a Statehouse employee who bragged about not missing an electrocution of a prisoner in the Ohio Penitentiary in the last fifteen years even though he had no business being there.

"Despite Jim's later assertions that 'I'm a damned good reporter,'" Budd recalled, "he was really too humane, too creative, too big to be a good reporter in the strictest sense."[2]

Nonetheless, Thurber drew many of the top assignments, a badge of honor for a reporter, and did a good job covering them. He covered Columbus City Council and bragged that he helped get an extra out when City Hall caught fire. He covered the opening of Ohio Stadium, an assignment that over ninety years later would still impress a lot of Columbus residents, and the opening of the James Theater, which qualified as a much bigger deal at the time than it seems today. He covered a clandestine Ku Klux Klan meeting, although he was frustrated by his editors' mismanagement of it. He also got to interview boyhood friend Daniel Ogden Stewart, who was visiting the city after his book *A Parody Outline of History* grabbed a lot of attention elsewhere. He even got sent to New York to review plays.

He eventually got his Sunday page, a kind of column called *Credos and Curios,* which offered him the creative license he coveted. When that was taken away from him after forty-two weeks in December, 1923, for reasons still not entirely clear, that helped convince Thurber that it was time to leave the newspaper—and Columbus. But he admitted years later that he never really left.

"Whenever I'm in the Midwest, I still wake up with a start, wondering what time it is and thinking I have to cover City Hall by one o'clock," he said. "After 36 years, my anxiety dreams are still about the *Dispatch,* where I'm with no paper, no pencils, a typewriter that won't work, Gus (Kuehner) glaring over my shoulder, and the clock frozen at ten minutes to one—with one o'clock the deadline."[3]

CHAPTER 33

An Ink-Stained Dinosaur

The *Columbus Dispatch* library has no file for Norman "Gus" Kuehner, which seems a little odd. Kuehner worked in the newspaper's editorial department for twenty-eight years. During that time, he served as
both city editor and managing editor, status that normally would have
rewarded him with a brown, 6 x 8 inch envelope bearing a few news clippings that illuminate his life.

Kuehner didn't even have an empty envelope with his name on it
among the hundreds in the library filing cabinets. If he had, it might have
been a sign that some absent-minded reporter had borrowed the old editor's life and forgotten to put it back. *No* envelope hints at a deeper
meaning.

"He probably took his file with him when he retired," one of the
paper's librarians said.

It was a good guess—and likely a wrong one. Kuehner probably didn't
have the chance. He was fired in 1936, a sad end to an impressive career.

Kuehner's memorial is really better than a rectangular envelope tucked
away in a library filing cabinet, anyway. He is immortalized in Thurber's "Newspaperman: Head and Shoulders" in *The Thurber Album* as
the prototype for the old-time city editor. The insult-wielding monster
Thurber describes almost with affection is an extinct creature, a cynical,
crime-loving, news-addicted journalist who learned his job by doing it.

Guys like Kuehner once existed on newspaper staffs all over America. He is as much a part of the past as Joseph Pulitzer or Benjamin Franklin now, a grim, ink-stained dinosaur who doesn't fit in a world of carefree people tweeting "news" on their cellphones, laptops, and iPads.

Kuehner's story has two distinct parts. The first is that of uncompromising, hard-bitten newsman who made Thurber's life as a young reporter prone to flowery prose a living hell. The second is a depressing tale of his life after the *Dispatch,* one that starts with a drinking problem and ends with his death of a heart attack at the age of forty-nine. Kuehner may have been born to be a newspaperman, but he died as a laborer at the Curtis-Wright Aircraft plant near Port Columbus International Airport, having written a sister a few months before he died that he still hoped to get hired back by the *Dispatch.*[1]

Kuehner actually had been born into a family of German cigar makers. He grew up with a brother and two sisters in a house at 526 City Park Avenue in German Village, two blocks south of Livingston Avenue and Interstate 70, the southern border of today's downtown Columbus. As a boy, he carried the afternoon *Dispatch* after school, and he had just completed the eighth grade when he landed a job as a copy boy at the paper he had been delivering. He was fifteen.

Longtime *Dispatch* printer Carlton C. Berry remembered when "he was but a kid climbing a ladder to post bulletins on the board at 45 North High Street,"[2] but the kid was deadly serious about working his way into a reporter's position, even at that early age. He worked like a demon, and because he often wore a scowl while performing his duties, one of the editors started calling him "Gus" after a popular comic strip character, Happy Hooligan's brother, Gloomy Gus.

"If Gus has been a dog," one of his friends said, "he would have bitten off his tail to keep it from wagging."[3]

This youthful Kuehner went to work early every day so he could practice typing on the office typewriters and hung out at the police station on Saturdays so he could pick up pointers from the paper's police reporters. Sometimes he even hitched a ride with the cops to the scene of the crime. At sixteen, he asked the paper's city editor to let him cover an electrocution at the Ohio Penitentiary. The editor's refusal didn't quell the copy boy's fascination with death. He dreamed of someday being the *Dispatch* police reporter, and he got there before his 20th birthday. He covered several executions before he became city editor and enjoyed sending newbie reporters to grisly death scenes to see if they had it in them to be newspapermen.

His promotion came with a higher salary and more responsibility. It didn't necessarily come with more happiness. Kuehner aspired to be a police reporter and he never really got over his attraction to violent crime. Deep down, he may have envied the writers he belittled. While an editor's job paid more, the frustration of being chained to a desk may have contributed to Kuehner's mincing manner. One day, he relentlessly rode a rewrite man until the victim tried to stab him with a desk spindle. Kuehner knocked him out.

Probably because he quit school in the eighth grade and came up with through the ranks, Kuehner didn't have much use for college graduates. He liked to say that "You get to be a newspaperman by being a newspaperman" and "You can't learn how by studying journalism in college under a broken down ex-editorial writer for the Hoboken Bugel."[4]

Thurber was quick to point out to his readers—and not to Kuehner—that J. S. Myers, then the head of the Ohio State department of journalism, had been managing editor of the *Pittsburgh Post* and editor of the *Pittsburgh Sun*. It doubtless wouldn't have changed Kuehner's mind if he had. Kuehner saw college journalism professors as failed newspapermen. He believed college graduates needed guidance from a real self-made editor like him to be successful journalists.

Thurber's *Dispatch* colleague George Smallsreed said that "Kuehner seemed to make a point of keeping Thurber's talent under his thumb—of course, he didn't see it as a talent."[5] Yet Thurber doesn't seem to have resented that. Thurber grew to respect Kuehner as an editor and he could identify an interesting character when he saw one, so he probably realized that the caustic city editor would someday be a topic of his writing.

Kuehner seems like a relic from another era today, and even almost a century ago, Thurber probably didn't know anyone else like him. At the urging of Karl Finn, a college chum who worked at the *Dispatch,* Thurber was hired in summer of 1920 by managing editor Charles "Heinie" Reiker while Kuehner was on vacation. But Kuehner had returned by Thurber's first day of work and the new reporter immediately found himself in the city editor's crosshairs. Thurber was sitting in the corner rewriting a few items from the *Lantern,* the Ohio State student newspaper, when Kuehner came in and saw him. He ignored the new hire's pleasant "Good morning," saw what he was doing and swept his copy to the floor. He "growled 'This isn't a college paper,' and strolled away with the grace of a wagon," then let Thurber sit at his desk the rest of the day doing nothing, Kuehner's standard treatment for new college hires.

For Thurber and all new reporters the "practically impossible assignments" came next. "If a new man handled one or two of these successfully, or came back with honorable scars that showed he had tried, the city editor softened a little, like an iceberg in April weather," Thurber wrote. "One cub reporter, sent to get a statement from a hospital patient whose room was closely guarded, borrowed an interne's [sic] white jacket, got hold of a stethoscope, and managed to reach the patient's bedside before he was unmasked and ejected from the hospital by way of the laundry chute. Kuehner thought he had made a good try and grunted something to that effect . . ."[6]

Kuehner assigned nicknames to most of his underlings, names that dripped with sarcasm. Thurber was "Hey" and "You" early in his apprenticeship. He became "Editor" when he Kuehner found out he had been one of Lantern's editors—"he called me "Editor" in a mocking falsetto, shouting the word so that everybody in the city room would hear it"—and became "Author" later when Kuehner discovered that Thurber wrote some of the theatrical material for the Strollers. "Author" was the name that stuck. Kuehner called Maud Murray Miller, who wrote the "Human Progress" column, "Mother." Smallsreed became "Parson" because the thin, bespectacled, man looked like a minister to him. A reporter who grew up on a farm became "Farmer." A former Army lieutenant became "Loot." Many of the nicknames were anything but flattering.

He called the women college graduates the paper hired "slob sisters" and could be especially tough on women who couldn't handle his torrent of insults. The woman who had her shoe snatched off her foot and tossed out the window probably wasn't surprised Kuehner did that or that he was unapologetic about it afterwards. She knew if she whined about it, it would only make matters worse.

Praise didn't come easy for him, either. When Thurber managed to get a photo of a boy who had drowned, an assignment that had gotten the paper's police reporter thrown out of the deceased boy's house, Kuehner surprised him with "What are you, sticky-fingered?" Thurber had actually gotten the group photo from the boy's high school principal, a performance which Kuehner eventually rewarded by giving Thurber better assignments.

It is doubtful that he grew to like Thurber's writing style, however.

"He was always a very wordy kind of a reporter," former *Dispatch* reporter Ruth Young White said, "because he loved words and he knew wonderful, beautiful words. . . . He was always more literary than we were, but we had a city editor who didn't go along with that well because he thought that a newspaper article should be written for people who were not educated and who could understand all of the words that were in the articles. Jim didn't like to write that run of the mine kind of thing. He liked to write the fancier sort of thing so that he and the city editor has a running battle.

"I don't think [Thurber] ever was imbued too much with this accuracy business that we all had been taught. He liked to write and he liked it to sound good. I think Norman Kuehner, the city editor that I was referring to, did help to make him a good reporter."[7]

Thurber described Kuehner as the kind of guy who would snap "Get a watch!" when asked for the time. He wasn't easy to please, especially when a reporter didn't see the world in the same nuts and bolts terms that he did.

"[Thurber] was a meticulous writer and liked to turn in colorful feature stories," Smallsreed said. "Kuehner didn't like them. He'd begin reading one, stand up slowly, rip it in two, say 'I don't like this stuff' and drop it in the wastebasket. Thurber would look like a beaten dog. . . . After six weeks on the job, Kuehner became less oppressive to Thurber and things got better for him."[8]

Thurber wasn't the only reporter to run afoul of Kuehner's rules. Miller wrote a story "about some uplift society" at which the chairman had dropped dead during his address. This was the only part of the story that interested Kuehner and Miller put it the last paragraph of her story. When the city editor read it and told Miller to "Turn this lady upside down," she was furious and began to scream at him. "Don't go around trying to hide bodies in the newspaper, Mother," he said.

Thurber's friend Joel Sayre worked as a reporter for the *Ohio State Journal* at the time and he was blunt in his assessment of the *Dispatch* city editor, calling Kuehner "a sadistic son-of-a-bitch."[9] But several of Thurber's *Dispatch* colleagues thought their friend painted an overly negative picture of Kuehner in *The Thurber Album*. One told Kinney that "underneath that crustiness was . . . a wonderful layer of kindness and humaneness." Maybe, as Kinney wrote, "Thurber just wasn't Kuehner's kind of man."[10] His elegant writing, sensitivity and humor stood in marked contrast to the characteristics Kuehner valued; even though he scored some successes during his three years at the *Dispatch,* some of his colleagues doubted that he was cut out to be a newspaperman.

James E. Pollard, later head of the Ohio State journalism department, worked for the *Dispatch* and the *Ohio State Journal* during this era, and he didn't recognize the man Thurber wrote about.

"I knew Norman Kuehner rather well, I thought," he said. "I began part-time work for the *Dispatch* as early as 1913, which is considerably before Thurber, and I never saw this hard-boiled side of Kuehner which Thurber develops in his chapter on Kuehner in the *Album* book. 'Dutch' was hard-nosed and all that and a great kidder, I thought, but I never saw the almost vicious side of him, the sadist side of him which Thurber brings out in his sketch."[11]

Stories about Kuehner that Thurber left out of his portrait of him in *The Thurber Album* do show that the irascible city editor had a good heart beneath that gruff exterior. On the first day Thurber was assigned to cover City Hall, an ornate building that stood across from the State-house on State Street where the Ohio Theater is today, a fire broke out during a city council meeting he was covering and destroyed the building. Thurber "saved" a large stack of blueprints he thought were irreplaceable, somebody's coat and somebody else's watch, and with the help of the managing editor got out a midnight "extra" about the fire. He had called Kuehner first, and the city editor refused to get out of bed ("Listen, Author, you're on an afternoon paper, remember?") and hung up on him.

For weeks, Kuehner rode him mercilessly about the stuff he "saved" from the fire, calling him "Chief" and asking why he hadn't saved any used carbon paper or rare old thumbtacks. He also gave Thurber a raise from $25 a week to $30 shortly after that. When Thurber approached him for another raise, many months later, Kuehner snapped at him.

"Sure," he said. "Go out and set the Statehouse on fire. That ought to get you another $7.50 a week." Then Kuehner immediately went back to editing copy, as if the matter were closed. But Thurber's next paycheck showed a $10 raise, a sign that the city editor appreciated the work the reporter did, even if he couldn't let anyone within hearing distance know it.[12]

The day Thurber left the newspaper, he wrote that Kuehner "said three things to me." The first, "So long, Oscar," was uttered "sourly," and was a reference to Thurber heading to the New York that Kuehner despised and associated with Oscar Hammerstein. He also said "Good luck, guy," in a low tone, "so that nobody else would hear him." Finally, as Thurber left the city room and headed toward the corridor that held the elevators, Kuehner loudly called out "Hey, Author, bring me a ladyfinger," so that everyone would hear.[13]

The latter was a verbal jab he had often taken at Thurber since he discovered the reporter sometimes stopped at a photo studio not far from the *Dispatch* where some newspapermen gathered to discuss literature and the arts. Tea and cookies were served as these affairs, and Kuehner suspected that a man who drank tea and discussed novels would probably end up in New York City. He hated New York City.

"If a woman screams in front of the post office in New York," he once snapped, "the AP wire carries a whole column on it."

In Kuehner's mind, the male tea drinker could also be capable "of such other feminine vices as running up a pair of dimity curtains or playing with embroidery cloths."[14]

Kuehner's tough guy image might have been more of an act than reality. Thurber admitted that the only time he visited the city editor's home during his time at the newspaper, he didn't find the same surly Kuehner who ruled the newsroom like an oppressive despot. Instead, he discovered a man intensely devoted to his wife, Esther, and two young sons, a man who "seemed oddly relaxed, as if the *Dispatch* were a tight-fitting collar he had taken off at his front door."[15]

The two-story, five-bedroom house at 442 South Drexel Avenue in Bexley Park where the Kuehners moved following its construction in 1922 might have served as the perfect model for a prosperous, happy family. Esther Kuehner's father, John D. Evans, likely built it. Evans was a successful contractor who family members say owned a lot of property;[16] one of his finest moments came in 1900 when he dismantled the stands of a baseball field for the city's professional team on Parsons Avenue on the city's South Side and moved it via Columbus Street Railway System to 512 Cleveland Avenue, where it was reassembled. He renamed it Neil Park after the owner of the land, Robert Neil, and it remained (a steel and concrete grandstand replaced the wooden bleachers later) as the site of professional baseball and football games for over forty years.[17]

The Kuehners lived with him at the Evans family home at 50 North Garfield Avenue following their marriage, and the widower and his housekeeper, Anna Jones, moved into the new house with them when it was finished. In a sweet touch of irony, Jones's son, Johnny, managed local theaters and later became a well-known local columnist for Kuehner's newspaper.

When Kuehner died, his granddaughter, Yvonne Kuehner Grosjean, was only four years old. But what little her father, Norman, told her about him would seem to confirm the *Dispatch* image of him.

"I guess he was a pretty strict man," she said. "My father said he was very tough."[18]

Kuehner actually softened up toward Thurber over the years, even if his caustic manner didn't change. Kuehner once telephoned him during a visit to New York for an editor's convention and asked him "Where do you get your lady fingers now, Author?"[19]

Thurber didn't know it then, but Kuehner was headed for a bad end. Thurber tried to soften it as much as possible in *The Thurber Album*:

> In 1936, [he] gave up his job suddenly, for reasons that have never been clear to me. He had got into a melancholy state, lost weight alarmingly and found it hard to keep his mind on his work. There was a persistent rumor outside the *Dispatch* that the paper had decided that its editors should all be college men. It is easy to see how the great disparager of college men on newspapers might have cracked under such a cruel, ironic blow.[20]

While the explanation sounds plausible, Thurber knew the real story; it had been relayed to him by his friend Smallsreed, who succeeded Kuehner as managing editor: Kuehner had become a heavy drinker and began to miss more and more of his work because of it. Harry P. Wolfe (his brother Robert had died in 1927) tolerated the absences for a while out of loyalty to a loyal employee who had given 28 good years to the paper but knew he had to do something. In January, 1936, Kuehner was offered a year's leave and paid-up round-the-world trip as an opportunity to straighten himself out. Kuehner refused the offer, promised to reform and pleaded for another chance.

Wolfe reluctantly gave it to him and Kuehner stayed on the straight and narrow for a month. Then he went another bender that lasted several days, and when he was asked for an explanation upon his return, Kuehner—likely either hung-over or still under the influence—answered with an obscenity-laced tirade that got him fired.

He went to work on the Alf Landon presidential campaign staff in Chicago that year and then got a job with the Unemployment Compensation Commission, in a building Thurber described as "close to the *Dispatch* and a million miles away." He eventually got the job with Curtis-Wright working the midnight to 8 a.m. shift in aircraft production.

Life wasn't good. His wife, Esther, died in Harding Hospital in 1942 at the age of forty-nine after what was described in the paper as a two-week illness; her death certificate listed "cardiac dilatation" as the primary cause of death. "Chronic alcoholism," scurvy, and pellagra—the latter two being vitamin deficiency diseases sometimes contracted by alcoholics—were also noted among her health issues. Coupled with his own drinking

problems, his wife's death offered more proof that Kuehner's personal life
had also deteriorated away from the newspaper.

In some ways Esther's illness produces more questions than answers
about how his life went horribly wrong. Kuehner wasn't even living in
the family's impressive two-story Bexley home when he died a year later;
after Esther's death, the house was put in son John's name and Esther's
father still lived there with John's family. Kuehner died in a German Village apartment he occupied at 527 City Park Avenue, in a house that like
the South Drexel address had been in his wife's name for years. Oddly, it
lay directly across the street from the house he grew up in.

He was living alone when he suffered fatal heart attack. His body was
discovered because he was filling the bathtub at the time and the water
overflowed, creating a leak in the ceiling of the apartment below him.

Thurber cut to the heart of the tragedy in his profile of Kuehner:

> This was the only item in the story of the death of Norman Kuehner, air-
> craft worker, that would have interested Gus Kuehner, newspaper editor.[21]

CHAPTER 34

Breakfast at Marzetti's

The only things Capitol Square Printing would seem to have in common with Marzetti's restaurant are the address and the four walls, and even those aren't all visible because of the wonders of renovation.

The space at 59 East Gay Street is still the space, though. When you see the before and after photos, and the last look at "before" happened over seventy years ago, you can tell that the dimensions are the same. Marzetti's was once here, all right, and so were all of the fascinating people who ate there. It filled this space from 1919 to 1940, and for the first six years this popular restaurant was located within a block of the city's three daily newspapers. The *Columbus Dispatch*, the *Columbus Citizen*, and the *Ohio State Journal* were clustered in an imaginary triangle around it and newspaper people were drawn to this place. During that period, it also stood less than a half-block from Keith's, the city's top vaudeville theater, so it also drew its share of entertainers. If the walls could talk, they could tell stories that didn't involve reams of paper, company envelopes, and four-color presses. Some of the stories they heard, even the ones they could repeat in the company of ladies, would doubtless be captivating.

You can almost see a youthful James Thurber sitting at one of the tables, telling his newspaper cronies an entertaining tale of an interview that blew up or a story that was butchered by an editor who thought the English language should be celebrated in as few words as possible. When

Thurber worked on the afternoon *Dispatch,* he regularly started his day here with other reporters, before he tackled the streets of Columbus in search of the next big story.

Today Marzetti's is a brand of salad dressing that can be found in most grocery stores. In those days it was a Columbus restaurant that started near the Ohio State campus, expanded into this downtown location on Gay Street where it first started commercially producing its dressings, and finally ended up on Broad Street across from the Statehouse. That's the location that nearly everyone in the city remembers today, including Marilyn Smith, the long-time owner of Capitol Square Printing.

"I've been here for 39 years and I had no idea Marzetti's was ever here," she said.

Smith knows Marzetti's; when it closed in 1972, it had enjoyed a long run as one the best-known restaurants in town. The salad dressing business had long since outgrown the alley side space of the Gay Street location and into a factory on the north side of town.

Smith didn't know that the company made dressing back there, either. Her business had started in that space, behind the space where most of the restaurant had been located until 1940.

"You know, when I started back there—and I was back there nine years before I took the rest of the building—this [storefront space on Gay] was empty most of the time," Smith said. "They kept renting it out to little delis and donut shops, and they would go out of business in the middle of the night. They would gone when I came in on Monday morning, and finally I just said 'I'll take the rest of the building.'

"They ran Gerald Ford's presidential campaign out of this. [Future speaker of the Ohio house of representatives] Jo Ann Davidson ran the campaign out of here. I met her when my shop was back there because I was doing printing for them. It was really great because it was really convenient for them. Bob Cupp, who was a judge, he and his wife worked in here during that time. They weren't married. They were just two kids right out of college. And then they got married and Bob eventually went to the Senate—I do all the work for the Senate—and when he left the Senate, he became a judge."

Columbus city directories show what a colorful life the space has enjoyed: Jehovah's Witnesses, the Lyon & Healy music store, and Pan Ohio Mortgage all occupied the space at various times and it also served as the Ohio headquarters for U.S. Senator John Glenn's campaign for president in 1974.

But if you could pick one moment in time to visit this long, rectangular place, it would probably be one of those mornings when Thurber had the rapt attention of his newspaper colleagues and competitors.

Thurber briefly recalled those days in "Memoirs of a Drudge," a piece that he did for the *New Yorker* in 1942 that was published in book form for the first time in *The Thurber Carnival* in 1945:

> Before going to France, I worked on the *Columbus Evening Dispatch,* a fat and amiable newspaper, whose city editor seldom knew where I was and got so that he didn't care. He had a glimpse of me very day at 9 AM, arriving at the office, and promptly at ten he saw me leave it, a sheaf of folded copy paper in my pocket and a look of enterprise in my eye. I was on my way to Marzetti's, a comfortable restaurant just down the street, where a group of us newspapermen met every morning. We would sit around for an hour, drinking coffee, telling stories, drawing pictures on the tablecloth and giving imitations of the more eminent Ohio political figures of the day, many of whom fanned their soup with their hats, but had enough good, old-fashioned horse sense to realize that a proposal to shift the clocks of the state from Central to Eastern standard time was directly contrary to the will of the Lord God Almighty and that the supporters of the project would burn in hell.[1]

Norman Budd, then a reporter for the afternoon rival *Citizen,* remembered in a 1962 article in the *Ohio State Monthly* that Thurber's best stories were not the ones he printed in the *Dispatch,* but his humorous "versions of city council meetings, or fires, or interviews he shared with the group at Marzetti's."[2]

Ohio State Journal reporter John McNulty, an Irishman from Lawrence, Massachusetts, who had been fired from numerous East Coast newspapers because of his excessive drinking and who later wrote for the *New Yorker,* was another member of the morning Marzetti's crowd and he became one of Thurber's fast friends.

One story Thurber doubtless told was of a brief interview with Columbus native Eddie Rickenbacker, the World War I flying ace and race car driver. One of his editors gave him one question to ask Rickenbacker, and he waited for him to land at the airport. He asked him shortly after he got off the plane.

The question should have elicited a thoughtful answer, but all Rickenbacker said was "I don't think so" and he walked away.[3] Thurber didn't know how to take that, whether it was intended as a negative response, or whether he meant that he didn't intend to answer the question.

Another Thurber tale doubtless involved his "shortest interview on the phone" with Harry M. Daugherty, a local lawyer who talked Warren Harding into running for president and later became his attorney general.

"I asked him some question or other," Thurber wrote later, "and he said 'Go to hell' and hung up."[4]

One can only imagine how the theatrical reporter embellished that tale in relaying it to his newspaper cronies in Marzetti's.

CHAPTER 35

"It's McNulty"

John McNulty slipped into Columbus like a soft, slow-moving rain, a novel approach for a guy who drank and stormed his way through several newspaper jobs in New York City. He was twenty-five going on either fifteen or fifty, too talented not to be offered a job at the *Ohio State Journal* and too impulsive to keep it. He arrived in 1921, in time to stretch Thurber's views on words, women, drinking and nightlife, and they became an almost daily companions and lifelong friends.

McNulty was born and raised in Lawrence, Massachusetts, in a neighborhood of Irish immigrants, a designation that included his parents. His bricklayer father fell to his death while building a chimney when John and his younger brother William were boys, a tragedy that created financial issues for the young family. His mother, a seamstress, changed course when her brothers bought her a small candy store to enable her to support her family.

John's mom was mischievous and witty, a bit of an actress and mimic who often did impressions of customers as soon as they were out of the door. It was one of many things that Thurber and McNulty had in common: performing mothers who bestowed acting talents and a love of attention on their boys. It probably explains why both came to act out stories and anecdotes at parties and in bars, and why Thurber and McNulty, though good friends, often competed for center stage.

McNulty wasn't handsome in a conventional way—his second wife, Faith, even described him that way—but she remembered his blazing blue eyes, true black hair and rough, masculine features that caused everyone to notice him when he entered a room.

He apparently met and got to know Thurber at the photo studio/salon near the *Dispatch* where the more serious Columbus writers hung out, although it could have also happened at Marzetti's restaurant on Gay Street. Faith McNulty, John's second wife, said her husband loved to tell people about those early days when he met Thurber:

> "Jimmy looked up to me," John told me, "because I was a writer from the big city of New York. He thought I must be worldly. He didn't stop to wonder why, if I was so sophisticated, I was there in Columbus, Ohio."[1]

The editors at the *Ohio State Journal* apparently never wondered that, either. McNulty's friends in New York contacted friends at the *Journal* and told them they had a crack New York reporter who might be willing to work there for a little while—they apparently didn't say why—and received a positive response. They escorted McNulty to the train with his pockets empty save a pack of Sweet Corporal cigarettes; he often spoke of how he sobered up during the train ride and realized the pathetic nature of his situation. Thurber claimed that the *Journal* hired McNulty for $60 a week, more than was being paid to any other reporter in town at the time, and in some ways at least, it was money well spent. Thurber wrote that before a year had passed his new friend knew more people in the city than he did, even though Thurber had been born and raised there.

"They included everybody from taxi drivers, cops, prizefighters, and bellboys to the mayor of the city and the governor of the state," Thurber wrote. "He wrote speeches for one successful candidate for governor, and in that, as in everything else, he had the time of his life."[2]

When they met, Thurber was covering city hall for the *Columbus Dispatch* and McNulty was a general assignment reporter for the *Journal,* then on Statehouse Square at 62 East Broad Street. Even though they worked on different papers, the offices were about a block apart. Thurber said he bumped into McNulty nearly every day, often at the corner of Broad and High Streets, the city's main intersection.

> He was invariably excited about something, the cabin lights of the (airship) Shenandoah which he had seen twinkling in the sky the night before, a girl at the James Theatre who sang "Roses Are Shining in Picardy,"

Donn Byrne's novel *The Changelings,* which he demanded I begin reading right away, there on that crowded corner, or a song called "Last Night
on the Back Porch," which he insisted on playing for me, then and almost
there. Actually, he took me around the corner to a music store and began
beating the song out on the first piano he came to, to the astonishment of
the store's staff. "It's McNulty," I explained to them in a whisper, and they
all nodded and breathed his name in unison, obviously believing he was a
great pianist, come to play Memorial Hall, who had suddenly been seized
by a rare moment of relaxation and frivolity.[3]

Moments of "relaxation and frivolity" weren't rare for McNulty, who
was eventually fired for drinking and then hired back when he showed up
at the *Ohio State Journal* offices the next day neat, sober and respectable
and told the editor "I understand there's a job opening."

Thurber became a regular companion on McNulty's drinking adventures, an experience that taught him how to handle the bootleg booze of
Prohibition and also altered his conservative, Midwestern feelings toward
"fallen" women.

Although Thurber and McNulty were the same age and Thurber had
briefly worked as a code clerk in Paris during the war, he needed McNulty's help on both counts. Years later, Robert Kanode, a reporter for the
Citizen in those days, recalled an occasion in 1921 when local officials
invited City Hall reporters including Thurber to a "possum dinner," where
near-beer, moonshine and white lightning were being served:

> For all his wit and worldly references to France, Thurber was extremely
> naïve and unsophisticated in those days. He was the only one at the din-
> ner who had no experience drinking the strong stuff in any amount. He
> was to direct the Scarlet Mask production of *Oh, My Omar!* at the State
> Penitentiary that night after the dinner. When the Mask people came to
> pick him up, they found him standing in the middle of the dinner table
> delivering a speech to the councilmen, who were either too tired or too
> drunk to understand what he was saying.
>
>   A couple of us helped his friends get Jim to the penitentiary, where we
> tried sobering him up by walking him up and down in front of the prison.
> But he got worse. Someone went in to explain the situation to the warden,
> who asked that they put the show on as best they could to avoid a prison
> riot. Another reporter, named McCoy, and I drove Thurber home. His
> parents had obviously never seen Thurber or anybody else in the family in
> that condition, which was a good thing. I explained that the possum had

made him sick and I think his mother accepted it, for all that Jim didn't
act sick. He was singing by then. It's a wonder any of us survived that
Prohibition stuff.[4]

Mame Thurber apparently talked about it for days, blaming the city's
poor government on "those awful possum dinners" that the city council-
men were always eating.

With or without possum, McNulty and Thurber became fast friends.
They found that that they had a lot in common besides their love of writing; competed for the stage wherever they were and loved to stage public
incidents together that amused and befuddled the poor, innocent souls
who happened to stumble across them.

McNulty would sometimes have Thurber approach him on the street
as a Ku Klux Klan recruiter, muttering manically all the while. "We are
looking for likely 100 percent Americans," Thurber would say, "so we can
build up in this city the biggest Kleagle in the country."

"*Klavern*," McNulty would say, correcting him. He would then loudly
proclaim his Irish heritage while an embarrassed Thurber slinked away,
mumbling. Thurber later wrote that "the word got around town that the
local Klan was made up of imbeciles."[5]

It would be fascinating to know the Columbus that McNulty knew.
He spent twelve years in the city, most of them during the Prohibition
Era, and it didn't slow him down. It's safe to say that McNulty knew
every speakeasy and illegal brewer and distiller in town.

Thurber introduced him to Donia Williamson, the sister of Ben, one of
his East High School classmates and Phi Psi brothers at Ohio State, and
she became the first Mrs. McNulty in 1924. She told Harrison Kinney
"John and Jim were a couple of funny guys. They alternately outdid one
another in appreciation of the other's gags."[6]

Thurber left for New York in 1924. McNulty left the *Ohio State Journal*—or maybe he was fired again—worked on and was probably fired
from the *Dispatch* and ended up on the staff of the *Columbus Citizen,*
where he was a crack rewrite man and later the theater critic. Rewrite
men would take a call from a reporter in the field, take in all the facts
and then crank out a compelling, fact-filled story in the time it would
take most of us to decide what to put in the first paragraph. Even when
he was the drama critic, McNulty figured in the coverage of the biggest
news stories, the famous Snook murder case, the Lorain, Ohio, tornado
and the Ohio Penitentiary fire among them. His lead for the ten pages or

so of copy that he turned in after that devastating tornado hit the Lake Erie port of Lorain?

"All hell blew in off the lake."[7]

As good as McNulty's stories were, the stories about him were even better. When he died in 1956, the *Columbus Citizen's* story about him included a tale about McNulty being sent south to a ribbon cutting of a new bridge across the Ohio River. Because the time of the ceremony bumped up against the afternoon *Citizen's* deadline, the office already had a story written and in place before the event occurred and sent McNulty there to make sure everything went as expected. The paper apparently didn't hear from McNulty that day, but three days later received a wire from him from Athens, Ohio, that read: "Please advise what I'm doing here."

He was eventually fired by the *Citizen* for the same old reasons, and he drifted to newspapers in both Cleveland and Pittsburgh where he encountered similar problems. In 1935, Thurber, by then a highly-successful writer for the *New Yorker*, visited Columbus and learned from friends Herman and Dorothy Miller that McNulty had gotten drunk and insulted the guests at a party they had thrown. Thurber spoke to McNulty about it and talked him into going with him back to New York. Thurber paid his train fare, helped him find a job and introduced him to *New Yorker* owner Harold Ross, whom he started lobbying for McNulty's hiring.

At Thurber's urging, McNulty was hired by the *New York Daily Mirror*, a Hearst tabloid whose managing editor, Stanley Walker, recalled the moment in a grateful letter to Thurber in 1957:

> [You] suggested that I hire him. I did so, at $50 a week to start, and he was great from the start. He was at this time, as you may recall, only a step out of the gutter, but he more or less pulled himself together.[8]

McNulty's best days were ahead. He gave up drinking, or at least he tried, got back with his wife Donia, who had left him, and finally got his life on track. He moved to the *New York Daily News* and started contributing to the *New Yorker*; a 1941 short story "An Atheist Hit by a Bus" gained him the national spotlight.

He met the Faith Corrigan, a copy girl at the *Daily News,* that same year. He fell in love with her and eventually divorced Donia, marrying Faith four years later despite a wide gap between their ages. When they met, she was twenty-one and he was forty-six. He had also just started contributing to the *New Yorker* on a regular basis, which became his vehicle to fame. He continued to do that until his death in 1956.

Many of his stories were based on the people he met in Tim and Joe Costello's Third Avenue saloon, a place frequented by many of his writer friends, including Thurber. The place was an old-style saloon, a low-key place with a long, mahogany bar with mirror on the wall behind it, shelves crowded with glasses and a tile floor. It remained that way until the 1950s when McNulty's writings made it famous and tourists and Madison Avenue advertising types started frequenting the place and changed its tone.

McNulty described that with a line in a story that was later attributed to New York Yankees catcher Yogi Berra: "Nobody goes there anymore. It's too crowded."

McNulty worked briefly in Hollywood—he married Faith in Los Angeles—but returned to New York, which was a natural fit for him.

"The days didn't go by for John McNulty," Thurber wrote, "they happened to him. He was up and out at six every morning, wandering the beloved streets and 'avenues' of his city, stopping to talk and listen to everybody. His week was a seven-day circus that never lost its savor."[9]

A book of McNulty's stories called *Third Avenue, New York* was published by Little, Brown in 1946 and got good reviews. A second collection of his stories, *A Man Gets Around,* was published in 1951. Hollywood bought "The Jackpot" which dealt with the problems experienced by a man who had won a radio quiz; besides the *New Yorker,* he also wrote for *Vogue, Holiday,* and *Women's Day.*

Despite his success, McNulty is little known in Columbus today and few traces of him remain in the city where lived for a dozen years. Both of the newspapers he worked at length for are long gone and so is the *Citizen's* building, which was demolished in 1960. It stood just to the south of the Renaissance Hotel on North Third Street. The building which housed the *Ohio State Journal* at 62 East Broad Street, became the home of the *Dispatch* editorial office in 2016 after the paper was sold, but there is nothing that indicates that the *Journal* had ever been published there.

McNulty loved the race track and he was known to frequent Beulah Park, which opened just south of Columbus in Grove City as the first thoroughbred race track in Ohio in 1923. McNulty liked race tracks as much for the characters he met there and the stories they gave him as he did for the $2 bets he placed. But the track closed in 2014 and took its license to Youngstown, where it became Hollywood Gaming at Mahoning Valley Race Course.

Even though few in Columbus know McNulty today, those who knew him in the old days never forgot him. When he died of a heart attack at the age of sixty in 1956, it became obvious that he had left an indelible imprint on the city, or at least on his former newspaper buddies.

Citizen sportswriter Lou Byrer recalled a Saturday night party McNulty attended at the home of one-time *Dispatch* sports editor Bill McKinnon. He wrote that "as midnight approached, John had disappeared and no one could get into the bathroom. Finally someone succeeded in breaking the lock, and there was John, calmly taking a bath. He seemed puzzled that anyone should think it was unusual.

"It's Saturday night, isn't it?"[10]

CHAPTER 36

※

Janitor of the Passing Show

The image would have made a terrific Billy Ireland editorial cartoon. Before the Elizabeth Ireland Graves Foundation donated $7 million to Ohio State University in 2009 to support the renovation of Sullivant Hall, the lone entrance to the Billy Ireland Cartoon Library & Museum lay at the end of a narrow pedestrian alley between Mershon Auditorium and the Wexner Center for the Arts. Staff members joked that the alley's lone garbage can served as the unofficial marker for it.

Fans of Ireland's work would have no trouble conjuring a mental picture of the cartoonist's imaginary drawing of that, possibly a plump, rumpled trash can bearing a caricature of his elfish face next to a caption questioning why a museum for legendary cartoonists can't command a more credible signpost than a garbage can that looked like him.

This is one Ireland battle didn't have to win with his drawings—he died of a heart attack at the age of 55 in 1935. But the sheer size of the donation required to give a fitting home to the museum and a fitting memorial to a talented cartoonist who may never gotten his due without it offers a strong hint at the value of his work. In the 1920s and 30s, Ireland probably could have accomplished as much or more with his drawings in the *Columbus Dispatch* as that $7 million donation did in 2009.

Today, the entrance to the museum is prominent on the north side of Sullivant Hall off a pedestrian mall that used to be 15th Avenue. Ireland's name is carved in a granite block in front of it. That memorial elevated a reputation that shouldn't have needed elevating, a slight that probably wouldn't have mattered much to the Chillicothe, Ohio, native. His lack of respect still represents a miscarriage of justice to those who admired him.

Before his name was attached to what was then simply the Cartoon Library and Museum, Ireland's relatively modest modern fame could be attributed to the fact that he had his own chapter—"Boy from Chillicothe"—in *The Thurber Album,* which was published in 1952. That put Ireland on equal footing with Thurber's parents, his favorite college professors, his ancestors and other important people in his Ohio background.

Ireland probably wouldn't have needed that boost from Thurber if had he been willing to move farther away from his hometown. His long career at the *Dispatch* shows how little that mattered to him. He worked for the *Chillicothe News-Advertiser* when he graduated from high school in 1898 and he fielded offers from newspapers in Columbus, Cleveland, and Pittsburgh. He took the job at the *Dispatch,* in part because Ohio's capital city was only about 50 miles from Chillicothe. After his work appeared regularly in the Columbus newspaper, editors of other big city papers recognized his ability and started to reach out to him, but their inquiries and job offers made no difference. Ireland fell in love with Columbus and developed a fierce loyalty to his adopted hometown. The opportunity to return to Ross County for a visit whenever the mood struck him allowed the *Dispatch* to give him a perk other papers couldn't match.

His southern Ohio roots provided entertaining subject matter for his drawings, especially after he began doing a full page feature called "The Passing Show" in the Sunday *Dispatch* on February 9, 1908. The first one was divided into four sections, one in which Ireland did a caricature of Dr. Karl Muck, conductor of the Boston Symphony that had appeared locally at Memorial Hall; one which depicted the trained monkeys on stage at B. F. Keith's theater; one focused on the local ice-boating fad; and one that dealt with the city's changing weather in several small drawings.

The following week, Ireland's feature morphed into a ten-section page, more typical of what the page would be for the next twenty-seven years. The page often consisted of even more sections, and rarely found itself constrained by boundaries in its commentary, observances, features and humor. That garbage can in the alley would have fit in perfectly.

In 1909 he started to feature the fictional antics of characters from Tick Ridge, a rural Ohio town that lived in his memories of southern Ohio. Uncle Jerry Smudge, Jedge Tish Lybold, Uncle Lafe Newberry, Doc Deniwitz, Tillie Metz, Uncle Willy Brush, and Mert Pettigrew all became part of a regular feature usually called "Jerry and the Jedge" or "The Jedge and Jerry" in the lower left corner of the page. Many of the witticisms Ireland used here were comparable to those of humorist Will Rogers, an Ireland friend and fan. (Rogers sometimes told people "I take two newspapers, the *New York Times* and the *Columbus Dispatch,* for Billy Ireland's page.")[1] Irvin Cobb and George M. Cohan also considered themselves fans, as did many entertainers who regularly played Columbus and got to see Billy's page while passing through.

Ireland portrayed himself as "The Janitor of the Passing Show," and depicted himself as a round figure in a pair of overalls. (Could he have put overalls on that trash can? Absolutely.) He used the immensely popular Sunday feature to promote various causes and endorse political candidates and ballots issues; he highlighted the need for better dams, advocated the cleanup of the downtown area near the Scioto River for the development of a civic center, called for the construction of a new football stadium at Ohio State and so forth.

In their 1980 book *Billy Ireland,* authors Lucy Shelton Caswell and George S. Loomis Jr., wrote that the Ireland was a writer as much as a cartoonist, an image which probably describes what he did as well as any:

> "The Passing Show" can best be understood not as a comic strip, but as a full-paged illustrated column. It was Ireland's vehicle to entertain, inform, persuade, lobby, and criticize, and he used it for these and many other purposes. He reflected ordinary life: annoyance with spring cleaning and troublesome coal furnaces, wonder at the beauty of the seasons, delight when roasting ears were ripe, and disgust at the 'malpractice' of certain tree surgeons. Although the illustrations and dialogue of "The Passing Show" cannot be separated, it was the text which most often conveyed Ireland's idea. It provides a documentary of events of over twenty-five years in Ohio, spiced with Ireland's humor and commentary.

Two of "The Passing Show" originals were on display at cartoon library at OSU's Sullivant Hall as this chapter was being written. The large, 28 x 22 paper sheets he drew on and the intricacies of the drawings and the lettering give the modern browser a peek at what a large weekly undertaking this must have been. (He also drew a daily editorial cartoon and other images for the *Dispatch* in addition the Sunday feature, which is what most modern fans remember.) "The Passing Show" appeared in color similar to today's Sunday comic strips, but Ireland apparently rarely applied color to the drawings. After he inked in his pencil sketches, he took the drawing to another artist who applied water color to the original drawing. Sometimes, Ireland specified which colors he wanted, although Walter Tucker, one of the aforementioned artists, said that Billy usually trusted the younger draftsmen's judgment.[2]

Ireland won many battles, big and small. He waged a campaign to have the log cabin where Ulysses S. Grant was born removed from the Ohio State Fairgrounds, where it has been on display for years, and taken back to its rightful place near Point Pleasant, Ohio.

His May 10, 1935, caption over drawings of the cabin on the Fairgrounds and in an idyllic setting in a park in Point Pleasant reads: "Why not—move the Grant Cabin from the State Fair Grounds where, for one week in the year, it is viewed with other more appropriate Fair attractions—and return it to a shrine in the beautiful hills where it belongs?"

He also played a role in the Republican governor Frank B. Willis' quest for a second term in 1916 against James M. Cox. Willis' consumed forty-eight chicken gizzards at a picnic, and Ireland seized on that demonstration of gluttony as fodder for his cartoons. All through the campaign, Ireland drew an image of Willis' private car followed by a string of boxcars labeled "Chicken Gizzards."[3] Willis lost.

Not all of Ireland's drawing centered on local issues. The Ku Klux Klan was one of his frequent targets, and on October 9, 1921, Ireland spelled out "The Passing Show" header in letters drawn on the chests of hooded figures mounted on horses and a frame on the same page featured a rooster saying to a chicken "Ku-cluck, cluck, cluck! Ku-cluck, cluck, cluck!" The caption under the drawing read "Is this where the name originated?"

Thurber, who once covered a local meeting of the Klan, relished the fact that Ireland took a prolonged public stand against it.

"His ridicule of the Ku Klux Klan in the early twenties was a significant force in the disintegration of the Klan's local Klavern," Thurber wrote. "Klansmen used to stand in full bedsheet regalia, on street corners, with lighted cigars protruding from the mouth-holes in their robes, and Billy's caricatures literally kidded them to death."[4]

More of his work would have found its way into other newspapers if he hadn't spent so much of his time on local topics. While his devotion to local issues didn't do much to enhance his national reputation, it made him a huge celebrity in Columbus and the cities, towns and counties surrounding it. Thurber doubtless knew of Billy Ireland and his work while growing up in Columbus; he was an Ireland fan before joined the

Dispatch staff and became an even bigger one after he got to know him. Ireland fascinated Thurber, both as an artist and as a Columbus celebrity.

He delighted in visiting Ireland's office at the newspaper, as did many *Dispatch* employees, friends, local citizens, and aspiring young cartoonists who wanted advice and a job.

"They were good friends," Joel Sayre said. "I mean, Ireland was extraordinary in that he could sit there at his drawing board and just work away and talk to people. . . . He worked on ["The Passing Show"] and this would take—well, a lot of night work was put in this thing. And he'd be drawing away at this and people would come in and he'd talk to them. And Thurber was a constant visitor there. He was always dropping in to see how he did it and being a doodler and scribbler himself, he loved to watch Bill work with his pen."[5]

Thurber's "doodles" were nothing like Ireland's detailed work, but Sayre thought the sessions still helped Thurber become Thurber.

"Ireland had a funny slant on things and Thurber may have got some poke from that," he said.

In 1925 an Ohio State freshman named Milt Caniff stopped by and asked for a part-time job in the newspaper's art department. Billy challenged him to draw something that would make him laugh and Caniff did, so Ireland got him a part-time job doing layouts for $17 a week. Caniff later drew the popular "Terry and the Pirates" and "Steve Canyon" comic strips that are sometimes featured in the cartoon library named for Ireland.

Billy's door was always open and he didn't stop drawing while he entertained visitors, sometimes spicing the conversation with stories of Ross County. Thurber wrote that he had plenty of them:

> I ran into him one day in 1922, walking along East Broad Street in Columbus, and his face wore the particular Ireland smile that meant he had just heard, or remembered, a good Ross County story.
>
> "This farmer down there," he began, "drove over to a preachers house in Chillicothe one day, with the mother of his five children and the kids themselves, running in age from six months to eleven years. 'Me and Elviry want to git married,' he said. The parson was surprised and said 'These, I take it, are children of a previous marriage.' The farmer shook his head. 'No, they ain't, Reverend,' he said. 'Y'see, me and Elviry's been plannin' to drive over here an' git hitched ever since I met her at the huskin' bee in 1909, but the roads has been too bad.'"[6]

As accommodating as Ireland could be to publicity seekers who wandered into his office with a good story, a blue chicken egg, a potato shaped like a buffalo, or any unusual item they thought might make "The Passing Show," he led a relatively private life. For more than 20 years, he had lunch with his closest friends—Haz and Perry Okey, Ed Penisten, Billy Wolls, Ed Nace, George Eckelberry and Phil Bradford—at the same table in the Athletic Club of Columbus at 136 East Broad Street.[7] He rarely participated in the city's social scene, other than its big social event on fall Saturdays: Billy was a devoted Ohio State football fan.

Ireland undoubtedly would have been popular even if he hadn't been a talented artist. Penisten, a *Dispatch* sportswriter, recalled a day in 1922 when Ireland and President Warren G. Harding were guests at a party at Buckeye Lake, a reservoir thirty miles east of Columbus that had originally built to provide a source of water for the Ohio and Erie Canal. While walking on the dock, they began to scuffle in a good-natured way and both fell in the water.[8] Today the secret service would have gone apoplectic; instead everyone enjoyed a good laugh.

There were lots of them when Ireland was around. Hillsboro, Ohio, native Hugh Fullerton, who rose to national fame as a baseball writer in Chicago and is celebrated as the first writer who suspected that the 1919 World Series was fixed, closed his newspaper career as the sports editor of the *Dispatch* in the late 1920s and early 30s. He was around for some of the best Ireland tales. In a May 29, 1935, story in the *Chillicothe News-Advertiser,* Fullerton remembered a day during the Depression years of the early 1930s when Ireland was stopped by a beggar who asked him for a dime. Ireland told the beggar he was using the wrong approach, and turned up his coat collar and looked desperate as he walked toward a gentleman and held out his hand: "Please, mister, I'm hungry," Ireland said, in a pathetic voice. He walked away with fifty cents, which he gave to the beggar and added 'See what I mean?'"[9]

His cartoonist friends from other cities went out of their way to visit him in Columbus because they knew it would be a good time. His home north of Broad Street at 264 Woodland Avenue on the city's East Side is gone, although the neighborhood still has impressive houses that link to Columbus royalty; artist Emerson Burkhardt and Baseball Hall of Famer Larry MacPhail both lived in homes on Woodland which are still occupied.

"Billy Ireland was one of the most entertaining companions I have ever known," artist H. T. Webster wrote, in a letter to Caswell and Loomis. "I visited him once during Prohibition and old Bob Wolfe (publisher of the *Dispatch*), who had to be away at the time, gave Billy the key to his liquor vault. This struck me as an acid test of affection and esteem, and that we produced no noticeable dent on the stock made us both a little ashamed. Wolfe had fitted Billy's office with a large, ornate and expensive desk, but Billy kept corn in it to feed the pigeons and continued using his battered old drawing table. Wolfe was so devoted to Billy that he was always ordering him to forget his work and take trips with him."[10]

Golf was another one of Ireland's loves and he regularly played with his pal Haz Okey, the longtime Franklin County court reporter. They usually played at the Columbus Country Club, a fine course which opened in 1903, was remodeled by famed golf architect Donald Ross several times between 1915 and 1940, and would someday host the PGA Championship (1964) and two other PGA events.

In October 1915, Billy wrote to his dentist, Dr. Gillette Hayden:

> "Albeit" with my upper and lower maxillaries slowly sluffing away, but in suppliant attitude I beg of you to allow me to "stay away from school" until the rough weather sets in. Please, Miss Mayden! If you knew the heart of a golf nut, you wouldn't refuse me. God never intended man to have his teeth "fixed" in sunshiny weather. I promise to be good just as soon as it rains.[11]

Billy probably loved nature even more than golf. His good friend Edward S. Thomas told Caswell about the time that Ireland and *Dispatch* editor Arthur Johnson Sr. decided to hike from Columbus to Chillicothe, a distance of forty-eight miles. When the dynamic duo reached Yellowbud, about thirty-five miles from Columbus, Ireland's feet were burning. He purchased two gallons of ice cream at a country store, asked for a pail, removed his shoes and socks and plunged his aching feet into the ice cream. Thomas said he didn't know whether they made it to Chillicothe on foot or needed a ride to complete the journey.

The hundreds of trips he made to southern Ohio were only part of Ireland's travel adventures. He visited a family cottage on Cape Cod every summer and often traveled to political conventions, boxing matches, and other national events. In his later years, he featured many of his trips in the "Gypsy Trail" section of "The Passing Show."

His love of travel probably explains why Robert Wolfe once gave Billy a new Packard for Christmas, which probably still ranks as the best Christmas bonus in the newspaper's 147-year history. But Ireland was a Wolfe friend and confidant literally to the end. In 1928, when the newspaper publisher fell to his death at eleven in the morning from the fifth-floor ledge of the *Dispatch* building at 34 South Third Street, Ireland's office was located next to Wolfe's. He is listed as a witness to the accident on his friend's death certificate.

A Fullerton tribute to Ireland for the cartoonist's hometown paper cut to the core of who Ireland was: "He loved Chillicothe and once said to me, 'Hughie, did it ever occur to you that my object isn't to get to New York but get back to Chillicothe?'"[12]

His relative lack of national fame compared to J. N. "Ding" Darling of the *Des Moines Register* and John T. McCutcheon of the *Chicago Tribune,* two friends whose drawings were similar may be as simple as that. The late Preston Wolfe, former president of the Dispatch Printing Company, told Caswell and Loomis that William Randoph Hearst offered to syndicate Ireland's cartoons and proposed setting up a Columbus engraving plant that could produce the plates necessary for the distribution of his cartoons through the syndicate. While there's no definitive word on why Ireland refused, it seems likely that he didn't want to submit to demands that would have altered his lifestyle. He enjoyed playing golf, traveling and roaming the southern Ohio hills, and all of these things may have had to be curtailed if he had gone into syndication. He also might have been forced to put aside his Columbus- and Ohio-based subject matter for more national issues, an approach which clearly didn't appeal to him.

Ireland never won a Pulitzer Prize the way Darling and McCutcheon did, but then they didn't get their names on a cartoon library or have a timeless profile of them written by James Thurber. Time will judge which measure of fame is the most valuable.

CHAPTER 37

From the 'Hood to Hollywood

Donald Ogden Stewart and Elliott Nugent are two of the twenty-three "players" featured on the ObscureHollywood.net website, which carries the subtitle "Neglected Films. Stars of the Past. The Obscure Revisited."

A time traveler from Columbus in the early 1920s would probably find their inclusion odd, but probably no less than the books, stories, and academic papers naming James Thurber one of the great American humorists. When Stewart and Nugent had already left Columbus and achieved a fair measure of national fame, their friend Thurber still worked as a relatively unknown newspaper reporter in his hometown and envied their success.

The Thurber comparisons with Stewart are especially intriguing. They were born eight days apart in Columbus in 1894. They attended Sullivant and Douglas schools at the same time—Thurber was a grade behind Stewart because of the accident with his eye—and both eventually achieved national renown as writers.

Stewart initially wanted to be what Thurber became—a famous humorist—and Thurber aspired to the success that Stewart had as a novelist and playwright. But Thurber ultimately enjoyed the most enduring success of the two, maybe in part because unlike Stewart he wasn't captured by Hollywood and sidetracked by politics.

While they shared the same hometown and many childhood memories, their backgrounds and view of life were remarkably different. Stewart's Harvard-educated father was a prominent Columbus lawyer and judge and young Don coveted a place in high society. He eventually went to private school at Phillips Exeter Academy in Exeter, New Hampshire. He got a summer job with the Citizen's Telephone Company as a favor from the company president, local business titan Frank Davis, who was a friend of his father. He graduated from Yale.

Like Thurber, Stewart might never have become a successful writer if fate hadn't intervened. He embarked on a business career after graduating from college, hoping to land a position that would eventually command a large salary and secure a high social position before realizing that a career as a writer called to him.

His early memories of his hometown were similar to Thurber's: The cast of characters and near-constant fighting at Sullivant School; the ten-acre Statehouse yard "full of squirrels and statues of Civil War heroes"; the O. P. his parents talked about in hushed tones (which he later learned referred to the Ohio Penitentiary); "the Lazarus Bros. store on High Street where you got a free baseball and bat whenever you bought a new suit"; the twelve-story Wyandotte Building ("the only tall building in town") where his father had an office; Hatton's Drug Store on High Street ("where I had my first ice cream soda"); The Exhibit movie theater/nickelodeon at High and Long ("I wasn't supposed to go to it, although I sometimes did"); "the exciting whistles from the trains in Union Depot"; Dobbie's Dry Goods store on High Street across from Lazarus "with its cashboxes whizzing by on overhead wires"; Tommy West's saloon on Long Street "out of which came exotic odors and an occasional (terrifying) drunk"; and Olentangy Park, a far north side amusement park accessible by trolley, where "there was everything a young heart and stomach could wish."[1]

Gilbert and Clara Stewart and their three kids—Bert, Anne, and Don—lived in "a six- or seven-room apartment" on the fourth floor of The Normandie, an apartment-hotel at 259 East Long Street that stood only a short walk from the center of town, and the family "took our meals in a large dining room on the top (seventh) floor." The Stewarts were much better off than the nomadic Thurbers, who moved from one rented house to another during this time period. Gilbert Stewart became a judge and belonged to the exclusive Columbus Club; by Thurber standards, the Stewarts were well-to-do. But at that point, their "wealth" didn't include their own house or even a car.

"There were few automobiles," Stewart wrote, "we couldn't afford a horse and carriage from Fred Atcheson's nearby Gay Street livery, and (the) streetcar rides were sheer joy."[2]

His first memory of Thurber is from recess at Sullivant, while Stewart was "hitting Beans Horne in the stomach" behind the school's outdoor toilets. Thurber's second wife, Helen, later recalled how Don had told her husband in the 1950s that he became a Marxist when he was beaten up by a bully at Sullivant and suddenly understood what it was like to be persecuted. Thurber, who thought of Don as the kid who "always owned the ball," had a different memory of the incident when his friend reminded him of it decades later.

"But Don," he said, "you *won* that fight."[3]

When Stewart was eight, he transferred to Douglas School "way out on 17th Street near Broad Street in the fashionable East End (that) necessitated a walk of over a mile each way." He wrote that why his parents moved him there "was never clear to me," but surmised they thought it was a better school in a better district.

"This may have been the beginning in me of a sense of class distinction," he wrote, because "most anybody who was anybody lived on or near East Broad Street." He admitted that "when I started at Douglas school, I gradually shifted my sights from the alleys and vacant lots around The Normandie to the grassy yards of East Broad."[4]

His sights shifted in other ways as well. The Stewarts soon moved from the Normandie to a house at 916 Madison Avenue so now he *lived* near East Broad Street. He attended East High School, which would become Thurber's alma mater, but some of the older students made fun of him and he grew to hate it. Stewart longed to be a star on the school's football team and made no impression. Even though many regarded East as the best of the Columbus high schools, Don was miserable. He "broke down" in a candid talk with his mother and told her how unhappy it made him to be such a "failure."

The next summer (1909), it thrilled him to learn that he had been accepted into Phillips Exeter Academy. This offered him the kind of opportunity he wanted, a chance to receive the best education possible at an exclusive Eastern school, to meet the right people and maybe even become an important lawyer like his father. He described himself as a "resolutely mediocre young man" until an English teacher suggested that he apply for the editorial board of the school newspaper, and after he surprisingly succeeded in getting named to it, he was chosen as the paper's managing editor for his senior year.

This small success, coupled with a friendship with a Yale-bound student, would eventually give him the confidence and desire to take his talents to New Haven. When his father was indicted for the theft of $2,000 while he was a judge, the scandal threatened to thwart him; his father was broke, his brother Bert urged him to give up the idea of attending Yale and take a job at the gas company and Don had to secure loans to stay in school.

Don went all-in on Yale and became less and less enamored with his hometown. He still returned home in the summer, but Thurber wasn't one of the Columbus pals Don hung out with when he returned and they might never have become close as adults if they hadn't both been so interested in writing.

However, Stewart experienced a few false starts as a businessman before he got there. Frank Davis got him a job interview with the American Telephone and Telegraph Company in New York, which excited him because he thought it would give him a chance to work and live in Manhattan. Instead, the company hired him and immediately dispatched him to Birmingham, Alabama, where he wasn't paid like a business-titan-in-waiting at $15 a week. The company transferred him to Pittsburgh and then Chicago, and after he had a brief stint in the Navy during the war, he went back to AT&T and got transferred to Minneapolis for a promotion to chief clerk.

While he had expected his next transfer to get him to New York, this still qualified as a nice promotion and it worked out better than he could have imagined. A friend of his in the Twin Cities introduced him to a St. Paul native and former Princeton student named F. Scott Fitzgerald. His new acquaintance told him he about a new novel he had just written, and "I got him to lend me a cardboard box full of *This Side of Paradise,* written in pencil."[5] They spent a lot of time together, discussing poetry and writing, pondering the frustrations of love—Fitzgerald has just broken off a relationship with Zelda Sayre, his future wife—and at times, drinking heavily. Fitzgerald filled an "educational void" created when Stewart had moved away from his Yale friends, and it wouldn't be long before their new friendship paid dividends.

While he was in Minneapolis, Stewart began to realize the business world might not be for him. He took one more real fling at it when he met a Yale grad named Harold Talbott Jr., who had made huge profits during the war manufacturing planes for the U.S. government. Talbott offered him a job in Dayton at twice his salary and he took it, only to become disenchanted when he discovered that Talbott didn't have much for him to do. So he quit his job in November, 1920, at the age of twenty-six. After a brief stop in Columbus to deposit his mother (who had been living with him) he went to New York to look for a job.

By this time, Fitzgerald's novel had been published by Scribner's and become immensely popular. He had married Zelda and moved to New York. When Stewart got there, his friend got him an interview at *Vanity Fair*; the guy who interviewed Stewart liked him, but said he didn't have a job for him. This wasn't the dead end it seemed to be: The editor asked for a sample of Stewart's writing that he might use to base a recommendation of him to other publications, and sensing that this presented an opportunity that he couldn't afford to miss, Stewart agonized over the possibilities.

He finally decided to do a parody of a Theodore Dreiser piece. The editor loved it, the magazine published it and his writing career suddenly showed promise. He sold another article to *Vanity Fair* and started to find other outlets for his work. He scored a hit in 1920 with *A Parody Outline of History,* a satire on H. G. Wells's *The Outline of History,* and when he stopped to Columbus in 1924 on a lecture tour, Thurber "interviewed" him for the *Dispatch.*

"Jim and I, with the aid of some bootleg whiskey, devised a 'crazy humor' interview which seemed screamingly funny to us at the time," Stewart wrote. "He listened very appreciatively to my stories about Benchley and Dorothy Parker, and I'm sure I must have given him some fatherly advice about how to succeed as a humorist (he was born six days [actually eight] after I was.) At any rate, the next time I heard of him was two or three years later when Benchley and Dorothy began telling me about the wonderful stuff he was writing for the *New Yorker.*"[6]

Thurber had some catching up to do. Because of Stewart's association with Benchley and Parker, who were editors at *Vanity Fair* when he started working there, he started having lunch with a group of writers in the dining room at the Algonquin Hotel. The group became famous as the Algonquin Round Table. Besides Benchley, Parker and him, the other regulars in the group included Robert E. Sherwood, Alexander Woollcott, Heywood Broun, Harold Ross, Edna Ferber, Ruth Hale, Franklin Pierce Adams, Jane Grant, Neysa McMein, Alice Duer Miller, Charles MacArthur, John Peter Toohey, Marc Connelly, George S. Kaufman, Beatrice Kaufman, Frank Crowninshield, Ben Hecht, Lynn Fontanne, Alfred Lunt, and Ina Claire.

Don Stewart was on a roll. After meeting Ernest Hemingway during a trip to Paris in 1924, he, Hemingway and a group of friends traveled to Pamplona, Spain. The trip inspired Hemingway's classic novel *The Sun Also Rises* and Stewart provided the basis for the character of Bill Gorton.

Stewart enjoyed more success with the novel *Mr. and Mrs. Haddock Abroad* in 1924, wrote *The Crazy Fool* in 1925, and adapted his own book, *Brown of Harvard,* as a film in 1926. Fellow Yale grad Philip Barry wrote the part of Nick Potter in the 1928 play *Holiday* with Stewart in mind and didn't have to try too hard to convince his friend to star in the play on Broadway. Stewart made other appearances as an actor during this period, some in concert with Nugent. Meanwhile, Thurber had started working at the *New Yorker,* which gave them an opportunity to rekindle their friendship. They shared many of the same friends.

Stewart recalled his "reunion" with Thurber one evening at Tony's in Manhattan in the late 1920s that hints at the way things were. During Thurber's interview of him in Columbus, the alcohol had helped lead them into a stirring rendition of *The Old Mill Stream* and alcohol worked its magic again:

> The reunion once more was a joyful one and once more included *The Old Mill Stream,* in which Robert Benchley and Dorothy Parker enthusiastically joined. Sometime around three in the morning Thurber, beginning to worry that (first wife) Althea might think he was out somewhere drinking, departed in the direction of home.
>
> Three minutes later, he was back at our table, with what might be described as a rather exalted look on his face. "Elephants," he announced happily, in the same awed tone in which one might report one's first impression of the cathedral at Chartres or a performance by Eleonora Duse. "Elephants . . . walking west along 52nd Street, holding each other's tails." We welcomed his seemingly imaginative contribution to our own crazy world with enthusiasm; it was only when he appeared doubtful that Althea would accept this as an excuse for his late return that we went to the door and witnessed a procession of Ringling Brothers animals on their way from the New York Central railroad yards to Madison Square Garden, where the circus was to open the following Monday.

Stewart summed this bizarre occasion succinctly. "Thurber's world was like that," he said.[7]

Stewart's world changed dramatically when he moved to Hollywood in 1930. Over the next several years he worked on twenty-five films including several in a short time period. But no matter where they lived or how much success either of them enjoyed, Thurber always seemed to be on the fringe of Stewart's life. In 1935, when Thurber was about to make Helen Wismer his second wife, she recalled a chance meeting with his old friend:

> Just before the wedding day, Jamie and I were at 21, where we ran into Don Stewart. When we told him we were going to be married, he insisted on being best man and even giving us the wedding. We said no, Bob Coates was the best man and my father was giving us the wedding, but Don, ever the pixie, alerted the press. As soon as we arrived in Colebrook, an hour before the wedding, my mother nervously started to serve us Heublein Manhattans. We were already hung over from the night before at the Coateses. I had the worst hangover of my life. During the ceremony, the phone kept ringing—it was Don Stewart's press calling—and when somebody finally took the receiver off the hook, the telephone company put a howler on it, so we had that for background music. We were all slightly hysterical and very hung over. When my father pronounced us man and wife, Jamie burst into tears. My father said to me afterwards: "What kind of man is this?" I honestly didn't know what to answer.[8]

The same question could have been asked about Stewart. If he sometimes felt guilty for eschewing literary works for Hollywood, that changed when he read *The Coming Struggle for Power* by John Strachey and converted to socialism.

"It suddenly came over me that I was on the wrong side," he wrote. "If there was this class war as they claimed, I had somehow got into the enemy's army. I felt a tremendous sense of relief and exultation. I felt I had the answer I had been so long searching for. I now had a cause to which I could devote all my gifts for the rest of my life."[9]

Stewart and Dorothy Parker met former Berlin journalist Otto Katz in 1936 and he told them about the disturbing events in Nazi Germany. They decided to join a group of entertainers concerned about the growth of fascism in Europe and establish the Hollywood Anti-Nazi League. Stewart eventually joined the American Communist Party and also became president of the League of American Writers, an organization that attempted "to get writers out of their ivory towers and into the active struggle against Nazism and Fascism."

His wife, Beatrice, didn't approve of his political activities and decided to leave him, about the same time he was falling in love with writer Ella Winters, the widow of muckraking writer Lincoln Steffins. This time

Stewart had found a woman who shared his politics. They were married in 1939.

Stewart continued to work in Hollywood throughout this period. His films included *The Prisoner of Zenda* (1937), *Holiday* (1938), *Marie Antoinette* (1938), *Love Affair* (1939), *The Night of Nights* (1939), *Kitty Foyle* (1940), and *The Philadelphia Story* (1940), which won him an Oscar for best screenplay.

But his politics began to interfere with his career. Stewart started working with I. A. R. Wylie, who had just published a novel entitled *Keeper of the Flame* in 1942. The book had been inspired by the activities of Charles Lindbergh and the America First Committee. But when the film, which starred Spencer Tracy and Katherine Hepburn, was screened for the Office of War Information's Bureau of Motion Pictures on December 2, 1942, Bureau chief Lowell Mellett disapproved of its anti-capitalist message.

Metro-Goldwyn-Mayer head Louis B. Mayer felt the picture equated wealth with fascism and according to Stewart, "walked out in a fury" of the New York City premiere when he realized "what the picture was really about."

Undeterred, Stewart continued to write film scripts, including *Forever and a Day* (1943), *Without Love* (1945), *Life with Father* (1947), *Cass Timberlane* (1947), and *Edward, My Son* (1949). But when the House of Un-American Activities Committee (HUAC) began investigating the entertainment industry after World War II ended, it's not surprising that Stewart was a target. He was one of 151 actors, writers, and directors listed as members of subversive organizations and blacklisted until they appeared in front of the committee and convinced its members they had completely renounced their radical past.

The "blacklist" convinced Don and Ella Stewart to move to England, where they spent the rest of their lives. They rented a house owned by Ramsay MacDonald, and Hepburn, a close friend from their days in Hollywood, helped the Stewarts renovate it. She wrote an introductory note for Stewart's 1975 autobiography.

In the spring of 1955, the Thurbers went to Europe for the first time in eighteen years, stopping in Paris first and visiting Elliott Nugent and his wife, and then going on to England, where Thurber wanted to visit several old pals including Stewart and former Time editor T. S. Matthews and his wife, Martha Gelhorn, whom the Thurbers had met when she was Hemmingway's wife.

The Thurbers also visited the Stewarts again in June 1958, when he planned to work on his play about *New Yorker* founder and editor-in-chief Harold Ross there. Thurber's letter to Stewart from Paris on October 14, 1958, shows how much fun they must have had reminiscing about old friends—and how connected they all were.

Thurber told of a night when he and Stewart's old pal, F. Scott Fitzgerald, drank for hours and "Fitz" had asked him for a "good girl" they could call on. Helen, Thurber's future wife, said "no" when he phoned her ("You and Fitzgerald both? You must think I'm crazy"), and Thurber's sometime flame Ann Honeycutt did, too. Finally, Paula Trueman took them in. "All he wanted to talk about was Zelda," she said.

Thurber mentioned that Thomas Wolfe had "broken Fitzgerald's record by arriving at our apartment in New York at 6 p.m. and staying until 9 a.m. . . . Scott later wrote to his daughter 'Wolfe's secret leaks out at every seam—he had practically nothing to say.' Ross said the same thing about (Alexander) Woollcott, but added 'and he says it all the time.'"[10]

Even Ohio State got a call in that letter to Stewart, although it served mostly as a foil for Thurber's humor:

> You have not asked for information about Ohio State University, probably through an oversight. So here are the facts: O.S.U. has not developed a writer since Nugent and Thurber, but it has found out how long a bee can live in a vacuum and how to cure soft foot in swine. They are now working on crab apple scab, but so far have succeeded only in spreading the disease to the cows and horses in the animal husbandry building. Professor Neff has sued the university on the ground that he has crabapple scab, too, but his wife says he always says that. Jesus, Don, I wish that Bob (Benchley) were here to get in on this. How do we keep on going without that laugh of his?[11]

Thurber closed its letter to his expatriate friend with a story about recently being introduced to a former underground agent who had been captured by the Germans during World War II, whose first words to Thurber were, "You are a Deke, I believe." Thurber told him he was mistaken, but that his friends Don Stewart and Jap Gude were and that Gude was at Brown when the agent was nearby in Vermont.

You can almost see Thurber chuckling when he penned his last line:

> You may now know the expression, but in America we often say "It's a small world." What do *you* often say, as Noel Coward would put it?

CHAPTER 38

The Boy
Thurber Put in Hysterics

Joel Sayre knew Thurber about as long as anyone outside of his immediate family, and he remained a loyal friend to him until the end.

He got to know Thurber as a boy at that ball field behind the Ohio School for the Blind on Parsons Avenue, not as players but as neighborhood spectators at games played by a team of the school's employees Thurber later immortalized with his tale about the "Blinkies."

The local boys played there too, but Thurber was six years older than Sayre and he couldn't play because of his eyesight; hence, it isn't surprising that Sayre didn't have a vivid recollection of the first time he met him. He was more concerned with his Thurber's older brother, Robert, the baseball star on those early fields of dreams.

Sayre didn't go to school with any of the three Thurber boys. Robert was the youngest of the three and he was four years older than Sayre—William was seven years older—and the star-struck kid sometimes came to their house to hang around with him. In order to avoid the tough atmosphere at Sullivant School, Sayre's parents sent him to Columbus Academy, a "a country day school that had just started up . . . on the outskirts of town.

"This building was kind of a nice colonial style structure," Sayre remembered. "It had been the biggest brothel, I guess, between New York and Chicago. This was a very famous brothel called Madame Jesse Brun-

er's Palace of Love. I think it finally got shut down because they'd begun
to introduce animals into some of their exhibitions.

"We moved into this school. I think the first faculty there had three
on it, including the headmaster. It was, on the whole, a most enjoyable
place. I got to know a great many kids from various parts of Columbus.
Some of them were rich kids, some of them were just, I don't know, lower
middle class. There were no poor kids there."[1]

But boys from all schools and all ages were drawn to the parks, and
the Thurbers and Sayres lived in the same general area of the east side of
town, even if they were miles apart financially.

Sayre's father, Joel G. Sayre Sr., was a partner in a glass company
(W. R. Jones and Co.), and the family lived near the rich and powerful
at 558 East Rich Street. Allen G. Thurman, former Congressman, U.S.
senator, chief justice of the Ohio supreme court, and candidate for vice-
president with Grover Cleveland in 1888 (he lost that year after winning
1884 and before winning again in 1892), had lived a few houses down on
the other side of the street. He died six years before young Joel was born,
but his parents knew the Senator well, and the Thurbers and the other
East Side boys played baseball and football on the spacious grounds that
surrounded Thurman's sprawling home. Harry Daugherty, who would
serve as U.S. attorney general under Warren G. Harding, and Dr. Samuel
B. Hartman, whose famous Peruna elixir made him millions, lived two
blocks away on Town Street. The three-story mansion of local brewer
Louis Phillip Hoster stood directly across Rich Street from the Sayres'
house, and it made quite an impression on young Joel:

> We lived a couple of blocks down (from the Blind School). Rich Street was
> a quiet street, so we used to play ball right out in the street. There was not
> much traffic generally. So we were playing ball and I was in center field.
> This was then a cobble street.
>
> There was only one authentically rich person, and that was a brewer
> named Hoster who lived right across the street from us. This was an old
> man and old woman. . . . They had horses, and they had coachmen with
> sort of stiff hats with cockades on the side. All the servants were German.
> Yes, this was quite a place. They had Hoster's beer there. . . . They had an
> immense sidewalk, the only big stretch of sidewalk in the neighborhood.
> This house took up almost three-fourths of the block. It was a really big
> one. We lived across the street.[2]

Sayre described the rest of the neighborhood as "middle-class, nobody was rich, nobody was poor," although "the Lutheran clergyman" who headed the family next-door was apparently the president of a Lutheran school he described as "just a little tin-pot place" called Capital University. This all may have seemed middle class to Sayre; then again, he recalled that his mother "had a long succession of German and Hungarian girls" who cooked and cleaned her house, a horse and a couple of carriages and a German coachman named August. He also attended a private school. Rich and poor are relative terms. If the Sayres weren't rich in the Hoster-Hartman sense, a lot of people whose incomes categorized themselves as middle class doubtless would have envied their position.

The Thurbers sampled that world only when they stayed with the Fishers on Bryden Road, but all of their many rented properties were in the same general area on the near east side. The kids in that area spent a lot of time on both the Thurman property and the blind school grounds, and Sayre and the other boys frequently attended the baseball games played by the blind school team that Thurber later wrote a funny tale about in *My Life and Hard Times*.

"This team was not made up of blind boys, but of people who worked at the blind asylum," Sayre said. "And they would have these games every Saturday on the blind asylum grounds on the ball field there. Jim has written a very funny piece about these games and the strange field they played on. I think that's where I first got to know him and then I used to see him frequently at the ball games and football games we used to have on the grounds of Senator Thurman.

"At those two places, there were all kinds of sporting events going on which the kids in the east end of town where we lived participated in. Jim Thurber was six years older and Robert was I guess about four. There's a great difference there, but I used to tag along. In those days, Robert was the most attractive of the Thurber brothers. He was very good looking. He was a terrific baseball player. He was a very good fighter. And he did all sorts of juggling tricks and was quite a hero among the kids. Well, that's where I used to see them. And both of them, but Jim particularly used to talk to me, and he found out he could make me laugh very easily. He could give me hysterics, put me in hysterics of laughter."[3]

While that was the beginnings of the Thurber-Sayre friendship, both moved on. It wasn't until the early 1920s when both ended up as reporters on competing Columbus newspapers that their paths merged.

The routes that brought them there couldn't have been more different. When America entered World War I, Thurber couldn't enlist in the Army because of his lost eye. Governor James M. Cox took a personal interest in Sayre and encouraged him to join the U.S. Army, but he was refused because of his age. He subsequently secured a fake birth certificate and succeeded in joining the Canadian Army and was sent to Siberia with its Expeditionary Force.

After the war he earned a degree in literature at Oxford University in England and briefly studied medicine at Heidelberg. He began his writing career doing features on the Methodist Church's tercentenary anniversary special section for the *Ohio State Journal* and became the paper's police reporter at the same time Thurber was covering City Hall for the *Dispatch*. Sayre said that was the first time he really got to know Thurber.

"I was just a cub reporter," Sayre said. "I wasn't any good. Thurber was much better than I was. He was a very good reporter, and it was a pity he wasn't on our paper because he would have been much more appreciated. . . . He would have been much better off on the *Journal*."[4]

Sayre felt this way because Thurber's early hero, Robert O. Ryder, edited the *Journal* and appreciated fine writing. Thurber worked for city editor Gus Kuehner, who was irritated by it. Sayre's older sister married *Dispatch* cartoonist Billy Ireland, a colleague and good friend of Thurber, another example of how small Columbus was. If you lived on the same side of town or worked in the same business, there was a pretty good chance that you knew each other.

Ironically, the Thurber-Sayre friendship flourished away from Columbus, after their writing careers led both of them to New York. Sayre worked briefly as a sportswriter for the *Boston Herald* and then became a reporter for the *New York World* and *New York Herald-Tribune*. After a stint on the *New York Post,* Thurber worked for the *New Yorker,* and Sayre became a contributor to the magazine.

Sayre specialized in crime reporting and his career blossomed. He covered the career of the notorious criminal, John Thomas "Legs" Diamond, and wrote *Rackety Rax,* a satirical novel about gangsters muscling in on college football. Sayre married *New York World* reporter Gertrude Lynahan shortly after that and they moved to Bermuda in the spring of 1932, where he wrote *Hizzoner the Mayor,* about two corrupt New York mayors.

When Thurber got the news that the movies had paid a thousand-dollar option on *Rackety Rax,* the family (including baby Rosemary) went to Bermuda for a month to help the Sayres celebrate. The two old friends enjoyed singing together and knew all of the barbershop harmonies. Sayre later remember an evening when Joel, Gertrude, Thurber and *Herald-Tribune* sportswriter Don Skene made up an all-night signing quartet.[5]

During the mid-thirties Sayre went to Hollywood to serve as a screenwriter on several films including *Annie Oakley, Gunga Din,* and *The Road to Glory*. On the latter film he collaborated with novelist William Faulkner.

He served as a foreign correspondent for the *New Yorker* during World War II, covering the Persian Gulf Command which supplied the Soviet Union with munitions through Iran. His articles were later collected and reproduced in his book *Persian Gulf Command; Some Marvels on the Road to Kazvin*. In 1945 the *New Yorker* sent him to Germany to cover the last phases of the war in Europe. His book, *The House Without a Roof*, about a Jewish family in the Third Reich, resulted from his experiences there. He continued to write for the *New Yorker* and other magazines after the war, lived in London for a time and finally took a teaching position at the Annenburg School of Communications at the University of Pennsylvania in 1960. He retired from teaching in 1971, eight years before his death.

He would be a good friend of Thurber's until he died in 1961, drinking with him in New York, visiting him when the Thurbers lived in Connecticut and supporting him as his blindness and illnesses worsened. He became a vocal critic of Burton Bernstein, when the *New Yorker* writer penned a biography of Thurber in 1975 that Sayre believed focused on his friend's problems and totally missed the mark in characterizing him:

> From my point of view, for my money, Bernstein's slams on Thurber were absolutely wrong. He took up Thurber when he was a sick man with a brain tumor and thyroid troubles. And anybody would be, shall I say, "trying" under those conditions. That wasn't the real Thurber at all. And everybody who'd known Thurber when he was right still loved him, I think.
>
> (Another) thing I disagree with very much . . . Thurber is painted by Bernstein as a boy who had a miserable childhood and who grew up very insecurely and was very unhappy. And his humor was an escape from this. And then also his mother and his first wife Althea were two dominating women and they whooped his character around. I think it's all too glib. I knew Thurber during his childhood. I don't think he was miserable at all. He seemed to me to be a very happy kid. He and his two brothers were very merry characters, especially Robert. And they were always having laughs. . . . The whole approach seems to me to have been mean. He made

up his mind that Thurber was no-good, a son-of-a-bitch, and then he used
everything he could find to prove this point, you know?[6]

Sayre was very protective of Thurber's reputation. He was one of the
few people who knew him well from boyhood to old age, so he had a
perspective on his old friend that few shared.

"I think of Thurber as two Thurbers," he said. "When I knew Thurber
first, well, that is after we both had long pants on, he didn't drink too
much, he was warm, generous, tremendously responsible. Thurber was
in those days, and I'm talking about the twenties, Thurber was always
worrying about getting his mother's life insurance paid up. He looked
after not only his wife, but he looked after his mother and I think he
looked after Robert most of his life and helped William out with his problems. He was always not only giving, but worrying about other people's
troubles."[7]

Sayre knew Thurber better than most, and he proved to be a good
friend to the end.

The Thurber family at their Gay Street house in 1936. From left: Robert, Charles, Mame, William, and James. (James Thurber Papers, Rare Books & Manuscripts Library of The Ohio State University Libraries)

LATER MATTERS

Going Away and Coming Home

*W*hen Thurber returned to Columbus after spending time in Paris as a code clerk during and after World War I, he found a job as a reporter with the *Columbus Dispatch*—and a new social life. Thurber had been involved with the Strollers and Scarlet Mask theatrical groups while he was in school, and even though he was no longer an Ohio State student, he continued that association.

He still had hoped for a career as a playwright, and wrote, directed and acted in musical comedies for the Scarlet Mask. There he became reacquainted with photographer Ray Lee Jackson, another budding playwright, and met Althea Adams, who would become his first wife. Jackson worked in Al Callen's photo studio in the Civil War era Gwynne mansion downtown, and Thurber and Adams were among those who attended Bohemian teas there in the afternoons.

When Thurber and Adams decided to get married, Adams' mother—a professor at OSU—chose the historic Trinity Episcopal Church on the other end of the block from Callen's for the ceremony, and Jackson was part of the wedding party.

Herman Miller, who had gone to school with Thurber and become a faculty member in the OSU English department, and his future wife, Dorothy, also became part of the Thurbers' social world. They would remain close friends and confidants long after he left New York. Miller also had his eye on a career as a writer, and Thurber visited him and his wife on nearly every trip to Columbus.

During most of those visits, Thurber stayed in the Deshler Hotel, the city's most elegant hotel since its construction in 1916 at Broad and High. Even after his mother and brother moved into an apartment in the Great Southern Hotel and lived there for many years, Thurber stayed at the Deshler on his trips home.

Ted Gardiner was another friend Thurber also made time for on his trips home. Gardiner had also attended OSU, but Thurber became close to him during the early 1920s, and he and Althea socialized with the Gardiners after they were married.

The Gardiners would continue to be close to Thurber in his later years, after Herman Miller had died and Dorothy Miller had moved away. Ted Gardiner was there the 1960 night that *A Thurber Carnival* opened in the Hartman Theater, which had been the site of some of those Scarlet Mask productions Thurber wrote and participated in.

At that point Thurber had only twenty-two months to live. After he died, Thurber's ashes were buried at Green Lawn Cemetery and Thomas Meek, another friend from his childhood days on the city's East Side, was one of the mourners. Meek belonged to the same fraternity as Thurber and worked with Thurber on the *Ohio State Lantern,* although he didn't pursue a writing career.

Meek became a stockbroker in New York and managed Thurber's assets for most of his life—and afterwards. As a member of the OSU development fund board, he spearheaded the effort to acquire Thurber's manuscripts, letters, and other material for the school—rare pieces now known as the Thurber Collection.

CHAPTER 39

•

Shooter of the Stars

A researcher on the trail of a radio or movie star from the 1930s or 1940s might encounter a chance meeting with Ray Lee Jackson. As photographer for the National Broadcasting Company during that period, Jackson took hundreds of portraits of famous and not-so-famous performers, many of which have landed in the Library of Congress. His name pops up on pictures all over the Internet—with few clues that he once inhabited Thurberville.

Jackson was born in 1890, four years before Thurber, and grew up in Columbus in a family of junk dealers. He lived most of his early life in the family home at 1157 East Long Street. His grandfather started W. S. Jackson and Son in the 1870s, and his father, Andrew, worked in the business, which became Jackson Brothers and Co.

It was a profitable business, but Ray had other ideas. He attended Ohio State, participated in the Strollers theatrical group on campus and took up photography. Jackson's friendship with Thurber began during Scarlet Mask musical comedy productions while both were students at Ohio State and continued with their involvement in that theater group after both had left school. Jackson directed and staged many of those performances and coached actors until 1924.

Jackson worked at the Al Callen's photo studio in the old Baldwin Gwynne mansion at the southwest corner of Fourth and Broad Streets in the late 1910s and early 1920s, where Thurber, future wife Althea Adams, Elliott Nugent, Ralph McCombs, Callen's artist-wife Emily, and others of a literary and theatrical mind and spirit attended afternoon teas. One block from the Statehouse, the Civil War era mansion stood directly across Fourth from another old mansion that still houses the Columbus Club. It was romantic setting for what Adams later described as "the nearest thing Columbus had to a Bohemian tea."

Thurber courted Adams during this period and when the couple married at Trinity Episcopal Church on the other end of the block from the studio, it is no surprise that Jackson would have been one of the ushers at their wedding.

Jackson and Callen went their separate ways after the Gwynne mansion was sold and demolished in the early 1920s, and for several years, Jackson had a studio at 118 South High and later at 186 Broad Street, in buildings that have also been torn down.

Like Thurber, Nugent, and others in the group, Jackson aspired to be a playwright and in 1925, his play *Friends Invited* made its debut at Wallack's Theatre on Broadway. Barron Callen—Barron was Al's middle name—had one of the five parts in it, but it closed after one performance.

Fortunately Jackson's photography talents exceeded his written ones. He moved to New York and established the photography department at the NBC in 1931. He took publicity photos of movie stars and radio stars who appeared at the microphones of the NBC Red and Blue radio networks in the 30s and 40s.

In the *Ohio State University Monthly,* he told of how fidgety comedian-singer Eddie Cantor sat still as a statue for Jackson: "I'm having the time of the life," he told Jackson afterwards. "If you had been chased around a bull ring for three months as I was in making *The Kid from Spain* you'd welcome the chance to sit still."[1]

Jackson also recalled his meeting with the new First Lady, Eleanor Roosevelt, whom he ranked among the most charming women he had photographed:

> She came down for pictures after making her first radio address following the election. As there was little time, we were a bit hasty entering the studio and she stumbled over a screen prop, plunging right into my arms. She lost her balance, but not her composure. "Well," she laughed. "Can you imagine? I didn't see that." And everything was all right.[2]

Another of his stories involved an afternoon shooting Ed Wynn and Graham McNamee, whom he said spent most of the time trading gags or striking comic poses.

"I wanted to photograph Wynn's ancient and much-patched stage shoes all by themselves," Jackson said. "He was reluctant at first but finally consented. The comedian removed the shoes, exposing a big hole in one sock. 'Look at that,' he moaned. 'Five thousand dollars a week and a hole in my sock. S-o-o-o, I am a perfect fool.'"[3]

In the April 27, 1945, issue of *Life*, NBC press department manager Sidney Eiges, in response to a story that had appeared on Gertrude Stein, contributed a photo of the back of Gertrude Stein's head, taken by Jackson for NBC. Why backward?

"She writes backwards, so I thought we should photograph her backwards," he quoted Jackson as saying.

Jackson's work was widely praised by those he photographed and those at the newspapers and magazines who used his publicity shots.

"He's the only photographer I know who can make Midwestern senators look like glamour boys," author H. L. Mencken said.[4]

Jackson quit NBC in 1952, his one-man department having grown to six employees and its production having grown to five thousand prints a week. Many of the radio stars he came to know well because of his photographic sessions had been lost in the transition to television and many of his friends had moved away. The kind of publicity photos he took were no longer as relevant because of the growth of TV. He also wasn't happy with the changing city.

"The big city just isn't what it used to be," he said. "It's not the same New York I went to years ago."[5]

He moved back to Columbus and brought his cosmopolitan lifestyle to a bachelor's pad he set up in an apartment at 580 East Town Street. He again opened his own studio in a stone house at 1271 East Broad Street and after a year he also became the head photographer for Baker Art Gallery, a historic Columbus photo business that had once boasted of four presidents—Rutherford B. Hayes, William McKinley, William Howard Taft, and Warren G. Harding—as clients.

He enjoyed cooking dinner for friends, collected over five hundred cookbooks and kept meticulous records of the meals so that a menu would never be repeated for guests. The dinner parties also enabled him to use the fine linens and tableware he collected during his European trips—steak knives from Paris, fine linens from Switzerland, a variety of Chinese plates and bowls, blue and white Royal Doulton china, a set of

Limoges china, and heirloom teapots. He limited guests to two cocktails
before dinner because he felt that more would limit appreciation for the
food.

Cooking was his hobby and he took it almost as seriously as his photography; he held a membership in the Wine and Food Society of London
and during trips to Europe he attended Dione Lucas's Le Cordon Bleu
cooking school.

Jackson died on January 15, 1964, at the age of seventy-six and was
buried in Green Lawn Cemetery. In its obituary, the *Ohio State University
Monthly* noted that the walls of his Townley Court apartment held an
etching of Chicago that had once belonged to actress Sarah Bernhardt; his
mother's wedding handkerchief framed against black velvet; sculptured
wood angels from Italy; a painting by Columbus artist Alice Schille; a
watercolor by Ohio State art professor and longtime friend Will Rannells;
and only one of his own photographs, a scene over a bridge on the Seine
River, printed in such a way that it resembled a soft watercolor."[6]

Some of his photos have since become part of the library holdings at
Ohio State.

CHAPTER 40

His Real-Life "Thurber Woman"

In a famous Thurber cartoon, a large, forbidding woman stares menacingly at her small, docile husband.

"I'm getting tired of you throwing your weight around," she says.

It is classic, real-life Thurber humor, a hen-pecked husband doubtless afflicted with the "Thurber nervousness," as he called it, and a strong, dominant woman who pretended this dictatorship of a marriage was a democracy.

Thurber both saw it with his parents and lived it with Althea Adams Thurber, the first wife whom he both worshipped and, by his own admission, sometimes feared.

Thurber's friends and family present contrasting images of her which are at times difficult to reconcile. But most agree that Thurber saw both his mother and Althea in the figure that came to be known as the "Thurber woman" in many of his cartoons.

Althea's assertiveness proved to be more than just good cartoon-fodder. If her decisiveness sometimes made Thurber uncomfortable, she was just what he needed at the time. She believed he had a thirst in him that Columbus ultimately couldn't quench and saw that he could never reach his full potential if he stayed in his hometown. While it's possible that Althea also saw Thurber as her ticket out of town—some family members, including his second wife, Helen, believed that—ultimately Althea's greatest contribution to Columbus was getting Thurber to leave

• 265 •

it. If Thurber hadn't met and married her, there's a chance he would have settled into a comfortable life as a local newspaper reporter or press agent and never taken the chances that put him on the road to literary fame.

Fate had to orchestrate a complicated plot to bring them together. Althea was born on April 28, 1901, in New York City, the daughter of Paul and Maude Gregory Adams. At the time of Althea's birth, Paul was a medical student in his last year of internship. He moved his family to Los Angeles the following year, and after a brief practice he became an Army surgeon. The family was living in Hawaii where he served with the Fifth Cavalry when he died of peritonitis in 1910. Althea was nine years old.

Mother and daughter moved back to California for a time before Maude's sister-in-law, Edith Adams Blake, and her husband, Professor Frederick C. Blake, dean of the Physics Department at Ohio State, invited them to come to Columbus and live with them. Maude Adams took them up on their offer, enrolled at OSU as a graduate student in home economics, and got a teaching job at the Columbus School for Girls. When she finished her schooling, she joined the university's home economics department as an assistant professor.

Probably as soon as they were financially able, Althea and her mother moved into an apartment one block from campus at 20 East 13th Avenue, an old brick building that today is mostly hidden by a modern façade and occupied by Formaggio's Bar and Grill, a pizza restaurant. Althea graduated from North High School in 1918 and went to the Western College for Women in Oxford, Ohio, for one year, before transferring to Ohio State in the fall of 1919. She attracted the attention of all of the sororities and eventually picked Kappa Kappa Gamma. Her popularity led to her being chosen as one of the nine "Rosebuds of Rosebush," whose criteria were an outstanding "womanliness, brightness, fairness and willingness to help others" and whose attitude "helped make the Ohio of today."

"I loved Althea, that beautiful, lovely girl," Minnette Fritts said. "We had no sorority house in those days but we lived not far from one another. We both liked to walk. We became very, very close friends."[1]

Althea's popularity extended to the opposite sex, although at 5-foot-9 she was tall for the women of her day. Her picture appears on a page of the 1921 school year book, the *Makio* (Japanese for "mirror"), as one of eight "Magic Mirror" girls, selected on the basis of womanly courtliness and bearing.

She was active in theater and recalled meeting Thurber at a rehearsal for one of the plays put on by the Strollers, which Thurber had rejoined after returning from France after the war. When Thurber finished his

workdays at the *Columbus Dispatch,* he usually spent his evenings working both on a Strollers drama and skits for Scarlet Mask. Althea had
joined the Strollers but hadn't met Thurber until a spring day in 1921
when he showed up at the campus chapel, which also served as the student theater, to discuss a scene he was writing for the next Scarlet Mask
show with Ray Lee Jackson. Jackson was directing a Strollers play with
Althea in the cast and Thurber's arrival interrupted the rehearsal and
resulted in their introduction.

"It could have been either of the two plays that Ray directed," Althea
said. "I was in *The Importance of Being Earnest* and one of three girls
in *The Girl with the Green Eyes.* Jim had recently returned from the
U.S. Embassy in Paris, a polished man of the world, and I was somewhat
bowled over by him, I suppose."[2]

Her attraction to Thurber caught most of his friends and acquaintances by surprise. She was pretty, popular, and very social. He seemed
shy and aloof to those who weren't among his close friends. But he was
six years older than she was, worked at the *Dispatch,* and had spent a
year in France; she had majored in romance languages with an emphasis
on French and must have been intrigued by his talk of returning to France
to live and work.

Thomas Meek, a Thurber friend who also worked on Scarlet Mask
productions, remembered his pal setting his sights on Althea and going
after her.

"As I remember it, Jim had a project going to conquer Althea, which
was quite a project since she was a Amazonian woman, both physically
and mentally," Meek said. "I considered it remarkable that he finally captured her. A lot of us sat around thunderstruck, trying to figure out how
he did it. They both had a passion for dogs. That was one thing, maybe."[3]

Their love of the literature and the arts was another.

"He was on the *Dispatch* and I was in college and at four P. M. on
many days a group of us would meet downtown for tea at the photography studio that Al Callen and Ray Lee Jackson ran," Althea said. "We
took turns bringing cakes. It was the nearest thing Columbus had to a
Bohemian tea. We had a wonderful time in an innocent way. There was
always good conversation."[4]

The participants at the photo studio must have felt like they were in
on something that the rest of Columbus wasn't, like they were part of
an elite group of intellectuals who would someday remake the world in
marvelous new ways.

This, too, must have been part of Althea's captivation with the older, more-worldly Thurber; he had moved beyond the campus scene and wanted to take her with him. But to many of their friends, their divergent backgrounds doomed their relationship.

Ralph McCombs, an early Mask participant, was one of those who didn't think the attraction would last.

"The Adamses didn't have a great deal of money, but they had status in that Althea was the niece of the dean of OSU physics department," McCombs said. "In North Columbus, where the Adamses lived, it mattered who you were, in the way that only a small Midwest city can insist on. The Adamses moved in socially respectable circles, both in Columbus and at the university. The Thurbers were considered raggedly pants by comparison."[5]

It didn't matter. In early 1922 Thurber asked Althea to marry him, and she consented. They originally decided on an October date, but they changed their minds and decided to do it in May. Althea's mother didn't oppose the marriage, but thought her daughter should wait until she finished college. The May date meant she wouldn't finish her junior year because married women were not qualified to attend undergraduate classes.

Althea didn't care. "I felt he was the complete man of the world," she told Kinney. "He was so much better read than I. He introduced me to good writing. Nobody could talk me into delaying the marriage."[6]

They were married on May 22, 1922, at historic Trinity Episcopal Church on Statehouse Square, at the corner of Third Street and the west end of the Broad Street block from the mansion where they had socialized at the photo studio.

Thurber's pal Elliott Nugent was traveling with his play *Kempy,* so Ed Morris took his place as best man. Professor Blake, Althea's uncle, gave her away. Thurber's brother Robert, who felt that Althea disrespected his family, claimed to be ill and didn't attend the ceremony.

The newlyweds went to Washington, DC, and New York for their honeymoon in a Ford coupe that belonged to Althea's mother and were houseguests of the Nugents in Westport, Connecticut. Elliott's lack of enthusiasm for the new bride bothered Thurber, who desperately sought his friend's approval. Nugent couldn't help it; he thought Althea was all wrong for Thurber. Although Thurber had frequently bragged to his friend about what a catch Althea was in letters written before that, he seldom mentioned her after that.

The young couple returned home and rented a small apartment on Linwood Avenue, where they lived for only a short time before moving into the Tionesta Apartments on Neil Avenue. They moved again to an apartment at 1371 Madison Avenue on the East Side, the frequent moves probably a good indication of how tight their finances were.

Their married life very much revolved around the campus theater groups. Thurber coauthored the 1922–23 Scarlet Mask production, and Althea helped with the lighting and sets. Thurber's $35 a week *Dispatch* salary didn't leave them with much spare cash, and Althea took tight control of the family budget. Their food budget was $20 per week and some evenings were designated "onion sandwich parties" according to Dorothy Miller, whose future husband, Herman, often brought Roquefort cheese and milk to the parties.

"She was very tough on poor Jim," McCombs said. "Every morning when he went off to work at the *Dispatch* she gave him just enough money for carfare and lunch. She watched over him like a mother hen."[7]

Thurber wrote several of the Scarlet Mask productions. He admitted later that they weren't very good, but he was paid $350 per show—about two months salary at the *Dispatch*—and both hoped they would lead to bigger, better things. In 1923 Thurber went to New York to review plays for the *Dispatch* and he visited the Nugents while he was there. He met a friend of Nugent's who owned a cottage in the Adirondack hamlet of Jay, New York, and the friend offered to let Thurber use the house in the summer of 1924 as a secluded spot where he could concentrate on his writing. Thurber had had his Sunday "Credos and Curios" feature/column cancelled by the *Dispatch* in December; bitter over the quasi demotion and already being pushed by the increasingly bored Althea to look toward broader horizons, Thurber thought the opportunity seemed like a good one. He quit his job at the *Dispatch* and they both went there.

Thurber saw this as a chance to turn his unproduced Scarlet Mask libretto *Nightingale* into a Broadway musical comedy and to write short stories and humorous essays that he thought might please the *Saturday Evening Post* editors. The libretto was never produced (Thurber later claimed it was lost, but a typescript is on file in the Library of Congress) and he sold only a few small items from their adventure. They returned to Columbus when the weather began to turn cold in the fall of 1924, with no money and no prospects, having accomplished nothing. Thurber no longer had a job the *Dispatch,* which had a policy that it would never rehire you if you quit. Neither of them found that especially distressing, but they did realize that the trip to the Adirondacks had been a bad idea.

"Of course nothing could possibly be more foolish than to start out to make your name by writing a musical comedy without any music and without knowing one single soul in the business," Althea said, "or anything, anywhere near it."[8]

Thurber had no more success selling his stories back in Columbus, but he picked up a variety of freelance publicity jobs and by the spring of 1925 was actually making more money than he was before he left. Althea was still convinced that her husband would never achieve success as a humor writer in Columbus and now she began to advance the idea that they should move to France, where all of the writers and artists were going. Joel Sayre said that it was tribute to her strength and perseverance than he finally agreed to go.

> I saw quite a bit of the Thurbers before I left Columbus. I could see that Althea was ambitious for Jim in a good way. It wasn't that she wanted him to be successful for her sake alone, but for his, too. She believed in his abilities; she knew he had more than Columbus could bring out. Poverty wasn't driving love out the window at the time. Neither had had much money and they were used to that. Althea was certainly no shrew. She had pink cheeks, beautiful blue eyes, was good-natured and a nice lady . . .
>
> It's easy, in light of what happened later, to take sides, to argue that if the marriage was wrong in the late twenties, it had been wrong all along, and that Jim succeeded despite Althea, not because of her. But that isn't true. Thurber acquired his great drive only after he got it going; he had acquired very little ego while in Columbus. I used to hear Althea tell a down-in-the-mouth Thurber, "You can write and you must write. You are a humorist and Columbus isn't the place to do humor." She was entirely unselfish about it. Jim was too good for his hometown, she felt. He was a worrier, timid and without confidence, and she responded as any person who loved him would. If she had believed he would be better off in Columbus, she would not have persuaded him to leave. She recognized the large charge Paris had given him, and that was the reason it made sense to her to help get him back over there.[9]

They saved enough money for two student-class tickets on the Leviathan and left Columbus for the second May in a row. This time it was for good, although they had no way of knowing that. Thurber's newspaper experience would serve them well in France, where he eventually landed a job with the Paris edition of the *Chicago Tribune*. When they returned to the States—separately, as it turned out—Thurber peddled his talents in New York and not Columbus.

Their marriage had started showing signs of strain while they were in France, and it continued to deteriorate even while Thurber started to make his mark in New York. Although they separated in 1929, Rosemary, Thurber's only child, was born in 1931 and they remained married until 1935.

In 1928–29, Thurber wrote several stories for the *New Yorker* that came to be known as the Monroe series (Althea and her mother had once lived on Monroe Avenue in Columbus) that draws almost literally on the couple's married life. Thurber tried to put Mrs. Monroe—Althea—in disguise as a small blonde, doubtless aware that his unflattering characterizations of her might not be taken in the spirit they were (or weren't) intended.

Althea married and divorced twice after her divorce from Thurber, a personal history that probably at least partially absolves him of the blame for the couple's marital failures. He defended her for years after their divorce, and continued to proudly declare that she was "one of the most beautiful girls in the country," as he did in a letter to Dale Kramer.[10] But after he had too many drinks, Thurber would often admit that "she always scared me."[11]

Nonetheless, Sayre believed that at least in some way, Althea deserves credit for Thurber's later success. She persuaded Thurber to take a chance and move away from Columbus during a period when he was doing well as a freelancer, which might have never happened otherwise.

She had roots in Columbus—her mother died there in 1950—but Althea never looked back after she and Thurber left there. When her second daughter (from another marriage) moved to Scotland, Althea followed her there and she died in Aberdeen on July 6, 1986, far from the scene of what surely must be considered her greatest success.

"Next to Nugent and Miller, Althea was the principal believer in, and catalyst for, Jim back then," Sayre said. "He didn't really begin to make the bell ring until he wrote about Columbus in the *My Life and Hard Times* series, and he would never have written about Columbus and his family that successfully if he had stayed there. How could any writer get perspective or lose a crippling self-consciousness if he decided to write about a family and city he saw on an everyday basis?"[12]

CHAPTER 41

—————
•

Married in History

Three churches faced Statehouse Square when James Thurber was a small boy. There is one now. It says a lot about the changing face of city, the difference between the Columbus that Thurber lived in and wrote about and the Columbus that exists today.

Trinity Episcopal Church, the place where he married Althea Adams on May 22, 1922, is an enduring landmark. It has stood at the southeast corner of Third and Broad Streets since 1869 and occupied another location on the square at 20 East Broad starting in 1833. When the bride's mother, Ohio State assistant professor Maude Adams, chose Trinity for the site of her daughter's wedding,[1] she chose wisely. The church's history and location demanded respect and prestige.

Trinity's roots are traceable almost to the beginnings of the city. In 1817 Reverend Philander Chase—founder of Kenyon College and uncle of future Ohio governor, Lincoln secretary of treasury, and Supreme Court justice Salmon P. Chase—met with many of the city's pioneers in the High Street house of storekeeper Lincoln Goodale. Thirty of them, including Philo Olmstead, Joel Buttles, and John Kilbourne, signed papers the 6-foot-4 Chase had prepared to bring Trinity Episcopal Church into existence.[2]

First Presbyterian Church dominated the city in those early days. It had been started in Franklinton in 1806 by settlement founder Lucas Sullivant and moved across the Scioto River to Columbus in 1814 and had a building at 167 South Front Street in 1815. It moved into a much larger building on Statehouse Square at the southwest corner of State and Third Streets in 1830 and would survive there until the dawn of the twentieth century. Its success partially explains why Trinity, without a building and sometimes without a rector, grew so slowly in the early years.

When the Greek Revival style church opened a few doors east of Broad and High in 1833, that provided a significant boost. Trinity couldn't approach the sheer numbers of the Presbyterians, but it had more of the well-to-do, well-connected local citizens than those of most of its rival churches. Stagecoach tycoon William Neil, owner of the Neil House hotel and the farm that would eventually become the site of Ohio State University, attended Trinity. So did well-known local newspaper publisher Samuel Medary, book publisher Isaac Whiting and prominent lawyers John W. Andrews and Phineas B. Wilcox, banker William Deshler, and eventual governor William Dennison. Alfred Kelley, a state lawmaker and railroad executive known as the father of the Ohio canal system, owned a huge Greek Revival mansion a few blocks east on Broad Street. He attended Trinity, too.

But in the 1850s, the congregation began to swell with families of more modest means and it became increasingly apparent that the original church wasn't large enough. The church purchased a lot at the southwest corner of Sixth and Broad and a foundation was laid; work stalled because of a lack of funds. The church sold the lot to the city's board of education—Central High School was eventually built on the foundation the church had laid—and Trinity put off the idea of building until its financial picture improved.

That finally happened in 1862, and Trinity bought the lot owned by then-governor Dennison at the corner of Broad and Third where the church now stands.[3] In 1863 the old church on Broad was sold for $10,000, and after the buyer died shortly thereafter it was sold again, this time to Peter Hayden, a banker, mining and railroad tycoon. After the old church was razed, Hayden erected a four-story brownstone office building on the site in 1869 that is the oldest commercial structure on Statehouse Square today.

The new church had moved only a block east and it found itself in more of a residential setting on Third. Houses lined the block to the south on Third Street, many of them owned by Trinity members. William Deshler's house stood catty-corner across Broad from the new Trinity, and First Congregational Church, built in 1856, stood next door to the Deshlers.

Construction on the new Gothic Revival building started in 1866 and the new church finally opened in 1869, albeit without a steeple. The steeple in the original plans was never built because of the cost, estimated at between $10,000 and $12,000.

Only two years after its opening, Trinity hosted the biggest wedding in its history and the only royal wedding ever held in the city of Columbus. On May 16, 1871, Amelia (May) Parsons, daughter of wealthy businessman George Parsons, wed Prince Alexander Ernst de Lynar of Bavaria. The couple had met while May was studying in Europe and the prince served as an aide to Emperor William I at the German embassy in Paris.

May had grown up in her father's huge two-story brick mansion. Their street, called East Public Lane when the house was constructed in 1847, marked the eastern edge of the city when it was built. Today it is called Parsons Avenue and runs less than a block to the east of Interstate 70, which forms part of the inner belt of freeways that circles downtown. George Parsons—an attorney, first director of the Franklin Bank, and director of the Hocking Valley Railway and the Columbus-Harrisburg turnpike—had a lot a half-mile deep and one thousand feet wide. The lavish parties he held for his daughter and his new son-in-law after the wedding weren't the first important ones he had held there. During the Civil War, Kate Chase, daughter of the former Ohio governor, went there to a party as the bride of wealthy Rhode Island governor William Sprague.

For all of those reasons, May Parsons' wedding doubtless would have been a huge social event in the still small state capital ever if she hadn't married a prince. As it was, it topped the city's 1871 social calendar. Crowds gathered outside the church hours before the wedding was scheduled to begin, enough ladies, according to the *Ohio State Journal,* "to make a good sized sewing society."

Everyone was allowed into the church for the service, including nosy girls on the way home from school. They must have been excited by the chance to see a real, live prince, and Alexander didn't disappoint them. He wore his ceremonial dress, with a "profusion of rings" on his fingers and decorations around his neck. May wore a white dress of heavy, corded silk with a moderate train, a lengthy overskirt looped with orange blossoms, a long tulle veil, and a diamond and pearl necklace.[4]

Police stationed near the entrance weren't needed. The bulging crowd behaved itself; it isn't every day that one of the local girls becomes a princess.

A case can be made that Thurber's marriage to Althea Adams was the second most important event in the history of Trinity Episcopal Church, although it could never have been mistaken for royal wedding. In fact, it delivered a touch of chaos that somehow seems fitting given the humorous family incidents Thurber chronicled in his later writing.

Roy Lee Jackson, a proprietor of the photo studio where Thurber and his bride spent a lot of time, was the only usher who made it to the church in time to seat the guests. The rest had ridden in one car after getting dressed at the Phi Psi house and were delayed by a minor accident on the way to the church. They arrived late, but the service itself went off without a hitch; the marriage didn't fare as well, as the couple was divorced thirteen years later.

The church had other big days. An 1887 wedding of Rutherford H. Platt and Maryette Smith was attended by former President Rutherford B. Hayes, who was the groom's uncle. In 1917 Ohio Governor James Cox, who would run for president against Warren Harding (and lose) in 1920, spoke at Trinity's one-hundredth anniversary celebration and noted that for one hundred years, "Trinity Church has cast a watchful, inspiring and sometimes restraining eye on the Statehouse. It is inspiring to know that this church has the age to guarantee sage philosophy and yet has a young and progressive spirit."[5]

The funeral for Samuel Prescott Bush, father of U.S. Senator Prescott Bush, grandfather of President George H. W. Bush and great-grandfather of President George W. Bush, was held at Trinity in 1948, even though the family attended St. Paul's Episcopal. Like Maude Adams, the Bush family must have felt that having the service in a historic church across the street from the Statehouse lent a weight to the occasion that it wouldn't have any place else.

CHAPTER 42

Thurber's "Closest" Friend

Thurber planned to make Herman Miller the last half of the one of the profiles in *The Thurber Album*. The former Ohio State English, speech and drama professor, one of Thurber's closest friends, didn't make the manuscript and ended up on the dedication page:

> To Herman Allen Miller October 25, 1896—April 20, 1949 whose friendship was an early and enduring inspiration

Thurber comes alive in many places in Columbus, but other than the Thurber House there may be none where his presence seems as noticeable as the log home along the Olentangy River in Worthington that belonged to Herman Miller and his wife Dorothy. Thurber visited the place they called "Fool's Paradise" on many of his visits to Columbus after he left the city for good in 1925.

Jesica Stevens, who describes herself as a nurse, intrinsic healer and communicator, has owned the property since 2011. She calls it "Gateway to Heaven," a description of it that feels more accurate than the one given to it by the Millers. If the 1.236-acre property at the foot of West South Street isn't a "gateway to heaven," it should be.

The second-floor terrace, once closed in as the Millers' bedrooms, offers a stunning view of the river and several huge sycamore trees, a few standing tall in her yard and others perched on the river's edge. The largest one, an ancient giant probably six feet in diameter, stands ten feet to the west of the house where it has served as a silent witness to hundreds of years of events big and small that have unfolded here.

Thurber's repeated visits probably trump the others as milestone moments, although the place's past as a Civil War camp and as the site of both a gristmill and a sawmill that served the frontier settlement of Worthington in the early days of the nineteenth century cannot be discounted. But the forgotten history might even top regular visits by one of America's greatest humorists: Early Indian tribes probably hunted, fished and camped here even more often than Thurber visited here, and there's no way for a modern observer to know how those events shaped our history.

"This is a magical place," Stevens said. "You can see why Thurber loved it here."

Thurber's love for the property is more than matched by his love for Herman Miller, whom he called "his oldest and in many ways my closest friend" in a letter to Dorothy written the day after her husband died. The two men knew each only slightly when were both students at Ohio State but they got to know each other better when they worked on theater productions together for the Scarlet Strollers drama group a few years later.

A production called *Psychomania,* a one-act spoof of the Freud craze raging at the time that was Thurber's only original contribution to the group's repertoire, proved to a milestone moment in the Thurber-Miller friendship.

"It was not until 1922 that I came to know Thurber very well," Miller wrote, in a 1940 story for the *Weekly Reader,* a classroom magazine for children. "In that year we acted together in an amateur production of some short plays, one of which he had written. At the performance one of our cast was so badly seized with stage fright that he couldn't utter a line. Thurber and I, working in relays, managed to speak all of his lines in addition to our own. Naturally, that didn't do the play any good, but it did begin a fine friendship. A love of good books, night-long talks and Roquefort cheese has cemented that friendship through many years."[1]

Like Thurber, Miller was a local boy. He grew up in a two-story, brick house at 578 South Sixth Street in German Village, and except for one year at grad school, lived there until he got married, thirteen years after his graduating from Ohio State in 1919. He got his Masters from Columbia in the spring of 1920 and joined the OSU faculty as an English instructor in the fall. Thurber and Miller both aspired to be playwrights. They laughed at the same things and shared a love of novelist Henry

James and the professor (Joseph Taylor) who introduced him to them, which also seems to have strengthened their bonding.

One of the students in Herman Miller's poetry class in 1922, a sophomore named Dorothy Reid who had grown up in Galion, Ohio, sixty miles north of Columbus, would become his future wife. She also founded a campus literary magazine called *The Candle* that encountered financial trouble almost immediately.

"He was the teacher in my poetry class; I thought he was wonderful," Dorothy said. "It wasn't till later the following spring that we got acquainted. He saw some of my poems and thought they were pretty good, and we really liked each other from then on. At the time, he and Jim were good friends, but I had not met him. He was working at the *Columbus Dispatch* doing a column."[2]

Herman told Thurber about the *Candle's* troubles, and he campaigned for it in three of his Credos and Curios pages in the *Dispatch*.

The Miller-Thurber friendship blossomed during a period when Thurber met and married Althea Adams, left the paper, tried to write a novel in an upstate New York cabin and moved back to Columbus. Herman offered him a sympathetic voice throughout this difficult period.

"Herman recognized, as did Althea, that Jim ought to get out of Columbus," Dorothy said.[3]

When the break was made and the Thurbers finally landed in New York after a brief detour through France, Miller remained a confidant. They frequently corresponded by mail, a practice they continued throughout their lives, and visits were common on both ends.

"I saw him down at Herman's house (on South Sixth Street) several times, when Jim would come down there," Dorothy said. "Or we'd go out to dinner and talk, He was not really doing a whole lot at that time, you see, except writing for the newspaper in New York or some of those places he was working. He was quite envious of my position, because I had a job with the American Insurance Union, which built what is now the LeVeque Tower. It was the AIU building then. I went in to do their publicity after I graduated from college. They also had a radio station, so in addition to getting out pamphlets and writing publicity, I was doing book reviews, writing radio plays and producing them every week for several years.

"So Jim thought that was very good. I know when his *Owl in the Attic* came out, I gave it a nice review on the station."[4]

Miller taught drama at OSU. He sometimes went to New York to catch Broadway plays and visited Thurber while in town.

"One evening in 1927, when he was a reporter for the *New York Evening Post,* I sat with him in his little apartment," Miller wrote. "He was almost surrounded by a restless Scottie pup he called 'Black Watch the Third' because his real name was 'Queenie.' He was unusually happy that night, for a humorist, but not a little worried. He had just been offered two jobs, and he is not a man to make any kind of decision easily. But that night he finally chose the position offered by editor Harold Ross of the *New Yorker* magazine."[5]

The two men shared lots of important moments. Thurber returned to Columbus in the fall of 1930 and he told Herman his marriage with Althea was finished. Dorothy, not yet married to Herman, recalled listening to the two men talk about this late into the night, a conversation that was finally interrupted by a call from Althea. She was about to have a wisdom tooth extracted and wanted Jim with her. Without hesitation, Thurber left on the train the next morning.

"It didn't seem to me the marriage was washed up," Dorothy said. "And the next thing Herman and I heard, a few months later, was that Althea was pregnant."[6]

Herman and Dorothy married in 1932. They moved into a house at 2633 Glen Echo Drive, in a wooded area on the north side of Columbus not far from Glen Echo Ravine. It hinted at the move the Millers would make to Fool's Paradise five years later.

When Joseph Taylor died in March 1933, Miller and Thurber exchanged letters on the topic. Miller said that he planned to write a book or play based on Taylor's life. Thurber later wrote Miller about how they both might adapt *The Ambassadors,* a James book both Taylor and Thurber admired, to the stage.

It was a pleasant thought that never came to fruition. Thurber's life was moving too quickly for that and Miller never really displayed the talent for such a union, despite his friend's affection for him. Not long after Althea filed for a divorce from Thurber, the Millers visited him in a friend's Fifth Avenue apartment where he was living in New York.

"We were getting ready to go out to dinner when Althea stopped by to get something," Dorothy said. "She was very polite and glad to see Herman, who had taught her at OSU. There was no squabbling, and I wondered why Jim didn't invite her to join us for dinner. I feel she would have accepted.

"Jim and Herman were in their zany mood. We walked to the Charles restaurant in the Village. Thurber had loosened the laces of one of his shoes and would suddenly kick it ahead of him on the sidewalk. It annoyed me, because Herman and Jim both laughed like fools when considerate people, including one sincere little man, retrieved the shoe for Jim."[7]

Thurber married Helen Wismer in June 1935. The following year he brought her to Columbus for a Thanksgiving with the family, OSU's homecoming football game with Michigan (he had drawn the cover for the program) and visits with local friends, including the Millers. Carl Sandburg, the poet and Lincoln biographer, came to Columbus to participate in a Harms Lecture Series at Capital University while Thurber was there. Thurber and Sandburg admired each other's work but had never met. Sandburg was staying with Mary Teeter Zimmerman, a noted librarian and literary connoisseur in the city, while he was in town. She knew Thurber, who asked to meet him and happily extended their stay at the Deshler-Wallick Hotel for the chance.[8]

After the second night's lecture, Dr. Louis Roth hosted about twenty people, including Sandburg, the Thurbers and the Millers at his two-story brick home at 168 South Dawson Avenue in Bexley.

"Some friends who knew Sandburg brought him," Dorothy Miller said. "We brought the Thurbers. Jim admired Sandburg, and Sandburg admired Jim. They just talked a blue streak, talked until about four in the morning. The rest of us sat around half asleep, I think, because, after all, there is a limit to the human system I don't care how interesting it is."[9]

Herman Miller said it was the first time he had seen two famous men trying to sit at one another's feet. Both men were at their pontificating best, and at one point, Sandburg strummed a guitar and sang and Thurber sang along. A delighted Thurber sent both Herman Miller and Sandburg drawings commemorating the long night—they portrayed himself as a small figure and Sandburg as very large—and he was always grateful to his friend for helping to set it up. Sandburg would later be among the numerous literary figures to visit Fool's Paradise when the Millers lived there.

The Millers didn't purchase the Worthington property until the following fall and although it needed some work to make it habitable as a year-round residence, it wouldn't take them long to move in. Herman was still teaching at Ohio State; the Thurbers visited Columbus in October, 1938, took in an OSU-Purdue football game with the Millers and spoke to the students in one of his classes. But Miller must have been contemplating quitting and discussed it with the Thurbers; he resigned from Ohio State on June 30, 1939, to devote all of his time to writing.

Fool's Paradise was the perfect place for his new avocation. Elmer E. Latham, a Worthington dentist, had originally constructed the cabin a mile and a half north on the river at the end of Wilson Bridge Road. But after he quarreled with his neighbors, he purchased the property at the end of South Street, and with the help of four local boys, took the cabin apart, floated the logs down the river and reassembled it there in 1904. Even though it had two stories and a basement, he and his family spent only summers and Christmases there.[10] It bore little resemblance to the beautiful larger house Stevens lives in today.

Ironically, when Stevens first saw it, she called it "the ugliest place I've ever seen." She had always lived in new homes and had no experience refurbishing old houses, but was drawn to this place in ways that only an intrinsic healer could explain.

"I was looking at the house across the street," Stevens said. "I really liked the land, and I was guided to this house, I believe that. This is not just another place. Can you get a sense of it?"[11]

Latham sold the property in 1920 and it passed through the hands of several owners before the Millers bought the place. Herman gave up his teaching job and devoted his time to writing there, putting his office in a loft on the second floor at the west end of the great room with a large fireplace. Bookcases teeming with books surrounded his work space there and the mammoth sycamore and the Olentangy River are visible from the window. Thurber supposedly wrote there during some of his visits, and the loft is still there, although it is a little smaller than the one Herman and Thurber used. Dorothy's office occupied a similar loft at the other end of the room, although Stevens had that one removed before she moved into the house to improve the room's natural lighting.

As a writer, Dorothy Miller proved to be more successful than her husband. In addition to writing poetry, she became editor and chief writer for the American Education Publishers' classroom newspaper *Current Events* in 1933 and worked there until her retirement in 1965. (She sold Fool's Paradise to Gordon Chandler in 1952 after Wesleyan University bought her company and moved the paper's editorial offices to Middletown, Conn. She lived in Connecticut until her retirement, when she moved to Fort Myers, Fla., where she died in 1999 at the age of 99.)

Thurber was working on *The Male Animal* with Elliott Nugent when the Millers moved there, and the play's success helped convince him that his friend made the right move by quitting his teaching job at OSU to devote all of his time to his writing. Thurber recalled how Miller had supported him when he and Althea were struggling to launch his writing career, bringing them cheese, crackers, and onion sandwiches, and he promised similar support.

"If you need any money for cheese and crackers until checks begin coming in," he wrote Miller, "there is no one you know who would more happily, or could more easily, thanks to Broadway, send it. (Thurber had just received a nice check from the sale of *The Male Animal* to Warner Brothers.) Don't forget that."[12]

Thurber apparently did end up helping the Millers financially; Herman wrote a manuscript about Alexander Hamilton and had difficulty finding a publisher for it. He submitted it to Harcourt Brace, at Thurber's suggestion; Thurber was sympathetic and anxious to help. He told Herman that if he got the manuscript back not to "be discouraged, but send it back to me and I'll try it out on another publisher."[13]

In the meantime, Thurber wrote a piece for The *New Yorker* called "A Friend to Alexander," which he said later was inspired by Herman Miller. It appeared on January 10, 1942.

"I got the idea from a friend of mine who was doing a study of Hamilton," Thurber said, later. "He called me one day and said "This is Aaron Burr." It occurred to me that you can become so engrossed in a historical project of that sort, you might become a part of it."

Thurber had such a deep affection for the Millers that he had difficulty seeing his friend's limitations as a writer, just as he had Joey Taylor. But others saw it, even if he didn't.

Ted Gardiner, another one of Thurber's Columbus friends, found the Miller-Thurber pairing odd.

"I never knew what Jim saw in Miller," Gardiner said. "He was usually such a rude, unpleasant intellectual."[14]

Helen Thurber liked Herman when he wasn't drunk.

"Herman always told his stories standing up, just like Jamie did," she said. "They were both perfectionists. When we visited Columbus after we were married, we always had to see Herman and his wife Dorothy— especially for dinner, which Herman loved to cook. I was fond of Herman but I also found him tiresome when he was drunk. Jamie thought he had more potential as a playwright than I did. He helped him out with money—and even considered making a play of *The Ambassadors* with him. It didn't work out."[15]

Thurber started work on a pastiche of James—an imitation of his work—in the winter of 1944. He worked on it for four months, put it aside for two years, and then started in on it again. He sent it to Herman Miller for his input in 1946, then wrote him a long letter about dramatizing *The Ambassadors*. A few months later, Thurber wrote to him again, saying that he had given up on the idea.

Health became an issue on both ends. Thurber still visited Columbus and the Millers, but his loss of sight was becoming a problem. He and Helen visited his mother over Mother's Day in 1948; they stayed at the Deshler-Wallick Hotel and they enjoyed a night of fun with the Millers. Helen told Kinney that had taken to memorizing his steps and "we didn't realize how blind he had become." Miller didn't feel good and no one realized how ill he was. He died unexpectedly the following April after a two-day stay at Mount Carmel Hospital at the age of 53.

The Thurbers were in Bermuda when they got the news. A distraught Thurber sat down and wrote Dorothy Miller a heart-felt letter that showed how deeply he cared about her husband:

Dearest Dorothy,

It is hard to write the day after Herman Miller's death, for it marks the end of my oldest friend, and in many ways, my closest. No matter how long it had been since we knew each other, an old communion was easily and instantly established. There was no other man who knew me so well and I took pride and comfort in his sensitive understanding. He remembered everything, over thirty–five years, and brought it with his special humorous soundness. There was more depth and pattern to our friendship than to any other, and I have nothing that can take its place. It was more pleasure to have his laughter and appreciation than anyone else's, because he was the one who completely understood all the references, sources and meanings. I have known nobody else in whom sensibility and intelligence were so perfectly joined.

I tried to make as much of a study of him as he did of me, and since I knew his gentleness as few did, it was a private joy of mine to watch him raise his shield against the dull and ordinary persons whom he kept on the outside. Not many got through to an appreciation of his aristocratic mind, his fine judgment of people and books, and his love of the wonderful, from the comic to the beautiful. For those he loved there was no code or key, though. It was all free and open, generous and devoted. One of the nicest things about him was that genuine shyness which at first couldn't believe that the ones he loved, loved him. His happiness was all the greater when he found out. There was never a moment when he wasn't important to me.[16]

Thurber broke off the letter at that point, then picked it up the following day:

I couldn't write any more yesterday, and since then I've been thinking about Herman's good old Henry James awareness, and his fascinated analyses of Joe and Esther Taylor, Billy Graves, Althea-and-me, and others. Helen delighted him like a Christmas gift, because he saw she was made to order for me—and a tough order that is. I keep remembering all our fine days together, the suppers at your home, the party at the Whites in New York, the old chalice in Brooklyn, the time I kept going to the bathroom in the chemistry building, waiting for Minnette, and Herman's magnificent laughter when she rode up in a car and he saw she was going to have to sit on my restless lap all the way to Broad and High. I got more pleasure out of Herman's laughter than anyone else's. It was wonderful when his sides actually began to ache and his eyes to stream. I will always remember it . . .

It is a deep sorrow that I couldn't have seen Herman again, and couldn't have been there with you. I didn't see him often enough, or write to him often enough, and I so wanted him to meet Rosemary. But I have long and loving memories or Herman Miller, and I will always have them.

We send you our deepest love, Dorothy. We mourn with you, and we will think of you constantly. God bless you.

Always,
Jim

CHAPTER 43

The Hotel That
Aged with Thurber

When Thurber was twenty-one years old, the Deshler Hotel opened on the northwest corner of Broad and High. It rivaled the finest hotels in the world at the time and its opening on August 23, 1916, was a gala affair; 102 chefs, waiters and captains were hired in New York and were brought to Columbus in chartered railroad cars. Opera stars and an international dance team entertained 525 invited guests

All of that doubtless made an impression on young Thurber. Through the years, his visits to Columbus usually meant a room at the Deshler. The Deshler lived most of its life as the finest hotel in the city and the advertising reinforced that reputation, calling it "the most beautifully equipped hotel in America." Whether it deserved that billing or not, the hotel's elegance couldn't be denied. The twelve-story brick and terra cotta structure cost $1.5 million to build, or about $35 million in today's dollars. The lobby floor was decorated by a mammoth Oriental rug that cost $15,000 in 1927, or $205,000 today.

The modern twenty-six-story One Columbus Center that sits on the site today now offers no hint of the plush hotel or the family that both settled the spot and gave the hotel its name. The city was five years old when David Deshler bought this lot in 1817 for the then-exorbitant price of $1,000—other lots in the new city were going for $100 or $200—and the young carpenter built a wooden house and shop on the site. They were still there in 1869 when David's son, William Deshler, began construction of the Deshler Block, a four-story brick building which housed the Deshler Bank, storerooms, and offices. Then in 1915, William's son, John Deshler, announced plans for a 400-room hotel—269 with baths—that would be the envy of most cities.

The hotel was leased to Ohioans and New York hoteliers Lew and Adrian Wallick. The Wallicks added 600 rooms next door in the new AIU building—known today as the Leveque Tower—which was reached via a "Venetian bridge" at the second story level. The hotel was renamed the Deshler-Wallick for another opening; New York mayor Jimmy Walker came and tried to have a ceremonial sip of wine in each of the 600 hotel rooms. Legend says he almost did it; it doesn't say whether he was still standing when he took his last sip.

Thurber's experiences there weren't quite as legendary, but there were many more of them.

He was invited back to town in 1930 as the principal after-dinner speaker for a Phi Kappa Psi Founder's Day banquet at the Deshler in honor of the fraternity's fiftieth anniversary. While Ted Gardiner and other good Columbus friends were drinking in a suite upstairs, Thurber sat through one boring speech after another at the banquet. When it was finally his turn to talk, an irritated and alcohol-fueled Thurber ditched his prepared remarks and instead grilled the fraternity system in general and took special aim at the OSU chapter of Phi Kappa Psi.

"I've listened to this ghastly bilgewater about the pure white flame of Phi Psi for two hours and fifteen minutes," he said. "The only reason I ever joined your fraternity was because of Elliott Nugent and Jack Pierce."[1]

He piled insult upon insult, and his Phi Psi brothers apparently took it for rich Thurber humor; all but a few of the fraternity's national officers cheered him wildly afterwards.

Not all of his Deshler visits were so dramatic. Whenever he came to town with Helen, his second wife, they often met his good friends Herman and Dorothy Miller for dinner there.

"He brought Helen to Columbus and they came up to our house so we could meet her," Dorothy Miller said. "[But] they always insisted on our coming down to the old Deshler. It was right in the heart of downtown, and had so many famous people stay there. Christopher Morley always came there and since he was a good friend of ours, we came there to see him a number of times, too. Jim and Helen always stayed there because, I guess, there was no place at his mother's house. All his different friends would have fought over him, he said, so they decided the easiest thing was to go there. They always had us come down and have dinner with them. Once in a while we did have them to our place in Worthington. . . . We got together every time they came to Columbus."[2]

As Thurber eyesight deteriorated into blindness, his familiarity with the hotel became more and more important.

"Once we went to see them at the Deshler-Wallick and hadn't realized his eyesight was getting so much worse," Dorothy Miller said. "He was showing us then, as he led us down. *There are six steps here, then you walk a little and there are five steps here.* He memorized all the steps in that staircase and he did that with everything. When he sat down at the table, Helen would tell him exactly where everything was so he could reach things."[3]

Mame and Robert Thurber were living in an apartment at the Seneca Hotel in 1955 when she was dying. Nurses were on twelve-hour duty there. When Mame suffered a stroke on November 23 and was moved to University Hospital, Thurber and Helen immediately took a train to Columbus. They stayed at the Deshler-Wallick for an almost a month until she died on December 20, 1955.

While staying at the Deshler, Thurber began a new series of fables. Thirty-seven of them ran in the *New Yorker* from May 12 to October 13, 1956, and they appeared in his book *Further Fables for Our Time.*[4]

The hotel aged with Thurber. President Harry S. Truman spoke there in 1946 at a conference of the Federal Council of Churches of Christ, and as the former president, he and wife Bess Truman stayed there on July 6–7, 1953, during a three-week road trip from Missouri to the East Coast and back in a 1953 Chrysler. But things were already changing. The hotel was sold in 1947 to Chicagoan Julius Epstein, who sold it five years later to the Hilton hotel chain, which renamed it the Deshler-Hilton.

In 1964 a company headed by Charles Cole bought and renamed it the Deshler-Cole. Cole eliminated the 600 rooms in the Leveque Tower and remodeled the hotel, but its decline was underway. It was sold one last time to Fred Beasley in 1966 and became the Beasley-Deshler. But it was closed in 1968 and was razed in September, 1969, eight years after Thurber died.

CHAPTER 44

Mame Slept Here

For a few minutes, the patrons in the bar in the Westin Columbus Hotel put away their politics, forgot about the Cleveland Browns' most recent embarrassment, quit watching that amazing You Tube video of the world's fastest violin player, stopped trying to dig their way out of an avalanche of e-mail, and focused on the woman who somehow seemed perfectly at ease standing on a chair in a crowded room of drinkers who might stumble into her and inadvertently send her to Grant Hospital in a speeding ambulance.

Halloween was only a few days away, and Susanne Jaffe, creative director of Thurber House, prepared to read a passage from Thurber's "The Night the Ghost Got In." This is why they came. Jaffe had a book in her hand and a glint in her eye. No PowerPoint. No seventy-inch video screen. Jaffe didn't even have a microphone. After a brief explanation of who she was and why she was here, she held up the book and started to read at family room volume, or at least it sounded that way from the other side of the room and the other side of the bar. It didn't take long before the patrons began to laugh. Those who could hear only parts of Jaffe's reading laughed from memory.

Thurber, who often came to this hotel when his mother and brother Robert lived here, was getting laughs from the grave. *This* was also "The

Night the Ghost Got In." The ghost was Thurber, and he did more than "get in." He was the center of attention—as always.

"It's still funny," a woman at the bar said. "It will always be funny."

Could there ever be a better endorsement for Thurber's work? More than a half-century after he wrote the words that many in the bar were straining to hear, dozens of people were chuckling over his description of the events that occurred on one bizarre night in his family's home—now called the Thurber House—on Jefferson Avenue.

This was a made-for-Thurber House event and it scored a bull's-eye, both because of the story—one of Thurber's best—and because of the location. The Westin Columbus was born as the Great Southern Hotel, which served as home to Mame Thurber and her son Robert from 1941 until 1955.

Mame and Robert lived in an apartment that bore room number 510, an address that no longer exists in the hotel's modern configuration. There are no rooms that resemble apartments on today's fifth floor.

"Room 510 sounds like the Thurber conference suite and meeting room now," Westin Columbus front office manager Daniel Nelson said. "It's kind of rectangular. I'm just going off of my training when I started here at the hotel, that the Thurber conference suite had at one point been a room and had been turned into a meeting space."[1]

The Thurber conference room is on the second floor, so it seems unlikely that this is would have room 510. A few days later, after checking with other hotel employees, Nelson had a different theory.

"They renumbered the entire hotel a couple of renovations ago," he said. "We can't confirm that [510] number for you, but room 401, or the presidential suite, may be where the Thurber family used to live. It's a pretty popular suite. It's rented just about every day."

Room 401 is on the fourth floor, which would seem to make it an unlikely choice. Two other hotel employees also said it was the Thurber family's apartment until they were pressed for details. As their resolve broke down, they qualified their answers with a less definitive "Well, I think they probably lived there."

That didn't surprise Donn Vickers, who held a lot of events at the Southern as the first director of the Thurber House.

"I don't think there's anybody who knows," Vickers said. "We had a good relationship with [the Southern] because they used to host a lot of things for us. But the damned management would change in that kind of business. About every two years, there was a brand new guy and I would have to say, 'I'm from the Thurber House. James Thurber was a great American blah, blah, blah . . .' and the guy would say, 'I think I've heard that.'"[2]

Whatever the true location of 510, painter Emerson Burkhart sketched Mame Thurber in that room one day in 1951, and then painted an oil portrait of that sketch in his home on Woodland Avenue. Robert and William Thurber thought the painting made their mother look old, not exactly an insult for a woman of eighty, and didn't want it; through a succession of sales and donations, it now resides at the Thurber House.[3]

Not all of the family's Southern Hotel memories were made in 510. Thurber's daughter, Rosemary, recalled a lunch in the hotel's restaurant, which at the time was likely located on the Main Street side of the hotel in space occupied by a meeting room today.

"We were having lunch I think at the Southern Hotel with my grandmother and my (uncles)," she said, in a 2011 interview. "William and Robert got into a sort of scuffle over the syrup and who was taking too much syrup. That's just how it must have been for Mame all the time they were growing up."[4]

Impressive as the Thurber connection looks on the building's resume, the old hotel at the southeast corner of High and Main didn't need James Thurber and his family for credibility. The hotel and its accompanying theater have a guest list that would dazzle a Hollywood gossip columnist, a who's who of politics, sports and theater. Mame Thurber may have been the longest celebrity resident. She was by no means the most famous.

Four United States presidents—William McKinley, William Howard Taft, Teddy Roosevelt, and Woodrow Wilson—have stayed there, as did Franklin Delano Roosevelt's first lady, Eleanor. The Grand Ballroom hosted a ball in celebration of McKinley's second inauguration in 1901.

Millie Kramer once recalled how she was a seventeen-year-old girl working at the soda fountain in 1919 when the Detroit Tigers stayed there while in town for an exhibition game. Future Baseball Hall of Famer Ty Cobb heard that there was a girl working there who was a real sports enthusiast—Kramer later played professional basketball—and he looked her up at the soda fountain and spent the afternoon talking with her there. For the rest of her life she remembered how the acerbic Baseball Hall of Famer, whom others knew as a nasty, combative jerk, was "a real gentleman."[5]

Most of the Southern Theater's actors stayed here during their visits to Columbus, and that list is also impressive. After the Broadway touring production of *In Gay New York* opened the theater in 1896, *An American Beauty* starring Lillian Russell followed it. During its early years, the royalty of the theatrical world played the Southern, including Ethel and Lionel Barrymore, John Philip Sousa, Al Jolson, Sarah Bernhardt, George M. Cohan, Harry Lauder, Lily Langtry, and W. C. Fields. Actress Maude Adams flew from the stage to the balcony in an early production of Peter Pan and dancer Isadora Duncan said she wouldn't play in Columbus unless she could play the Southern. Poet James Whitcomb Riley read at the Southern. Al G. Field's Minstrels, which were based in Columbus, opened its season there for many years.

That the hotel and theater were there at all seemed like an act of fate. In the 1890s the hotel site was part of a South Side that was predominantly German; the freeway (I-70) that has since divided German Village and Downtown was more than a half-century in the future. The area boomed when the National Road entered the central city on Main Street and turned north on Broad Street in 1831, but when the railroads arrived in the 1860s, the action shifted to the north end of Downtown.

The first Union Station stood on the north end in the vicinity of today's Hyatt Columbus Hotel at Nationwide Boulevard and High Street, and construction surged up and down High in both directions. The Chittenden Hotel was part of this building frenzy at the northwest corner of Spring and High Streets. Henry Chittenden built his first hotel there in 1889. That building burned down in 1890, so he built another, six stories tall with two theaters. But on November 24, 1893, it also burned down, taking the Park and Henrietta theaters with it. Chittenden immediately began building a third hotel, but the sudden room shortage in the city was all the impetus South Siders needed to start a fund-raising campaign to build an impressive hotel on their end of town and maybe regain some of the area's lost magic. More than four hundred South Siders subscribed to stock to help finance its construction. South Side brewer Nicholas Schlee was the president of the group (The Great Southern Fire Proof Hotel Company), and future United States senator and Grover Cleveland vice-presidential candidate Allen G. Thurman was vice president of it; Thurman's law offices were located in an old building on the site. The money poured in and the 222-room Great Southern Fireproof Hotel and Opera House—with 56 private bathrooms and 8 public baths—opened in 1897, shortly after its accompanying theater.

Chittenden had already opened his third Chittenden Hotel at Spring and High by then, and he followed the South Siders' lead in going all-in on making sure that the building was fireproof; constructed of tile, brick, iron, steel, and concrete, it also became a familiar part of the city's downtown landscape. The final Chittenden remained open until 1972 and was subsequently torn down, and the Southern might have met a similar fate.

Ralph Lazarus was one of the original board members, and in 1900 the Lazarus family, whose department store launched the Federated Department Store chain that exists today as Macy's, bought the hotel and operated it for seventy years.

But after decades of maintenance issues, the family sold the facility to a realtor who had plans of turning it into an apartment building and garage. That never happened and the Southern's doors were closed in 1979. Fortunately the hotel and theatre were purchased by local developers who decided to renovate the hotel in 1982. Marcus Corporation finally purchased the hotel in 1996 and restored and refurbished it to its grandeur and glory. It remains as the oldest hotel in the city.

Columbus has been home to many impressive hotels, but the Great Southern's longevity seems appropriate. Long before the Thurbers landed, the hotel and theater attracted plenty of attention on its own. The Southern Theatre was one of the first commercial facilities in Columbus to use electricity. The complex generated its own water supply from three wells in the basement. The hotel's rooftop garden, lit by electric arches like those that illuminated High Street and lavishly decorated with potted shrubbery, featured a cabaret and restaurant above the hotel's main ballroom that became a social center for Germans who lived in that part of town.

Columbus Dispatch artist Bill Arter told a story about a young newspaperwoman, Mrs. Millicent Easter, who lived at the hotel and worked as its press agent. When she heard that Mame Thurber was house-hunting, she invited her to the Southern and gave her the grand tour, showing her several suites that were available for rent.

After the tour ended, they returned to Easter's room to continue their discussion, and Mrs. Thurber said firmly, "This is the one I want."

Easter gracefully gave up her apartment to her and Mrs. Thurber and her son, Robert, began their long residence at the hotel.[6] Because it has been restored to its former glory, it lives as one of the best places in Columbus to celebrate Thurber's legacy.

CHAPTER 45

The Wonderful Gs

Of Thurber's close Columbus friends, Fred R. "Ted" Gardiner is the only one who didn't come from the old neighborhood or attend Ohio State with him. Thurber met Gardiner after college when he was dating first wife Althea Adams, who was friends with Ted's wife, Julia. The foursome would go out on dates together, and the two men hit it off.

They shared the same sense of humor, knew many of the same people and became good drinking buddies. The marriage to Althea didn't last. The friendship with Ted and Julia Gardiner did.

"I knew Althea for a long time, because she and Ted both went to North High, and then I knew her at Ohio State where she was in Kappa Kappa Gamma sorority," Julia Gardiner said. "I went with no one but Ted. Sometimes I wish I had been in more activities, instead of always scheming about meeting Ted. We were married in 1921, in April—I quit school the latter part of my junior year. We used to double date, the four of us. Later, they wanted us to go to Europe with them—I don't know just why we didn't. They became even better friends when Jim came back on visits. He was so thankful, he said, just to be with us and not be hounded by strangers at big mob-scene cocktail parties."[1]

Gardiner was four years younger than Thurber. The family lived in several different locations around town—his father Richard was the secretary and superintendent for the Builders and Traders Exchange—but when Ted was old enough to go to Ohio State they were living at

1694 North High Street, across the street from the Ohio State campus at Twelfth Avenue.

His older brother, Lyle, started a movie equipment business, which given the growing popularity of movies proved to be an astute move. Their father managed the firm and Ted also went to work there after college. He sold theater supplies and distributed films to theaters in the Columbus area, which he told Kinney proved to be the perfect setup for jokes after the Thurbers moved to New York and he returned to the area unannounced:

> Thurber was absolutely psychic in knowing when to call and be someone else. Once when I didn't know he was in town, he telephoned and pretended to be an irate manager of a convention hall who had rented a couple thousand chairs from us. He was mad as hell and wanted to know why my people had set up all the chairs facing the rear instead of facing the platform. As it turned out, just the day before I'd contracted to set up two thousand chairs in a convention hall. I had new help I wasn't sure of and it all could have happened the way Thurber described it. I had a dreadful time calming Thurber, who wanted his money back, was threatening to sue and to take the matter to the Better Business Bureau. I was still trying to build my business and he nearly gave me a heart attack.
>
> Another time he called as the manager of a local theater. He was slightly hysterical but rational enough to point out that although a Clara Bow movie was being shown, the marquee was advertising a William Hart film. "You're sending people into my theater expecting to see Bill Hart when I've got Clara Bow on the screen," Thurber shouted at me. Actually, I'd just been through an identical mix-up with the same theater and I thought I'd straightened it out. He seemed to sense what would work. He took me in every time, even when he made a big scene because my employees had delivered equipment to 165⅞ Main Street instead of 165½. It took me a few minutes to realize that no Columbus address contains a ⅞ fraction.[2]

The Gardiners and Herman Miller and his wife Dorothy became Thurber's closest Columbus friends. Ted and Julia had a house built at 2016 Devon Road in Upper Arlington and Thurber sometimes stayed there when he was in town.

When Althea was in the process of hiring a lawyer in late summer of 1934 to legally separate from him, Thurber decided he needed to get away to think and drove to Columbus with Robert Coates, the New Yorker's art critic and one of his closest friends at the time, and the pair landed at the Gardiners' house shortly after they arrived. While they were there, he learned by telephone that Althea had filed for divorce in Connecticut on the grounds of "intolerable cruelty." Thurber knew this was the beginning of an ugly court case.

"We all went out and got drunk as goats," Gardiner said. "Jim, Coates and I picked up Herman Miller and various other people along the way, and we went to the Rocky Fork Country Club. As I remember it, it was a very bad evening. Some coquettish girl at the club got drunk, and Jim, Coates and Miller all tried to make her. They began to fight over her and, of course, none of them succeeded. Jim was in a bad way that night. He carried a small torch for Althea, I think, in spite of their troubles. Later on, he used to say 'Nobody knows what to do about Althea or Nasser.'"[3]

Gardiner always visited Thurber when in New York, which he said made for some fascinating experiences:

> Once he kept me in a bar drinking until just prior to my train departure, and I had to dogtrot to Grand Central. Thurber let me get a head start and then began running frantically after me, shouting "Stop that man! That's my suitcase!" Luckily that sort of thing doesn't even draw attention in New York and I made my train. They closed the gate right after I got through, leaving Thurber shaking the bars and shouting that I'd never get away with this. He put everything he had into the gag and it was plenty. There's no one around now who could make the world the wild and funny place that he could.[4]

The Gardiners had finished an attic in their house with a spring door stairway. One night, Thurber led several others up there and sketched drawings in blue chalk on brown plasterboard, in some cases adding captions. One line, thought to have been put there by Thurber "and keep them for pallbearers" was a shortened version of an old expression that began with an expletive—"[screw] all but six, and keep them for pallbearers." Others joined in, which was fine with Thurber, and given his growing celebrity, the Gardiners were somewhat reluctant to leave the sketches when they moved to 2120 East Broad Street in Bexley in 1943. Fortunately the new owners left them alone and the people who bought the house in 1963—Richard and May Setterlin—thought enough of the drawings to try to salvage them when they were building a new home in October, 1970. A story about their efforts ran in the *Dispatch Sun-*

day Magazine and they were eventually removed and became part of the Thurber Collection at Ohio State.[5]

The Gardiners would have been disappointed if they had been lost. Their two daughters, Julia Hadley and Patricia McGuckin, grew up in a house where Thurber was an occasional houseguest, and they enjoyed his company almost as much as their parents did. Patricia eventually became a reporter for the *Columbus Dispatch*. Hadley, who graduated with a degree in English literature from Ohio State, conducted tours at Thurber House for many years.

McGuckin's prose in an unpublished paper she wrote in 1962 gives a good indication of what the Gardiner girls thought of Thurber:

> As far back as I can remember, the pattern of our family life was marked and brightened periodically by Jim Thurber's visits. [The] visits were always awesome occasions for me. . . . Though I was too young to appreciate his writing and mind, I instinctively knew that this tall, kind friend of my father's, with his restless gestures and his rapid-fire, sometimes incomprehensible manner of speaking, was no ordinary man. . . . Evenings at our house usually followed the same pattern—the dinner, then long hours of talk and laughter, most of the talk by Thurber, who was once called by a friend a "a night-blooming monologist."

In interviews with Rosemary Joyce in the 1970s, the three women made it clear that one of the family's lasting memories of Thurber was that it was difficult to get him to go to bed. They said he had no concept of time, and as McGuckin said, "he'd always stay up talking until four in the morning."[6]

"He never had to get up early either," their mother countered. "He used to sleep all morning."

During one of his visits with the family, he wrote what the Gardiner girls called the "looking glass limericks," backwards limericks in which he used the names of their two cocker spaniels, Polly and Molly. When he later rewrote the limericks and used them in *The 13 Clocks,* the girls he had composed them for were tickled. He dedicated his extended fable/fairytale *The Wonderful O* to the Gardiner family.

The tribute isn't surprising. When Thurber came to town, he could count on Ted Gardiner for whatever he needed, from companionship to taxi service. A 1953 visit to Columbus during the Christmas season concluded with Ted taking Jim and Helen to Union Station, as Thurber recounted in a humorous letter to the his family:

We got on the train all right in spite of the fact that no redcap showed up until after the trains got in. Ted loaded our seven bags on a truck and wheeled them to the gates himself. The station master, a friend of Ted's, kept saying everything would be fine, but he also kept calling me Mr. Gulick. We did get on the train only to find our space had been sold twice, the second time to a Mr. and Mrs. Gulick, who were put out of the compartment shouting and cursing. . . . We have to go to town Sunday to hear Elliott Nugent in a television version of "The Remarkable case of Mr. Bruhl." His place has probably been taken by Gulick.[7]

When Thurber was given the chance to both author and appear on stage in the 1960 revue *A Thurber Carnival,* an adaption of many of his stories given the title of his famous 1945 book, he agreed to have the show open in the Hartman Theater in Columbus rather than in East Coast venues that normally serve as the farm system for Broadway.

Ted Gardiner attended some of the rehearsals and he and his family were there on opening night—January 7, 1960—although Ted had been bothered by some the things he saw during the run-throughs in advance of the play.

"There was lots of changing done in the rehearsals—sometimes I could help," he said. "But I was disturbed by some of the rehearsals—by the presentation of some of the scenes. In the story 'If Grant Had Been Drunk at Appomattox,' they had General Grant appearing in white long balbriggans and I thought that was bad taste; and it shocked the pants off me, not because I'm a purist and there's anything wrong with balbriggans but it detracted from the grandeur of Grant. It was the sight gags that Thurber, being almost totally blind, wasn't aware of. The night of the opening I was watching the audience carefully, and their reactions were not hilarious. It worried me so much that I left, and rode around the streets. I came back just in time to see Burgess Meredith, the producer, racing across the foyer toward the balcony. My first reaction was 'My God, they're throwing things from the gallery!' All he was doing was trying to get up to the gallery to see how it looked from up there. It was considered a success in spite of my super-critical attitude."[8]

After a three-night run in Columbus, the show went on a six-week tour of the Midwest before its Broadway opening at the ANTA Theatre on February 26, 1960. It generally received good reviews and seemed to be doing well until an actors' strike shut it down after seventeen weeks. It reopened on September 12 and lasted three months with Thurber playing himself in the skit from "File and Forget." As chance would have it, the

Gardiners had come to New York for a visit and were there on that final, fateful night.

Jap Gude, producer Haila Stoddard, the Thurbers and the Gardiners all met at Ruby Foo's afterwards and the Thurbers especially couldn't understand why Helen Bonfils, who had bankrolled the production, couldn't continue to do that as a tax write-off.

Ted Gardiner listened to all of that blather, but he viewed the evening through the eyes of a close friend. In an interview with Kinney, he remembered that night as "the last time Jim was doing what he really liked."

Thurber was dead a little more than twenty months later.

<hr>

•

CHAPTER 46

Bookends of a Stage Career

The Hartman Theater is a vivid memory for many of Columbus older residents and a blank page to most of its younger ones. It stood on South Third Street on the southern-most part of the property where the Sheraton on Capital Square is today; before the theater died at the age of sixty in 1971, it lay next to the ten-story Hartman office building on the southwest corner of State and Third streets, the structure that gave its life for the construction of that hotel building.

Thurber would doubtless be disappointed that the theater didn't survive; it practically bookended Thurber's stage life. In the 1920s it was the site of some of the Scarlet Mask productions that Thurber wrote, directed and acted in. In January, 1960, with Thurber's spirit sagging and his health in decline, it hosted the opening of *A Thurber Carnival,* the musical revue that proved to be the last real triumph of his life.

With or without Thurber, the Hartman was one of the city's primary entertainment venues for decades, opening a few steps from Statehouse Square in 1911 when Thurber was sixteen years old. Its intimate surroundings made it a popular site for touring Broadway plays, and it was the site of many events, major and minor. Al Jolson (*Sinbad*), Maude Adams (*Peter Pan*), George Arliss (*Disraeli*), and Otis Skinner (*The Honor of the Family*) were among the early stars who appeared on the Hartman stage, and on September 20, 1912, presidential candidate Woodrow Wilson gave a speech to one thousand local businessmen there. Helen Hayes first appeared at the Hartman in *Babs* in 1921 and appeared in *Candle in the Wind* and *Victoria Regina* later. Tallulah Bankhead starred in *The Little Foxes* and *Design for Living*; Katherine Hepburn, Joseph Cotton, and Van Heflin appeared in *The Philadelphia Story*; and the Barrymores—Ethel, Lionel and John—all played the Hartman at various times. John Barrymore captivated audiences with his performance as *Hamlet* in the 1920s and returned with his farewell show, *My Dear Children,* in the early 1940s. George M. Cohan starred in *I'd Rather Be Right* during the same time period. The theater was chosen as the venue for the world-premiere of Eugene O'Neill's play *A Moon for the Misbegotten* on February 20, 1947, long before Thurber agreed to have *A Thurber Carnival* open in his hometown.

That revue came at a good time for him, his life having fallen in a downward spiral of ill feelings and ill health. His intermittent thyroid issues had flared up again, and *The Years With Ross,* his dual biography of publisher Harold Ross and the *New Yorker,* was still on the best seller list and still causing him problems with some of his dearest friends at the magazine. They were unhappy with his treatment of Ross, the magazine and them. It didn't set well with him that the *New Yorker* had taken to rejecting some of his submissions, or that he didn't agree with some of the editing decisions on the ones that were accepted.

Actress Haila Stoddard quelled these waves of negative vibes by proposing that some of his writings and cartoons be laced together and merged with original music as a stage production. Stoddard had been a fan of Thurber's since she was girl and she roughed out a script and showed it to her friend—Elliott Nugent—who showed it to Thurber. He asked her to read it to him and Helen in their suite at the Algonquin Hotel, and the session impressed him enough to give her the go-ahead. He had fielded many such proposals over the years, but she had picked most of his favorite pieces to include in revue. After struggling to complete his own plays to succeed *The Male Animal* for years, he must have realized that he would never finish his own plays and this might be his last shot at Broadway.

Stoddard had a wealthy friend in Denver named Helen Bonfils who was interested in theater and liked "to do things for fun and tax purposes." She told Stoddard she could have all the money she needed to get the show to Broadway. As it turned out, the number was $350,000.

Stoddard chose Burgess Meredith, a friend of Thurber's, to stage and direct it, and a pleased Thurber went to work writing and rewriting the show.

"I wanted someone who cared about Thurber's work as much as I," Stoddard said, about her decision to hire Meredith. "There wasn't a word in the final production that wasn't Thurber's."[1]

They decided to open in Columbus where there would be a receptive audience, and tour in the Midwest rather than use the traditional circuits of eastern cities on the road to Broadway. It was an interesting choice given that Thurber's relationship with his hometown had been all over the map; as recently as 1957, he had written to Dorothy Miller, "We haven't been to Columbus since my mother died in December, 1955, and don't want to go out again. It has become an enormous, vulgar and dispiriting city."[2] But the thought of having his revue open in the Hartman, where he experienced so much joy in his Scarlet Mask days, must have pleased him.

Seven weeks before the revue opened, Thurber came to Columbus to receive a Headliner Award from the Press Club of Ohio. He was lured by the fact that World War I flying ace Eddie Rickenbacker, golfer Jack Nicklaus, former international track star Jesse Owens, former Cleveland Indians pitching great Bob Feller, and cartoonist Milton Caniff were among the other honorees. That was all well and good until he got to the black tie affair at the Neil House hotel and he sat through media honors for eleven reporters, ten of whom were from local newspaper and television stations. He suddenly got the idea, partially inspired by alcohol, that he was merely being honored by the Columbus Press Club, and that he was had been duped into attending by organizers who made it seem like a statewide affair.

An annoyed Thurber visited the *Dispatch,* where he spoke insultingly to some staff members, who insulted him back. A female reporter told him that she had read his book on Harold Ross and didn't like it; an angry Thurber began spewing insults about the newspaper and its conservative policies.

George Smallsread, the paper's managing editor and Thurber's friend since their reporting days together, decided he had had enough. He vowed that not another line about Thurber would ever appear in the *Dispatch*.

That might not have presented a problem for either of them until it was announced that *A Thurber Carnival* would open in Columbus with a three-day run in early January. No apologies were forthcoming from either man; they acted like two angry six-year-olds. Publicist Virginia Hall Trannette said that she feared the worst and lobbied for reconciliation, but got nowhere:

Smallsread was still mad and said the *Dispatch* wasn't interested in the
Thurber revue. Thurber wouldn't apologize. I nearly went crazy with the
two of them acting like big babies. I finally blew my stack and told Smallsread that the opening of a future Broadway play in his city, its author
recognized by mayor and governor, was news and that he was acting like
a fool. Smallsread gave in. Then I got to Thurber and told him he'd better
behave himself, and that if I had to keep an eye on him, I'd even accompany him to the bathroom to prevent his damaging the press relations I'd
finally mended for the moment.[3]

Thurber behaved himself and his disposition improved. Two days
before the opening, Thurber was ushered into Mayor Ralston Westlake's
office to be honored as "a distinguished native son,"[4] the first award of its
kind in Columbus. Local photographers, not realizing that Thurber was
blind, tried to get him to pose reading the citation. Thurber got a laugh
out of that, and offered as a suggested headline "Blind Author Regains
Sight in City Hall!"[5]

After Governor Mike DiSalle read a proclamation on local TV declar-
ing it "James Thurber Week" in Ohio, a now conciliatory Thurber wrote a
story for the *Dispatch* on the importance of taking good care of the eyes.
"I felt the week should in some way be turned into something larger than
a person's private enterprise," he said.[6]

After the earlier storm of petulance, Thurber seemed to enjoy his
interaction with the local media. The cast rehearsed and he continued to
rewrite the revue.

"James stayed here much of the time, maybe a week or 10 days,"
Doral Chenowith said. "I did [the production] for *Newsweek* as a stringer;
I worked at the *Columbus Star*. I went over there every day in the afternoon; maybe I was star struck. I sat with him and we would go to a little
club sandwich shop off lobby of the Hartman Theater and we would have
grilled cheese sandwiches."[7]

Chenowith later became known as the "Grumpy Gourmet" and served
as the *Columbus Dispatch* food critic for over twenty years, so it's probably not surprising that he remembers every detail of those lunches at the
Club Restaurant:

It was just a few tables. I remember he liked grilled cheese, thick and
toasted and he wanted them on white bread. I can remember a discussion,
they were putting pimento on those sandwiches right out of a jar and he

objected to it and they followed his directions and dropped that. But every day he wanted those grilled cheese sandwiches.

I probably still have bruises on my left wrist. When you walked with him, he would hit you on the left wrist to see if you were still there.[8]

Opening night proved that the decision to open in Thurber's hometown was a good one; more than sixteen hundred attended what turned out to be a lavish, social affair at which some men wore black tie. The audience reacted favorably to the production, even though it clearly needed some work.

"A bunch of them went to Danny Deeds' Maramor for the cast dinner after the first night's grand opening, kind of the way they do Sardi's in New York," Chenowith said. "Of course in Columbus there were only a couple of reviews."[9]

The show played the Hartman for three days. Although the reviews were favorable. Thurber and Meredith spent their early afternoons in a hotel room reworking the sketches, Thurber dictating to a production secretary, Elinor Wright.

Stoddard knew better than to let all of the compliments go to her head.

"There's too much Thurber adulation around Columbus," she said. "We'll know better what line changes and cuts to make in other cities."[10]

The show played in Detroit, Cleveland, St. Louis, Cincinnati, and Pittsburgh before it finally opened at the ANTA Theatre on Broadway on February 26, 1960. It ran there for seventeen weeks before an actors strike interrupted production. When it resumed in September, it had lost some of its cast members and some of its momentum, but it had Thurber playing himself in the skit of "File and Forget."

The production lasted but three more months, and probably wouldn't have lasted that long if Thurber hadn't been in the cast. But the investors made money, much to Bonfils's disappointment, and Thurber had enjoyed a kind of farewell tour in his hometown before he died.

It probably meant more to him than he let on.

CHAPTER 47

•

The Neighborhood Kid Who "Collected" Thurber

When a visitor is buzzed into the Rare Books and Manuscripts Room at The Ohio State University's Thompson Library and handed a file that holds original Thurber letters or a folder containing the first draft of a Thurber manuscript, he probably has no idea that the exchange couldn't have happened without an assist from one of the kids from Thurber's east side Columbus neighborhood.

Thomas Bradfield Meek was three years younger than Thurber and knew him initially as one of the older kids at the ball field behind the Ohio School for the Blind. As a young boy, he didn't know him that well and had no reason to think he would. Instead, he became another one of Thurber's childhood acquaintances who regularly turned up in his life.

Their destinies drew them together repeatedly, even after Thurber was dead. When Thurber landed in New York and began scaling the heights as a young writer, Meek had taken a position as a stockbroker there and hence became one of his drinking companions. When blindness and illness conspired to make Thurber miserable later in life, Meek often provided solace and support. When Thurber's ashes were buried in Green Lawn Cemetery in Columbus, Meek was among the mourners. When Thurber's letters, manuscripts, and photos were close to being donated to Yale University several years after his death, Meek used both his position as chairman of the Ohio State development fund board and his money to help create the Thurber Collection that scholars use today.

Like most boys on the city's near east side, Tommy Meek was drawn to the blind school ball field, which he later called "a great Mecca for all of the boys that Jim would know."[1] The Meek family lived in a two-family house at 49 South Monroe Avenue, five blocks north of the athletic field, then moved to 240 South Eighteenth Street, about three blocks east of the school yard, in 1907.

Tommy's father, William, worked with his father in a saddlery and harness manufacturing business—J. W. Meek and Company on East Spring Street—that his dad had started in the 1870s.

Tommy followed Thurber to Sullivant, Douglas, and East High School. They shared the same English teacher in Miss Mary Ferrell and truthfully not much else. Meek became the editor of the East High school newspaper, the *X-Rays*—even Thurber never did that—and decided to go into journalism at Ohio State. In part because Thurber dropped out of school for a year, they ended up working together on the campus newspaper.

"Our relationship became much closer through our experience together on the *Ohio State Lantern*," Meek said. "I entered the school of journalism as a freshman and we had a system then of news editors. One of the junior students would be assigned a day each week to be the editor of the day and I was fortunate enough to be a cub reporter under Jim during that period and I always stuck around the *Lantern* offices until two or maybe three in the morning when we put the *Lantern* to bed."[2]

This gave both of them a chance to walk over to Minnette Fritts's place, toss stones at her window and try to convince her to join then for a late night snack; both possessed a romantic interest in her and also considered her a friend. Even though they had grown up within a half mile of each other, Meek said his experience with Thurber on the *Lantern* gave him his first real peek at the playful Thurber mind:

> We had some interesting experiences on the *Lantern*. We had a one-eyed linotype operator named Morris Hewlett and, of course, he and Thurber had a great affinity because of their common affliction. He would come storming out of the type setting room and say "What do you think we've got back here, rubber type?" Because, as you know, when you write headlines, the width of the column is limited and you have to know how many characters are in each line—which depends on whether you use one or more columns or the size of type and so on. And when we wrote our headlines, we'd have to gauge that so it would fit. And Jim, just the pixie

nature in him, would quite often put too many characters in there and that caused Mr. Hewlett's distress. But they were always good friends. And once in a while he would slip in an item that really didn't belong in the *Lantern* and leave it up to Hewlett to catch it.[3]

This was the mischievous Thurber, who Meek saw a lot of during those *Lantern* days. Meek remembered a night when the *Lantern* had a page to fill and nothing to put in it. As chance would have it, he peered out of the window of the Shops Building (later called Welding Engineering Laboratories), where the *Lantern*'s offices were located, and happened to notice strange lights in the northern sky. Thurber decided that it must be the Aurora Borealis, and told Meek to write a story about it. Meek called up Professor Lord, the head of the astronomy department, and Lord explained that the northern lights hadn't been seen in Columbus in fifteen or twenty years. Whether that's really what Meek saw or not, it was the kind of random story that could fill up a page.

Even if he lucked into this one, Thurber couldn't always be trusted to exercise good judgment.

"Those little items he would inject might be something about a bulldog seducing a coed or something highly unlikely," Meek said.[4]

As fate would have it, Meek pledged Phi Kappa Psi, where their mutual friend Elliott Nugent was also one of the brothers. Meek would eventually try to get Thurber in, a tough sell even for the handsome, popular Nugent. Meek was Thurber's friend, but he could understand why.

"Even while Jim amused us with his jokes and charm, even while he was trying so hard to be a regular guy, there was a conflict in him," Meek said. "You could feel it. He wasn't ever a complete fraternity man because there was an antisocial streak in him. He had other interests and leaned toward what we used to call 'the masses.' He hated Republicans—and we were all Republicans—because, I suppose, of what they did to his father. He amused us, but he was a little odd. He didn't have many close friends."[5]

Thurber left school to become a code clerk during World War I, and after he returned, he and Meek both became involved with the Scarlet Mask theater group associated with the university. They collaborated on several productions and their friendship tightened, but both moved on— and were eventually reunited in New York.

After majoring in journalism, Meek landed a job with New York investment firm S. W. Strauss and Company in 1922 and he moved to Jackson, Boesel and Company as syndicate manager for the distribution of common stocks five years later. This was about the same time Thurber joined the staff of the *New Yorker,* so they were on a parallel rise. They shared common friends and drank in many of the same places during a period when Thurber often seemed out of control.

"It was difficult being with Jim," Meek said. "He seemed to like misbehaving, being the bad boy. It was an antisocial strain in him. One time, Tony threw him out of his speakeasy for acting up, and another time, during dinner at Elliott Nugent's place, Jim started to smash furniture, insulted everyone and even got into some scuffling. He was perverse, like a small boy, taking the opposite point of view just to annoy and provoke you. It was sort an intellectual exercise, I suppose, just to see what would happen. For instance, I am a Republican. Jim knew that full well, yet he launched a tirade against Republicans whenever I was around. At Costello's one night, he had too much to drink and called me a "cold, calculating capitalist." I resented it, but I was amazed when he phoned me the next day to apologize, which he rarely did then. But I respected Jim as a genius. What can you do with a genius?"[6]

As Thurber became more and more successful financially, Meek handled his investments. On January 9, 1940, when *The Male Animal,* the play cowritten by Thurber and Nugent, opened on Broadway at the Cort Theater, Meek threw a theater party for them jammed with all of the OSU alumni Meek he could corral.[7]

Meek maintained a strong loyalty to Ohio State, even during a period when Thurber distanced himself from it. He was active in the New York Alumni Association and served as president of it on several occasions. He also served as president of the Ohio Society of New York. In the meantime, he became manager of the midtown offices of the New York brokerage firm of Harris, Upham and Co., in 1954—he later became vice-president of the company which would merge with Smith Barney and Co. in the 1970s—and served as a volunteer in the New York area for the university's development fund. That in turn helped him land a position on the university's development fund board in 1957.

After Thurber died in 1961, his friend became an important advocate for him within the university. Meek eventually became chairman on the board, which positioned him perfectly for the lobbying needed to make the harvesting of material that became the Thurber Collection happen.

"It started in the Development Fund," Meek told Lewis Branscomb, who would become the curator of the collection. "You could come before the board every year for a request for $10,000 for the library enrichment fund and I think I inquired at the time whether any of that was being used for collection of some of Thurber's works because I realized that the threat of material going to Yale still existed. I felt along with many other people that his works should be at Ohio State and in Columbus. Well, word came back that you (Branscomb) were picking up some manuscripts and books and various items whenever you could get your hands on them, so I decided that my annual contribution to the President's Club would be directed toward the Thurber Fund."[8]

Meek did more than contribute a substantial amount of money for the acquisition of the material. From his position on the board, he put pressure on the university to "properly fit up the room so that the works that he hoped to acquire would just have a proper home."

This meant a lot to Helen, Thurber's second wife. She wouldn't have contributed the material she did without that assurance, and having a friend involved—Meek—must have made it easier for her to commit it to Ohio State.

"She was pretty adamant that she wanted the collection, whatever material she wanted to give to the university, should be properly housed and properly presented," Meek said. "After talking it over with her, I wrote a letter to President [Novice] Fawcett and Vice President [Gordon] Carson and just stated bluntly that they either had to put up some money or else they were going to lose the very valuable manuscripts that she had."[9]

They did, and so did Meek. In 1965 he was a major contributor for a $9,750 purchase of material from Thurber's brother, Robert, that included Thurber's childhood drawings, report cards, photographs, a twenty-two-page "western" written in high school and dozens of books, many autographed by Thurber.[10]

Hundreds of guests descended upon the Thompson Library for the dedication of the James Thurber Reading Room in 1970. A happy Branscomb thanked Meek—"a lot of the work in helping us get this room was done by the Class of 1917, Thurber's classmates, under the direction of Thomas B. Meek."—and proudly declared that "we now have the largest collection of Thurber in the world."[11]

It is a both a fitting tribute to Thurber and to a friend from the old neighborhood, who did everything in his power to make it happen.

CHAPTER 48

The Last Flower

James Thurber must have suspected that he would end up at Green Lawn cemetery, even if he had other ideas. The 360-acre cemetery on the south side of Columbus served as the final earthly address for both his parents and grandparents and a small army of relatives, friends, mentors and colleagues. It only seemed logical that he would join them.

Most of us aren't anxious to go to our final resting place and Thurber was no different. Almost two years before he died, Thurber prepared to visit Columbus while his health deteriorated, and he made a joke of it in a letter to the Van Doren family that he counted among his good friends:

> We are leaving for Columbus tonight and hope to return in a week or so, especially since I do not want to be buried in Green Lawn cemetery there, in which my once bickering, but now silent, family occupies a good square mile of space.[1]

Thurber biographer Burton Bernstein treated this like a serious request not to be buried there, then made it sound as if Thurber's explicit instructions had been ignored. He didn't explain why Thurber would have made that request to the Van Dorens, and not to those who would actually have a say in the matter.

He had once written that he wished his ashes to be strewn on the seas between New York and Bermuda, but again, this doesn't exactly qualify as a formal request. When he died on November 2, 1961, after nearly a month in a coma and Helen Thurber had him cremated, she discovered that his brothers were angry with her for having done that. At that point, she didn't dare bury him anywhere but in Columbus with his family.[2]

A brief graveside service with a small group of friends covered it. Helen, Thurber's daughter Rosemary and her husband Fred, brothers Robert and William, James Pollard and John Fullen from Ohio State, *Dispatch* managing editor and newspaper colleague George Smallsread, former OSU classmates and lifelong pals Elliott Nugent and Thomas Meek, actor Burgess Meredith (who had directed *A Thurber Carnival*) and friend Jap Gude gathered under the awning tent to hear Reverend Karl Scheufler of the First Methodist Church of Columbus read some brief prayers and a verse from the Methodist hymnal:

> Now the laborer's task is over;
> Now the battle day is past;
> Now upon the further shore
> Lands the voyager at last.
> Father, in Thy gracious keeping
> Leave we now Thy servant sleeping.

"I kept it very brief," Reverend Scheufler said. "I didn't know the family well, but I'd preached at Mame's funeral, and I suppose that was why I was asked to preside at this one."[3]

For a Columbus native who achieved fame in part because of his humorous stories about the people, places and things he remembered from the city, Green Lawn actually proved to be a fitting location for his ashes. Since the cemetery's founding in 1848, much of the city's royalty had been buried there, including some city pioneers who were originally interred in the old North Graveyard that occupied an eleven-acre, four-block area in the vicinity of the North Market.

They were *all* supposed to have been moved to Green Lawn in the 1870s and 1880s when a new Union Station was under construction in today's Short North across High Street from the graveyard. But in recent years when the city has had to dig sewer lines in that area, workers have discovered the bones of early settlers who didn't make the trip with their tombstones to the south end of town.

Some did, especially when their graves were well marked and local families knew where their relatives were. John Kerr, one of the city's proprietors and its second mayor, is *supposed* to have been moved there from the North Graveyard, but there is no way to be sure. The remains of Lucas Sullivant, who founded the settlement of Franklinton on the west side of the Scioto River that preceded Columbus by fifteen years, were moved from the Franklinton Cemetery to Green Lawn, as were those of his wife, Sarah.

Green Lawn became the prestige address for deceased early Columbus pioneers and heroes. Its second permanent occupant was Dr. Benjamin F. Gard, who died of cholera on July 12, 1849, after responding to a cholera outbreak at the Ohio Penitentiary,

Many local business titans were interred in Green Lawn including Eddie Rickenbacker, World War I flying ace, race car driver, one-time owner of the Indianapolis Motor Speedway, and CEO of Eastern Air Lines; P. W. Huntington, founder of Huntington Bank; Samuel Medary, nineteenth-century newspaper politician and publisher whose antiwar newspaper *The Crisis* enjoyed a national circulation during the Civil War; and Samuel Bush, local industrialist and grandfather of President George H. W. Bush and great-grandfather of President George W. Bush. Thurber's family, including most of the Fisher clan and Aunt Margery Albright; the three Ohio State professors he wrote about in *The Thurber Album*; former *Dispatch* city editor and Thurber nemesis Norman "Gus" Kuehner; and OSU martinet George L. "Commy" Converse are also Green Lawn neighbors, so the bronze urn containing his ashes is certainly in familiar territory.

"The thing that most impressed me at that burial," Smallsreed said, "was how Meredith, Gude and I simply stared at that tiny urn, as if we were trying to convince ourselves that this could be all that remained of that powerful force, James Thurber."[4]

There weren't many flowers—the family had requested contributions to "Fight for Sight" in their place—and the service was remarkably brief.

News of Thurber's death made the front pages of the *New York Times* and other newspapers around the world. The day after the funeral, the *New Yorker* weighed in with its own epitaph.

William Shawn's part of the obituary paid homage to Thurber's part in the magazine's tradition and noted that "his work was largely unclassifiable, it was simply Thurber." The tribute that his friend and *New Yorker* colleague E. B. White wrote nailed it the way no one else could:

The whole world knows what a funny man he was, but you had to sit next to him day after day to understand the extravagance of his clowning, the wildness and subtlety of his thinking, and the intensity of his interest in others and his sympathy for their dilemmas—dilemmas he instantly enlarged, put into focus and made immortal, just as he enlarged and made immortal the strange goings on in the Ohio home of his boyhood. His waking dreams and his sleeping dreams commingled shamelessly and uproariously. Ohio was never far from his thoughts, and when he received a medal from his home state in 1953, he wrote, "The clocks that strike in my dreams are often the clocks of Columbus." It is a beautiful sentence and a revealing one.

He was both a practitioner of humor and a defender of it. The day he died, I came on a letter from him. "Every time is a time for humor," he wrote. "I write humor the way a surgeon operates, because it is a livelihood, because I have a great urge to do it, because many interesting challenges are set up, and because I have the hope that it may do some good." Once, I remember, he heard someone say that humor is a shield, not a sword, and it made him mad. He wasn't going to have anyone beating his sword into a shield. That "surgeon," incidentally, is pure Mitty. During his happiest years, he did not write the way a surgeon operates, he wrote the way a child skips rope, the way a mouse waltzes.

Although he was known for *Walter Mitty* and *The Male Animal,* the book of his I like best is *The Last Flower.* In it, you will find his faith in the renewal of life, his feeling for the beauty and fragility of life on earth. Like all good writers, he fashioned his own best obituary notice. Nobody else can add to the record, much as he might like to. And of all the flowers, real and figurative, that will find their way to Thurber's last resting place, the one that will remain fresh and wiltproof is the little flower he himself drew, on the last page of that lovely book.[5]

An image of that flower is carved into his gravestone at Green Lawn. It marks a fitting end to a remarkable life.

Herman Miller and Althea and James Thurber with three unidentified friends at Buckeye Lake in 1922. (James Thurber Papers, Rare Books & Manuscripts Library of The Ohio State University Libraries)

The Rest of Thurberville

Ohio Avenue School

Thurber started first grade in the fall of 1900 at the Ohio Avenue School, while the family was living at 921 South Champion Avenue. He was in the second grade there in April, 1902, when his father, who had been appointed to a U.S. Justice Department commission the previous fall, moved the family to Washington, DC.

The school, located at 505 South Ohio Avenue, was built in 1895 and it is still in use today; it was one of several Columbus schools that were earmarked for the wrecking ball in the early 2000s and was renovated instead. After a $9 million renovation that started in 2003, the school reopened in the fall of 2007.

When the family returned from Washington in June, 1903, and took up residence at 625 Oak Street, the boys attended Sullivant School.

Doc Marlowe

The fabulous Doc Marlowe, the medicine show man who made elixir that he supposedly called Black Hawk Liniment, and who wore a ten gallon hat with kitchen matches stuck in the band, was one of Thurber's most fascinating Columbus characters. But his real name wasn't Marlowe but Marler, and his pain reliever was actually called "Sioux Liniment."

Thurber's piece on him first appeared in the *New Yorker* on November 2, 1935, well after Daniel Marler died. But given the nature of the story, in which it's clear that his subject was a bit of a scoundrel, it's easy to see why a writer might want to give him an alias. Marler was a boarder with Aunt Margery Albright for years, and when Thurber profiled her in "A Daguerreotype of a Lady" in *The Thurber Album,* he called the medicine by its real name. But he still referred to the Doc as Marlowe and not Marler, which is how he is listed in the city directories during those years.

"Doc Marlowe wore scarred leather leggings, a bright-colored bead vest that he said he got from the Indians, and a ten-gallon hat with kitchen matches stuck in the band, all the way round. He was about six feet four inches tall, with big shoulders, and a long, drooping moustache. He let his hair grow long, like General Custer's. He had a wonderful collection of Indian relics and six-shooters, and he used to tell me stories of his adventures in the Far West. His favorite expressions were "Hay, boy!" and "Hay, boy-gie!," which he used the way some people now use "Hot dog!" or Doggone!" He told me once that he had killed an Indian chief named Yellow Hand in a tomahawk duel on horseback. I thought he was the greatest man I had ever seen. It wasn't until he died and his son came from New Jersey for the funeral that I found out he had never been in the Far West in his life. He had been born in Brooklyn."[1]

Actually, Marler was born in Ohio. He had a shooting gallery with John Williamson at 188 North High Street in 1887 and a saloon at 143 North Third Street in 1888. The following year city directories listed him as a "horse dealer" at 662 North High. By 1902, he had become a carpenter. There are plenty of gaps in listings for him in the directories, times when he presumably could have been traveling around the west killing Indians or simply peddling his drugs at the traveling medicine shows he told the young Thurber about.

Either way, he seems to have settled in at Aunt Margery's house around 1906–07, and remained there until he died on June 26, 1924, five years after his landlord died and left the house to her widowed daughter, Belle Harte. At the time of Marler's death, Harte was listed as an employee of Sioux Liniment, described in an ad in Ohio State's *Sundial* humor magazine as "A Columbus Made Liniment with a Middle West Reputation."

Marler once admitted to Thurber that he had called it "snake oil" before he brought it to Columbus.

Reverend E. Stacy Matheny

Thurber wrote about Reverend E. Stacy Matheny, his mother's first cousin, in "Daguerreotype of a Lady," his portrait of Aunt Margery Albright in *The Thurber Album*. Matheny was a frequent visitor of Thurber's grandparents, William and Katherine Fisher, and one of the relatives Thurber saw often in his youth.

Matheny aspired to be an architect as a boy and studied with the Scranton School of Architecture before he was called to the ministry. He never lost interest in architecture, and he became known to his friends and parishioners as "The Preacher Architect" because he helped design homes, churches and schools while serving as a minister.[2]

He served in several southern Ohio communities—Byer, Chillicothe, Piketon, Portsmouth, and Crooksville, the latter where he designed and built a new church and parsonage. After he became a deacon in 1900, he was ordained as elder in the King Avenue M. E. Church in Columbus. He would serve at several Columbus churches, including the Reeb Avenue M. E. Church, the Cleveland Avenue M. E. Church, and the Independent Protestant Church, while also practicing architecture.

He died in 1949 and was buried in Green Lawn Cemetery.

Julius Ziegfeld

Thurber dedicated one of his portraits in *The Thurber Album* to Julius A. Ziegfeld, an old friend and carpenter "who could fix anything that was broken in a house, from cellar to attic." Most of "Snapshot of Mr. Ziegfeld" centered on Election Day 1916, when Thurber served as the Republican registrar and Ziegfeld served as Democratic registrar at their polling place. Ziegfeld wanted to argue with Thurber about politics, about God and about any other matter that was suitable for debate, and Thurber didn't, but he never forgot the long day they spent together.

Thurber described Ziegfeld as a legendary coffee drinker. He told Thurber he could drink fifty cups of coffee on the day of a crisis, but admitted he rarely drank more than twenty a day. He said in the corner of Holland where he grew up, babies sipped coffee in their cribs.

Ziegfeld was a stubborn Dutchman, the son of a baker named Carl Ziegfeld who owned a bakery and confectionary at 422 East Main Street (originally 346 East Friend before the street name and street numbers were changed). Julius had been born in Amsterdam in 1867, and worked

in his father's bakery in his younger years, but became a respected crafts-
man who did work for the wealthy families who lived in many of the
large houses on East Broad Street and Bryden Road.

He moved into a house at 78 South Washington Avenue in 1899, and
lived there with his wife, Emma, for the rest of his life. His oldest son,
Carl, told Thurber that his father "had a carpentry shop at the rear of
our home, which served less as a workshop than as a collecting place
for all the material he gathered from the many buildings he repaired. He
refused to throw anything away and even saved pipe fittings that had
rusted through or that had burst from freezing."[3]

Ziegfeld had nine children, some of whom continued to live in the
house on South Washington after their father died on April 27, 1946.

Columbus Metropolitan Library

The Carnegie Library, today known at the main branch of the Columbus Metropolitan Library, was a frequent haunt of both Thurber and his
father, Charles. It got its impetus from a $200,000 grant from philan-
thropist Andrew Carnegie in 1901 when Thurber was seven years old. At
the time, the property at 96 South Grant Avenue was the site of a house
built by Noah H. Swayne in 1848 that had been leased to the state as the
residence for six Ohio governors, including future President Rutherford
B. Hayes. The house was razed early in 1903, to make room for the new
library. It was dedicated on April 4, 1907, and twelve-year-old Thurber
signed up for a library card with his grandparents' Bryden Road address
the day after it opened. The building was 2½ blocks from the Fisher house
and all of the Thurber boys doubtless spent some time there. But after old
City Hall was destroyed by fire on January 21, 1921, temporary offices
were set up in the library building, and Thurber, then a reporter for the
Columbus Dispatch, often set up shop there in the library's reading room.
Early library plans showed two reading rooms, one on the north end of
the first floor and one on the north end of the second floor with newspapers and periodicals. That room, which could correspond to today's Carnegie room, seems the likely destination for the young newspaper reporter.
Years later, a reporter digging into Thurber's background asked an old
librarian if she remembered seeing Thurber in the reading room there
often and she replied that certainly she did and she saw his father there
just as often. Today, the original building is at the front end of a much
larger library complex that underwent a massive remodeling in 2015–16.

Buckeye Lake

Thirty miles east of Columbus, Buckeye Lake has been a popular destination for central Ohio residents since the nineteenth century. It was built as the Licking Summit Reservoir in 1826 as a feeder lake for the Ohio and Erie Canal project and in 1835 Thomas Minthorn opened the first hotel in the vicinity. By the 1910s, Buckeye Lake boasted an amusement park on its north shore and twenty-one hotels and boarding houses for visitors who flocked there from around the state, mostly on the interurban electric railcars. There were two dance pavilions, an arcade, a beach, a bathhouse, picnic grounds, and a ballpark. It's difficult to know how many times Thurber visited there, although he definitely visited with new wife Althea in 1922 with close friend Herman Miller and other friends. Thurber later recalled winning "a canary bird throwing baseballs at bells" at Buckeye Lake in 1923.[4] He mentioned it in a "Sequence of Servants" in *My Life and Hard Times*. In describing one of the Thurber servants, Gertie Straub, he wrote that she "came in after two o'clock one night from a dancing party at Buckeye Lake and awakened us by bumping into and knocking over furniture. 'Who's down there?' called mother from upstairs. 'It's me, dearie,' said Gertie, 'Gertie Straub.' 'What are you doing?' demanded mother. 'Dusting,' said Gertie.[5] Buckeye Lake State Park was created there in 1949. The amusement park closed in 1970, although the lake and surrounded communities remain a magnet for boaters and fishermen.

Douglas School

Old Douglas School, where Thurber attended the seventh and eighth grades, was 101 years old when it was demolished in 1976 for the construction of a new Douglas. The new building occupied the same site as the old one at 43 South Douglass Street, two blocks south of East Broad Street on the city's Near East Side, but its service to the school system didn't last as long. It closed in 2010. Thurber moved from Sullivant to Douglas in 1907 when the family moved in with the Fishers on Bryden Road from the Norwich Hotel, and he remained there when they lived at 568 Oak Street in 1908–09. Thurber was elected the 1909 "class prophet," and wrote a class prophecy that was seventeen typewritten pages long. It is regarded by Thurber scholars as his first writing that showed a hint of his later promise. Some even believe it had traits of "The

Secret Life of Walter Mitty." Graduation from Douglas was the last he
would see of childhood sweetheart Eva Prout for eleven years. She left
school after the eighth grade to pursue a professional acting and singing
career.

Olentangy Park

Olentangy Park was a grand amusement park that featured a dance pavil-
ion, theater, swimming pool, bowling alleys, rental boat docks on the river
and rides—roller coasters, Ferris wheels, loop-the-loop, shoot the chutes,
etc. It occupied the property about a mile north of the Ohio State campus at 2907 North High Street where Olentangy Village, a sprawling red
brick complex of condominiums, stands today.

Robert M. Turner opened a park called The Villa there in 1893 and
the Columbus Street and Railroad Co. bought the site in 1896; the street
car line's North High Street route ended here. It added picnic grounds
and some facilities for amusement including gambling, and renamed it
Olentangy Park. In 1899, the Dusenbury brothers purchased the park and
expanded it. The theater included 2,248 elegant opera chairs, was illuminated by nearly 2,000 electric lights and featured the largest orchestra pit
in Columbus. Summer theater flourished here.

This was one of Thurber's favorite places while growing up, which
could probably be said of most kids in Columbus. In 1906 at the age of
eleven, Thurber and cousin Earl Fisher took the trolley here, spent the day
and were down to their last fifteen cents—their trolley fare. Instead they
spent the money riding on the loop-the-loop ride—and walked the eleven
miles home.[6] At the end of his freshman year at Ohio State, Thurber spent
the summer of 1914 working here selling tickets at the Panama Canal
exhibit. During the summer of 1917, he worked as a publicity agent for
the park. After Thurber quit his job at the *Columbus Dispatch* in 1924
and he took a hiatus with first wife Althea to work on a novel in a cabin
in upstate New York, he returned Columbus without a job and briefly
went back to publicizing Olentangy Park and a few other entertainment
venues. It was his last association with the old amusement park.

The park was sold to L. L. LeVeque in 1938 and torn down so that
Olentangy Village could be built. The park's merry-go-around is in use at
the Columbus Zoo.

Una Soderblom

When Thurber was a senior in high school during the fall and winter of 1912–13, he had a job working at a small tobacco store at 327 North 20th Street—the Soderblom Cigar Company—just north of the corner of Mt. Vernon Avenue.

The store was run by Una Soderblom, a Swede who was four years older than Thurber. Most of the patrons were workingmen and the majority of them worked for the Pennsylvania Railroad, which had its machine shops ten or twelve blocks north. Thurber described most of the patrons at "engineers, firemen and brakemen."

"My memory of their problems is dim," Thurber wrote. "But I think that their greatest one was waking up in time to get to their trains. Often they turned over and went back to sleep after being telephoned by the official Caller. . . . He was a slight, grayish man who never wore a collar, but always wore a back collar button anyway, and he sat at a table with a telephone on it in the rear of the store. Just why his office was in the tobacco shop I never found out.

"He studied in his spare time what he called 'Physic.' Physic was, in reality, the science of psychic phenomena, especially hypnotism. Most of the engineers and firemen scoffed at his studies, but there was one fireman named McCready who was a pushover for the Caller. The Caller used to hypnotize McCready every time he came into the store. He would do this by spinning a small top on one of the glass cigar counters, and make the fireman stare at it; then he would speak to him in a low, commanding voice and McCready would stiffen all over and begin to flop around as if he were a mechanical fireman instead of a live one. Most of the engineers who saw these performances were not very crazy about making runs with McCready.

"Another interesting character was an engineer who could spit fifteen feet, and there was a fireman who had been runner-up for two successive years in the speed races of the Central Ohio Ice Skating Carnival. I remember one day he came into the shop and said he had just bought a blue suit "with a red stripe into it." And that's all I got out of my experience with railroad workers. In those days I didn't think much about the plight of the workingman, if, indeed, I knew that he had one, and anyway I was elected president of my senior class at high school while I was working at the shop, which made me feel superior to everybody that came into the place, even Mr. Soderblom."[7]

Soderblom was only in the cigar business for four or five years after Thurber worked there. He managed the Mid-Star Loan Company and eventually became a salesman in a clothing store. He died in 1940 at the age of forty-nine.

John D. Harlor

Thurber told *Time* in 1951 that his mother asked Harlor, the principal at East High School while Thurber was in school there, not to give him the editorship of the high school newspaper *The X-Rays* because of his eyesight. However, the paper did print Thurber's first published story, "The Third Bullet," in May, 1913.

The Harlors lived across Franklin Avenue from the school and let Chic Harley, the school's athletic hero, live with them for a school year after his family moved to Chicago. But Harlor left his job as principal after six years and became a teacher at North High. He subsequently became the superintendent of the Franklin County Children's Home.

At the age of fifty, he was too old for service in World War I, but became a member of the Spalding Educational Unit that served overseas. After the war, he returned to East High as a teacher and retired from the Columbus Public Schools in 1934. He lived near Westerville during his retirement years and died in March, 1954, at the age of eighty-six.

John Hance

In "The Figgerin' of Aunt Wilma," which first appeared in the *New Yorker* of June 10, 1950, and was later included in the book *Thurber Country,* Aunt Wilma squabbles with exasperated grocer John Hance over the two cents she thinks he owes her after he runs out of pennies to give her in change. Aunt Wilma was really Thurber's Aunt Margery, but Hance was Hance.

Just as Thurber wrote, Hance's grocery stood "on the south side of Town Street, just east of Fourth" near the Central Market. Hance's operated the store at 207–209 East Town, for thirty-eight years, a block from Aunt Margery's house at 185 South Fifth. It explains why Thurber described its "wide oak floor board . . . worn pleasantly smooth by the shoe soles of three generations of customers." Hance opened his grocery in the late 1870s and the old Civil War veteran continued to operate it until he was seventy years old in 1914, two years before his death.

For most of this time he lived in a house that is still standing at 1093 East Long Street and he died there. At the time of his death, he also owned the John W. Hance Casting Company in Westerville with his two sons, Harry T. Hance and J. Marston Hance. It is doubtful that any of them were ever able to square the books with Thurber's Aunt Margery.

Buckeye Steel Castings

Thurber worked for part of a summer while he was in high school at this steel factory at the intersection of Parsons Avenue and Frank Road on the south side of Columbus, a plant that was called Columbus Castings when it was sold and closed in 2016. Thurber likely got the job because the father of Ed Morris, his best friend at the time, owned a local iron works company with connections to the plant.

Thurber had the job when Samuel Prescott Bush was the president of the company. Bush held that position from the 1908 to 1928; he was to become the respective grandfather and great-grandfather of President George H. W. Bush and President George W. Bush.

The company started as the Murray-Hayden Foundry, which made iron farm implements, but became successful when it started manufacturing railroad couplers. The company was closely associated with rail baron E. H. Harriman and for a while was under the control of Frank Rockefeller, the brother of oil magnate John D. Rockefeller.

Miss Naddy's Dancing Academy

This place apparently became one of Thurber's favorite tales—and one he never wrote about. When Thurber asked Minnette Fritts to go to the Phi Kappa Psi dance during the Christmas season of 1917, he was conscious about how poor of a dancer he was compared to Fritts' other suitors, so he decided to take dance lessons.

This led him to Miss Naddy's Dancing Academy, which Helen Thurber recalled in her forward to the posthumous Thurber book *Credos and Curios*, published in 1962.

"This was a favorite Thurber recitation told with nostalgic relish," she wrote, "and I will never forget the picture of the dancing class, over a bowling alley very much on the wrong side of the tracks, and so delight-fully different from the prim, white-gloved school where I learned to one-step. At Miss Naddy's (forgive me if I misspell her name—I have only heard it spoken), most the students smoked cigars and packed guns, but their teacher was pretty tough herself, and never daunted. 'All right, now we'll try another moonlight waltz,' she would yell, after three previous attempts by candlelight had failed, ending in what could hardly be called waltzing, 'and this time I want you guys to stay out from behind them palms!'"

In fact, Margaret A. Naddy taught at the Emerson Dance Academy at High and Warren Streets, in the heart of today's Short North. She mar-ried William Henry Turkopp on January 8, 1917 in St. Joseph Cathedral; Turkopp also taught dance there. She died of influenza on March 29, 1920, at the age of forty.

1104 Fair Avenue

The Thurbers were living in this two story frame house on March 13, 1913, "The Day the Dam Broke."[8] The family apparently didn't live in this house long, possibly less than a year; it was one of the fourteen differ-ent addresses that the Thurber family occupied in Columbus from 1892 to 1918.

Reverend Karl W. Scheufler

Reverend Karl W. Scheufler lived a full life before presiding at the grave-side service for James Thurber in 1961. The Sandusky, Ohio, native attended Ohio Wesleyan University, Columbia University, Union Theo-logical Seminary (NY), Harvard, and Boston University, receiving the AB, AM, and STB degrees. After he was ordained a minister in the Method-ist Church, he was ordained an elder in the Methodist Church and he and his wife Ada went to China for five years for missionary work. The Karl and Ada Scheufler Papers are now in the archives of Yale University Divinity School Library serving as a source of history for this period in China.

In the 1930s and 1940s Karl was the pastor of Trinity Methodist Church in Cincinnati until he returned to the Army as a chaplain during World War II. On December 19, 1942, Karl joined the 355th AAA Searchlight Battalion as a captain and was with them in North Africa and Europe. After the war, the family moved to 946 Bryden Road in Columbus and he pastored for the nearby First Methodist Church, on the southwest corner of Bryden Road and Eighteenth Street.

He said he kept his remarks at the graveside service "very brief" because he didn't know the family well. He thought he was chosen for the service because he had presided over Mame Thurber's funeral in December, 1955.[9]

Tionesta Apartments

After Thurber married Althea Adams on May 20, 1922, they moved into this sprawling, sixteen-room, 2½-story, red brick building that looks a like two houses have been combined. This handsome building is still in use at 868–870 Neil Avenue, on the southeast corner of Neil and Wilber Avenues, one block south of West First Avenue.

George Karb

George Karb was elected mayor of Columbus twice, from 1891 to 1894 and again from 1912 to 1920. He went to the mayor's chair the first time from his job as city police commissioner and the second time from the job as Franklin County sheriff.

Karb was a likable guy and a tireless promoter of the city, a son of German immigrants who came to Columbus in 1844, fourteen years before he was born. He grew up on the south side of Columbus and owned his own pharmacy at the corner of Fourth and Main streets before he became mayor.[10] He made for a memorable figure while strutting around town in his long black coat, wing collar and pince-nez glasses, greeting citizens with an energetic "Good morning, Colonel!" that gave the impression that the city was in good hands.[11]

Karb did a good job as mayor, presiding during the city's transition to home rule, citywide city council elections and a new city charter, but he is most remembered for his description of the city as "good old Columbus town." The phrase lived on long after his death in 1937.

Dr. John M. Dunham

Dr. John Milton Dunham, described by Thurber as one of Aunt Margery Albright's "favorites," arrived too late to the house at 251 Parsons Avenue to deliver baby James Thurber and received a scolding from Albright: "You might have spared your horse. We managed all right without you." But then she asked him if the baby's hairy head meant that he wouldn't be too bright. "I believe that holds good only when the hair is thicker at the temples," he said. Dunham was born in 1840 in Warren County, Ohio. He had office at 222 East Town Street, a block from Albright's house on South Fifth, for more than forty years. He died in 1928.

227 South Seventeenth Street

Charles Thurber and his family lived in this spacious, eight-room house from 1909 to 1912. Robert Thurber remembered that the family moved away from here "because of the high cost of heating by steam."

Park Hotel

When the Thurber family moved back to Columbus from Washington, DC, in 1903, they moved into the Park Hotel, at the northwest corner of High and Goodale Streets. The four-story structure had opened at that location on December 1, 1878, on what is now a cap over I-670. Capital University had been located at the back end of this building in a structure large enough to serve as both a dormitory and recitation hall. But the school moved to the Columbus suburb of Bexley in 1876 and that building became part of the Park Hotel when it was built.

The Thurbers were still living here in 1904 when Charles Thurber became seriously ill with what was likely some type of influenza, and in 1905, the family moved back in with the Fishers. Not long after that, the Park became the Northern Hotel and later the Railway YMCA. Part of the building survived as the Goodale Hotel until the building was demolished on January 1, 1957.

Karl T. Finn

Karl Finn knew Thurber since their days at East High School. He was editor of the *X-Rays*, the school newspaper; his aunt, Anna Finn—Miss Finn to students—had taught German at the school since the day it opened and she must have been a good influence on him as a writer.

He attended Ohio State and worked at the student *Lantern* with Thurber, competed with his friend for the affections of Minnette Fritts, and wrote about former East star Chic Harley, just as he had for the *X-Rays*. He eventually got a job at the *Columbus Dispatch* as campus correspondent and stayed on as a reporter after his graduation. He helped convince the editors to hire Thurber as a reporter.

While Thurber went on to a career as a writer, Finn eventually went in another direction, leaving Columbus for Cincinnati in 1928 to become president and general manager of the Cincinnati Better Business Bureau. He left for a job in newspaper advertising at the *Cincinnati Times-Star* in 1940; he was advertising director for the paper for many years and later assistant to the publisher for public relations. He also served as retail advertising director for the *Cincinnati Post*. He became editor and publisher of the Williamsburg Gazette in Clermont County following his retirement. He died in a Cincinnati nursing home on December 3, 1985.

Norwich Hotel

After Charles Thurber recovered from a near fatal illness in 1905 that William Thurber described as "a brain disease"[12] (which was probably some type of influenza) the Thurbers moved out of the Fisher home on Bryce Road and into an apartment in the Norwich Hotel, at the northeast corner of State and Fourth Streets. They lived in the building in 1906 and part of 1907, while Charles resumed work as a free-lance stenographer.

The Norwich had been constructed by Henry A. Lanham as an office building in 1890 and converted into a hotel in 1895. In 1985 it was remodeled and converted back into an office building.

H. E. Cherrington

Harold Edgar Cherrington was born in Gallia County in southeastern Ohio in 1888. His father, Clement, was a teacher, and the family lived in both Wellston and Huntington Township. H. E. landed a job at the *Columbus Dispatch* as a reporter in 1912. He became the newspaper's music and drama critic in 1914 and shared the Sunday page with Thurber's "Credos and Curios" column in 1922.

Cherrington married vaudeville performer Harriet Eastman, who retired from the stage after the wedding. She subsequently operated an antique shop in the Virginia Hotel, which stood on the site of the present Renaissance Columbus Hotel at the corner of Third and Gay Streets, for many years. The couple lived in a two-story brick house at 785 East Broad Street which she had inherited. It was likely constructed in 1863.

Cherrington left the paper in the 1930s and spent the rest his life doing public relations work. He died on September 18, 1956. His wife died in 1965.

Guy Harold "Hal" Cooley

Thurber met Cooley at one of the "teas" at the Callen photo studio in 1921 and was impressed with his work as a photographer and movie maker. Cooley, four years younger than Thurber, grew up in a house at 97 North Terrace Avenue on the city's West Side. He made a short Civil War film called *Over the Garden Fence* that had William Thurber, Althea Adams, and Thurber's Phi Kappa Psi fraternity brother Ralph McCombs among the cast. It premiered at Memorial Hall while Cooley was in Grant Hospital with bad cuts from cutting and splicing film. The opening was a disaster and they tried again at the Knickerbocker Theater with more bad results.

But Thurber was impressed with Cooley, and in 1922 the two of them conceived the idea of starting a news service together in Europe, which never happened. Cooley didn't go on to make huge Hollywood motion pictures, but he must have had an interesting life. In 1928 he survived a plane crash in Portland, Oregon, while he and another motion picture photographer were taking off for a trip to Seattle. In 1930 he was living on a houseboat in Sausalito, California, with his wife, Esther, an Oregon native, and working as a laborer in a boat shop. They were back in Portland in 1940, still living on a houseboat, and he was supervising a photo project. In 1942 he patented a photo printing device. In 1943 he helped retrieve the bodies of ten Vancouver shipyard workers from the tug boat May, which sank off the Oregon shore ferry landing. He died in Monterrey, California, in 1967, and was buried in Portland.

Dr. Virgil "Duke" Damon

Damon was the president of Phi Kappa Psi when Thurber was pledged to the fraternity. He lived in the Phi Psi house for the seven years he was on campus as a pre-med and medical student, and recalled how difficult it was get Thurber in. He moved to New York and became a nationally known Park Avenue obstetrician to celebrities and delivered Rosemary, Thurber's only child, in 1931. In 1937 Thurber wrote to Damon and asked him for a recommendation for a good eye man to deal with his deteriorating vision. Thurber sometimes socialized with Damon while he living in New York and Connecticut, and Damon was a frequent visitor during the month leading up to his death. Damon died in 1972 in Darien, Connecticut.

Frank Gullum

Thurber's chemistry teacher at East High School was also Chic Harley's football coach. A native of Hamden, Ohio, he graduated from Ohio University in 1907. He worked as analytical chemist for the Rock Island Railroad in Chicago for a year, and then taught high school science in Chillicothe, Ohio, for two years before going to East in 1910. He returned to Ohio University and Athens in 1918 as an assistant professor of chemistry, and he served as head coach of both the football and basketball teams for two seasons. He also coached the Ohio baseball team in 1919 and served as the school's athletic director for a number of years. He earned his masters of science in 1923. When he retired in 1955 after thirty-seven years as a faculty member and a dinner party was given in his honor, a Thurber cablegram from Paris was read to the guests. He died in Athens in 1965 at the age of seventy-nine.

Alfred Barron Callen

Al Callen and his wife Emily Barnes Callen ran the photo studio in the old Civil War–era Gwynne mansion at the southwest corner of Broad

and Fourth Streets (Ray Lee Jackson also worked there), where Thurber, Althea Adams, Hal Cooley, and others often went for tea and conversation about literature, art, and theater, among other things. Before he married Emily, it was called Barnes-Callen, Portraits by Photography. Callen was a photographer. Emily was an artist.

Al was born in Columbus in 1879 and was raised there. Emily's father, Hiram P. Barnes, was a preacher who attended Lane Seminary in Cincinnati and must have moved around some; she was born Portage County, Ohio, spent time growing up in Muskingum County, and ended up in Columbus.

A play Jackson wrote titled *Friends Invited* made its debut on at Wallack's Theatre on Broadway in 1925, and Barron Callen—Barron was Al's middle name—had one of the five parts in it. It closed after one performance. Whether the experience affected Callen is hard to say, but he and his wife were living in Manhattan by 1930 and he was using the name "Barron" Callen. He stayed in the area until at least 1944, when he was sixty-five years old.

By at least 1947, the Callens were living in Monterey, California, and he was managing the Star Theater, a position he kept until at least 1953. He later managed the Rio Theater and was still on the job in 1960, at the age of eighty-one. He died in 1969. Both he and his wife were buried in the Dresden Cemetery in Muskingum County, Ohio.

Ludwig Lewisohn

Lewisohn taught German and German literature at Ohio State from 1911 to 1919, during Thurber's days there. In 1922 he wrote the autobiographical book *Up Stream,* which especially impressed Thurber. The book took both OSU and Columbus to task, and Thurber was impressed enough with Lewisohn's thoughts that he wrote to his friend Elliott Nugent about it.

In a chapter titled "The Business of Education," Lewisohn wrote:

> Our students, then, came to the university not to find truth, but to be engineers or farmers, doctors or teachers. They did not want to be different men and women. . . . I suppose that these state universities do turn out very fair engineers, farmers and vegetarians. But when their job leaves these men free they are but little different from people who have not gone to college. They go to foolish plays, read silly magazines and fight for

every poisonous fallacy in politics, religion and conduct. A professor of geology in the university of Central City was publicly converted by Billy Sunday. The fact that he was not thereupon privately "fired," that he was still thought capable of teaching his science, symbolized the situation in its naked horror.

Lewisohn was a Columbia grad. He worked on the editorial staff at Doubleday and spent a year at the University of Wisconsin before taking the position at Ohio State. Upon leaving OSU in 1920, he became the dramatic editor of the *Nation,* where he worked until 1924. From 1924 until 1943 when he became editor of *New Palestine,* lecturing and writing became his career and only means of support. When he left in 1948, he became one of the thirteen original faculty members at Brandeis University, holding the position of Comparative Literature professor until his death in Miami Beach, Florida, on December 31, 1955.

He wrote numerous books, most notably the 1928 novel *The Island Within.*

John C. Harlor

John C. Harlor was the son of East High principal John D. Harlor. He attended East with Thurber, but admitted that he didn't know Thurber well until both ended up in the Scarlet Mask theatrical group. Thurber wrote and directed many of the plays and at the time, and Harlor was "very interested" in the theater. Harlor remembered that the group often took the plays on the road during the Christmas holiday season, "Sandusky, Toledo, Pennsylvania someplace"[13]—so they knew each other well.

He graduated from OSU with a law degree in 1922 and became a senior partner in the law firm of Wright, Harlor, Morris and Arnold, which merged with the law firm of Porter-Stanley in the late 1950s. Harlor specialized in banking and insurance law and argued one case before the United States Supreme Court.

When Harlor was in high school, his father invited star athlete Chic Harley to stay with the family when Harley's family moved to Chicago. As a result, John C. became Harley's roommate during the second part of his junior year at East High School. He gave the eulogy at Harley's funeral in 1974, and died in 1985 before his eighty-seventh birthday.

James E. Pollard

Pollard worked on the *Ohio State Lantern* with Thurber and graduated from Ohio State in 1916. He was the telegraph editor of the *Ohio State Journal* in 1922 when Thurber worked as a reporter at the *Columbus Dispatch,* and eventually returned to OSU as a journalism professor.

Pollard became the director of the OSU department of journalism and also served as the university historian until 1956; he wrote the *History of Ohio State University, 1873–1948* and *Ohio State Athletics, 1879–1959.*

In 1981 the James E. Pollard Memorial Scholarship was established, to be awarded to a journalism or communications student displaying above average academic achievement.

Ed Morris

Edward Ellsworth Morris was one of Thurber's best friends at East High School, although their families were on different ends of the economic spectrum. While the Thurbers moved from one rented house to another, the Charles E. Morris family lived in a thirteen-room, three-story, 6,423-square foot mansion at 875 East Broad Street that had been built in 1895 and survives today.

Charles Morris owned the C. E. Morris Company, a local ironworks business that was located on the north side of Curtis Avenue near Jefferson Avenue. It manufactured structural steel work. Probably because it did a lot of business with Buckeye Steel Castings, Morris' father got both of the boys a job at that plant one summer.

Morris and Thurber both attended Ohio State and both were rushed by Chi Phi, but the fraternity accepted Morris and rejected Thurber. Their relationship cooled as Morris spent less and less time with Thurber, but they remained friends. On May 20, 1922, when Thurber married Althea Adams at Trinity Episcopal Church, his good friend Elliott Nugent couldn't attend the wedding because he was on the road in a play and Morris served as best man.

Morris graduated from Ohio State with an engineering degree and became a mechanical engineer with the family company. He worked there for years and lived with his wife, Iala, and his daughter, Janet, in a big 2½-story frame house at 1643 Franklin Avenue. His oldest brother Willard was the company president. Ed's late arrival probably didn't help him here; he was the fifth son in a large family.

He and his wife lived in the Columbus suburb of Bexley for several years, and eventually moved to San Marino, California. They lived at 2632 Monterey Rd., near Pasadena, and he worked for the Pacific Iron and Steel Company until he died at the age of fifty-nine in 1955. He and his wife are buried in San Gabriel Cemetery.

Miss Daisy Hare

Thurber isn't the first writer to bury someone alive, and he must have been glad that an old friend, Patricia McGuckin, daughter of close friend Ted Gardiner, was the one who eventually tracked the would-be corpse down and interviewed her. Alice Daisy Hare was Thurber's first Latin teacher, and he referred to her in a correction to a 1959 interview done with him by *Time* in which he used an incorrect Latin phrase about his piece "Midnight at Tim's Place."

Thurber remarked that "the late Daisy Hare," who had taught him Latin at East High School nearly fifty years before, would have been shocked by his carelessness. It wasn't long before he received a letter informing him that Hare was alive and well in Columbus. McGuckin found her living in the East Side house where she had been for almost fifty years and did a story on her in the *Columbus Dispatch*. Far from being insulted, Miss Hare couldn't have been more gracious.

"I keep in touch with many of my former students, and I'm very proud of James," she said. "I would say the mistakes James made in his Latin merely reflect on my ability as his teacher back then."[14]

Hare was the Columbus-born daughter of Christopher and Elizabeth Hare. She never married, and she lived on the city's East Side all her life, having long stints (with her parents, who both died in 1930) at 179 East Mound Street and 802 East Main before moving with them to 396 Kendall Place. She graduated from Ohio State, taught school all her life, and actually outlived Thurber by three years. She died November 17, 1964, and joined him in Green Lawn Cemetery.

Ralph L. McCombs

Ralph McCombs was another one of Thurber's East Side childhood pals who went to Ohio State with him, worked with him on the *Ohio State Lantern,* the *Sundial,* and on and in Scarlet Mask productions.

McCombs was almost two years younger than Thurber and also had childhood memories of the Ohio State School for the Blind with a different twist: his blind father, James, was the music instructor at the school and had once lived there. Ralph was the youngest of five children and spent most of the first forty years of his life on Franklin Avenue, his family moving from 686 Franklin when he was about ten to 825 Franklin Avenue, where he lived until the early 1940s.

McCombs founded the Scarlet Mask musical-comedy organization at Ohio State with four others in 1920 after doing a production with the OSU men's glee club that the director didn't approve. He wrote and directed *Tain't So,* the club's first production. He was one of several of Thurber's theatrical friends who regularly attended the teas at the Callen photographic studio at Fourth and Broad streets and worked on several productions with Thurber. They collaborated on the all of the lyrics for *Tell Me Not,* a play Thurber wrote that played at the Hartman Theater the second week of January, 1925.

A lifelong bachelor, McCombs worked as instructor at Columbus Academy in the early 1920s. He worked at the *Ohio State Journal* and served as the music critic of the *Columbus Citizen* in the 1930s. He eventually went into public relations and was serving as the manager of the Columbus Symphony Orchestra when he died at his summer home in Creola, Ohio, in Vinton County, in 1957, at the age of eighty-one.

Johnny Jones

Longtime *Columbus Dispatch* columnist and East High grad Johnny Jones was born in 1900 in Oak Hill, Ohio. The family moved to Columbus when he was nine years old. He attended Garfield Elementary, Mt. Vernon Junior High, East High School, and Ohio State, but was a few years behind Thurber.

Jones was an unabashed Chic Harley fan, as was every East student and graduate, and a cheerleader at OSU in 1920. He was kicked out of school after two years.

"Officially, I got kicked out because I flunked economics with a grade of 69⅞," he said. "Unofficially, it was because I took five co-eds on a football special train to Chicago to see an Ohio State game, and co-eds didn't do that in those days."[15]

Jones was a *Dispatch* correspondent while in school and worked briefly at the *Ohio State Journal* before taking a job as a press agent for the Majestic Theater on High Street opposite the Statehouse. When Thurber and his wife, Althea, returned from New York in September, 1924, and Thurber needed a job, Jones was the manager of the Majestic and hired him as a press agent.

Jones managed several theaters, including the Southern, worked as promotion man for the organization that did the ground work for the founding of the Columbus Zoo and worked for the Columbus Chamber of Commerce. He "just happened" to be walking by the Ohio Penitentiary when it caught fire in 1930 and went to work as a reporter for the *Dispatch,* without informing the city editor. Thus began a career that saw him write a daily column—*Now Let Me Tell You*—from 1940 until his death in 1971. In it he often wrote flatteringly of fellow East High grads and longtime friends James Thurber and Chic Harley.

When he died in 1971, he was buried in Oak Hill next to his mother, Anna, whom he revered.

James Theater

Thurber covered the opening of the James Theater for the *Columbus Dispatch* in 1921. At the time, that seemed like a much bigger deal than it does today. When the James opened at 39 West Broad Street, it was the largest movie house in Ohio with three thousand seats, more than twice as many as the average large theater of its day. The James' vertical sign was called the most elaborate in the Midwest, "with 3,000 lamps . . . flashed to give motion effect."

Less than seven years later, owner Billy James sold the theater to Loew's and United Artists, who renamed it the Broad. It reopened on August 21, 1927, with Lillian Gish in *Annie Laurie* and a stage show headed by the Ritz Brothers. Headliners who appeared on stage at the Broad include Ted Lewis and his Orchestra, Eva Tanguay, Lupe Velez, and Victor Herbert.

The Loew's Broad closed on March 31, 1961, and was razed to make room for the Huntington Trust Building, which occupies the site opposite the Leveque Tower today.

NOTES

Notes to the Introduction

1. British Broadcasting Company, "The Private Life of James Thurber," December 2, 1961.
2. James Thurber, "The Car We Had to Push," in *My Life and Hard Times* (New York and London: Harper and Brothers, 1933).
3. Ibid.
4. Thurber response to his receiving the Ohio Sesquicentennial Medal, October 24, 1953, in *Thurber on Humor*, a pamphlet printed by the Martha Kinney Cooper Ohioana Library Association, Columbus, Ohio, 1953.
5. *Ohio State Journal,* February 14, 1959.
6. David McCord, "Djinn Rummy," *Saturday Review* (June 7, 1952), 17.
7. *Life,* August 4, 1947.
8. James Thurber, "More Alarms at Night," in *My Life and Hard Times* (New York and London: Harper and Brothers, 1933).

Notes to Chapter 1

1. James Thurber, "Preface: My Fifty Years with James Thurber," in *The Thurber Carnival* (New York: Harper & Brothers, 1945).
2. James Thurber, letter to John O'Hara, October 29, 1949.
3. James Thurber, "Daguerreotype of a Lady," in *The Thurber Album* (New York: Simon and Schuster, 1952).
4. James Thurber, "Preface."
5. William Thurber, interview with Harrison Kinney, 1962.

Notes to Chapter 2

1. Mame Thurber, interview with *Time's* Richard Oulihan, 1950.
2. Robert Thurber, interview with Harrison Kinney, 1962.
3. James Thurber, "Gentleman from Indiana," in *The Thurber Album* (New York: Simon and Schuster, 1952).
4. Ibid.
5. Harrison Kinney, *James Thurber: His Life and Times* (New York: Henry Holt, 1995).
6. Mame Thurber, interview with *Time's* Richard Oulihan, 1950.
7. Mame Thurber, letter to James Thurber, July 28, 1950.
8. James Thurber, "Gentleman from Indiana."
9. William Thurber interview with Lewis Branscomb, February 14, 1972.
10. Joel Sayre, interview for his memoirs, 1973. *Joel Sayre Papers.* The New York Public Library Manuscripts and Archives. Astor, Lenox, and Tilden Foundations.
11. *Columbus Sunday Dispatch*, May 15, 1932.
12. James Thurber, "Gentleman from Indiana."
13. Burton Bernstein, *Thurber* (New York: Dodd, Mead, 1975).

Notes to Chapter 3

1. James Thurber, "Lavender with a Difference," in *The Thurber Album* (New York: Simon and Schuster, 1952).
2. Ruth White, "James Thurber: His Life in Columbus," *Columbus Dispatch*, March 10, 1940.
3. Mame Thurber to Beverly Smith, *Columbus Dispatch Sunday Magazine*, June 1, 1952.
4. "Everybody is Getting Serious," *New Republic,* May 26, 1958; reprinted in *Conversations with James Thurber,* edited by Thomas Fensch.
5. "James Thurber: In Conversation with Alistair Cooke," *Atlantic Monthly,* August, 1956.
6. James Thurber, "Lavender with a Difference."
7. Ibid.
8. Samuel B. Baker thesis, op. cit.
9. James Thurber, "Lavender with a Difference."
10. Suzanne Fisher Hutton, interview with Bob Hunter, November 7, 2014.
11. *Columbus Dispatch,* "Life Beginning at 50, Says Thurber On Visit to City," January 14, 1946.
12. James Thurber, "Lavender with a Difference."
13. Ruth White, "James Thurber: His Life in Columbus," *Columbus Dispatch*, March 10, 1940.
14. Charles S. Holmes, *The Clocks of Columbus, The Literary Career of James Thurber,* 9.

15. James Thurber, "Lavender with a Difference."
16. Clifford Fisher, interview with Alice Leighner.
17. Mame Thurber, letter to Dr. Gordon Bruce, October, 1940.
18. Kinney, *James Thurber,* 17–18.
19. Joel Sayre, interview with Harrison Kinney, 1962.
20. James Thurber, acceptance speech for the award of the Ohioana Sesquicentennial Medal, October 14, 1953.

Notes to Chapter 4

1. James Thurber, "Daguerreotype of a Lady."
2. Ibid.
3. Ann Honeycutt, interview with Harrison Kinney.
4. William Thurber, interview with Lewis Branscomb, February 14, 1972.
5. James Thurber, "Daguerreotype of a Lady."
6. Ibid.
7. Ibid.
8. Ibid.

Notes to Chapter 5

1. James Thurber, "Adam's Anvil," in *The Thurber Album* (New York: Simon and Schuster, 1952).
2. Ibid.
3. Ibid.
4. Ibid.
5. Ibid.
6. Obituary clipping, Thurber Collection, The Ohio State University.
7. James Thurber, "Adam's Anvil."
8. Clifford Fisher, letter to Alice Leighner, Columbus, Ohio, October, 1969.
9. James Thurber, "Adam's Anvil."

Notes to Chapter 6

1. James Thurber, "Man with a Rose," in *The Thurber Album,* (New York: Simon and Schuster, 1952).
2. Ibid.
3. Robert Thurber, interview with Burton Bernstein.
4. *Of Thurber and Columbustown,* Rosemary Joyce, 7.
5. James Thurber, "The Luck of Jad Peters," in *The Middle-Aged Man on the Flying Trapeze* (New York: Harper & Brothers, 1935).

6. William Alexander Taylor, *Centennial History of Columbus and Franklin County, Vol. 1.*
7. James Thurber, "Man with a Rose."
8. James Thurber, "The Car We Had to Push."
9. Ibid.
10. James Thurber, "Draft Board Nights," in *My Life and Hard Times* (New York and London: Harper and Brothers, 1933).
11. Ibid.
12. James Thurber, "Man with a Rose."
13. Joel Sayre, WNDT, New York television talk show.

Notes to Chapter 7

1. James Thurber, "Conversation Piece," in *The Thurber Album* (New York: Simon and Schuster, 1952).
2. Suzanne Fisher Hutton, interview with Bob Hunter, November 7, 2014.
3. James Thurber, "Conversation Piece."
4. Kinney, *James Thurber*, 36.
5. James Thurber, "Conversation Piece."
6. Ibid.

Notes to Chapter 8

1. James Thurber, "Time Exposure," in *The Thurber Album* (New York: Simon and Schuster, 1952).
2. James Thurber, "The Autobiography of Judge Stacy Taylor," as reprinted in "Time Exposure," *The Thurber Album* (New York: Simon and Schuster, 1952).
3. E. Stacy Matheny, "The Matheny Family Tree," 1913, Fairfield County District Library, Lancaster, Ohio.
4. Ibid.
5. Williams Brothers, *The History of Franklin and Pickaway Counties* (1880), 78; corrections, 97.
6. James Thurber, "Time Exposure."

Notes to Chapter 9

1. Jim Stoner, interview with Bob Hunter, August 4, 2014, Sugar Grove, Ohio.
2. Ibid.
3. Ibid.
4. James Thurber, "Conversation Piece."
5. Ibid.

6. Stoner, interview.
7. William Fisher, Thurber's grandfather and Jake Matheny's brother-in-law, bought this two-hundred-acre property in 1888. He sold it to Jake's wife in 1904 for $700. Because the Fishers lived in Columbus all through this period, it seems plausible that Mathenys had been living there for a long time when they gained title to it. Thurber referred to his Uncle Jake's two-hundred-acre farm in an unpublished account of the reunions, and this was the only farm of that size in the area. He also wrote that "nothing had changed about (Sugar Grove) since my mother was a little girl and spent her school vacations there with her own brothers and cousins," and because the property belonged to Colonel Jackson in those days, she may well have gone there.
8. Matheny, "Matheny Family Tree."
9. 'Stoner, interview.
10. James Thurber, "Conversation Piece."
11. Ibid.
12. Ibid.
13. James Thurber, "The Luck of Jad Peters."
14. David Shiltz, telephone interview with Bob Hunter, August, 2014.

Notes to Chapter 10

1. Kinney, *James Thurber*, 89.
2. William Thurber, interview with Harrison Kinney, 1962,
3. William Thurber, interview with Lewis Branscomb, 1972.
4. James Thurber, interview with Harrison Kinney, 1948.
5. Helen Thurber, interview with Burton Bernstein.
6. William Thurber, interview with Lewis Branscomb, 1972.
7. James Thurber, letter to Ann Honeycutt, undated, quoting letter from Mame Thurber to James Thurber, circa 1933–34.
8. James Thurber, letter to John and Donia McNulty, November 21, 1937.
9. William Thurber, interview with Harrison Kinney, 1962.
10. William Thurber, interview with Lewis Branscomb, 1972.
11. William Thurber, interview with Harrison Kinney, 1962.
12. William Thurber, interview with Lewis Branscomb, 1972.
13. William Thurber, interview with Richard Oulihan, *Time*, 1950.
14. James Thurber, letter to William Thurber, 1940.
15. James Thurber, letter to Elliott Nugent, July 27, 1948.

Notes to Chapter 11

1. Rosemary O. Joyce, *Of Thurber & Columbustown*, 8.
2. James Thurber, letter to to E. B. White, January 1, 1938.

3. Joel Sayre, "Remembering Thurber," *Washington Post Sunday Book World,* October 22, 1992.
4. Alan Miller, "Thurber's brother dies at age 90," *Columbus Dispatch,* July 21, 1987.
5. James Thurber, letter to Robert Thurber, March 18, 1919.
6. Bernstein, *Thurber,* 203.
7. Robert Thurber, interview with Harrison Kinney, 1962.
8. Robert Thurber, letter to Harrison Kinney, 1972.
9. Mame Thurber, letter to Minnette Fritts, August 3 1939.
10. *Columbus Dispatch,* July 21, 1987.
11. James Thurber, letter to E. B. and Katharine White, June, 12, 1951.
12. Bernstein, *Thurber,* 415–16.
13. James Thurber, letter to E. B. and Katharine White, July 10, 1951.
14. James Thurber, letter to William Thurber, November 7, 1956.
15. Donn Vickers, interview with Bob Hunter, December 16, 2014.
16. Ibid.
17. Ibid.
18. Ibid.

Notes to Chapter 12

1. James Thurber, "Lavender with a Difference."
2. Ibid.
3. William Thurber, interview with Lewis Branscomb, February 14, 1972.
4. James Thurber, "Lavender with a Difference."
5. Ibid.
6. Ibid.

Notes to Chapter 13

1. James Thurber, "Man with a Rose."
2. Lawrence Abramson, interview with Bob Hunter, 2014.
3. James Thurber, "Man with a Rose."
4. Ibid.
5. Ibid.
6. Ibid.
7. Abramson, interview.
8. Ibid.
9. James Thurber, "Conversation Piece."
10. James Thurber, "Man with a Rose."
11. Kinney, *James Thurber,* 12.
12. James Thurber, "Conversation Piece."

Notes to Chapter 14

1. James Thurber, "Daguerreotype of a Lady."
2. William T. Martin, *History of Franklin County: A Collection of Reminiscences of the Early Settlement of the County; with Biographical Sketches and a Complete History of the County to the Present Time* (Columbus, OH: Follett, Foster and Company, 1858).

Notes to Chapter 15

1. James Thurber, "I Went to Sullivant," in *The Middle-Aged Man on the Flying Trapeze* (New York: Harper & Brothers, 1935).
2. Ibid.
3. Ibid.
4. Helen Thurber, to Burton Bernstein, *Thurber,* 25.
5. Donald Ogden Stewart, *By a Stroke of Luck! An Autobiography* (New York: Paddington Press, 1975), 14.
6. James Thurber, "I Went to Sullivant."
7. James Thurber, letter to Mrs. Rachel Rowe Macklin, 1959.
8. James Thurber, letter to John and Donia McNulty, November 21, 1937.
9. Stewart, *By a Stroke of Luck*, 16.
10. James Thurber, "I Went to Sullivant."

Notes to Chapter 16

1. James Thurber, "The Tree on the Diamond," in *The Thurber Album* (New York: Simon and Schuster, 1952).
2. Ibid.
3. Joel Sayre memoirs, October 30, 1973, Joel Sayre Papers, New York Public Library.
4. Ibid.
5. James Thurber, "The Tree on the Diamond."

Notes to Chapter 17

1. Eva Prout, interview with Lewis Branscomb, 1973.
2. Ibid.
3. James Thurber, letter to John and Doris McNulty, November 21, 1937.
4. James Thurber, letter to Elliott Nugent, March 25, 1920.
5. Eva Prout, interview with Lewis Branscomb, 1973.
6. Ibid.
7. James Thurber, letter to Elliott Nugent, April 4, 1920.

8. Eva Prout, interview with Lewis Branscomb, 1973.

9. Ibid.

10. James Thurber, letter to Elliott Nugent, June 9, 1920.

11. Eva Prout, interview with Lewis Branscomb, 1973.

Notes to Chapter 18

1. Suzanne Fisher Hutton, interview with Bob Hunter, November 7, 2014.

2. William M. Fisher II, interview with Bob Hunter, November 24, 2014.

3. James Thurber, "Man with a Rose."

4. William Alexander Taylor, *Centennial History of Columbus and Franklin County, Volume 1* (Chicago, IL, and Columbus, OH: The S. J. Clarke Publishing Co., 1909), 623.

5. Ben Hayes, "Old Blocks," *Columbus Citizen-Journal.*

6. William M. Fisher II, interview.

7. Hayes, "Old Blocks."

8. James Thurber, "Man with a Rose."

9. Taylor, *Centennial History of Columbus and Franklin County, Volume 1,* 624.

10. William M. Fisher II, interview.

Notes to Chapter 19

1. James Thurber, "The Day the Dam Broke," in *My Life and Hard Times* (New York and London: Harper and Brothers, 1933).

2. George Smallsread, interview with Harrison Kinney, 1962.

3. George Smallsread, letter to James Thurber, May 18, 1951.

4. Carlton C. Berry, *Memory Sketches of Over Fifty Years in Newspaper Composing Rooms* (Columbus, OH: The Dispatch Printing Company, 1954).

5. James Thurber, "The Day the Dam Broke."

6. Ibid.

7. Neil Martin, "Thurber Hits New High in Album," *Columbus Citizen Magazine,* June 22, 1952.

8. Joel Sayre, during a roundtable discussion of *My Life and Hard Times* on WNDT, New York.

Notes to Chapter 20

1. Thomas Meek, interview with Burton Bernstein for *Thurber.*

2. Bob Hunter, *Chic: The Extraordinary Rise of Ohio State Football and the Tragic Schoolboy Athlete Who Made It Happen* (Wilmington, OH: Orange Frazer Press, 2008).

3. *Time,* July 9, 1951.

4. Robert Thurber, letter to Charles S. Holmes.

Notes to Chapter 21

1. Donn Vickers, interview with Bob Hunter, December 16, 2014.

2. Luke Feck, interview with Bob Hunter, October 2, 2015.

3. Dave Timmons, interview with Bob Hunter, September 30, 2015.

4. Feck, interview.

5. Vickers, interview.

6. James Thurber, "The Night the Ghost Got In."

7. Robert Thurber, interview with Harrison Kinney.

8. James Thurber, letter to Bill Arter, *Columbus Dispatch Sunday Magazine,* April 2, 1967.

9. *Thurber House Organ,* open citation.

10. Ibid.

11. *Columbus Evening Dispatch,* April 28, 1904.

12. Anne Touvell, interview with Bob Hunter, October 29, 2014.

13. Earl Fisher, interview with Alice Leighner, October 1969.

14. Anne Touvell, interview with Bob Hunter, October 29, 2014.

15. *Thurber House Organ,* open citation.

16. Patty Dohaney Geiger, interview with Bob Hunter, May 8, 2014.

17. Mark Van Doren, interview with Burton Bernstein, *Thurber,* 480.

18. *Ohio State Journal,* November 19, 1868.

19. Anne Touvell, interview with Bob Hunter, October 29, 2014.

20. James Thurber, letter to Edmund Wilson, 1959.

21. Feck, interview.

Notes to Chapter 22

1. Elliott Nugent, *Events Leading Up to the Comedy,* (New York: Trident Press, 1965).

2. Ibid.

3. Ibid.

4. Ibid.

5. Dr. Virgil "Duke" Damon, interview with Burton Bernstein, *Thurber.*

6. Nugent, *Events Leading Up to the Comedy.*

Notes to Chapter 23

1. James E. Pollard, *History of The Ohio State University: The Story of Its First Seventy-Five Years, 1873–1948* (Columbus: The Ohio State University Press, 1952).
2. James Thurber, "University Days," in *My Life and Hard Times* (New York and London: Harper and Brothers, 1933).
3. Ibid.
4. Kinney, *James Thurber*, 146–47.
5. Pollard, *History of The Ohio State University*.
6. Kinney, *James Thurber*, 163.
7. Pollard, *History of The Ohio State University*.
8. *Columbus Citizen*, July 25, 1944.

Notes to Chapter 24

1. Minnette Fritts, interview with Rosemary O. Joyce, in *Of Thurber & Columbustown* (Columbus, OH: The Thurber House, 1984).
2. Minnette Fritts, interview with Lewis Branscomb, 1973.
3. Fritts, interview with Joyce.
4. Fritts, interview with Branscomb.
5. James Thurber, letter to Elliott Nugent, July 16, 1918.
6. Fritts, interview with Branscomb.
7. James Thurber, letter to Elliott Nugent, October 15, 1918.
8. Fritts, interview with Branscomb.
9. Ibid.
10. Minnette Fritts, interview with Burton Bernstein, in *Thurber* (New York: Dodd, Mead, 1973).
11. James Thurber, letter to Katharine White, April 24, 1948.
12. Fritts, interview with Branscomb.
13. Kinney, *James Thurber: His Life and Times*, appendix C.

Notes to Chapter 25

1. *X-Rays*, East High School, Columbus, Ohio, 1914.
2. *Columbus Dispatch*, October, 1922.
3. Robert D. Thomas, "Charles W. "Chic" Harley," in *Columbus Unforgettables: A Collection of Columbus Yesterdays and Todays* (Columbus, OH: Robert D. Thomas, publisher, 1983).
4. *Columbus Dispatch*, September 13, 1912.
5. *Columbus Dispatch*, November 26, 1912.
6. *Columbus Dispatch*, October 7, 1916.
7. James Thurber, letter to Elliott Nugent, September, 1922.

8. *Ohio State Journal*, November 19, 1948.

Notes to Chapter 26

1. Kinney, *James Thurber*, 154.
2. James Thurber, "Man with a Pipe," in *The Thurber Album* (New York: Simon and Schuster, 1952).
3. Ibid.
4. Ibid.
5. James Thurber, letter to James Fullington, March 18, 1952.
6. James Thurber, "Man With a Pipe."
7. Stafford Taylor, interview with Alice Leighner for Harrison Kinney, 1969.
8. James Thurber, letter to Mrs. C. H. Schwenke, November 8, 1950.
9. *Ohio State Alumni Monthly*, October 1933.

Notes to Chapter 27

1. James Thurber, speech for the dedication of Denney Hall, April 1960.
2. Ibid.
3. Ibid.
4. James Thurber, "Length and Shadow," in *The Thurber Album* (New York: Simon and Schuster, 1952).
5. Ibid.
6. Joseph Denney biography file, Ohio State University Archives.
7. James Thurber, "Length and Shadiow."
8. Charles S. Holmes, *The Clocks of Columbus: The Literary Career of James Thurber* (New York: Atheneum, 1972), 266.
9. James Thurber, "Length and Shadow."

Notes to Chapter 28

1. Kinney, *James Thurber*, 159.
2. *Ohio State Alumni Monthly*, June, 1941.
3. William Graves biography file, Ohio State University Archives.
4. James Thurber, "Beta Theta Pi," *The Thurber Album*.
5. *Ohio State Alumni Monthly*, March, 1941.
6. Ibid.
7. James Thurber, letter to Dorothy Miller, 1950.
8. Earl Wilson, *New York Post*, March 8, 1944.
9. James Thurber, "Beta Theta Pi," in *The Thurber Album* (New York: Simon and Schuster, 1952).
10. Ibid.

11. Ibid.
12. William Graves biography file, Ohio State University Archives.
13. James Thurber, letter to Elliott Nugent, 1951.
14. Charles S. Holmes, *The Clocks of Columbus*, 266.
15. James Thurber, letter to James Fullington, March 18, 1952.

Notes to Chapter 29

1. Cody Griffiths, interview with Bob Hunter, September 14, 2015.
2. Kyle Andrews, interview with Bob Hunter, September 4, 2015.
3. Ibid.
4. Dave Timmons, interview with Bob Hunter, September 30, 2015.
5. Wendell Postle, interview with Rosemary O. Joyce, in *Of Thurber & Columbustown.*
6. Virgil "Duke" Damon, interview with Harrison Kinney, 1962.
7. Elliott Nugent, *Events Leading Up to Comedy*, 63.
8. Buckeye Phi Psi, March, 1937.
9. Norm Spain, "Thurber House After Twenty Years," *The Shield of Phi Kappa Psi*, Spring 2005.

Notes to Chapter 30

1. *The Lima (Ohio) News*, August 9, 1916, 2.
2. C. Alphonso Smith, *O. Henry Biography* (New York: Doubleday, Page and Co., 1916).
3. Dr. John Thomas, letter to C. Alphonso Smith, in *O. Henry Biography.*
4. O. Henry, letter to G. P. Roach, May 18, 1898, in *O. Henry Biography.*
5. Ibid.
6. O. Henry, letter to Mrs. G. P. Roach, July 8, 1898, *in O. Henry Biography.*
7. James Thurber, "Loose Leaves."
8. O. Henry, letter to Al Jennings, 1901–02, in *The Caliph of Bagdad* (New York: D. Appleton and Co., 1931), 170.
9. *The Lima (Ohio) News*, August 9, 1916, 2.
10. James Thurber, "Loose Leaves."

Notes to Chapter 31

1. James Thurber, "Loose Leaves."
2. James Thurber, "Franklin Avenue, U. S. A.," in *The Thurber Album* (New York: Simon and Schuster).
3. Kinney, *James Thurber*, 138.
4. James Thurber, letter to Harvey Breit, November 25, 1949.

5. James Thurber, "Franklin Avenue, U. S. A."
6. Ibid.
7. *Ohio State Journal,* December 19, 1919.
8. James Thurber, "Franklin Avenue, U. S. A."
9. Ibid.
10. Robert O. Ryder and Harry J. Westerman, *The Young Lady Across the Way* (Boston, MA: John W. Luce, 1913).
11. James Thurber, "Franklin Avenue, U. S. A."
12. Ibid.
13. *Ohio State Journal,* March 17, 1936.
14. James Thurber, "Franklin Avenue, U. S. A."
15. Ibid.
16. Ibid.
17. Joel Sayre, interview with Lewis Branscomb.
18. Ryder and Westerman, *The Young Lady Across the Way.*
19. Harvey Taylor, *Detroit Times,* January 13, 1960.

Notes to Chapter 32

1. George Smallsread, interview with Harrison Kinney, 1962.
2. *Ohio State University Monthly,* January, 1962.
3. *Columbus Dispatch Magazine,* December 13, 1959.

Notes to Chapter 33

1. James Thurber, "Newspaperman—Head and Shoulders," in *The Thurber Album* (New York: Simon and Schuster, 1952).
2. Berry, *Memory Sketches.*
3. James Thurber, "Newspaperman—Head and Shoulders."
4. Ibid.
5. George Smallsread, interview with Harrison Kinney, 1962.
6. James Thurber, "Newspaperman—Head and Shoulders."
7. Ruth Young White, interview with Lewis Branscomb.
8. George Smallsread, interview with Harrison Kinney, 1962.
9. Joel Sayre, interview with Lewis Branscomb.
10. Kinney, *James Thurber.*
11. James Pollard, interview with Lewis Branscomb.
12. James Thurber, "Newspaperman—Head and Shoulders," early draft.
13. Ibid.
14. James Thurber, "Newspaperman—Head and Shoulders."
15. Ibid.
16. Yvonne Kuehner Grosjean, interview with Bob Hunter, 2014.

17. Bob Hunter, *A Historical Guidebook to Old Columbus* (Athens: Ohio University Press, 2012).
18. Grosjean, interview with Hunter.
19. James Thurber, "Newspaperman—Head and Shoulders."
20. Ibid.
21. James Thurber, "Newspaperman—Head and Shoulders."

Notes to Chapter 34

1. James Thurber, "Memoirs of a Drudge," in *The Thurber Carnival* (New York: Harper and Brothers, 1945).
2. *Ohio State Monthly,* January, 1962.
3. James Thurber, "Notes of an Old Reporter," *The Bermudian,* June, 1951.
4. Ibid.

Notes to Chapter 35

1. Faith McNulty, "John As He Was," in *This Place on Third Avenue: The New York Stories of John McNulty* (Washington, DC: Counterpoint, 2001).
2. James Thurber, "My Friend McNulty," introduction to *The World of John McNulty*
3. Ibid.
4. Robert Kanode, interview with Alice Leighner, 1962.
5. James Thurber, "My Friend McNulty."
6. Donia Williamson (McNulty) Karpen, letter to Harrison Kinney, October 18, 1962.
7. Lew Byrer column, *Columbus Citizen,* July 30, 1956.
8. Stanley Walker, letter to James Thurber, August 23, 1957.
9. James Thurber, "My Friend McNulty."
10. Byrer column, *Columbus Citizen.*

Notes to Chapter 36

1. James Thurber, "Boy from Chillicothe," in *The Thurber Album* (New York: Simon and Schuster, 1952).
2. Lucy Caswell and George A. Loomis Jr., *Billy Ireland* (Columbus: The Ohio State University Libraries Publications Committee, 1980).
3. James Thurber, "Boy from Chillicothe."
4. Ibid.
5. Joel Sayre, interview with Lewis Branscomb.
6. James Thurber, "Boy from Chillicothe."
7. Caswell and Loomis, *Billy Ireland.*

8. Ibid.
9. Hugh Fullerton, "Life of Billy Ireland, Story of Kindliness, Good Fellowship," *Chillicothe News-Advertiser,* May 29, 1935.
10. Caswell and Loomis, *Billy Ireland.*
11. Ibid.
12. Hugh Fullerton, "Life of Billy Ireland, Story of Kindliness, Good Fellowship."

Notes to Chapter 37

1. Stewart, *By A Stroke of Luck,* 15.
2. Ibid.
3. Helen Thurber to Burton Bernstein, *Thurber,* 25.
4. Stewart, *By A Stroke of Luck,* 16–17.
5. Ibid., 86.
6. Ibid., 135.
7. Donald Ogden Stewart, "Death of a Unicorn," *New Statesman,* November 10, 1961.
8. Thurber to Bernstein, *Thurber,* 251.
9. Stewart, *By A Stroke of Luck,* 216.
10. James Thurber, letter to Donald Ogden Stewart, October 14, 1958.
11. Ibid.

Notes to Chapter 38

1. Joel Sayre, reminiscences, October 30, 1973, 19–20.
2. Joel Sayre, reminiscences, October 30, 1973, 13–14.
3. Joel Sayre, interview with Lewis Branscomb.
4. Ibid.
5. Kinney, *James Thurber,* 512.
6. Joel Sayre, interview with Lewis Branscomb.
7. Ibid.

Notes to Chapter 39

1. *Ohio State University Monthly,* March, 1933.
2. Ibid.
3. Ibid.
4. *Ohio State University Monthly,* February, 1964.
5. Ibid.
6. Ibid.

Notes to Chapter 40

1. Minnette Fritts, interview with Lewis Branscomb, 1973.
2. Ibid.
3. Thomas Meek, interview with Burton Bernstein, *Thurber.*
4. Althea Adams, interview with Lewis Branscomb.
5. Ralph McCombs, interview with Harrison Kinney, 1962.
6. Kinney, *James Thurber, His Life and Times,* 261.
7. Ralph McCombs, interview with Lewis Branscomb.
8. Adams, interview with Branscomb.
9. Joel Sayre, interview with Harrison Kinney.
10. James Thurber, letter to Dale Kramer, April 23, 1951.
11. Burton Bernstein, *Thurber,* 121.
12. Sayre, interview with Kinney.

Notes to Chapter 41

1. Kinney, *James Thurber: His Life and Times,* 261.
2. Lisa M. Klein, *Be It Remembered: The Story of Trinity Church on Capitol Square* (Wilmington, OH: Orange Frazer Press, 2003).
3. Ibid.
4. Ibid.
5. Ibid.

Notes to Chapter 42

1. Herman Miller, *Weekly Reader,* 1940.
2. Dorothy Miller, interview with Rosemary O. Joyce.
3. Dorothy Miller, interview with Harrison Kinney, 1966.
4. Miller, interview with Joyce.
5. Herman Miller, *Weekly Reader,* 1940.
6. Miller, interview with Kinney.
7. Ibid.
8. Rosemary O. Joyce, with Michael J. Rosen and Donn F. Vickers, *Of Thurber & Columbustown,* 24.
9. Miller, interview with Joyce.
10. "Alice Latham Wood remembers," *This Week Worthington,* April 28, 2003.
11. Jesica Stevens, interview with Bob Hunter, June, 2015.
12. James Thurber, letter to Herman and Dorothy Miller, March 19, 1940.
13. James Thurber, letter to Herman and Dorothy Miller, August 6, 1942.
14. Burton Bernstein, *Thurber,* 114.
15. Ibid.
16. James Thurber, letter to Dorothy Miller, April 21, 1949.

Notes to Chapter 43

1. Ted Gardiner, interview with Harrison Kinney, 1962.
2. Miller, interview with Joyce.
3. Ibid.
4. Kinney, *James Thurber: His Life and Times*.

Notes to Chapter 44

1. Daniel Nelson, interview with Bob Hunter, 2014.
2. Donn Vickers, interview with by Bob Hunter, December 16, 2014.
3. Christine Hayes, "Burkhart Portrait of Thurber's Mother Mame Full of Mischief and Merriment, "*Short North Gazette,* December 2002.
4. Joe Blundo, "Thurber's world and welcome to it; sites in Columbus associated with author," *Columbus Dispatch,* October 30, 2011.
5. Bob Hunter, "Sipping Sodas with Ty Cobb at city's Great Southern Hotel," *Columbus Dispatch,* March 14, 2012.
6. Bill Arter, "Great Southern," *Columbus Vignettes IV,* 62.

Notes to Chapter 45

1. Julia Gardiner, interview with Rosemary O. Joyce, in *Of Thurber & Columbustown.*
2. Ted Gardiner, interview with Harrison Kinney, 1962.
3. Ted Gardiner, interview with Burton Bernstein, in *Thurber.*
4. Ted Gardiner, interview with Kinney.
5. Bob Waldron, "Thurber in the Attic," *Columbus Dispatch Sunday Magazine,* October 18, 1970.
6. Rosemary O. Joyce, with Michael J. Rosen and Donn F. Vickers, *Of Thurber & Columbustown.*
7. James Thurber, letter to the Thurber family, January 5, 1954.
8. Ted Gardiner, interview with Rosemary O. Joyce, in *Of Thurber & Columbustown.*

Notes to Chapter 46

1. Haila Stoddard, interview with Harrison Kinney, 1993.
2. James Thurber, letter to Dorothy Miller, May 15, 1957, in *The Clocks of Columbus,* Charles S. Holmes.
3. Virginia Hall Trannett, interview with Harrison Kinney, 1962.
4. *Newsweek,* January 13, 1960.
5. *Pittsburgh Sun-Telegraph,* February 16, 1960.

6. *Newsweek,* February 1, 1960.
7. Doral Chenowith, interview with Bob Hunter, September 11, 2015.
8. Ibid.
9. Ibid.
10. Haila Stoddard, interview with Harrison Kinney, 1993.

Notes to Chapter 47

1. Thomas Meek, interview with Lewis Branscomb.
2. Ibid.
3. Ibid.
4. Ibid.
5. Thomas Meek, interview with Burton Bernstein, in *Thurber.*
6. Ibid.
7. Kinney, *James Thurber: His Life and Times,* 749.
8. Meek, interview with Branscomb.
9. Ibid.
10. "OSU Buys Thurber Collection," *Ohio State Lantern,* April 1, 1965.
11. "Dedication Set Thurber Room," *Ohio State Lantern,* March 12, 1970.

Notes to Chapter 48

1. James Thurber, letter to the Van Doren family, November 12, 1959.
2. Kinney, *James Thurber: His Life and Times,* 1075.
3. Reverend Karl Scheufler, interview with Alice Leighner.
4. George Smallsread, interview with Harrison Kinney.
5. E. B. White, *New Yorker,* November 11, 1961.

Notes to the Appendix

1. "Doc Marlowe," *New Yorker,* November 2, 1935; also *Let Your Mind Alone* and *The Thurber Carnival.*
2. E. Stacy Matheny, "The Matheny Family Tree," 1913, Fairfield County District Library, Lancaster, Ohio.
3. James Thurber, "Snapshot of Mr. Ziegfeld," *The Thurber Album.*
4. Resume for house organ for appearance on NBC radio show "Information Please" in 1939, as reported by Harrison Kinney, *James Thurber: His Life and Times.*
5. "A Sequence of Servants," *My Life and Hard Times.*
6. Samuel B. Baker, *Ohio State Alumni Monthly,* December, 1961.

7. "Notes for a Proletarian Novel," *New Yorker,* June 9, 1934; also Michael J. Rosen, editor, *Collecting Himself: James Thurber on Writing, Writers, Humor and Himself,*

8. Robert Thurber, letter to Harrison Kinney, October 3, 1971.

9. Reverend Karl W. Scheufler, interview with Alice Leighner.

10. *A Centennial Biographical History of Columbus and Franklin County,* 936–37.

11. *Columbus: The Story of a City,* Ed Lentz, 108.

12. Kinney, *James Thurber His Life and Times,* 36.

13. John C. Harlor, interview with Rosemary O. Joyce, in *Of Thurber & Columbustown.*

14. Patricia McGuckin, *Columbus Dispatch,* April 17, 1959.

15. Johnny Jones, *Now Let Me Tell You,* 2.

BIBLIOGRAPHY

Abramson, Lawrence. Interview with Bob Hunter. 2014.

Adams, Althea. Interview with Lewis Branscomb. 1973. James Thurber Papers. Columbus, OH: Rare Books & Manuscripts Library of The Ohio State University Libraries.

Arter, Bill. Columbus Vignettes. Columbus, OH: Nida-Eckstein Printing, 1966.

———. *Columbus Vignettes II.* Columbus, OH: Nida-Eckstein Printing, 1967.

———. *Columbus Vignettes III.* Columbus, OH: Nida-Eckstein Printing, 1969.

———. *Columbus Vignettes IV.* Columbus, OH: Nida-Eckstein Printing, 1971.

———. "The House That Came Down the River." *Columbus Dispatch Sunday Magazine,* July 22, 1962.

Barrett, Richard E. *Images of America, Columbus 1860–1910.* Charleston, SC; Chicago, IL; Portsmouth, NH; and San Francisco, CA: Arcadia Publishing, 2005.

———. *Images of America: Columbus 1910–1970.* Charleston, SC; Chicago, IL; Portsmouth, NH; and San Francisco, CA: Arcadia Publishing, 2006.

Bernstein, Burton. *Thurber.* New York: Dodd, Mead, 1973.

Berry, Carlton C. *Memory Sketches of Over Fifty Years in Newspaper Composing Rooms.* Columbus, OH: The Dispatch Printing Company, 1954.

The Birth of Ohio Stadium. Produced by Brent Greene. Columbus, OH: WOSU, 1999. Television documentary.

Blundo, Joe. "Thurber's world and welcome to it; sites in Columbus associated with author." *Columbus Dispatch,* October 30, 2011.

Brandon, Henry. "Everybody is Getting Serious." *New Republic,* May 26, 1958. Reprinted in *Conversations with James Thurber,* edited by Thomas Fensch. The Woodslands, TX: New Century Books, 2000.

British Broadcasting Company. "The Private Life of James Thurber." December 2, 1961.

Brooks, Candy. "Alice Latham Wood Remembers." *This Week* (Worthington, Ohio), April 28, 2003.

Byrer, Lew. "McNulty Was Legendary as Columbus Journalist." *Columbus Citizen,* July 30, 1956.

Caswell, Lucy, and George A. Loomis, Jr. *Billy Ireland.* Columbus: The Ohio State University Libraries Publications Committee, 1980.

Collins, Harriett D. "Billy Graves Dies, Alumni Mourn Everywhere." *Ohio State University Monthly,* October 1943.

Columbus Citizen. "One of Oldest West Point Grads Says Fighting Japs Like Indian Wars." July 25, 1944.

———. "Thurber to Direct Scarlet Mask Play." September 30, 1924.

Columbus Dispatch. "Broadway Bows Nightly to Ohio State Men; Nugent, With Lead in 'Kempy,' and Mitchell, Are Acknowledged Leaders." October 20, 1922.

———. "East Squad Put Into Scrimmage." September 13, 1912.

———. "Life Beginning at 50, Says Thurber On Visit to City." January 14, 1946.

———. "Norman Kuehner, Former Managing Editor, Dies." December 25, 1943.

Columbus Evening Dispatch. "Life of T. T. Tress Snuffed Out by Sad Accident." April 28, 1904.

———. "Married Today at Lakeside, Mr. and Mrs. Norman Kuehner." August 7, 1915.

———. "Commission Man Is Stricken." October 16, 1918.

Columbus Sunday Dispatch. "Thurber's Service Includes Numerous Republican Roles." May 15, 1932.

Cooke, Alistair. "James Thurber: In Conversation with Alistair Cooke." *Atlantic Monthly,* August 1956.

Damon, Dr. Virgil "Duke." Interview with Burton Bernstein. In Bernstein, *Thurber.*

Davidson, Harold. "William L. 'Billy' Graves, Professor of English at Ohio State University, City Has Many Talented Musicians Who Practice Their Art Nonprofessionally." *Ohio State Journal,* 1933.

Davis, Robert H., and Arthur B. Maurice. *The Caliph of Bagdad, O. Henry.* New York: D. Appleton and Co., 1931.

East High School. *100 Years of Excellence: East High School 1898–1998, Columbus, Ohio.* Columbus: Central Ohio Graphics, 1998.

Fensch, Thomas. *The Man Who Was Walter Mitty.* The Woodlands, TX: New Century Books, 2000.

Fisher, Clifford. Interview with Alice Leighner. In Kinney, *James Thurber: His Life and Times.*

Fisher, William M. II. "Spittoons and Tarantulas, The Old Commission House." n.d.

Fritts, Minnette. Interview with Lewis Branscomb. 1973. James Thurber Papers. Columbus, OH: Rare Books & Manuscripts Library of The Ohio State University Libraries.

Fullerton, Hugh. "Life of Billy Ireland, Story of Kindliness, Good Fellowship." *Chillicothe News-Advertiser,* May 29, 1935.

Gardiner, Ted. Interview with Harrison Kinney. 1962.

Garrett, Betty, with Edward R. Lentz. *Columbus, America's Crossroads.* Tulsa, OK: Continental Heritage Press, Inc., 1980.

Grauer, Neil A. *Remember Laughter: A Life of James Thurber.* Lincoln: University of Nebraska Press, 1994.

Grosjean, Yvonne Kuehner. Interview with Bob Hunter. 2014.

Hampton, Pat. "Classmate says Thurber was brilliant, studious." *Columbus Dispatch,* December 9, 1984.

Hayes, Ben. "Old Blocks," *Columbus Citizen-Journal.* n.d.

Hayes, Christine. "Burkhart Portrait of Thurber's Mother Mame Full of Mischief and Merriment," *Short North Gazette,* December 2002.

Hinds, Conrade C. *Columbus and the Great Flood of 1913: The Disaster That Reshaped the Ohio Valley.* Charleston, SC: The History Press. 2013.

The History of Franklin and Pickaway Counties. Cleveland, OH: Williams Brothers, 1880.

Holmes, Charles S. *The Clocks of Columbus: The Literary Career of James Thurber.* New York: Atheneum, 1972.

Honeycutt, Ann. Interview with Harrison Kinney. In Kinney, *James Thurber: His Life and Times.*

Hooey, Robert E. "That's No Hooey," *Ohio State Journal,* November 19, 1948.

Howe, Henry. *Historical Collections of Ohio, Vol. 1.* Columbus, OH: Henry Howe and Son, 1889.

Howells, William Dean. *Years of My Youth.* New York and London: Harper and Brothers, 1916.

Hunter, Bob. *Chic: The Extraordinary Rise of Ohio State Football and the Tragic Schoolboy Athlete Who Made It Happen.* Wilmington, OH: Orange Frazer Press, 2008.

———. *A Historical Guidebook to Old Columbus.* Athens: Ohio University Press, 2012.

———. "Legend Loses Step to Time, Years Have Clouded Memories of Chic Harley, OSU's First Superstar." *Columbus Dispatch,* August 27, 2000.

———. *Saint Woody: The History and Fanaticism of Ohio State Football.* Washington, DC: Potomac Books, 2012.

———. "Sipping Sodas with Ty Cobb at city's Great Southern Hotel." *Columbus Dispatch,* March 14, 2012.

Hutton, Suzanne Fisher. Interview with Bob Hunter. November 7, 2014.

Joel Sayre Papers. The New York Public Library Manuscripts and Archives. Astor, Lenox, and Tilden Foundations.

Jones, Johnny. *Now Let Me Tell You.* Columbus: The Dispatch Printing Company, 1950.

Joyce, Rosemary O., with Michael J. Rosen and Donn F. Vickers. *Of Thurber & Columbustown.* Columbus, OH: The Thurber House, 1984.

Kinney, Harrison. *James Thurber: His Life and Times.* New York: Henry Holt, 1995.

———, editor, with Rosemary A. Thurber. *The Thurber Letters: The Wit, Wisdom, and Surprising Life of James Thurber.* New York: Simon & Schuster, 2002.

Klein, Lisa M. *Be It Remembered: The Story of Trinity Episcopal Church on Capitol Square.* Wilmington, OH: Orange Frazer Press, 2003.

Lee, Alfred E. *History of the City of Columbus, Capital of Ohio.* New York: Munsell, 1892.

Lentz, Ed. *As It Were: Stories of Old Columbus.* Dublin, OH: Red Mountain Press, 1998.

———. *Columbus: The Story of a City.* Charleston, SC: Arcadia Publishing, 2003.

Lewisohn, Ludwig. *Up Stream: An American Chronicle.* New York: Boni and Liveright, 1922.

Life. "Movie of the Week: The Secret Life of *Walter Mitty,*" pages 89, 91–92, and 95. August 4, 1947.

The Lima (Ohio) News. "O. Henry, Inmate of Ohio Penitentiary for Years; Noted Author Buffers for Crime Another Man Committed," page 2. August 9, 1916.

Martin, Neil. "Thurber Hits New High in Album." *Columbus Citizen Magazine,* June 22, 1952.

Martin, William T. *History of Franklin County: A Collection of Reminiscences of the Early Settlement of the County; with Biographical Sketches and a Complete History of the County to the Present Time.* Columbus, OH: Follett, Foster and Company, 1858.

Matheny, E. Stacy. "The Matheny Family Tree." Fairfield County District Library, Lancaster, Ohio: 1913.

McCabe, Lida Rose. *Don't You Remember?* Columbus, OH: A. H. Smythe, 1884.

McCombs, Ralph. Interview with Lewis Branscomb. 1973. James Thurber Papers. Columbus, OH: Rare Books & Manuscripts Library of The Ohio State University Libraries.

McCord, David. "Djinn Rummy." *Saturday Review,* June 7, 1952.

McNulty, Faith. "John As He Was." In *This Place on Third Avenue: The New York Stories of John McNulty.* Washington, DC: Counterpoint, 2001.

McNulty, John. *Third Avenue, New York.* Boston: Little, Brown. 1946.

———. *The World of John McNulty.* Garden City, NY: Doubleday, 1957.

McKinnon, W. F. "North Gets Four Men On All-High Eleven." *Columbus Dispatch,* November 26, 1912.

Meek, Thomas. Interview with Lewis Branscomb. 1973. James Thurber Papers. Columbus, OH: Rare Books & Manuscripts Library of The Ohio State University Libraries.

Miller, Alan. "Thurber's brother dies at age 90." *Columbus Dispatch,* July 21, 1987.

Miller, Herman. *Weekly Reader.* Columbus, OH: 1940.

Morsberger, Robert E. *James Thurber.* New York: Twayne Publishers, 1964.

Newsweek. "Theater: First Night of James Thurber's 'A Thurber Carnival,'" January 18, 1960.

Newsweek. "Advice from a Blind Writer." February 1, 1960.

New York Public Library. "Joel Sayre Memoirs." Tape 1, October 30, 1973.

Nugent, Elliott. "Brother James Thurber." *Buckeye Phi Psi,* April 1962.

———. *Events Leading Up to Comedy.* New York: Trident Press, 1965.

Obituary clipping. Jacob Fisher. Thurber Collection. The Ohio State University.

Ohio State Journal. "Bob Ryder Dies in Sleep in His California Home." March 17, 1936.

———. "Burning of Lunatic Asylum." November 20, 1868.

———. "The Fire at the Lunatic Asylum, Inquiries Answered." November 23, 1868.

———. "Terrible Disaster, Central Lunatic Asylum Destroyed by Fire." November 19, 1868.

Ohio State Lantern. "New York Man Is Elected New Fund Chairman." January 29, 1965.

———. "OSU Buys Thurber Collection." April 1, 1965.

———. "Thurber's Collection Displayed in Library." January 6, 1966.

Ohio State University Archives, Director of Athletics (Record Group 9/e—1/8), "Harley, Charles W. Correspondence: 1919, 1922, 1924, undated."

———. Joseph Denney biographical file, author unknown.

———. Joseph Russell Taylor biographical file, author unknown.

———. *The Makio,* yearbooks for 1912–1924. Columbus: The Ohio State University.

———. William Lucius Graves biographical file, author unknown.

Ohio State University Monthly. "The Academic Scene: Billy Graves: Joins the Great Triumvirate." January 1944.

———. "Billy Graves Weds." November 1941.

———. "Friends Pay Tribute to Joey Taylor." November 1933.

———. "Jackson Snaps Celebrities Who Go On Air for NBC." March 1933.

———. "Joseph Russell Taylor Dies." April 1933.

———. "Miller Drama Gift." February 1950.

———. "Roy Lee Jackson Dies." February 1964.

———. "Tom Meek Joins Firm." May 1927.

———. "William L. Graves." June 1941.

Park, Jack. The Official Ohio State Football Encyclopedia. Champaign, IL: Sports Publishing, 2001.

Pittsburgh Sun-Telegraph. February 16, 1960.

Pollard, James E. *History of The Ohio State University, The Story of its First Seventy-Five Years, 1873–1948.* Columbus: The Ohio State University Press, 1952.

———. *Ohio State Athletics, 1879–1959.* Columbus: Ohio State University Athletic Department, 1959.

Prout, Eva. Interview with Lewis Branscomb. 1973. James Thurber Papers. Columbus, OH: Rare Books & Manuscripts Library of The Ohio State University Libraries.

Robertson, Bob. "Wandering Thurbers to Lose One of Many Onetime Homes." *Columbus Citizen,* July 31, 1958.

Rosen, Michael J., ed. *Collecting Himself: James Thurber on Writing and Writers, Humor and Himself.* New York: Harper & Row, 1989.

Ryder, Robert O., and Harry J. Westerman. *The Young Lady Across the Way.* Boston, MA: John W. Luce, 1913.

Sauer, Doreen N. Uhas, and Stuart J. Koblentz. *Images of America: The Ohio State University Neighborhoods.* Charleston, SC: Arcadia Publishing, 2009.

Sayre, Joel. Interview for his memoirs. 1973. New York Public Library.

———. Interview with Lewis Branscomb. 1973. James Thurber Papers. Columbus, OH: Rare Books & Manuscripts Library of The Ohio State University Libraries.

———. "Remembering Thurber." *Washington Post Sunday Book World,* October 22, 1992.

———. Roundtable discussion about *My Life and Hard Times.* WNDT, New York.

Scheibeck, Irven. *Chic Harley, the one and only. Columbus Dispatch Sunday Magazine,* September 18, 1966.

Sheridan, Phil. *Those Wonderful Old Downtown Theaters.* Columbus, OH: Phil Sheridan, 1978.

Shiltz, David. "James Thurber's Ties to Fairfield County." n.d.

———. Telephone interview with Bob Hunter. August 2014.

Smallsread. George. Interview with Harrison Kinney. 1962.

Smith, C. Alphonso. *O. Henry Biography.* New York: Doubleday, Page and Co., 1916.

Spain, Norm. "Thurber House After Twenty Years," *The Shield of Phi Kappa Psi,* Spring 2005.

Stevens, Jesica. Interview with Bob Hunter. June 2015.

Stewart, Donald Ogden. *By a Stroke of Luck! An Autobiography.* New York: Paddington Press, 1975.

———. "Death of a Unicorn," *New Statesman,* November 10, 1961.

Taylor, Harvey. *Detroit Times,* January 13, 1960.

Taylor, Stafford. Interview with Alice Leighner for Harrison Kinney. 1969.

Taylor, William Alexander. *Centennial History of Columbus and Franklin County, Ohio, Vol. 1.* Chicago, IL, and Columbus, OH: The S. J. Clarke Publishing Co., 1909.

Thomas, Robert D. *Columbus Unforgettables: A Collection of Columbus Yesterdays and Todays.* Columbus, OH: Robert D. Thomas, publisher, 1983.

———. *More Columbus Unforgettables, A Further Collection of Columbus Yesterdays and Todays, Vol. 2.* Columbus: Robert D. Thomas, publisher, 1986.

Thomson, Tom. "Thurber Connection, Episode 55" *Short North Gazette,* December 2002.

Thurber, Helen. Interview with Burton Bernstein. In Bernstein, *Thurber.*

———. Introduction, *Thurber & Company.* New York: Harper & Row, 1966.

Thurber, Helen, and Edward Weeks, editors. *Selected Letters of James Thurber.* Boston: Little, Brown, 1980.

Thurber, James. "Adam's Anvil." In *The Thurber Album.* New York: Simon and Schuster, 1952.

———. ""Beta Theta Pi." In *The Thurber Album.* New York: Simon and Schuster, 1952.

———. "Boy from Chillicothe." In *The Thurber Album.* New York: Simon and Schuster, 1952.

———. "The Car We Had to Push." In *My Life and Hard Times.* New York and London: Harper and Brothers, 1933.

———. "Conversation Piece." In *The Thurber Album.* New York: Simon and Schuster, 1952.

———. "Daguerreotype of a Lady." In *The Thurber Album.* New York: Simon and Schuster, 1952.

———. "The Day the Dam Broke." In *My Life and Hard Times.* New York and London: Harper and Brothers, 1933.

———. "Draft Board Nights." In *My Life and Hard Times.* New York and London: Harper and Brothers, 1933.

———. "Franklin Avenue, U. S. A." In *The Thurber Album*. New York: Simon and Schuster.

———. "Gentleman from Indiana." In *The Thurber Album*. New York: Simon and Schuster, 1952.

———. "I Went to Sullivant." In *The Middle-Aged Man on the Flying Trapeze*. New York: Harper and Brothers, 1935.

———. *If You Ask Me*. P. M., Oct. 22, 1940.

———. "Lavender with a Difference." In *The Thurber Album*. New York: Simon and Schuster, 1952.

———. "Length and Shadow." In *The Thurber Album*. New York: Simon and Schuster, 1952.

———. Letter to Harvey Breit. November 25, 1949.

———. Letter to John O'Hara. October 29, 1949.

———. "Loose Leaves." In *The Thurber Album*. New York: Simon and Schuster, 1952.

———. "The Luck of Jad Peters." In *The Middle-Aged Man on the Flying Trapeze*. New York: Harper and Brothers, 1935.

———. "Man with a Pipe." In *The Thurber Album*. New York: Simon and Schuster, 1952.

———. "Man with a Rose." In *The Thurber Album*. New York: Simon and Schuster, 1952.

———. "Memoirs of a Drudge." In *The Thurber Carnival*. New York: Harper and Brothers, 1945.

———. "More Alarms at Night." In *My Life and Hard Times*. New York and London: Harper and Brothers, 1933.

———. "My Friend McNulty." In *The World of John McNulty*. Garden City, New York: Doubleday, 1957.

———. *My World—and Welcome to It*. New York: Harcourt Brace, 1942.

———. "Never Another Taylor." *Ohio State University Monthly*, October 1933.

———. "Newspaperman—Head and Shoulders." In *The Thurber Album*. New York: Simon and Schuster, 1952.

———. "The Night the Ghost Got In." In *My Life and Hard Times*. New York and London: Harper and Brothers, 1933.

———. "Notes of an Old Reporter." In *The Bermudian*. June 1951.

———. Ohioan Sesquicentennial Medal acceptance speech, October 24, 1953, in *Thurber on Humor*, pamphlet printed by the Martha Kinney Cooper Ohioana Library Association, Columbus, Ohio, 1953.

———. "Preface: My Fifty Years with James Thurber." In *The Thurber Carnival*. New York: Harper and Brothers, 1945.

———. "Snapshot of Mr. Ziegfeld." In *The Thurber Album*. New York: Simon and Schuster, 1952.

———. "'Them . . . the days' Is Thurber Theme in Reminiscence." In *Buckeye Phi Psi*. March 1937.

———. *Thurber Country*. New York: Simon and Schuster, 1953.

———. "Time Exposure." In *The Thurber Album*. New York: Simon and Schuster, 1952.

———. "The Tree on the Diamond." In *The Thurber Album*. New York: Simon and Schuster, 1952.

———. "University Days." In *My Life and Hard Times*. New York and London: Harper and Brothers, 1933.

———. "When Chic Harley Got Away." *Columbus Dispatch*, 1922.

Thurber, Mame. Interview with Beverly Smith. *Columbus Dispatch Sunday Magazine*, June 1, 1952.

———. Interview with Richard Oulihan. *Time*. 1950.

Thurber, Robert. Interview with Burton Bernstein. In Bernstein, *Thurber*.

———. Interview with Harrison Kinney. In Kinney, *James Thurber: His Life and Times*.

———. Letter to Charles S. Holmes. *The Clocks of Columbus*.

Thurber, William. Interview with Harrison Kinney. 1962.

———. Interview with Lewis Branscomb. February 14, 1972. James Thurber Papers. Columbus, OH: Rare Books & Manuscripts Library of The Ohio State University Libraries.

———. Interview with Richard Oulihan. *Time*, 1950.

Tibbetts, Robert A. "The Columbus Connection, or the Theatrical Adventure of Two Ohio State Phi Psis and the Way Thereto." *The Shield of Phi Kappa Psi*, November 1982.

Van Doorn, John. "John McNulty, One-Time Citizen Writer Who Attained Fame, Dead." *Columbus Citizen,* July 30, 1956.

Vincent, Robert. "Always a Newspaperman." *Columbus Dispatch Sunday Magazine*, December 13, 1959.

Waldron, Bob. "Thurber in the Attic." *Columbus Dispatch Sunday Magazine*, October 18, 1970.

White, E. B. *New Yorker,* November 11, 1961.

White, Ruth. "James Thurber: His Life in Columbus." *Columbus Dispatch*, March 10, 1940.

Williams Brothers. "Hamilton Township." In *The History of Franklin and Pickaway Counties*, 1880.

Wilson, Earl. *New York Post,* March 8, 1944.

Wood, Alice. "Looking Back, A Great Experience." Worthington, OH: n.d.

Wood, Dick, "Oral History, Alice Latham Wood (102 years), With Son, Dick Wood." April 28, 2003.

The X-Rays. Columbus, OH: East High School, 1914.

Microfilms and hard copies of the following newspapers and magazines were also consulted extensively:

The Columbus Dispatch

The Columbus Citizen

The Ohio State Journal

The Ohio State Lantern

The New York Times

The Ohio State Quarterly

The Ohio State Monthly

The city directories for Columbus published by R. L. Polk & Co. were also frequently consulted for the years 1880 through 1996.

INDEX

‗

•